To my children

Contents at a Glance

Beginning C for Arduino, Second Edition

Learn C Programming for the Arduino

Jack Purdum, Ph.D.

Apress®

Beginning C for Arduino, Second Edition: Learn C Programming for the Arduino

Jack Purdum
Ecosoft, Inc.
Cincinnati, Ohio, USA

ISBN-13 (pbk): 978-1-4842-0941-7   ISBN-13 (electronic): 978-1-4842-0940-0
DOI 10.1007/978-1-4842-0940-0

Library of Congress Control Number: 2015944814

Distributed to the book trade worldwide by Springer Science+Business Media New York, 233 Spring Street, 6th Floor, New York, NY 10013. Phone 1-800-SPRINGER, fax (201) 348-4505, e-mail orders-ny@springer-sbm.com, or visit www.springeronline.com. Apress Media, LLC is a California LLC and the sole member (owner) is Springer Science + Business Media Finance Inc (SSBM Finance Inc). SSBM Finance Inc is a Delaware corporation.

For information on translations, please e-mail rights@apress.com, or visit www.apress.com.

Apress and friends of ED books may be purchased in bulk for academic, corporate, or promotional use. eBook versions and licenses are also available for most titles. For more information, reference our Special Bulk Sales–eBook Licensing web page at www.apress.com/bulk-sales.

Any source code or other supplementary material referenced by the author in this text is available to readers at www.apress.com. For additional information about how to locate and download your book's source code, go to www.apress.com/source-code/. Readers can also access source code at SpringerLink in the Supplementary Material section for each chapter.

Contents

About the Author

Jack Purdum is a retired professor from Purdue University's College of Technology. Dr. Purdum has authored 18 programming and computer-related textbooks. He has been involved in university teaching for more than 25 years. He continues to contribute to magazines and journals, and he has been a frequent speaker at various professional conferences. He was the founder and CEO at EcoSoft, Inc., a company that specialized in programming tools for the PC. He continues to be actively engaged in onsite training and instruction in object-oriented programming analysis and design. Dr. Purdum has developed numerous programming and teaching methodologies, including the Right-Left Rule, The Bucket Analogy, The Five Programming Steps, Sideways Refinement, and code benchmarks (Dhampstone); he has been recognized for his teaching endeavors. He received his BA from Muskingum University, and his MA and PhD degrees from The Ohio State University.

About the Technical Reviewer

Terry King has designed broadcast stations, recording studios, broadcast equipment, intelligent machines, and special computer languages for IBM. He has worked as a broadcast journalist covering elections, fires, riots, and Woodstock.

He has taught electronics at SUNY and IBM, and "Bits&Bytes" at many high schools.

Terry received an Outstanding Technical Achievement award from IBM for the software architecture of IBM Chip Test systems.

He is now "retired" and writing about Arduino/embedded systems (`http://ArduinoInfo.info`) and running YourDuino.com with his friend from China, Jun Peng, and his library designer wife, Mary Alice Osborne. Since "retirement," Terry has lived and taught in Africa, China, the Middle East, and Italy. Now he is "home again" in rural Vermont and working 40+ hours a week on ArduinoInfo.info, firewood cutting, woodworking, and electronics.

Acknowledgments

No one writes a book in isolation. Perhaps without even knowing it, many people present me with ideas for teaching examples, better ways to get a point across to my students, and provide feedback on what works and what doesn't. It's not uncommon for nonprogramming friends to listen to me explain something and ask questions that ultimately points me to the heart of a lucid explanation. I must thank some of these people: Jane Holcer, Katie Mohr, John Purdum, Joe and Bev Kack, John Strack, Mike Edwards, and Dennis Kidder. I would also like to thank Terry King, the technical editor of this book, for his suggestions and keen eye in reviewing this manuscript. I also want to thank all of the vendors in Appendix A, whose contributions made it possible to test the programs that appear in this book. Also, many thanks to Kevin Walter, Michelle Lowman, and a host of other people at Apress who worked to make this a better book.

Introduction

Shortly after Gutenberg's big breakthrough, I was teaching a graduate-level statistics course and had to have a calculator with a square-root function. At the time, the least expensive I could find, even with an educator's discount, cost $150. Now I look down on my desk and see an Arduino Nano that's about the size of my thumb, costs under $5, and has more computing power than some early computers. I can't imagine where things will be 50 years from now.

The path I took to this moment in time is different than many of you reading this text. My primary area of expertise has been software engineering. However, I have always loved electronics and have dabbled in it since I first got my amateur radio license over 60 years ago. Yet, with all of the technological advances that are embodied in that thumb-sized board that sits in front of me, it's little more than a lump of silicon unless someone tells it what to do. Programming gives life to lumps of silicon, and I find that power pretty heady stuff.

The primary goal of this textbook is to teach you the C programming language as it exists in the Arduino integrated development environment (IDE). I just Googled "Arduino C programming books" and got 1.1 *million* hits! Some people are probably rolling their eyes, thinking: "Just what we need … another C programming book." I hope to convince you over the ensuing pages that this book is different.

First, many C programming texts designed for the Arduino environment relegate programming to the back seat, concentrating instead on the electronics. Indeed, some give you the feeling that programming is a necessary evil you must work through to get to the good stuff. Not this text. The truth remains that so-so software is doomed to produce so-so results with the hardware. Crafting good software can be every bit as rewarding as a well-engineered piece of hardware.

A second factor that makes this book different is my teaching experience. I had a programmer work for me who was perhaps the most gifted programmer I know. One summer I assigned an intern to him and, within a week, she quit in tears, saying he was impossible to work with—let alone learn something from him. Just because you are a brilliant programmer doesn't mean you can impart that knowledge to others. It's not until you have 150 sets of eyes staring at you like a deer in the headlights that can you appreciate what you thought was a great way to explain something obviously isn't. This trial-and-error process of teaching for more than 25 years has helped me develop techniques that lift students over the most likely stumbling blocks.

Finally, teaching programming does not have to be a dry or boring process. I have tried to make this text read as though you and I are talking face-to-face about programming. Although you are the final judge, I hope you come away with the enjoyment and appreciation for programming that I have. The power to make a piece of hardware dance beautifully to your commands is most addicting.

Assumptions About You

First, I am going to assume that you do not have to master C by next week. A major reason students who try to learn on their own fail is because they don't invest the time it takes to truly absorb the material being presented. You *must* take the time to type in the sample programs and run them yourself. This also means really working through the exercises at the end of the chapters. There are little programming nuggets to be learned from those exercises, and you owe it to yourself to ferret out those nuggets.

Second, maximize your learning experience means you *must* invest in the hardware necessary to test your code. I have tried to minimize the hardware necessary to write the programs in this book. Other than for the projects in Chapter 13, an Arduino board, a breadboard, a couple of LEDs, a few resistors, and some wire is all you need.

Third, I realize that many of you have some project in mind and that's the primary reason you are reading this book. You'll have a temptation to skip ahead to try and find out why your project isn't working. Don't. The sequencing of chapters and their content is such that each chapter builds on those that precede it. You need a strong foundation to build a solid understanding, and that means reading all of the chapters in the sequence in which they are presented.

Finally, take the time to enjoy the journey. If I say, "Think about it," I mean for you to really stop and think about what you just read. If you just finished reading some topic, perhaps how to write a *for* loop, stop and take the time to write a simple program of your own design to use a *for* loop. While you may think this will slow you down, it will actually speed up the learning process. Mentally telling yourself "I got that!" and actually writing your own program to implement the concept are two entirely different animals. As mentioned earlier, make sure you do the exercises at the end of the chapters. I didn't take the time to write those just to kill off a few extra trees. Try to answer them without looking at my solution. One of the neat things about programming is that there is more than one correct answer.

Resources

There are many places where you can go for additional help if you feel you need it. If you have a particular area of interest or question, your first stop should be a Google search. In most cases, just prefixing a Google search on the area of interest with the word "Arduino" (e.g., Arduino *for* loops) will produce many supplemental resources for you to investigate. Apress also has a number of electronics books that can be used to supplement this book.

Appendix A has a number of suggestions as to where to purchase various hardware components. In this edition, I have listed a number of Arduino "starter kits" that contain everything you need to test every project in this book.

The Arduino web site has numerous forums that can provide answers to many of the questions you might have. You can find the major topic areas at `http://forum.arduino.cc/index.php`.

I find that students find the "Programming Questions" forum especially useful. Because the Arduino IDE is an open source platform (i.e., people sharing ideas and resources), there are always people reading the forums who are willing to help. Just make sure you read any posting guidelines that appear at the top of the forum before posting your question. In the spirit of open source software and hardware, if you find some unique way of solving a problem, make a post of your own to a forum and give back to the community.

Finally, full-color images for all figures included in the print edition can be found in this book's source code bundle, which is available through `www.apress.com`. You can visit `www.apress.com/source-code` for more information on how to locate the source code.

Okay … enough of this. Let's start our journey to learn C….

CHAPTER 1

■ ■ ■

Introduction

There is one primary goal for this book: to teach you how to use the C programming language. The environment for reaching that goal is the Atmel family of microcontrollers. While C can be used to program other microcontrollers, our emphasis is on the Atmel controllers. Given that there are probably a bazillion C programming books available to you, why should you choose this one? Good question, and there's no single answer. However, I can give you some facts that might help with making your decision.

First, this book is specifically written for the Arduino family of microcontroller boards using the Atmel family of microcontroller chips. As such, the book is couched within the framework of an integrated development environment (IDE) that is available as a free Internet download. An *IDE* is a single program that combines all of the functions required to progress from the C language source code you are writing to an executable program. In essence, an IDE is a text editor, compiler, assembler, and linker all rolled into one program. Having the free Arduino IDE means you will not have to buy additional programming tools to learn C.

Second, the implementation of C provided with the IDE is not quite a full American National Standards Institute (ANSI) implementation of the C programming language. This implementation of the C language, which I will henceforth call Arduino C, is a robust, and virtually complete, subset of ANSI C. (The most obvious missing feature is the *double* data type, although *float* is supported.) In fact, the underling compiler you will be using throughout this book is the open source C++ compiler (GCC), which is full-featured. You will learn more about the language features available to you as we proceed through the book.

Why Choose This Book?

Even in light of the considerations mentioned, there are still probably dozens of books that cover Arduino C. So, why choose this book over the dozens that remain available to you?

First, this is a programming book and that is where the emphasis is. True, there are some small hardware projects to exercise your code, but the real purpose of the projects is to test your understanding of the C programming language—not the hardware. Once you have mastered C, Apress has a family of books that are centered on the Arduino microcontroller that you may use to extend your hardware expertise.

Second, I will take you "under the hood" of the C language, so you gain a much deeper understanding of what the code is doing and how it is done. This knowledge is especially useful in a programming environment where you have only a few pico-acres of memory available to you. There are those who say you really don't have to understand a language with any real detail to use it. To reinforce their argument, I have often heard the comment: "You don't have to know how to build a car to drive one." True, but if your car

Electronic supplementary material   The online version of this chapter (doi:10.1007/978-1-4842-0940-0_1) contains supplementary material, which is available to authorized users.

© Jack Purdum 2015
J. Purdum, *Beginning C for Arduino, Second Edition*: Learn C Programming for the Arduino, DOI 10.1007/978-1-4842-0940-0_1

breaks down 200 miles north of Yellowknife, NWT, I'll bet you'd wish you had a better understanding of the details that make a car tick. The same is true for programming. The better you understanding what is going on with the language, the quicker you will be able to detect, isolate, and fix program bugs. (A program *bug* is an error in the program that prevents it from performing its designed task correctly.) Also, there are often multiple solutions possible for any given programming problem. A little depth of understanding frequently yields a more efficient and unbreakable, yet elegant, solution.

Third, since I first began using C in 1977, I have gained a lot of commercial programming experience with C that just might come in handy. My software company produced C compilers and other development tools for the early PCs back in the 1980s. Also, I wrote my first C programming book more than 30 years ago. Still, the biggest advantage that has some worth to you is my teaching experience. Honestly, there are likely thousands of programmers who can code circles around me. Indeed, one of my employees was such a person. However, to be a good author, it matters little how good you are as a programmer or an engineer if you cannot convey that experience to others.

I have more than 30 years of university-level teaching experience, and I know where you are most likely to stumble in our upcoming journey. The bad news is that you *will* stumble along the way. The good news is that there have been thousands before you who have stumbled on exactly the same concepts, and I have managed to develop effective teaching methods to overcome most (all?) of them. I also think you will find the book's style both engaging and informative.

Finally, I genuinely enjoy programming with the C language. Of all the different languages I have used since I first began programming in the late 1960s, C remains my favorite. It is a concise, yet powerful, language well suited for microcontroller work. I think you're going to like it, too.

This chapter details what you need to use this book effectively, including some comments about the expectations I have about you. You will learn about some of the features that different Arduino-compatible boards have, their approximate cost, and where they can be purchased. Also, there are many Arduino Starter Kits available now and they are a wonderful way to get started because they usually contain the Arduino board plus numerous electronic components with which you can experiment. (Details about some suppliers can be found in Appendix A.) Suggestions are also made about some additional hardware items you may wish to purchase. The chapter then tells you where and how to download and install the IDE for the Arduino IDE. The chapter closes out with a short C program to verify that the IDE installation went as expected. When you finish reading this chapter, you will have a good understanding of what you need to use this book effectively.

Assumptions About You

Clearly, I'm targeting this book for a specific reader. In so doing, I have made certain assumptions about that reader: *I assume the reader knows absolutely nothing about C or programming in general.* In fact, I hope you don't know anything. That way, you can start with a clean slate. Often, someone who knows some programming aspects brings along a lot of bad habits or ill-conceived practices that need to be "unlearned." Starting off with no programming experience is, in this case, a very good thing.

I assume you know nothing about electronics. Indeed, this book is not meant to be an electronics book. However, there are a few hardware concepts used throughout the book, but you will be taught what you need to know to make things function properly. If you want to gain a deeper understanding of the electronics, I'd suggest finishing this text and then buying one of the other Apress books that targets your specific hardware area of interest.

I assume you will do the programming exercises found at the end of each chapter. Most of the exercises are software-based, meaning they require little or no additional electronic components to complete the exercise. Clearly, some hardware is needed to test even a purely software exercise: you must have a microcontroller board to type in and run the software in the exercise. This means you need to invest in a microcontroller board and some additional components. I've made every attempt to keep these component costs as low as possible while still demonstrating the point at hand.

Appendix A presents a list of vendors from whom you can buy various components at reasonable cost. Failing that, almost all of the components can be bought from a local Radio Shack outlet. (Alas, Radio Shack just filed for bankruptcy.) Appendix B presents a list of the miscellaneous hardware components you will need to complete all of the projects in this book. Obviously, some of these components can be ignored if certain projects are not attempted. As mentioned earlier, there are some great Arduino experimenter kits that not only include an Arduino-compatible board, but also dozens of components and other devices that can be used to make some really interesting projects. I especially like the MAKER Version Electronic Brick Starter Set from yourduino.com and the Ultimate Kit from oddWires.com. Both kits contain components to do all of the exercises in this book, plus many, many more (see Appendix A).

Finally, I assume you don't have to know C by this weekend. That is, I assume you will do the exercises and take the time to study and understand the code in the examples before moving on to the next chapter. Learning C is a building process whereby the concepts learned in the current chapter become a foundation for subsequent chapters. A crumbly understanding of the concepts of one chapter will likely cause a collapse of that understanding in later chapters. Take your time, pause and think about what you're reading, and *do the exercises*. It's easy to read something and say "I understand that." It's quite another to start with a blank page and write a program that uses what you've read. Simply stated: Do the exercises. If you try to take shortcuts and bypass the exercises, then your depth of knowledge will be less than it would be otherwise. Take your time and enjoy the ride.

What You Need

In addition to this book, there are several things you will need, plus some things you should have but could live without. Consider the components and factors discussed in the following sections.

An Atmel-Based Microcontroller Card

You will need to have access to an Atmel microcontroller board. (Let's use "μc" for "microcontroller" from now on.) Atmel produces a wide variety of μcs and there are literally dozens of clone boards available. You should consider purchasing an Arduino board based on one of those listed in Table 1-1. So, how do you decide which one to purchase? It really depends on what you want to do with the μc. If all you want to do is blink an LED or control a toaster, then one of the least expensive boards listed in the table probably will do just fine. If you are setting up some kind of experiment that must sample several dozen sensors every second, then you will probably want to use a μc that has a lot of digital and/or analog I/O pins. If your application is going to have a lot of program code associated with it, then obviously you should pick one with more memory. (Note that 2K to 8K of flash memory is eaten up by the bootloader. A *bootloader* is a small program that allows your μc to communicate with the outside world, so plan accordingly.)

The Arduino IDE is run on your PC, so most of the actual program development takes place on your PC. When you think the program code is in a state that can be tested, you compile and "upload" your code to the μc via a USB cable connected between your PC to the μc.

Most μc boards are shipped with the required USB (A to B) cable. If your board did not include one, often you can steal your printer cable and use it until you can find a replacement. Also note that some boards do not have a USB connector on the board. While these boards are less expensive, they require an external programming interface, which is less convenient. For the time being, only consider a board that has a USB connector on it. Again, look online for the USB cables and you should be able to buy one for less than a few dollars.

Types of Memory

With regard to memory, you will want to consider what's outlined in the following sections.

Flash Memory

The programs you develop using this book are written on your PC. When you have the program code to a point where you think it is ready to test, you upload that program code from your PC to the µc board via the USB connection. The program code is stored in the Arduino's flash memory. *Flash memory* is nonvolatile, which means that, even if you disconnect the board from its power source, the contents of the flash memory remain intact. It is probably obvious that your program must fit within the limits imposed by the amount of flash memory on your Arduino board.

As mentioned, 2K to 8K of flash memory is used for the software (i.e., the bootloader) that allows your program to communicate with the outside world, including your PC. Therefore, if your Arduino has 32K of flash memory, your program code actually must be less than 24K to 30K in size, depending on the size of your bootloader code. Also, flash memory has a finite life in terms of the number of times that you can rewrite it reliably before it gets a little flaky. Most set the safe write cycle at 100,000 writes. So, according to the documentation, if you save the program 10 times a day, you only have 27 years of reliability available to you.

SRAM

Simply stated, the static random-access memory (SRAM) is where your program variables (data) get stored during program execution. You should assume that the data stored in SRAM is lost when power is removed from the controller board.

Because SRAM is used to pass data back and forth between functions, creating temporary variables as the program executes, SRAM plays an important limiting factor in the amount of data your programs can use. I will have more to say about this in later chapters, but for now, the more SRAM, the better.

EEPROM

Electrically Erasable Programmable Read-Only Memory (EEPROM) is an area of nonvolatile memory where one often stores data that needs to be retrievable each time the program is run. Like flash memory, data values stored in EEPROM survive power removal.

However, EEPROM has two drawbacks when compared to flash memory: it is a little slower to access than flash memory, and like flash memory, it too has about 100,000 read/write cycles before it becomes unreliable. Because of these factors, EEPROM memory is often used to store configuration or other types of information that are needed when the system powers up, but are not often changed. For example, you might have some sensors that need to have certain values sent to them before they can be used, or other devices that need to be initialized with specific data. EEPROM would be a likely candidate for storing such configuration data. Again, I will have more to say about this type of memory later in the book.

Making the Choice

So, should it be the amount of memory, I/O pin count, processor speed, or something else that dictates your µc choice? Again, it depends on what you hope to do with the µc, but for most readers, the amount of flash and SRAM memory will likely be the most important limitations. But even those two parameters have trade-offs.

For example, you might want to have a program that generates a sine wave for a function generator. Because μcs are not that fast, you decide not to calculate the sine values on the fly, but rather to store pre-calculated sine wave values in a table stored in memory. When you look at the program, you see that the program code is pretty small but the amount of memory to store the sine table is large. Therefore, the limiting factor in your design is the amount of SRAM needed to hold the table, not the flash memory for the program instructions. (You might also store the table in EEPROM memory.) If you don't have a specific program task in mind, buy a board that has the most flash and SRAM memory your pocketbook allows.

Table 1-1 shows some of the compatible boards that you may want to consider for use with this book.

Table 1-1. *Atmel Microcontrollers Commonly Used in Arduino Boards*

Microcontroller	Flash memory (bytes)	SRAM (bytes)	EEPROM (bytes)	Clock speed	Digital I/O pins	Analog input pins	Voltage
Arduino Uno	32K	2K	1K	16Mhz	14	6	5V
Arduino Nano	32K	2K	1K	16Mhz	14	8	5V
Digispark Pro	16K	2K	1K	16Mhz	14	10	5V
RoboRED	32K	2K	1K	16Mhz	14	6	5 or 3.3V
ATmega1280	128K	8K	4K	16Mhz	54	16	5V
ATmega2560	256K	8K	4K	16Mhz	54	16	5V
Arduino Leonardo	32K	2.5K	1K	16Mhz	20	12	5V
Arduino Due	512K	96K	-	84Mhz	54	12/2[1]	3.3V
ChipKIT Max32[2]	512K	128K	-	80Mhz	83	16	3.3

1. The Due has two analog input pins.
2. This is not an Atmel chip, but produced by Diligent and can be programmed using C and an IDE that looks virtually identical to the Arduino IDE. It is based on the PIC32 (32-bit) microcontroller.

Board Size

The physical size of the μc card may also be important to you, depending on your planned application. As you might expect, larger available memory and more I/O pins dictate a larger footprint for the card. Figure 1-1 shows several popular μc boards. To get some perspective, the center board is a little smaller than the size of a deck of cards. The Digispark board (bottom right in Figure 1-1) is about the size of a postage stamp. You can also "roll your own" board using an 8-pin ATTiny85 chip (8K flash, 512 bytes SRAM and EEPROM) creating a really small board size.

Figure 1-1. *Sizes of two different Arduino boards, one based on the Atmega1280 (left) and one based on the Atmega328 (right) relative to a standard playing card.*

Input/Output (I/O) Pins

As you might expect, a μc with more memory and I/O pins cost a little more. For example, some ATmega328-based boards can be purchased for under $5 and those based on the ATmega2560 for under $15. The Due (pronounced "do-eh") costs around $25, whereas the Leonardo is about $10. (Table 1-1 is only a partial feature list. Consult the spec sheets for those boards you are considering.) Appendix A presents a list of suppliers that you may wish to consider. Note that there are numerous clones available for each member of the Arduino family. (For a good discussion of clones, compatibles, derivatives, and counterfeit boards, see http://arduino-info.wikispaces.com/Arduino-YourDuino.) As a general rule, buy the "biggest" you can comfortably afford that is consistent with the project(s) you have in mind. Hardware projects are often subject to "feature creep," where more and more functionality is requested as the project goes forward. "Buying bigger than you need" is often a good idea if you can afford it.

Breadboard

A *breadboard* is used to prototype electronic projects. By using jumper wires that plug into the holes on the breadboard, it is easier to create and modify an electronic circuit. The hardware elements found in this text are not a central feature. Indeed, I have tried to limit the hardware requirements as much as possible. Still, a breadboard is a useful addition to your tool chest and you should consider investing in one. Figure 1-2 shows a typical breadboard. I like this type of breadboard because it has two sets of power feeds and four banks of tie points. (The one shown has 2,800 tie points—the little "holes" where you can insert wires, components, ICs, and so forth. This is about twice the size you will likely need, but it's what I had on hand.) You also need some jumper wires to connect the tie points. I purchased the breadboard shown in the figure with 150 jumper wires for less than $20. There are smaller, less expensive breadboards available.

If your breadboard doesn't come with jumper wires, then make sure you purchase some—you'll need them! Note that jumper wires are sold as male-to-male, male-to-female, and female-to-female and with different lengths. As to the type to get, I would get a mixture of all three types, although you will likely use the male-to-male most often. I would lean toward the longer lengths (e.g., 10″). I prefer the Dupont-style jumper wires, as they tend to be a little more durable.

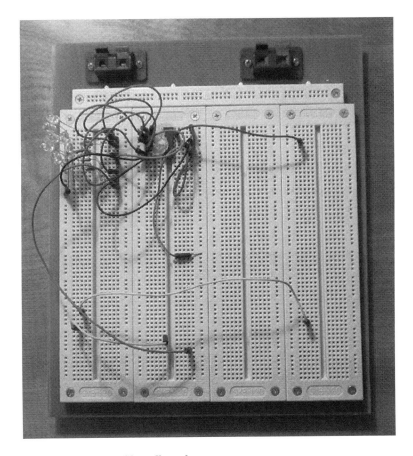

Figure 1-2. A typical breadboard

Miscellaneous Parts

Every attempt has been made to minimize the number of electronic parts you need to complete an exercise. In many cases, we reuse components between exercises. Appendix B presents a list of the parts that you need to complete all the exercises found in this book. With some judicious shopping on eBay, you can probably buy all of the components for less than $15 (excluding the breadboard and μc boards). While you are at it, you might look for some "rubber feet" that can be stuck to the bottom of your board. That way, if you slide the board across a table, it won't scratch it. I won't even mention what can happen if you slide a naked board across a table that has a paperclip on it.

I've already stated that several experimenter kits are available. If you buy one of these kits, you will have all of the components necessary to do any of the projects listed in this text. Some even come with a carrying case that keeps the components organized. I've only recently started using starter kits, and I find them to be very useful and convenient. This is especially true if you're just getting started with μcs.

Although you could read this book without buying anything else, not having minimal components and a compatible Arduino-based board would seriously dilute the learning experience. You really should have the electronic components available to you. You might also find out if your community has a local amateur radio (i.e., ham radio) club. Club members are always willing to offer advice about where you can find various electronic components at reasonable cost. Your local community college or university is another possible source of information, as might be the local teacher of the high school physics class. Indeed, when I taught at Butler University, the Physics department opened its lab on Saturday mornings to people who had an interest in learning electronics. To his credit, Dr. Marshal Dixon was the instructor who ran the program free of charge. Perhaps your community has a similar program. It doesn't hurt to check. Also, there are very active MakerSpaces in many communities that often have faires with Arduino/Electronics sections. With a little effort and a few dollars, you should be able to buy what you need.

Installing and Verifying the Software

A μc without software is about as useful as a bicycle without peddles. Like any other computer, a μc needs program instructions for it to do something useful. Arduino has provided all the software tools within their (free) IDE that you need to write program code. The remainder of this section discusses downloading, installing, and testing the software you need.

Start your Internet browser and go to http://arduino.cc/en/Main/Software. There you will find the Arduino software download choices for Windows, Mac OS X, and Linux. Click the link that applies to your development environment. Because I use the Windows operating system for program development, the file that was downloaded was named arduino-1.5.8-windows.zip. The latest Arduino IDE available at the time this is being written is Release 1.5.8 Beta. (Just before we went to press, Release 1.6.0 was announced. It's too late to change all the narrative and retest, but the latest release should work just fine.) You are asked to select the directory where you wish to extract the files. I named my directory Arduino1.5.8 and placed it off the root of the C drive (e.g., C:\Arduino1.5.8.) Regardless of the exact number of the release, you should see something similar to that shown in Figure 1-3 when you start extracting the files from the download.

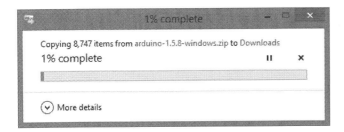

Figure 1-3. Extracting the Arduino programming tools

Inside the Arduino directory you just created, double-click the `arduino.exe` file. In a few moments, you may see a splash screen similar to that shown in Figure 1-4.

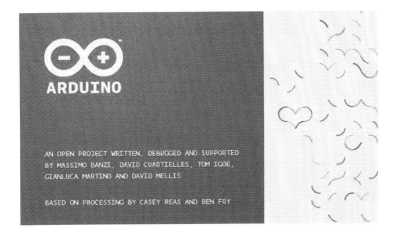

Figure 1-4. Arduino IDE splash screen

In a few more seconds, you should see the Arduino IDE. It should look similar to that shown in Figure 1-5.

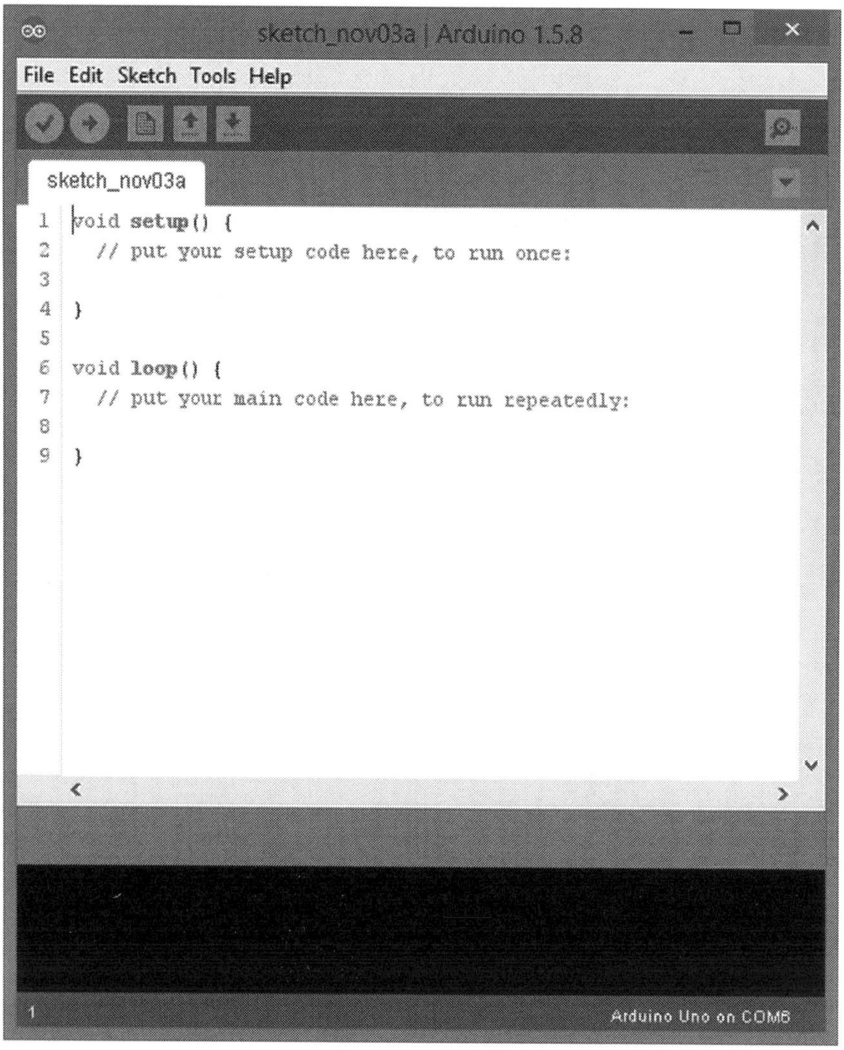

Figure 1-5. *The Arduino integrated development environment*

If you see the IDE as seen in Figure 1-5, you can be fairly certain that the software download and installation was performed successfully. Note that the IDE automatically provides two "empty" functions, *setup()* and *loop()*. Because all Arduino programs require these two functions, the IDE automatically provides empty shells for them. You fill in these shells as needed to get your program to do your bidding.

■ **Note**   The Diligent chipMAX family is not part of the Atmel family of μcs. The compiled program code is different from that for the Arduino boards. The chipMAX IDE, however, looks and feels almost identical to the Arduino IDE. You should be able to compile and upload the programs presented in this book using the chipMAX family of boards. You can download the chipMAX IDE at `http://chipkit.net/started/`. You might consider the chipMAX because it has a little more horsepower than most Arduinos.

Now that you have the software installed, we can check to see whether your controller board is functioning properly.

Verifying the Hardware

Now that you have the Arduino IDE software installed, let's connect your computer to the μc board, load a small program, and verify that all components are working together. First, you need to connect the USB cable to your μc board and then plug the other end of the USB cable into your computer.

Attaching the USB Cable

Figure 1-6 shows the μc board with the USB cable connected to it. Most companies give you the A-B type USB cable when you buy the μc board. As you no doubt have figured out, the unattached end of the USB cable should be plugged into a USB port connector on your computer.

The minute you connect the USB cable to your powered-up computer, power is applied to the μc board and an LED will light on the μc board. Obviously, the USB connection is supplying the voltage necessary to drive the μc board. The USB 2.0 specs suggest that the cable must supply between 4.4 and 5.25 volts at a maximum current of 500mA. This is not a lot of power. However, most μc boards also provide a small power jack (the black barrel-like "thingy" located on the lower left corner of the board in Figure 1-6) where a "wall wart" with greater power can be plugged into the power jack to drive the system. Wall warts supplying 9V at 1A are a common choice. None of our projects require more current than can be provided by the USB connection. (If you are using a USB hub, then make sure the hub provides 500mA to each port.)

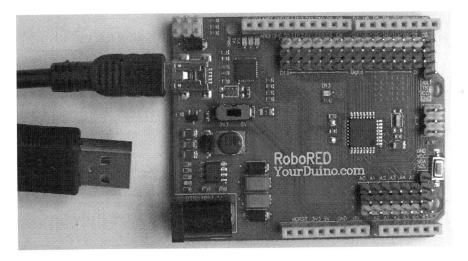

Figure 1-6. The μc board with USB cable attached

Selecting Your μc Board in the Integrated Development Environment

The Arduino IDE supports a variety of different μc boards. Therefore, you must tell the IDE which board you will be using for writing your program code. Figure 1-7 shows the menu sequence (Tools ➤ Board) that you use to select your μc board. In this example, I have selected the *Arduino Uno* menu choice.

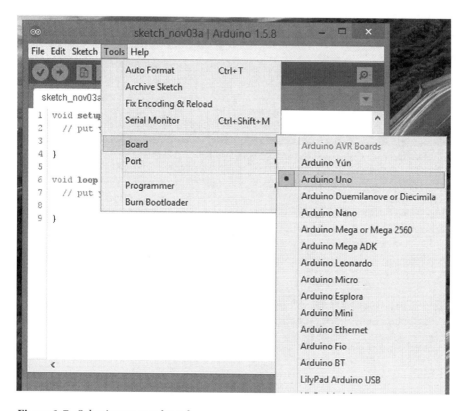

Figure 1-7. *Selecting your μc board*

You should select the menu choice that matches the μc board you are using. If you change μc boards at some future date, then simply come back to this menu and select the board to which you are changing. Also, depending upon what other devices you have connected to your PC, you may have to reselect the COM port, too.

Port Selection

The IDE does a pretty good job of automatically figuring out which USB port you have selected to power and communicate with the μc board. To determine which port is being used, simply use the Tools ➤ Port menu sequence, as shown in Figure 1-8. For my particular setup, COM port 6 is being used to communicate with the μc board.

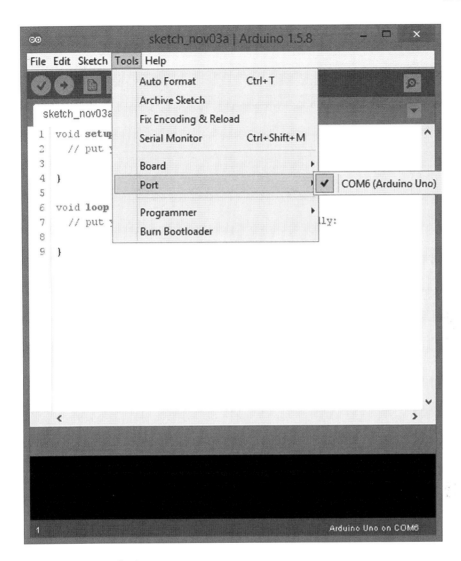

Figure 1-8. *Port selection*

If you are having difficulty determining which port should be used, then you can use the Windows Control Panel to examine which ports are assigned to what. For example, using Windows 8, the first step is to select the Device Manager option from the Start Panel list. Then select the Ports option, as shown in Figure 1-9. You should see the Arduino Uno (or the board you selected) listed. If you do not see the device listed, you can install the device driver yourself.

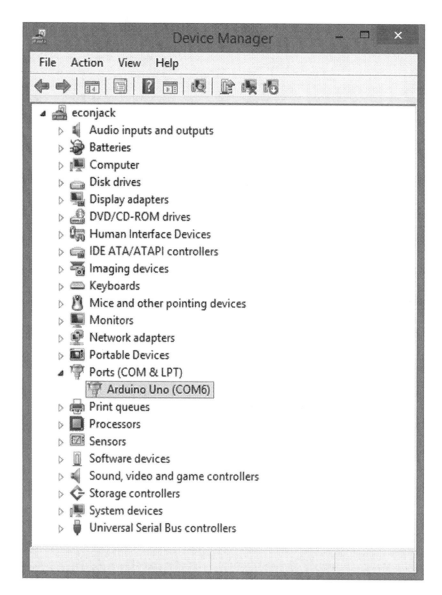

Figure 1-9. *Selecting the Device Manager from the control panel*

To install the Arduino device driver, run the Windows File Explorer. You can find this by right-clicking the lower-left corner of the display and selecting File Explorer. Once you have the File Explorer running, do the following:

1. Move to the directory where you installed the Arduino IDE. For me, it was
    C:\Arduino1.5.8. Looking in that path, I find the information shown in Figure 1-10.

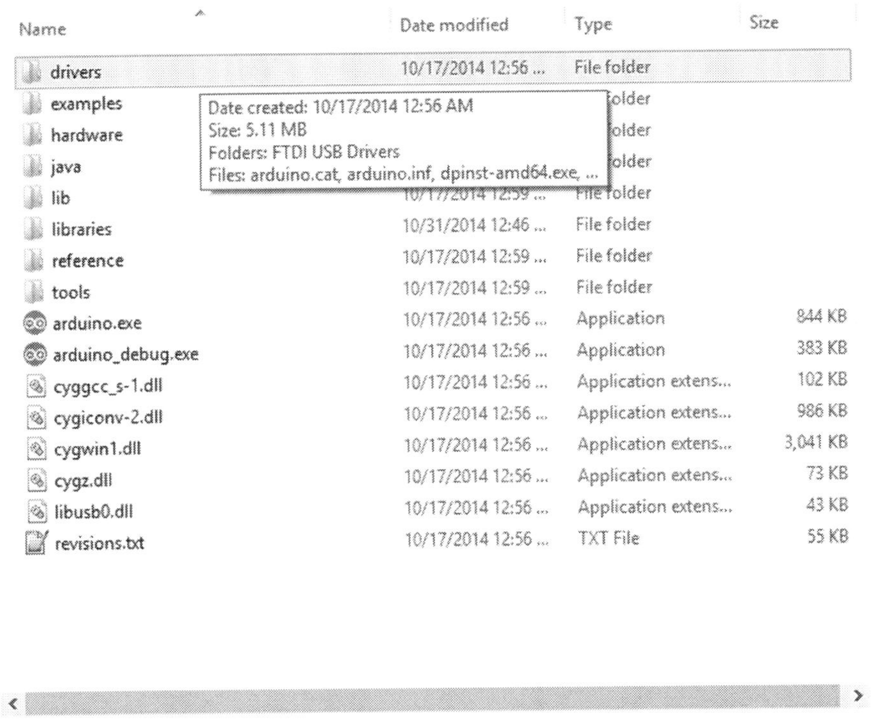

Name	Date modified	Type	Size
drivers	10/17/2014 12:56 ...	File folder	
examples		older	
hardware	Date created: 10/17/2014 12:56 AM	older	
java	Size: 5.11 MB	older	
lib	Folders: FTDI USB Drivers	older	
	Files: arduino.cat, arduino.inf, dpinst-amd64.exe, ...		
libraries	10/31/2014 12:46 ...	File folder	
reference	10/17/2014 12:59 ...	File folder	
tools	10/17/2014 12:59 ...	File folder	
arduino.exe	10/17/2014 12:56 ...	Application	844 KB
arduino_debug.exe	10/17/2014 12:56 ...	Application	383 KB
cyggcc_s-1.dll	10/17/2014 12:56 ...	Application extens...	102 KB
cygiconv-2.dll	10/17/2014 12:56 ...	Application extens...	986 KB
cygwin1.dll	10/17/2014 12:56 ...	Application extens...	3,041 KB
cygz.dll	10/17/2014 12:56 ...	Application extens...	73 KB
libusb0.dll	10/17/2014 12:56 ...	Application extens...	43 KB
revisions.txt	10/17/2014 12:56 ...	TXT File	55 KB

Figure 1-10. *Selecting the drivers folder in the Arduino directory*

2. Click the `drivers` folder and double-click the file named `dpinst-amd64.exe`. (If you have an older computer, you may have to use the file named `dpinst-x86.exe`.) From there, just answer the questions as they appear (they're pretty obvious), and the new drivers are installed. When the program finishes, you should see a COM port allocated to the Arduino, similar to that shown in Figure 1-9.

If you change port devices at some point in the future, it is possible that you will need to reselect the port using the menu sequence Tools ➤ Port. If the port check box that is shown is not checked, make sure you check it before proceeding. Once the port is selected, the IDE knows which port to use to send any data to the PC via the USB cable.

Now that you are reasonably certain that the software and hardware seem to be connected and working properly, let's load a small program into the IDE and see whether we can run it.

Loading and Running Your First Program

The Arduino IDE has gone through numerous revisions over the years. The current version is the first to carry the "Arduino 1" moniker, suggesting that the IDE software is now considered stable. Earlier versions of the IDE generated a default secondary file name (file extension) of "pde," which reflected that the source files (also called "sketches") were written under the Processing Development Environment (pde). With the latest release, the default secondary file name has been changed to "ino." The change was made so there wouldn't be conflicts with the source files that were created with earlier versions of the IDE. (Thus far, I have not found out why "ino" was selected. So, I'm just going to assume that it is because it squares with the last three letters in Arduino.) The latest version of the IDE can read the earlier "pde" files but resaves them as "ino" files by default.

Writing Your First Program

Rather than use one of the example programs that is distributed with the Arduino IDE, let's actually write a short program of our own. Go to the directory where you installed the Arduino IDE and double-click the file named arduino.exe. (You may want to make a shortcut for the EXE and place it on your toolbar.) In a moment, you should see the IDE, as shown in Figure 1-5.

Our goal at this point is to write a short program and test whether everything is working properly. As such, I won't spend too much time explaining *why* we are doing things; that will come later. You should simply follow the instructions for now and feel safe that you will learn what you are doing in later chapters.

Now add the following two lines to the *setup()* function shown in Figure 1-5:

```
Serial.begin(115200);
Serial.println("This is my first Arduino program!");
```

Your IDE should now look similar to Figure 1-11.

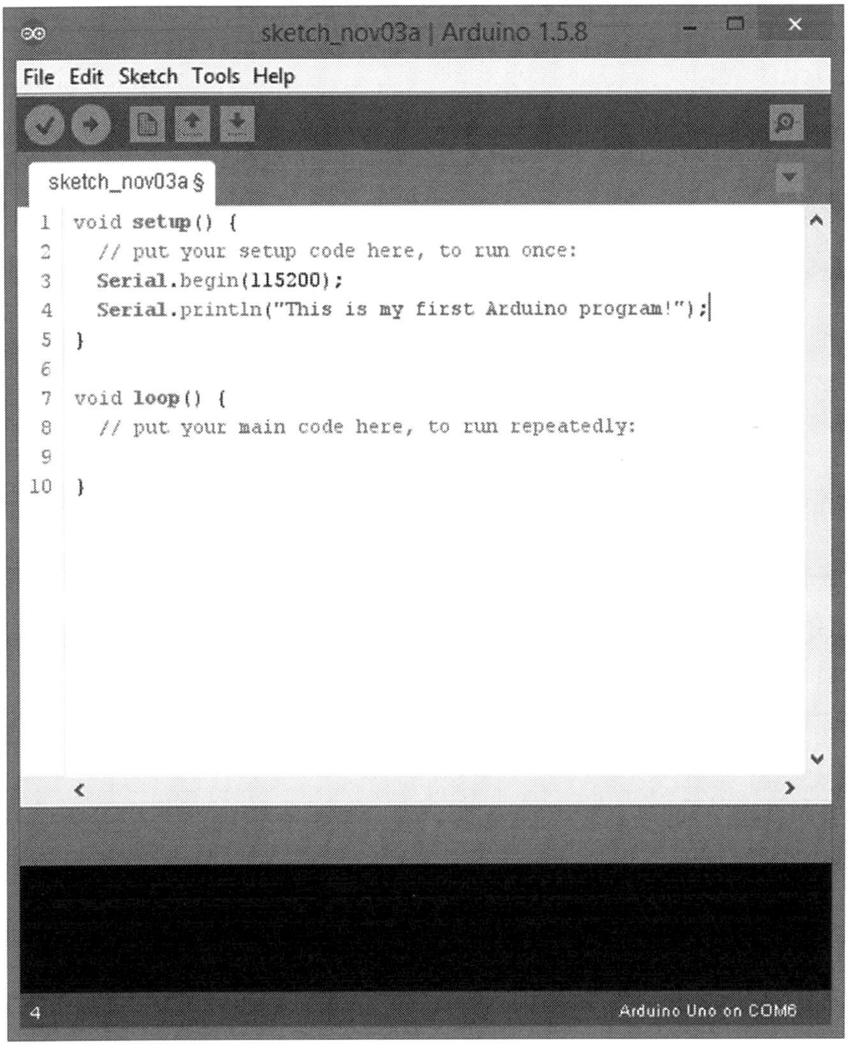

Figure 1-11. *The IDE after adding the two new source code lines*

What the Program Does

So, what should happen when we compile, upload, and then run our program? First, notice that we added our two lines after the two lines:

```
void setup() {
// put your setup code here, to run once:
```

Without going into detail, *setup()* is a C programming language function that must be present in every program you write. The opening brace ({) at the end of the first line marks the starting point of the code that will define what the *setup()* function does. If you look immediately after the two lines we added in Figure 1-11, you will see a closing brace (}). Everything between the opening and closing braces is called the *function body* for *setup()*. In other words, the braces mark the start and the end of the program statements that tell us what the function is expected to do.

So, what does our program do? The first line creates a *Serial* object and sets the communication rate (i.e., the baud rate) to 115200 bits/second. (Note that many of the sample programs shipped with the IDE use the slower 9600 baud rate. You need to adjust the *Serial* monitor accordingly, as shown in Figure 1-14. I tell you how to change the baud rate shortly.) The second line says that we want to "print" a message to the *Serial* object that says: "This is my first Arduino program!" Because there are no more source code statements in our program, that's all this program does. The program simply displays the message on the *Serial* object.

Serial object?

The Arduino IDE in conjunction with the bootloader includes the ability to communicate between your PC and the μc board via the USB cable. To make that communication possible, the IDE has a predefined program object called a *Serial* object. You initialize the *Serial* object by calling a method, or function, named *begin()*, which is buried within the *Serial* object. (In C, we use the term *function* as a programming unit. In object-oriented programming (OOP) languages, like C++, functions are called *methods*. The difference from a practical point of view is mostly semantic.) The *begin()* method is responsible for initializing the *Serial* object (e.g., setting the baud rate, parity bits, etc.) so it can communicate with your PC via the USB cable. Once *begin()* finishes its tasks, other methods buried within the *Serial* object can be used to communicate with other devices, like your PC.

One of the other methods available within the *Serial* object is called *print()*, which our program uses to send the message to your PC for display. In our simple program, we use the *print()* method to display our message on the *Serial* device associated with the *Serial* object.

Serial device? What *Serial* device?

Figure 1-12 shows you how to activate the Arduino *Serial* device. The IDE menu sequence Tools ➤ *Serial* Monitor (or the keystrokes Ctrl+Shift+M, or click the "magnifying glass" in the upper-right corner of the IDE) activates the *Serial* device. Once you have compiled and uploaded the code to the Arduino board, your message is displayed on the *Serial* device. If you are running Windows, the *Serial* device is little more than a pop-up window where the message is displayed (see Figure 1-14).

Note that you cannot activate the *Serial* monitor until after the program has been compiled and uploaded to the μc board. If you try to activate the *Serial* monitor before those tasks finish, the request is simply ignored.

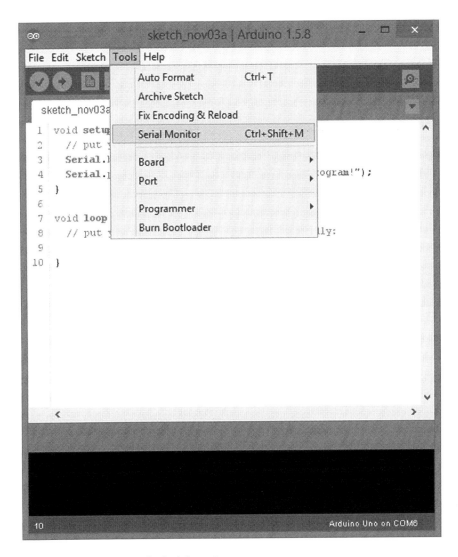

Figure 1-12. Activating the Serial monitor

Compiling and Uploading a Program

Once you have typed the new source code lines, you are ready to compile the program. The process of compiling a program refers to the process where a piece of software embedded within the IDE (i.e., the compiler) takes the C program statements you wrote and converts them into machine code instructions that the central processing unit (CPU) of your selected Arduino board understands. These machine code instructions are ultimately binary data (i.e., 1s and 0s) that cause the CPU to execute the code you wrote.

If there are no program errors detected by the compiler, you can send the compiled code from your PC to the Arduino board, where that code is executed. Figure 1-13 shows you the basic parts of the IDE to write, compile, and upload your program.

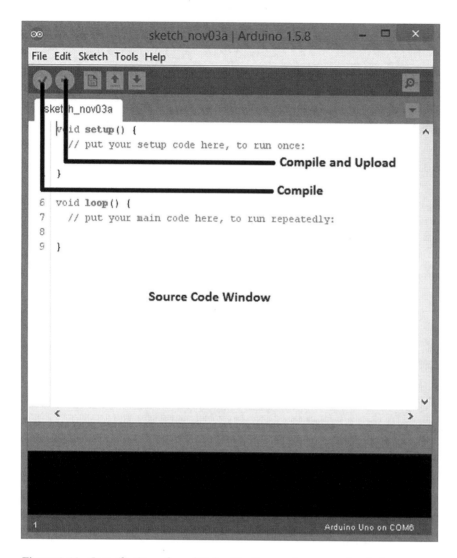

Figure 1-13. *Compile, Compile and Upload buttons and source code window*

If you just want to see if your program code contains any compiler errors, you could just click the Verify button, which is the circular button with the check mark on it near the top of the IDE. Clicking the verify button causes the compiler to check your program source code for errors and, finding none, it generates the executable code associated with your program. It does not, however, automatically upload that executable code to the Arduino board.

Assuming there are no program errors detected by the compiler, you can click the Upload button (i.e., the one with the arrow on it, just to the right of the Compile button). Clicking the Upload button causes the source code to be compiled and that code to be transferred from your PC into the flash memory on the Arduino board. Once the transfer is completed, the program code is immediately executed. In our case, this means the message is displayed on the *Serial* monitor, as shown in Figure 1-14.

Figure 1-14. Program output displayed on Serial monitor

Note the message at the bottom of the IDE. The IDE refers to your program as a sketch. The message tells you that your program used 1,932 bytes of flash memory out of 32,256 maximum memory bytes. It also tells you that 216 bytes of SRAM memory is used to actually process the variables used in the program, leaving 1832 bytes of SRAM unused. (Table 1-1 told you there was 2K of SRAM available on an Arduino Uno board.)

Another thing to notice is that, in the window for the *Serial* monitor, the monitor's baud rate is set to 115200 to match the baud rate in the *Serial*.begin(115200) program statement. If the two baud rates don't match, the output will be something looking like Mandarin, or you may not see any output at all. You can change the *Serial* monitor's baud rate by clicking the down-arrow at the end of the baud rate box. I'll explain the other aspects of the *Serial* monitor in later chapters.

Summary

In this chapter you learned about the Arduino development environment and some of the board choices you can use that support the Atmel chip family. Some of the hardware details about the boards were discussed to help you decide which board to use while you learn about programming the board using Arduino C. You then downloaded the Arduino development environment and installed the IDE. As a check on the IDE installation, you wrote a simple program and compiled and uploaded it to the board, and ran the program to verify that everything was installed correctly. You are now ready to start learning Arduino C.

CHAPTER 2

▨ ▨ ▨

Arduino C

The C programming language began its march to become formally defined by the American National Standard Institute (ANSI) with the formation of the X3J11 committee in 1983. The committee's work was completed and the standard passed in 1989. Ever since then, the language is often referred to an "ANSI C". The standard is also recognized by the International Organization for Standardization (ISO), so sometimes you'll hear it referred to as "ISO C". For all practical purposes, ANSI C and ISO C are the same. In a world that is overly hung up on political correctness, you will also hear both versions called "standard C". There have been several additional "upgrades" to the language (e.g., 1999 and 2011), but we will simply refer to it as standard C.

The C you are about to learn is not standard C. Instead, you will be learning an almost complete subset of standard C. The flavor of C used by the Arduino IDE is missing several elements of standard C (e.g., the *double* data type), but the absence of those features is not a crippling blow by any means. You will soon discover that the subset version of standard C, which we will call *Arduino C*, is more than able to perform just about any task you can throw at it. The missing features can usually be worked around, albeit sometimes in a less elegant manner.

Another difference between Arduino C and standard C is that the underlying compiler for Arduino C is actually the Open Source C++ compiler. As such, you will discover that most of the libraries used with the Arduino IDE are written using C++. This means that, even though you are writing your programs in Arduino C, much of the glue holding things together "under the hood" is written in C++. Indeed, you are free to mix C with C++ in the Arduino IDE. Still, we concentrate on Arduino C in this book, even though we have added a chapter near the end of the book to give you a light introduction to C++. So, from this point forward, when I write about the C language, I am actually referring to C as it is implemented in the Arduino IDE.

So, with that caveat in mind, let's start learning Arduino C.

The Building Blocks of All Programming Languages

All programming languages, from Ada to ZPL, are built from four basic elements:

- Expressions

- Statements

- Statement blocks

- Function blocks

The last element, function blocks, may be called different names in different languages, such as methods in C++, C#, and Java, procedures in Pascal, subroutines in Basic or Fortran, or perhaps some more exotic name in lesser-known languages. Regardless of their name, *function blocks* tend to be blocks of code designed to address some narrowly defined task. Programs are little more than arrangements of these elements in a way that solves a problem.

© Jack Purdum 2015
J. Purdum, *Beginning C for Arduino, Second Edition*: Learn C Programming
for the Arduino, DOI 10.1007/978-1-4842-0940-0_2

Expressions

An *expression* is created by combining operands and operators. Simply stated, an *operand* is typically a piece of data that is acted upon by an operator. An *operator* is often a mathematical or logical action that is performed on one or more operands. For example,

```
a + b
m - 3000
g < d
```

are examples of expressions. In the first example, the operands *a* and *b* are added (the + operator) together in a math expression. In the second example, the numeric constant 3000 (an operand) is subtracted (the – operator) from the operand named *m*. In the last example, operand *g* is compared to operand *d* to see if *g* is less than (the < operator) *d*. In this last example, a relational operator (i.e., the "less than" operator, or "<") is used instead of a math operator. In all three examples, the two operands are used in conjunction with a single operator to form an expression.

The first example is an addition expression, the second is a subtraction expression, whereas the last example is a relational expression. In each of these expressions, there are two operands and one operator. That's why you often hear such expressions referred to as binary expressions. *Binary expressions* are expressions that use a *binary operator*. Binary operators (e.g., +, –, and <) always use two operands. Another important thing to keep in mind is that any expression ultimately resolves to a value. There are *unary operators* that have only one operand and *ternary operators* that require three operands. However, the binary operators are the most common in C.

Expressions can be combined. For example, suppose A = 1, B = 2, and C = 3. You can write a complex expression as:

```
A + B + C
```

Because all expressions resolve to a value, you can resolve the first subexpression, A + B, to:

```
1 + 2 + C
```

Because the first subexpression is now pure numbers, you can resolve the first subexpression to the value 3. You can then resolve the complex expression to:

```
3 + C
```

Note what happened here. You took a complex expression with two operators and three operands and resolved one of the subexpressions (i.e., A + B) to 3. However, in the process, you reduced the complex expression to a single (binary) expression, 3 + C. Now you can resolve the remaining expression to

```
3 + C
3 + 3
6
```

and the complex expression with two subexpressions is now resolved to a single value, 6. Often you will hear the process of simplifying a complex expression called *factoring an expression* or *resolving an expression*.

What about the relational expression *g < d*? Suppose *g* = 5 and *d* = 4, then:

```
g < d
5 < 4
false
```

The expression resolves to "false" because 5 is greater than 4, not less than 4.

You might be thinking: "Wait a second! You just said that all expressions resolve to a value. 'False' isn't a value, it's a word." True, but in programming languages, logic *true* and logic *false* expressions do resolve to a value. In most languages, logic *true* resolves to a non-zero value (e.g., –1 or 1) and logic *false* is zero. *Relational expressions are designed to resolve to a logic true or false state*, so they ultimately do resolve to a value that can be used in a program.

Statements

A *statement* is a complete C instruction for the computer. All C statements end with a semicolon (;). The following are examples of C statements:

```
i = 50;
a = b + c;
m = d / 2;
```

In the first example, the equal sign (=) is called the *assignment operator* and is used to "assign" the value on the right side of the equal sign to the operand on the left side of the assignment operator. Therefore, the value 50 is assigned to variable *i*. Note how this first statement example is nothing more than an expression using the assignment operator with a semicolon at the end of the line. The operands are 50 and variable *i*.

So, what is a variable? Simply stated, a *variable* is nothing more than a location in memory that's been assigned a name. You will read much more about variables in Chapter 3.

In the second statement, you have a complex expression with a semicolon at the end. In this example, the value to assign into variable *a* is not yet known, so you must resolve the expression *b* + *c* first to get a value. If *b* = 4 and *c* = 5, then we can resolve the complex expression to:

```
a = b + c
a = 4 + 5
a = 9
```

The last expression assigns the value 9 into variable *a*. By adding a semicolon at the end of the line, the expression becomes a statement that causes variable *a* to change its value to 9. Remember in Chapter 1 I told you the C compiler is responsible for changing the English-like syntax of C into the 1s and 0s that the μc understands? Well, it is the semicolon that makes the C compiler finish whatever task the statement wants to be done. If you have a complex statement like

```
x = a + b - c + g + h + k;
```

then the compiler must resolve all of the intermediate expressions (i.e., *a* + *b*, *c* + *g*, *h* + *k*) before it can determine what new value to assign into *x*. It is the semicolon at the end of the statement that tells the compiler it has all the intermediate expressions it needs to resolve the statement.

■ **Note** The first kind of programming mistake you will likely make is forgetting to place a semicolon at the end of a statement. Because the semicolon is a *statement terminator*, each program statement must end with a semicolon. Without the semicolon, the compiler would not know when it has all of the information necessary to process the statement.

Operator Precedence

Suppose you have the following statement comprised of several expressions:

```
j = 5 + k * 2;
```

where $k = 3$ and the asterisk (*) is the multiplication operator. Now ask yourself: Does j equal 16 (i.e., $16 = 8 * 2$) or does it equal 11 (i.e., $11 = 5 + 6$)? The statement appears ambiguous because we aren't sure about the order in which the complex expression is resolved. Which of the following is it?

```
j = 5 + k * 2;        j = 5 + k * 2;
j = 5 + 3 * 2;        j = 5 + 3 * 2;
j = 8 * 2             j = 5 + 6;
j = 16;               j = 11;
```

Clearly, the results differ because of the order in which we resolve the complex expression. C resolves such ambiguities by assigning each operator a precedence level. *Operator precedence* refers to the order in which complex expressions are resolved. A partial C precedence table can be seen in Table 2-1.

Table 2-1. *Operator Precedence*

Precedence level	Operator
1	* (multiplication), /, %
2	+, -

In Table 2-1, you can see that multiplication, division, and modulo expressions are resolved before addition and subtraction expressions. Therefore, in the preceding expressions, the correct answer for j is 11 because the multiplication expression is resolved before the addition expression. If there is a tie between math operator precedence levels, they are resolved by solving the subexpressions in a left-to-right manner. Resolving subexpressions in this manner means that the math operators are left associative. The term *left associative* means that operator precedence ties are factored by processing the subexpressions in a left-to-right order. Because there are more operators than are presented in Table 2-1, I will be expanding the precedence table as you learn more about C.

Statement Blocks

A *statement block* consists of one or more statements grouped together so they are viewed by the compiler as though they are a single statement. For example, suppose you are an apartment manager and, if there is 4 or more inches of snow on the ground, you need to shovel the sidewalk. Assuming the >= operator is read as "greater than or equal to," you might write this expression as:

```
if (snow >= 4) {
        // Next 3 statements form a statement block body
        PutOnSnowRemovalClothes();
        GetSnowShovel();
        ShovelSidewalk();
} else {
        GoBackToBed();
}
```

Statement blocks start with an opening brace character ({) and end with a closing brace character (}). All statements between the opening and closing braces form the *statement block body*. In our example, it appears that when 4 or more inches of snow exist, we will put on our coat, grab a snow shovel, and shovel the sidewalks. If there is less than 4 inches of snow, a different statement block is executed (i.e., we go back to bed). You can place any type of valid C statements you wish within the statement block. You will see lots of examples of this in later chapters. For now, just think of a statement block as being defined by the opening and closing braces.

Function Blocks

A *function block* is a block of code that is designed to accomplish a single task. Although you may not be aware of it, you actually used a function block in the previous section. That is, *PutOnSnowRemovalStuff()* is a function that is designed to have you put on your coat. The actual code might look like this:

```
void PutOnSnowRemovalStuff(void) {
        if (NotDressed) {
                PutOnClothes();
                PutOnShoes();
        }
        GoToCloset();
        PutOnBoots();
        PutOnCoat();
        PutOnGloves();
        PutOnHat();
}
```

In this example, the function block also starts with an opening brace ({) and ends with a closing brace (}). However, well-designed function blocks are usually written to create "black boxes" in which the details of *how* we are doing something are buried in the function. For example, you might be thinking of writing the code to control a robot that requires sensors to detect whatever lies ahead. You might write a *TurnRight()* function that turns your robot 90 degrees to the right. This probably involves turning one of the wheels, perhaps applying a greater number of digital pulses to a stepper motor to cause the front two wheels to turn to the right. However, perhaps at a later time you decide to change your robot from four wheels to three wheels. Now you don't need to turn two wheels; only one needs to turn. By hiding the details of what has to be done to turn your robot to the right in the *TurnRight()* black box, you only need to change the program code in that one function block, rather than in a whole bunch of places where a right turn might be needed. By writing a *TurnRight()* function, you can avoid duplicating all of the statements that are in the *TurnRight()* function each time a right turn is called for in the program.

Another example might help. Suppose you are writing an application that inputs a phone number from a keypad. Your application requires home, cell, and work phone numbers. To make sure a valid phone number was entered, you need to check that it fits the 1-123-456-7890 format. Now you could duplicate the format checking program code three times in the program, or you could write a *CheckPhoneFormat()* function and simply "call" it three times. (For now, you can think of the term "call" as meaning to execute the body of code associated with the function. I have more to say about this in "The Backpack Analogy" sidebar later in this chapter.) Let's see ... write, test, and debug the code three times, or write a function and test and debug it once. Kinda seems like a no-brainer to me. Also, using functions means that you will be using less memory resources by not duplicating the code.

If you think of a computer program as a sequence of smaller tasks, function blocks are used to delimit the code for each of those smaller tasks. As you will soon find out, the Arduino programming environment has hundreds, if not thousands, of pre-written function blocks that you can use in your own programs. This means you don't have to reinvent the wheel each time a common programming task steps in front of you.

You just grab one of the existing function blocks from the library of pre-written function blocks and stick it into your program. Life is good ... and often easier because you can stand on the shoulders of programmers who have previously contributed to a C programming library that you can use!

Every program you can think of is built from the four basic parts discussed in this section. Indeed, the rest of this book is nothing more than showing you how to use these simple parts in an effective way to solve a particular programming problem.

Ah, but therein lies the problem. There are an infinite number of ways to combine these elements into a computer program, and some will work and others won't. In fact, even if you get your program to work, it doesn't mean there's not a different (better?) way to accomplish the same task. For instance, suppose you want to sort a group of numbers into a list, going from the smallest to the largest number in the group. There are dozens of ways to sort a list of numbers into ascending order, each with its own advantages and disadvantages. In fact, you'll find that your range of programming choices increases as you learn more about programming in general. Even something as simple as scanning a sequence of text looking for a particular pattern can be done many different ways (e.g., Brute Force vs. Boyer-Moore algorithms). The more programming knowledge and experience you gain, the more you'll be able to craft an elegant solution to a given programming problem. After all, if the only tool you have is a hammer, it shouldn't be too surprising that all your problems look like a nail.

Beginning programmers tend to lose sight of the fact that a function really should only perform one task. Their tendency is to craft a function that is a Swiss Army knife—trying to do too much in a single function. While a Swiss Army knife is convenient, it really doesn't do any of the tasks as well as a dedicated tool does. Which would you rather do—use a Swiss Army knife's saw blade to cut down a tree, or use a chain saw?

Further, as the complexity of a given task increases, so do the ways in which you can solve the problem. If someone came to you and asked you to write a fire alarm system for a hotel, there are probably a bazillion different ways to accomplish that task. Now the question is: Where do you start? That's the topic of the next section.

The Five Program Steps

When I was teaching programming courses, we would have in-class quizzes from time-to-time. Time allotted for the quizzes was usually about 30 minutes, and the programming task was always manageable within that time line. Virtually all of the students started banging on their keyboards the instant the clock started.

Bad move.

Ah, but there was always a student or two who stared at the ceiling, scribbled some notes on a piece of paper, all before they started writing a single line of code. While they often starting writing code five or ten minutes later than the other students, they always turned in a worthy solution. How come? Why?

The reason is because they thought about their plan of attack *before* they started throwing statements on the screen. Most students seem to think movement or activity means a solution. Not so; yet most students didn't seem to know where or how to start solving a programming problem. That's the purpose of this section: to give you a way to begin to organize a solution to a programming problem.

The simple fact is that every program you can think of can be reduced to five basic program elements, or steps. When you first start to design a solution to a programming problem, you should think of that program in terms of the following Five Program Steps: 1) Initialization, 2) Input, 3) Processing, 4) Output, and 5) Termination. Let's consider these steps in a little more detail.

1. Initialization Step

The purpose of the *Initialization Step* is *to establish the environment in which the program will run.* For example, if you've ever used Microsoft Excel, Word, or similar programs, the File command frequently has a list of the most recently used files. Internet browsers allow you to define a home page. A print program often has a default printer that is initialized. A database program often establishes a default network connection.

In all of these cases, data is fetched from somewhere (i.e., a data file, memory, EEPROM, the registry) and is used to establish some baseline environment in which the program is to run.

Simply stated, the Initialization Step does whatever background preparation must be done before the program can begin execution to solve its primary task. It's the same in the world of μcs. Ports need to be initialized, sensors have to be activated, thermocouples need to stabilize, plus a host of other possible events.

As a general rule, the program statements in the Initialization Step are only performed once when the program first begins execution. The code in the Initialization Step is not executed again, unless the μc is reset or power is lost and reapplied.

2. Input Step

Every computer program has a task that is designed to take some existing state of information, process it in some way, and show or otherwise use the new state of that information. If you are writing a fire alarm system, you take the information provided by the fire sensors, interpret their current state, and, if there is a fire, do something about it. If the sensor shows no fire, perhaps a second set of sensors are read and the process repeated. Indeed, your program may do nothing for decades but take new readings every few seconds and determine if some remedial action is necessary. Alas, the day may come when a fire is sensed and remedial actions are taken. Still, the entire process depends upon inputting fresh data from the sensors in a timely fashion.

The Input Step is the sequence of program statements that are necessary to acquire the information needed to solve the task at hand. That information, or data, may come from a sensor, a potentiometer, a file handle, a database or printer connection, a Wi-Fi signal—the list of data sources is almost endless. Regardless of the source, however, the purpose is to provide input that proves useful to the solution of the problem at hand.

3. Process Step

Continuing with our fire alarm example, once the input from the sensors is received, some body of code must be responsible for determining if the sensors are detecting a fire or not. In other words, the voltage (i.e., temperature) must be read (input) and then interpreted (i.e., the data processed) to determine the current state of the sensors. In a desktop application, perhaps the data input is the price and quantity of some item purchased by a customer. The Process Step may perform the task of determining the total cost of the purchase to the consumer.

Note that a program may have multiple Process Steps. For example, with our consumer, there may be a process to determine the sales tax due on the purchase. In this case, the process of determining the total cost of the order becomes an input to the process that calculates the sales tax due. The sales and taxes due could be the inputs to yet another process (e.g., consumer billing or updating a database).

In all cases, however, the Process Step is responsible for taking a set of inputs and processing it to get a new set of data.

4. Output Step

After the Process Step has finished its work, the new value is typically output on some device or sent to some other entity for further processing. In our consumer sales example, we might now display the total amount the consumer owes us. The Output Step, however, isn't limited to simply displaying the new data. Quite often, the new data is saved or passed along to some other program. For example, a program may accumulate the sales figures throughout the day and then update a database at night so some other program can generate a sales report for management to review the next morning. In our fire alarm example, the Output Step may cause an LED for a particular sensor to continue to display a green color under normal conditions. If a fire is sensed, perhaps the LED displays red, so whomever is in charge can see what area of the building is on fire.

The Output Step could be the Input Step for another program. For example, the Output Step might be an average of several temperature readings where, if a certain temperature is reached, two vats of chemicals are mixed together. It this example, the Output Step of the temperature program becomes the Input Step for a vat-mixing program.

Simply stated, the Output Step is responsible for using the results of the Process Step. This utilization could be as simple as displaying the new data on a display device or passing that new value on to some other program or process.

5. Termination Step

The Termination Step has the responsibility of "cleaning up" after the program is finished performing its task. In desktop applications, it's common for the Termination Step to perform the Initialization Step "in reverse." That is, if the program keeps track of the most recent data files that were used, the Termination Step must update that list of files. If the Initialization Step opens a database or printer connection, the Termination Step should close that connection down so unused resources are returned to the system.

Many μc applications, however, are not designed to terminate. A fire alarm system is likely designed to continue running forever, as long as things are "normal." Even then, however, there may still be a Termination Process that is followed. For example, if the fire alarm system has a component failure, the Termination Process may try to identify the failed component before the system shuts down for repairs. Perhaps the Termination Process deactivates the alarm system before a maintenance shutdown.

Simply stated, the Termination Process should allow for a graceful termination of the currently running program. In most of the projects you examine in this book, the Termination Step is not used. It is assumed that the program continues until power is removed or there is a component failure.

The Purpose of the Five Program Steps

I can't even begin to guess how many times I've given an in-class coding problem only to have the students say: "I don't even know where to start." Well, clearly they weren't paying attention, because that's the purpose of the Five Program Steps—to serve as a starting point for designing a program. As mentioned earlier, there is a tremendous urge to just start banging out source code on the keyboard the minute the programming task is defined.

Big mistake.

Even a one or two sentence statement for each of the Five Program Steps is probably enough to get you started on the design and coding of a given program. An *algorithm* is nothing more than a formal statement of how a given set of inputs are manipulated to produce a desired result. An algorithm is like a recipe or a set of blueprints: it describes what you need to do to reach a desired goal or endpoint. And so it is with programming: the Five Program Steps can be used to formulate a plan for solving a given programming problem. Although algorithms are more closely tied to Steps 2 and 3 (i.e., Input and Processing), the Five Program Steps should help you formulate an algorithm to solve whatever task is at hand.

Fight the urge to "look busy" by just hacking away at the keyboard without a program design based on the Five Program Steps. Creating a program design may seem like too much work, but trust me, you'll save a ton of time in the long run. (Where did the phrase "a ton of time" come from? Is time a resting place for Higgs-boson particles?)

A Revisit to Your First Program

Listing 2-1 shows the program code that you loaded and ran in the previous chapter. Let's look at that program in terms of our Five Program Steps. First of all, Listing 2-1 is the source code for your first program. *Source code* refers to the series of C language statements that constitute the program. It is the source code that the C compiler *parses* (i.e., reads and checks for syntax and semantic errors) and ultimately translates into binary code (i.e., the 1s and 0s) that the μc understands. Almost all of the source code is built up from C language statements … but not all.

Listing 2-1. The Source Code for Your First Program

```
void setup()
{                       // Start of setup() function body

  Serial.begin(115200);// Step 1, Initialization

  // Step 2, Input (the letters between the quotes)
  // Step 3. Process - Serial object formats data for display
  // Step 4. Output - Display the message on the monitor
Serial.println("This is my first Arduino program!");
}                       // End of setup() function body

void loop()
{                       // Start of loop() function body
}                       // End of loop() function body
```

The setup() Function

Every Arduino program *must* have a *setup()* function. While it is common to have program statements and directives appear before the *setup()* function, it is the *setup()* function that marks the actual start of the program. The purpose of the *setup()* function is to set the environment in which the program is run. In Listing 2-1, the Initialization Step initializes the *Serial* object for use in the program with the following statement:

```
Serial.begin(115200);// Step 1, Initialization
```

Note that the statement ends with the semicolon. The two slash marks (i.e., the //) are used to introduce a *comment* in the program. I will have more to say about program comments later in the chapter. For now, just think of program comments as little notes to help clarify what the code is doing.

This is the only remaining statement in our short program:

```
Serial.println("This is my first Arduino program!");
```

However, that single statement is really doing a lot of work. First, the sentence that appears between the two double quote marks is a sequence of characters that represents the input data for the program. As such, it serves as the Input Step (Step 2) of the Five Program Steps. The sequence of characters is the message that you want displayed on the *Serial* device.

Once the data is provided by Step 2, those characters within the quote marks are prepared for display by the *Serial* object. The result is that Step 3, the Process Step, converts what appears on the screen into the host character set. For the Arduino, the characters are processed using the *ASCII* (American Standard Code for Information Interchange) character set. For example, when you see a capital A displayed on your monitor, what the processor sees is the integer value 65. (A complete ASCII table can be found at www.bibase.com/ascii.htm.) When the Process Step is completed, your message is ready to be displayed.

As mentioned in the previous chapter, the *println()* method of the *Serial* object does the actual work moving your message to the output device for display. In this program, the output device is the *Serial* monitor. Therefore, the Output Step, Step 4, is tasked to the *println()* method, which results in your message appearing on the *Serial* monitor on your PC. (Recall that C++ uses the term method in lieu of the C term function. For all practical purposes, they are the same. However, I try to use the term *method* when the code is part of a C++ class, and I reserve the word *function* when the code is written in C.)

The loop() Function

At this point, the program proceeds to the *loop()* function, which appears at the bottom of Listing 2-1. Similar to the *setup()* function, every Arduino program *must* have a *loop()* function. However, in our simple program, there is are no statements in the statement body for the *loop()* function. That is, no program statements appear between the opening and closing braces of the *loop()* function.

Because there are no further program statements in the program source code in Listing 2-1, our program is finished. After all, if there are no more program statements, there's nothing left for the program to do, so our program ends. We have reached Step 5, the Termination Step.

Well, not really.

Arduino programs are designed in such a way that they proceed to the *loop()* function after the *setup()* function's closing brace is reached, even if there are no statements in the *loop()* function body. In other words, even though you can "see" it, after your message is displayed on the *Serial* monitor, it merrily proceeds to the *loop()* function and spins around inside of it doing nothing! Stated differently, your program never ends … there is no Step 5, or Termination Step. Indeed, you program continues to spin around in the empty *loop()* function doing nothing until you remove power or there is some kind of component failure.

■ **Note**   You can prove that *loop()* runs forever by looking at the C code file named main.cpp in your Arduino directory at hardware/arduino/avr/cores/arduino/main.cpp.

Because you may not know enough C to decipher what appears in the file at this moment, after a few more chapters you can return to that file and you'll be able to confirm that *loop()* does get called, even if it is empty, and that it does continue to execute forever.

You can demonstrate that *loop()* repeatedly executes with one simple change to the program shown in Listing 2-1. Simply move the last program statement in *setup()* into *loop()*. Your modified program should look like Listing 2-2.

Listing 2-2. The Source Code for Your First Program, As Modified

```
void setup()
{                       // Start of setup() function body

 Serial.begin(115200);// Step 1, Initialization

// Step 2, Input (the letters between the quotes)casll
// Step 3. Process - Serial object formats data for display
// Step 4. Output - Display the message on the monitor

}                       // End of setup() function body
```

```
void loop()
{                       // Start of loop() function body

 Serial.println("This is my first Arduino program!");

}                       // End of loop() function body
```

Now recompile and upload the new version of your program and invoke the *Serial* monitor. Any change in the displayed output?

If you modified the program correctly, the output on your *Serial* monitor should look like Figure 2-1. As you can see, the program message is displayed over and over because the *loop()* function is executing over and over. In other words, the purpose of the *loop()* function is to execute the statements in its function body over and over, *ad infinitum*.

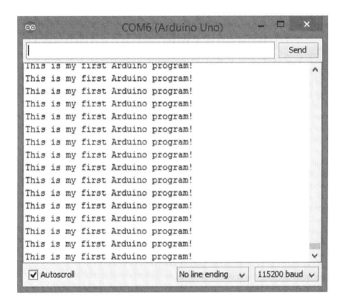

Figure 2-1. Output from the modified first program

So, how useful can it be to just repeat the same sequence of instructions over and over? Actually, it can be very useful. You might have a building with 100 fire sensors scattered throughout the building. One statement in *loop()* causes the program to go out and read the sensor to see if there is a fire. Finding no fire, the code changes some kind of sensor index, and the code goes out and reads the next fire sensor. Finding no fire, it increments the sensor index and reads the next sensor, and continues doing so until all 100 sensors have been read. Assuming all is well, the loop repeats itself and we visit sensor 1 again. The program constantly repeats this sequence until either there is a fire, or the power is removed, or some component in the system fails. The hypothetical *loop()* function might look something like this:

```
void loop()
{
   int sensorIndex;
   int fire;
```

```
for (sensorIndex = 1; sensorIndex <= 100; sensorIndex = sensorIndex + 1) {
  fire = ReadSensor(sensorIndex); // Return 1 if fire, 0 otherwise

  if (fire == 1) {    // If fire, do the following statements...
          SoundAlarm();
          TurnOnSprinklerSystem();
          CallFireDepartment();
          WaitForAllClear();
  }
  // If fire equals 0, go read the next sensor
  }
}
```

Although you are not ready to completely understand the code fragment presented here, you can see we define two variables named *sensorIndex* and *fire*. A *for* loop starts by setting the index equal to 1, and then calls a function named *ReadSensor(sensorIndex)*, sending the index number of the sensor we want to read (*sensorIndex*) to the function. Evidently, the *ReadSensor()* function returns a value of 0 if there is no fire detected and a value of 1 if there is a fire. The *if* statement checks to see if a fire was detected or not. If there is a fire, the four function calls within the *if* statement block are called. If there is no fire, those statements are skipped and we look at the next sensor.

Even though I have not discussed *for* loops or *if* statements, it's pretty easy to see what the intent of the program is. Clearly, the program is designed to monitor and protect the building "forever." Only when there is a fire does the code deviate from its simple repeated sampling of the sensors.

Arduino Program Requirements

The following are important lessons to learn in this section:

- Every Arduino program must have a *setup()* function.

- The *setup()* function is only executed once when the program first starts, making it a good candidate for Step 1, Initialization code.

- Every Arduino program must have a *loop()* function.

- The *loop()* function is repeatedly executed until power is removed, a program is reset, or a component fails. Programs Steps 2 through 4 usually appear within *loop()*.

The Blink Program

The Arduino IDE has numerous sample programs distributed with it. One of the sample programs is the Blink program. To load Blink into the IDE, use the File ➤ Examples ➤ Basics ➤ Blink menu sequence, as shown in Figure 2-2.

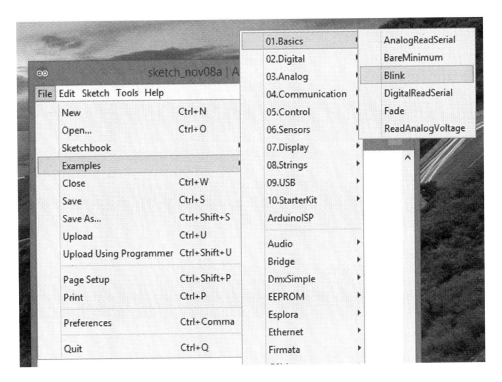

Figure 2-2. *Menu sequence for Blink example*

The source code for the Blink program is shown in Listing 2-3.

Listing 2-3. The Blink Program

```
/*
Blink
Turns on an LED on for one second, then off for one second, repeatedly.

Most Arduinos have an on-board LED you can control. On the Uno and
Leonardo, it is attached to digital pin 13. If you're unsure what
pin the on-board LED is connected to on your Arduino model, check
the documentation at http://arduino.cc

This example code is in the public domain.

modified 8 May 2014
by Scott Fitzgerald
*/

// the setup function runs once when you press reset or power the board
void setup() {
// initialize digital pin 13 as an output.
pinMode(13, OUTPUT);
}
```

```
// the loop function runs over and over again forever
void loop() {
  digitalWrite(13, HIGH); // turn the LED on (HIGH is the voltage level)
  delay(1000);            // wait for a second
  digitalWrite(13, LOW);  // turn the LED off by making the voltage LOW
  delay(1000);            // wait for a second
}
```

As mentioned earlier, the program *source code* refers to the series of C language statements that constitute the program. It is the source code that the C compiler parses (i.e., reads and checks for syntax and semantic errors) and ultimately translates into binary code (i.e., the 1s and 0s) that the μc understands. Almost all of the source code is built up from C language statements ... but not all. (As mentioned earlier, most Arduino literature refers to Arduino program source code as *sketches*. However, I prefer to use the term "program" rather than sketch.)

Program Comments

I mentioned program comments before, but now we want to consider them in greater detail. The first dozen or so lines in the Blink program are as follows:

```
/*
Blink
Turns on an LED on for one second, then off for one second, repeatedly.

Most Arduinos have an on-board LED you can control. On the Uno and
Leonardo, it is attached to digital pin 13. If you're unsure what
pin the on-board LED is connected to on your Arduino model, check
the documentation at http://arduino.cc

This example code is in the public domain.

modified 8 May 2014
by Scott Fitzgerald
*/
```

If you look closely at these lines, you can see that none of them ends with a semicolon. That is, none of the lines forms a C program statement since all program C statements must end with a semicolon. If that's the case, what are they and why are they part of the source code?

The preceding lines are called comment lines. *Comment lines* are used to document what's going on in a program for whomever may be reading the code. There are two basic types of comments: single-line and multi-line.

Single-Line Comments

You saw several examples of single-line comments in Listings 2-1 and 2-2. Single-line comments begin with a pair of slash (//) characters. There can be no spaces between the two slashes. (Otherwise the compiler might think it was looking at the division operator.) Upon seeing the two slash characters, the compiler knows that what follows from the two slashes *to the end of the current line,* is a program comment that does not need to be compiled. As such, comments that begin with // must appear on the same line as the two slash characters. If you fold a comment to the next line without the leading slashes, it will be seen as a syntax error by the compiler.

Again, the following is an example of this type of comment:

```
// Pin 13 has an LED connected on most Arduino boards.
// give it a name:
```

Multi-line Comments

Multi-line comments begin with a slash-asterisk pair (/*) and end with an asterisk-slash pair (*/). There are no spaces between the two character pairs. Everything in between these two character pairs is treated as a comment and is ignored by the compiler. Unlike single-line comments, multi-line comments can span multiple lines. You can see an example of a multi-line comment at the top of Listing 2-3.

Note that you could write the multi-line comment at the top of Listing 2-3 as

```
// Blink
// Turns on an LED on for one second, then off for one second, repeatedly.
```

and the program would behave exactly the same. However, multi-line comments are useful for long comments that span many lines because they take fewer keystrokes to implement. The compiler could care less which you use. The important thing to remember is that *comments invoke no penalty in terms of memory space or the performance of the program*, so there's no reason not to use them as needed.

When to Use Comments

Well, what does "as needed" mean? Fair question. Comments should be used any time you wish to document what a program is doing or about to do. Reading code isn't always easy and it might be hard for the reader to figure out what's going on in a particular section of code. In such cases, a comment may make it easier for someone to decipher what the code is supposed to do. For example, if you have a black box function that implements some really scary mathematical equation, you might add a comment to explain what's going on. If the function is really complex, it's not uncommon to put a multi-line reference comment into the code that has a book and page number (or perhaps an Internet URL address) where the reader can go for further information.

At first blush, it may seem that comments are directed to someone other than the person who actually wrote the code. Frequently, that is true, especially if you write code in a commercial environment with other programmers who may have to work with your code. However, even if you are the only person who will ever see the code, you'll be amazed how a piece of code that was so easy to understand this morning may as well be written in Sanskrit six months from now. Comments should be used to help the person reading the code … whomever that may be.

Yet, the question still remains: When do you add comments to a program? Too few comments often make the code difficult to understand. There simply are not enough comments to be helpful to your understanding of the code. However, too many comments can have the same effect because they "get in the way" of understanding the code. Comments are clutter if they don't contribute any real benefit to understanding the code.

There are no hard-and-fast rules for commenting the program source code. My preference is to use a multi-line comment before most function blocks or any line (or lines) of code that do something unusual or "tricky." You will see examples of function block comments in later chapters.

You should use single-line comments when you do something unusual that may take a few seconds or more to understand. For example,

```
x = y / 2.0;
x = y * .5;        // Divide the number in half
```

Both statements produce the same result for floating point numbers; they divide the number held in variable *y* in half. However, the second form is slightly faster because division is the slowest math operation you can use. The comment simply jogs the reader's mind as to what's being done. (Normally, you would not do this anyway. It would only be noticeable if the calculation was being done thousands of times in a big program loop.)

As a general rule, comment those lines of code that do something that makes you pause to understand what that line is doing. Commenting every line is almost never necessary in a program. Commenting obvious program statements is a waste of time:

```
x = x + 1;        // Take the value of x and add 1 to it.
```

Really? If the reader can't figure out what the preceding statement is doing without reading the comment, they really shouldn't be reading the program source code in the first place. The correct use of comments should result in relatively few comments in a program. I'll have more to say about comments as you gain more programming experience.

The setup() Function in Blink

There is only one program statement in the *setup()* function:

```
pinMode(13, OUTPUT);
```

This statement activates (or "calls") a function called *pinMode()*, which is a function provided to you with the Arduino IDE. We know this function must be buried within the IDE because we don't see the program source code for it in Listing 2-3. Therefore we can deduce that *pinMode()* is a function that is part of the "standard function library" that is part of the IDE. As pointed out in Chapter 1, a function is a small collection of program statements that is designed to perform a specific task. Some tasks are so common to almost all programs that they are collected together into a function library. A *function library* is nothing more than a collection of pre-written functions—each designed to perform a specific task—that you can reuse in your own programs. This collection of related functions is grouped together into a library. The *pinMode()* function is one of the functions found in the Arduino function library. Indeed, a good amount of your learning effort is to discover what tasks have already been solved for you by one of the functions in the function library.

Okay, so how do you find out what those functions are and what they do?

How to Find Information About Library Functions

If you want more information about a function that you think is in the Arduino standard library, visit `http://arduino.cc/en/Reference/HomePage`, and you will see a page similar to that seen in Figure 2-3.

Reference Language I Libraries I Comparison I Changes

Language Reference

Arduino programs can be divided in three main parts: *structure*, *values* (variables and constants), and *functions*.

Figure 2-3. Using the Arduino Language Reference

Note how I have typed *pinMode()* into the search bar. If you then click the small magnifying glass on the right edge of the text box, the search program will search for more details on whatever you typed into the search text box (e.g., *pinMode()* in our case). The search brings up a Google page for the *pinMode()* function. Usually, the first reference shown is the one you would select. However, if you double-click the word "pinmode" to highlight it, then right-click and select *Find in Reference*, the page seen in Figure 2-4 is found and displayed.

Reference Language I Libraries I Comparison I Changes

pinMode()

Description

Configures the specified pin to behave either as an input or an output. See the description of digital pins for details on the functionality of the pins.

Figure 2-4. The pinMode() description

If you read the complete description, you will find that the *pinMode()* function is used to set the way in which a pin is to be used in the program. In the Blink program, the reference tells us that the statement

```
pinMode(13, OUTPUT);
```

means that Arduino pin number 13 is going to be used as an OUTPUT pin. Simply stated, the symbolic constant OUTPUT is also defined within the Arduino IDE, which means that we will be outputting data on pin 13. If we wanted to read some device or sensor attached to pin 13 as a data source, we would use the following:

```
pinMode(13, INPUT); // If we want to read a device attached to pin 13
```

All of the digital pins on the Arduino can be configured as OUTPUT or INPUT pins.

So, why pin 13?

As it turns out, almost all Arduino (and compatible) boards have a built-in LED tied to pin 13. By defining pin 13 for use as an OUTPUT pin, we can turn this onboard LED on and off under software control, hence the program name "Blink".

I don't like seeing numeric constants, like the preceding 13, simply stuck in a program's source code. It would be much better if there were a way to give meaning to the number. I call such numbers *magic numbers* because their purpose or derivation is often a mystery … especially if you are reading source code you didn't write. You will see how to reduce the number of magic numbers in a program in Chapter 4.

■ **Note**   Although I have never found an Arduino-compatible board that didn't have an onboard LED, this could be the case for a "homegrown" board. If that were the case, you could attach the anode of an LED to pin 13, and connect the cathode to a resistor (220 ohm to 1000 ohm, 1/10W or larger is fine) , and run the other end of the resistor to ground (GND on the Arduino board). This would pulse the external LED when the Blink program is run.

The *pinMode()* function call is the only statement in the *setup()* function, so our Initialization Step consists of a single statement. Obviously, more complex programs can be expected to have more statements in *setup()*.

It is important for you to remember that the *setup()* function is only called once when the program first begins execution. This is why we can refer to *setup()* as the Initialization Step in our program. If you wish to call *setup()* a second time, you would have to press the Reset button on the μc board. The Reset button halts the current execution of the program and restarts it by calling *setup()*. You can also reset the board by removing and reapplying power to the board. The *setup()* function is called automatically (on most newer Arduino boards) each time you upload a new version of the program code from your PC to the μc board.

THE BACKPACK ANALOGY

You will often read the phrase "calling a function" as well as "returning from the function" or even "return to the caller". These are common idioms used by programmers, and they have a specific interpretation. Think of a function as a black box with front and back doors. Think of yourself as the person who marches through the program causing each program statement to execute.

The term "calling a function" means that any time a "function is called," you put on a backpack, stuff it with any information this function may want (e.g., 13 and OUTPUT for our *pinMode()* function call, which are called *function arguments*), and then set off to "call on the function." The door to the black box opens and you walk in and start executing whatever instructions are contained in the black box. If the black box needs information from the outside world, it takes that information (13, OUTPUT, which are now called *function parameters*) from your backpack before it begins its task. (I go into more details about parameters vs. arguments in Chapter 6.) The black box then does its thing, and upon completing its task, it may (or may not) put some new information in your backpack. It then ushers you to the back door and sends you back to the point immediately following the program point that caused you to visit the black box in the first place.

This process of going back to that precise program point is called "returning to the caller" or "returning from the function." Therefore, calling a function is nothing more than a journey to some set of pre-written program statements that are designed to accomplish a specific task. Once that task is complete, program control returns to the statement immediately following the function call.

So what is the second function argument in *pinMode()*, named *OUTPUT*, all about and where is it defined in the program? A *function argument* is simply a piece of data that the function needs to have to complete its task. *OUTPUT* is a symbolic constant that can be thought of as a variable name that is embedded within the compiler. A *symbolic constant* is a name that is tied to a specific data value. There is a programming convention (not a rule) where symbolic constants are written in uppercase letters. Because C is case sensitive, you could define a variable named *output* and the compiler knows that it is a different variable than its own symbolic constant named *OUTPUT*.

Why use symbolic constants? Simply stated, one reason is because it makes the program code easier to read. Which of the following would you rather read in a program?

```
pinMode(LED, OUTPUT);
```

or

```
pinMode(13, 1);
```

There are other reasons for using symbolic constants. I will explain them in later chapters. For now, however, simply think of symbolic constants as a series of uppercase letters that are tied to some predefined value with the intent of making the code easier to read.

The loop() Function

After the *setup()* function completes its work, every Arduino C program automatically calls the *loop()* function. Stated differently, when the Initialization Step (Step 1) is completed via the function call to *setup()*, we are ready for Step 2, the Input Step. Because there are no more statements in *setup()*, the remaining Program Steps must be in the *loop()* function. The code for the *loop()* function is reproduced as follows:

```
// the loop function runs over and over again forever
void loop() {
  digitalWrite(13, HIGH); // turn the LED on (HIGH is the voltage level)
  delay(1000);            // wait for a second
  digitalWrite(13, LOW);  // turn the LED off by making the voltage LOW
  delay(1000);            // wait for a second
      }
```

Inside the *loop()* function, the program calls a pre-written function named *digitalWrite(13, HIGH)*, passing in two arguments to the *digitalWrite()* function: the I/O pin number to write to and the state we wish to place the I/O pin into (*HIGH* in this case). Once again, *HIGH* is a symbolic constant held within the compiler and is interpreted to mean we want to turn the pin on, which supplies a voltage (5V) to I/O pin 13. This voltage then turns on the LED.

Note the purposes the *digitalWrite()* function serves. First, it tells the function which I/O pin to change and what state to place the I/O pin in. Once the function receives these two pieces of information (via your backpack!), it places the LED in the desired state. In this case, the function turns the LED on. In other words, passing in the two pieces of information to *digitalWrite()* serves as the Input Step (Step 2) of our Five Program Steps. *digitalWrite()* also serves as part of the Processing Step (Step 3) because it takes the input data from the Input Step and changes the state of the LED according to the inputs it just received. Given these inputs, the LED is turned on at this point. That is, the function processes the input data and the LED "displays" (Step 4, Output Step) light.

You can probably guess what the *delay(1000)* call does. When the *delay(1000)* function call program statement is reached, the program puts the number 1000 into your backpack and you trundle off to the *delay()* black box. Once you're inside the black box named *delay()*, the code within the black box takes the value 1000 from your backpack and executes the code contained within the black box. In other words, *delay()* needs some information, called a function parameter, from the "outside world" to complete its task. If you look up the description for *delay()* (http://arduino.cc/en/Reference/Delay), you will find that the function returns no value to the caller. Therefore, when *delay()* is finished doing its thing, it hands you an empty backpack and shows you the back door of the black box. Program control, therefore, resumes execution with whatever the next statement is after the *delay(1000)* statement.

The *delay(1000)* function call causes the program's execution to pause for 1000 milliseconds (or one second). Because the LED is turned on, the one-second time delay has the effect of letting us observe the LED with illumination. If the calls to *delay()* function were left out of the program, the LED would be turned on and off for such a short period of time that our eye would not even be able to tell it was blinking. In an operational sense, therefore, the *delay()* function call serves as an extension of the Output Step (Step 4) of our Five Program Steps by letting us observe the current state of the LED.

As you probably guessed, the next call to *digitalWrite(13, LOW)* and its subsequent call to the *delay(1000)* function turns the LED off for one second. This is still part of the Process and Output steps. Turning the LED off is just as much an Output process as turning it on.

Once the *delay(1000)* function is finished, the closing brace of the *loop()* function is read. However, because *loop()* establishes what's called a *program loop*, program execution returns back to the first statement in the *loop()* function body and performs a second pass through the loop starting with *digitalWrite(13, HIGH)* again. This turns the LED back on. This sequence repeats until power is removed from the circuit, which means the LED simply sits there and blinks until the power is removed from the μc board, a component fails, or the cows come home.

Because the program is designed to loop forever, there really is no Termination Step (Step 5). Most microcontroller programs are written to chug along until they are stopped by some outside force (e.g., losing power or component failure). There are exceptions to this generalization, but they are relatively rare.

delay(): Good News, Bad News

The *delay()* function is an easy-to-use way of injecting a time delay into a program. That's the good news. The bad news is that, during the delay time period, the Arduino board is essentially brain dead. That is, the central processing unit (CPU) is concentrating so hard on getting the time delay right, it can't do anything else. In many applications, this isn't a problem. However, imagine our fire alarm sensor situation with the new World Trade Center. In a building that large, there might be 10,000 fire sensors. If you used a polling method to read each sensor, and it takes a hundredth of a second for each "visit," a round-trip through the sensor list will take 100 seconds. Now further suppose that the instant you leave a given sensor, it immediately detects a fire. It would be 100 seconds before you knew about the fire. Giving a fire a 100-second head start is not a good thing.

Because of this limitation of the polling method for reading sensors, most programmers would use what's called an Interrupt Service Routine (ISR). Simply stated, all of the sensors are tied to an interrupt pin on the Arduino board, and if a fire breaks out, the sensor *immediately* sends a message to the interrupt pin and executes the code associated with the ISR, even if it's not that sensor's turn to be read. Therefore, using an ISR effectively does away with the 100-second delay.

Well ... maybe.

If you are using *delay()* in your program, the Arduino CPU is comatose while *delay()* is doing its thing. That means that no ISR can be serviced until after the delay period is finished. So if you do a *delay(600000)* call in your fire alarm program, the fire could get a 10-minute head start before you even know a fire has started!

There are better ways to put a delay in your program, which we will explore later on. If you're curious right now, look at the program named BlinkWithoutDelay (File ➤ Examples ➤ Digital ➤ BlinkWithoutDelay). This program shows how to put a delay into a program, but still allow ISRs to interrupt things if necessary.

Summary

In this chapter you learned how to build program statements from operands and operators. You then saw how statements can be enlarged to statement and function blocks, ultimately leading to a complete program. You also learned the Five Program Steps and how they can be used to help design a program. Finally, these concepts were applied to a dissection of the Blink program example. With these preliminaries behind you, you can move on to learn about the various types of data you can use in your programs.

EXERCISES

1. Name the basic building blocks of a programming language.

   Answer: Operands, operators ➤ Expressions ➤ Statements ➤ Statement blocks ➤ Function blocks

2. What is a binary operator?

   Answer: A binary operator is an operator that requires two operands to create an expression.

3. Why is an understanding of operator precedence important in an expression?

   Answer: Operator precedence dictates the order in which subexpressions are evaluated in complex statements. Without this understanding, it is possible that a complex statement will not have the subexpressions evaluated in the order you wish, leading to erroneous results.

CHAPTER 2 ▦ ARDUINO C

4. Which of the Five Program Steps is least likely to appear in your programs, and why?

   Answer: The Termination Step. The reason is because many μc programs are designed to run forever and may never reach a termination point unless power is removed or a component fails.

5. What is the purpose of the /* and */ character pairs?

   Answer: This sequence of characters mark the start and the end of a multi-line comment in a program. They are also useful in "commenting out" a chunk of code during program testing and debugging.

6. What does "calling a function" mean?

   Answer: It means that program control is transferred from its current place in the program to the code associated with the function that is to be executed.

7. What does "return to the caller" mean?

   Answer: Return to the caller occurs when program control finishes executing the code associated with a function and program control returns to the point at which the function was called.

8. When would using *delay()* be a poor program choice?

   Answer: Because *delay()* prevents communication with any of the Arduino's I/O pins while the *delay()* is being processed, it would be a bad choice with programs that use Interrupt Service Routines.

9. Write a general purpose accounting system for your Arduino.

   Answer: Naw … just kidding.

44

CHAPTER 3

▨ ▨ ▨

Arduino C Data Types

When we refer to a C data type, we are referring to the attributes that a piece of program data has. As you will learn, certain data types are better suited to specific tasks than other data types, even though more than one data type might work. Selecting the right data type often results in a program that runs faster and uses less memory. In the μc world, where speed and memory are rare commodities, it pays to know what your data type choices are. In this chapter you will learn about the data types the Arduino C brings to the table. Arduino C supports almost all of ANSI C's data types.

As mentioned in Chapter 2, a *variable* is little more than a chunk of memory that has been given a name. When you define a variable, you must also tell the compiler what type of data is to be associated with that variable. The *data type of the variable is important because it determines how many bytes of memory are dedicated to that variable, and what type of data can be stored in the variable.*

Byte?

As you probably know, computers only know two things: On (1) or Off (0). Decades ago, computer manufacturers decided to arrange these binary digits, or *bits*, into groupings of 8 bits. Each group of 8 bits taken as a unit is called a *byte*. Because a byte can only have two states, 1 or 0, bytes are most happy using base 2 arithmetic, rather than the base 10 that you are used to. If you recall your high school math, 2^8 is 256. So a byte can have its bits arranged in 256 unique combinations. Because 0 is a valid number, a byte of computer memory can represent the values 0–255. I will have more to say about binary data later.

As you will learn later in this chapter, there are two basic types of variables: value types and reference types. If the variable is defined as a value type, there is a very specific range of numeric values possible with that data type.

A list of the basic *value data types* is presented in Table 3-1.

© Jack Purdum 2015
J. Purdum, *Beginning C for Arduino, Second Edition*: Learn C Programming
for the Arduino, DOI 10.1007/978-1-4842-0940-0_3

Table 3-1. *Arduino C Value Data Types*

Type	Byte length	Range of values
boolean	1	Limited to logic *true* and *false*
char	1	Range: –128 to +127
unsigned char	1	Range: 0 to 255
byte	1	Range: 0 to 255
int	2	Range: –32,768 to 32,767
unsigned int	2	Range: 0 to 65,535
word	2	Range: 0 to 65,535
long	4	Range: –2,147,483,648 to 2,147,483,647
unsigned long	4	Range: 0 to 4,294,967,295
float	4	Range: –3.4028235E+38 to 3.4028235E+38
double	4	Range: –3.4028235E+38 to 3.4028235E+38
string	?	A null (`'\0'`) terminated reference type data built from a character array
String	?	An reference data type object
array	?	A sequence of a value type that is referenced by a single variable name
void	0	A descriptor used with functions as a return type when the function does not return a value

■ **Note**   There are several other data types that are defined for the Arduino IDE (e.g., *long long*); however, because doing anything with them is relatively inefficient, I do not discuss them here.

Keywords in C

Each of the data types shown in Table 3-1 (i.e., *boolean, char, int,* etc.) is a keyword in C. A *keyword is any word that has special meaning to the C compiler.* Because keywords are reserved for the compiler's use, you cannot use them for your own variable or function names. If you do, the compiler will flag it as an error. If the compiler didn't flag such errors, the compiler would get confused as to which use of the keyword to use in any given situation.

There are other C keywords that cannot be used to name a data type in your programs. Many of these keywords are for language constructs (e.g., *for, while, struct,* etc.) that are an integral part of the language. You will learn these keywords as we progress through the book. In other cases, pre-written functions like the *delay()* function you used in the last chapter should not be used for your own variable names. While not exhaustive, you can find a partial list of reserved C keywords at http://arduino.cc/en/Reference/HomePage.

Variable Names in C

If you can't use keywords for variable or function names, what can you use? There are three general rules for naming variables or functions in C. Valid variable names may contain the following:

1. Characters a through z and A through Z

2. The underscore character (_)

3. Digit characters 0 through 9, provided they are not used as the first character in the name

Just about everything else is not acceptable, including the C keywords. Note that the rules also mean that punctuation and other special non-printing characters are not allowed either.

If you happen to use a variable name that is also the name of an Arduino library function, you will run into problems when you try to use the two in the same program. If you named a variable *delay* and then tried to call the *delay()* function, the compiler would get cranky and complain because it is confused by the variable and the function that share the same name. The rule is simple: Don't do that! Surely you can think of a variable name that doesn't collide with an existing function name.

Valid variable names might include the following:

```
jane            Jane            ohm             ampere          volt
money           day1            Week50_system   XfXf
```

Using the same rules, the following would not be valid names:

```
^carat          4July           -negative       @URL
%percent        not-Good        This&That       what?
```

As an exercise, explain to yourself why each of these erroneous variable names is wrong.

Given these limits, how does one create a "good" variable name? As a general rule, I like variable names that are long enough to give me a clue as to what they do in a program, but short enough that I don't get tired of typing their name. Using this notation, variable names begin with a lowercase letter, with each subword capitalized. (This form of notation is often referred to as *camel notation*.) The following are examples of camel notation style:

```
myFriend        togglePrinter       emptyPaperTray       closeDriveDoor
```

I think this style makes it easy to read the variable names. C could care less which style you use. However, keep in mind that it is unlikely that you will write perfect (error-free) code every time you write a program. Using variable names that make sense and are easy to read makes debugging just that much easier. Also keep in mind that C is case sensitive, which means that *myData* and *MyData* are two different variables.

With that in mind, let's examine the common data types available for use in your C programs.

The boolean Data Type

The *boolean* data type is limited to two values or states: *true* or *false*. These two values are unchangeable (i.e., constants) that are defined within the compiler and are the only two values a *boolean* variable can assume. Therefore, the following is a valid data definition for a *boolean* variable:

```
boolean mySwitch = false;
```

This is probably going to be used to store the state of a switch (e.g., the switch state is *true* when the switch is On and it is *false* when the switch is Off). However, you may also see code like the following fragment:

```
boolean switchState;
    // some more program statements
switchState = ReadSwitchState(whichSwitch);
if (switchState) {
    TurnSwitchOff(whichSwitch);
} else {
    TurnSwitchOn(whichSwitch);
}
```

Walking Through the Function Call to ReadSwitchState ()

Even though we don't cover the *if* statement until the next chapter, you can probably figure out what's going on here. The *ReadSwitchState()* function returns a *boolean* value that is *true* if the switch is on, or *false* if the switch is off. Recall from Chapter 2 what the function call statement means. When you call the *ReadSwitchState()* function, you grab your backpack, stuff the current value of *whichSwitch* into it, and jump to the black box that contains the *ReadSwitchState()* code. Once inside, the code takes the value of *whichSwitch* out of your backpack and uses it to process the code in its function block. Note that the *ReadSwitchState()* function sends a value back to the caller. We know that because of the assignment operator (=) that appears before the function call statement. Therefore, just before you leave the black box, the function grabs your backpack and puts a value in it that was calculated as the result of the function call. The function then tells you that you are free to return to the caller.

However, when you return from the call to the *ReadSwitchState()* function, the assignment operator causes the code to grab your backpack, take out the value put there by function call, and assign that value into *switchState*. (Technically, your backpack is actually something called the program stack, but we'll flesh out that detail later in the book.) Because *switchState* is defined as a boolean variable, we know that is the type of data that is being returned from the function call to *ReadSwitchState()* (i.e., that's the type of data the function stuffed into your backpack). Therefore, because *switchState* is defined as a *boolean* data type, only the values *true* or *false* can be stored in *switchState*.

Binary Numbers

Because digital computers only understand two states, On (1) and Off (0), they use a binary (base 2) numbering system. Alas, you and I grew up with the base 10 numbering system, so base 2 seems a bit strange at first. However, it's not hard to understand how a base 2 number is constructed.

Consider Table 3-2. You can think of a computer *bit* (binary integer) as a small unit of data that can assume only one of two values: on (a value of 1) or off (a value of 0), which is consistent with the binary nature of digital computers. Most CPUs group bits together into a single entity called a *byte*. Each *byte is comprised of 8 bits*. Most programming languages start counting things with the number 0 rather than 1. Therefore, the bits in a byte begin with bit 0 and end with bit 7.

Because the "high" bit for an 8-bit byte is bit 7, that bit is used as the *sign bit* if the data can have positive and negative values. If the sign bit (i.e., bit 7) is turned on for a *char* data type, for example, the number is interpreted as a negative value. If you add up all the values "to the right" of bit 7 (i.e., line 2 in Table 3-2, or 64 through 1), you'll find that it totals to 127. If you look at the range for a *char* data type in Table 3-1, you'll see the highest positive value is 127. If bit 7 is turned on for a *char*, the interpretation is that this is a negative number, so the value becomes –128. This should help you understand how the ranges are set for the different data types. For an unsigned data type (e.g., *unsigned char, unsigned int, unsigned long*), there is no need for a sign bit—all values are positive, so the high bit is just another positive bit available for use. This explains why the maximum value for an *unsigned* number is about twice that of a signed data type.

Table 3-2. *The Base 2 Interpretation of an 8-Bit Data Value*

	Bit 7	Bit 6	Bit 5	Bit 4	Bit 3	Bit 2	Bit 1	Bit 0
Power of 2	2^7	2^6	2^5	2^4	2^3	2^2	2^1	2^0
Decimal value	128	64	32	16	8	4	2	1
Binary number	0	1	0	0	0	0	0	1
Decimal value		64						1

Now, let's examine Table 3-2 in greater detail. You can see how the bit positions correspond to various powers of 2. For example, if you take the value 2 and raise it to the 6th power, the resulting value is 64. If you recall your high school math, any number raised to the 0th power is 1. Moving from Bit 0 to the left, you can see in row 2 how the value doubles as you move to the next higher bit position.

The question becomes: How can I form a binary value? Suppose you want to form the decimal (base 10) value 65. To create that value, you would need to turn on bits 0 and 6 (see the last row in Table 3-2.) Because 2 to the 0th power is 1, and 2 to the 6th power is 64, adding these two values together produces 65, binary 01000001. So, how would you create the value 5? If you turn on bits 2 and 0, you get a value of 5 (i.e., 00000101). What about the value 10? In that case, turn on bits 3 and 1 (i.e., 00001010).

Wait a minute! It appears that shifting all the bits to the left one position is the same as multiplying the number by 2. Likewise, shifting all the bits to the right one place is the same as dividing by 2. That's exactly right. Arduino C supports *bit shifting*. You may see examples of bit shifting in some code you look at down the road. I will have more to say about that later on. Bit shifting only works with integral data types.

The char Data Type and Character Sets

When computers first came into existence, all of the characters that were deemed necessary could be represented with relatively few values. Your keyboard, for example, probably has fewer than 127 keys on it. Because of the relatively small number of characters needed, the American Standard Code for Information Interchange (ASCII) character set was developed based on 8-bit (i.e., 1 byte) values. By treating the eight bits as an unsigned quantity, the ASCII character set was later extended to include limited graphic characters, too. The ASCII character set was the norm for decades. However, as computers fanned out across the globe, the need to extend the character set became obvious. The Japanese Kanji character set, for example, has almost 2,000 characters in it. Clearly, these characters cannot be represented in an 8-bit byte. For this reason, the Unicode character set was developed.

The *Unicode character set* is based upon a 2-byte value for each character. From a programmer's point of view, Unicode characters are unsigned quantities, hence over 65,000 characters can be represented. (See the 2-byte range of values in Table 3-1. For details on the Unicode character set, see www.unicode.org/ charts. For the ASCII character set, see www.asciitable.com.) Because of the desire to "internationalize" computer software, more and more programmers moved to the Unicode character set. However, there were diehard ASCII programmers, too. Perhaps as a compromise, there are Unicode character sets for different bit lengths. For example, UTF-8 is the Unicode Transform Format for 8-bit character sets. Now you can select from UTF-8, UTF-16, and UTF-32.

We will stick with the ASCII (1 byte) character set in this book. If you need Unicode in your software, you can cobble it together using Arduino C. However, I will leave that as an exercise for you, if you're interested.

Generating a Table of ASCII Characters

One of the sample programs included with the Arduino C IDE is one that can generate a table of the ASCII character set. You can see the menu sequence to follow in Figure 3-1. The File ➤ Examples ➤ 04.Communication ➤ ASCIITable menu sequence loads the source code for the program. Compile and upload the program as you did in Chapter 1 by pressing the button with the arrow on it (the Compile/Upload button). Now select the Tools ➤ *Serial* Monitor menu choice or simultaneously press the Control, Shift, and M keys at the same time. This loads the *Serial* monitor so you can view the data being sent back to your PC.

Once again, we won't go through the code because we don't have enough under our belt yet to make it worthwhile. (You will write your first program in the next chapter.) For now, the ASCIITable.ino program will at least allow you to see the ASCII characters displayed as characters, decimal (base 10), hexadecimal (base 16), octal (base 8), and binary (base 2) numbers.

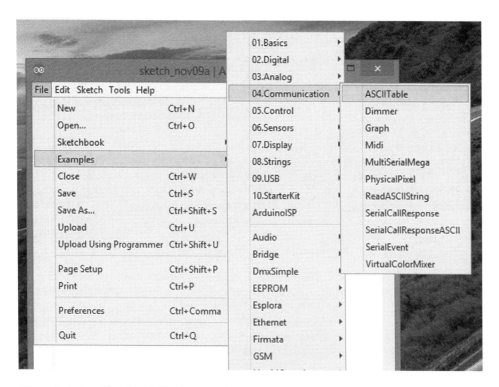

Figure 3-1. *Loading the ASCIITable sample program*

Figure 3-2 presents part of the output from the ASCIITable program. By examining the output from the program, you can see the relationship between the different numbering systems.

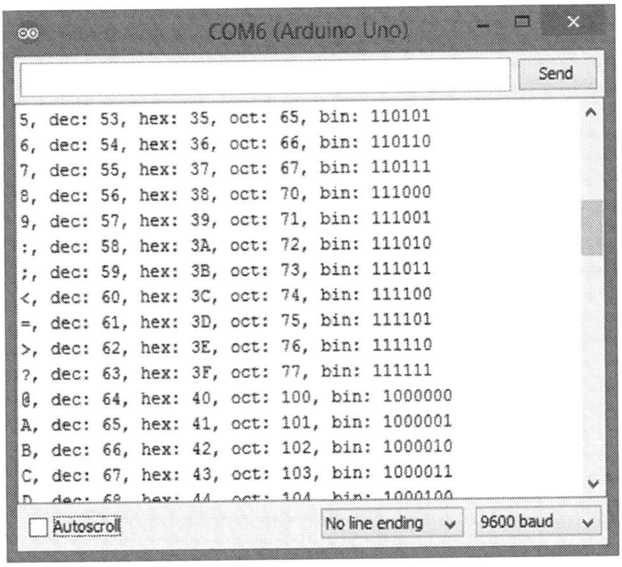

Figure 3-2. *Part of the ASCII character set*

If you look at the extreme left edge of Figure 3-2, toward the bottom, you'll see the character 'A'. If you wanted to create a variable and initialize it to the value for the letter 'A', you could use this:

```
char c = 'A';
```

After the compiler processes this statement, variable *c* would contain the letter 'A'. Note that *character constants* that are used in an assignment statement are surrounded by *single quote marks*. If you read the 'A' line in Figure 3-2, you can see that the numeric value 65 represents the letter 'A'. What this means is, when you touch the Shift key and the letter A on your keyboard, the value 65 is transmitted to your computer. If you prefer to think in base 16 numbers, the value 41 is sent (i.e., $16 * 4 + 1 = 65$). In base 8, the value is 101 (i.e., $8 * 8 + 0 + 1 = 65$). However, since computers only understand 0s and 1s, what the computer actually receives for the keyboard character 'A' is the binary value 01000001. (Figure 3-2 leaves the leading 0 off of the binary display for the ASCII table because the 8th bit is always 0.)

The byte Data Type

The *byte* data type is also an 8-bit value, but there is no sign bit, so its range is almost twice that of a *char*. (Can you explain why an *unsigned char* has the same range as a *byte*? Think about it.) You may use the *byte* data type to store any value between 0 and 255. If you ever find yourself in a situation where you are running out of memory for data storage, changing the data from an *int* data type to a *byte* might save the day.

Given that *byte* and *unsigned char* have the same range of values, how can you decide which to use? Well, from the compiler's point of view, it doesn't matter. However, as you gain experience, you'll find yourself falling into conventions that most C programmers use. That is, if you are reading data from a sensor, many sensors route their data through a port one byte at a time. As a result, programmers often use the *byte* data type to represent raw data coming in through a data port. On the other hand, all flavors of the *char* data type are often associated with textual (i.e., ASCII) data. The choice is yours.

The most commonly used 8-bit data type is the *char*. However, *byte* is available when you need it.

The int Data Type

The *int* data type is an integer value in C and is a signed quantity. Because an *int* is a signed quantity, an *int* can assume either positive or negative whole numbers (see Table 3-1).

Fractional values are not allowed for any integer data types. If a math operation with integer values yields a fractional value (e.g., 9 / 5), that fractional value is truncated (*not* rounded) and only the whole number is retained (i.e., the result is 1, *not* 1.8 or 2).

In Arduino C, an *int* data type is a 16-bit value, as shown in Table 3-1. In some other languages (e.g., Java, C#, C++) an *int* is usually a 32-bit (4-byte) entity. If you have programmed before in some of these other languages, you need to be aware that an *int* in Arduino C has a smaller numeric range than it carries in other programming languages. (Often these other languages refer to a 16-bit *int* as a *short int*. The actual bit-size of an *int* data type is the bit size of the registers in the host μc. A register is an internal piece of hardware buried within the μc that is designed to hold a group of bits. For the Arduino boards we are using, these registers are designed to hold 8 bits.)

Because you can also have *unsigned int* data types, you can increase the upper limit of positive values by almost a factor of two. However, the price of this greater range is that unsigned data types cannot store negative values. The *int* data type is used more frequently than the *unsigned int* data type in most programs.

The word Data Type

As you can see in Table 3-1, the *word* data type has the same storage requirements and range of values as an *unsigned int*. Given that's the case, why even have a *word* data type when an *unsigned int* could be used instead? The term *word* is actually more associated with assembly language programming and reflects the largest group of bits that can be handled by the CPU with a single instruction. While there is no hard-and-fast rule about using the *word* data type, you tend to see it used most often as a variable that is involved with bit manipulations or when hexadecimal (base 16) numbers are being used instead of decimal (base 10) numbers. You will study bit manipulations in a later chapter. For the moment, you can think of the *word* data type as being similar to an *unsigned int,* but used to suggest low-level data manipulations.

The long Data Type

Because the *long* data type uses 32 bits (4 bytes), it has an approximate range of values of between plus or minus two billion. Like the other data types discussed so far, the *long* data type is also an integer data type and, as such, cannot be used to represent fractional values. However, because there are 2^{31} possible values (the 32nd bit is the sign bit again), the range of values is very large. As a general rule, if you are certain that all possible data values for a program fall within the range of an *int*, using an *int* is a better choice than a *long* if for no other reason than the memory requirements for a *long* are twice that of an *int*. Also, the Atmel family of μcs that we are using here all use 8-bit (1 byte) registers. Therefore, shuffling 2 bytes of data for an *int* will usually be faster than moving 4 bytes of data for a *long*. Although the performance hit for a *long* may not be noticeable except where you're spinning through a tight loop of values, it's still worth keeping the data type trade-offs in mind.

The float and double Data Types

Arduino C does allow you to use floating point numbers. That is, you can have data values in your program that use fractional values. In fact, if you look at the Arduino.h header file (usually located at \hardware\ arduino\cores\arduino), you will find symbolic constants defined for *PI*, *TWO-PI*, and so forth. In that file, *pi* is defined as:

```
#define PI 3.1415926535897932384626433832795
```

So, you could define a *float* as

```
float pi = PI;
```

and the compiler will substitute the number 3.1415926535897932384626433832795 for *PI* and assign that value into *pi*. (Recall that C is case sensitive, so *pi* and *PI* are viewed as different entities in C.) The range of values for a *float* is roughly plus or minus 3.4 times 10 to the 38th power. That's a big number: A value with up to 38 digits. Each *float* requires 4 bytes of storage space.

In most languages, a *double* data type has twice the storage requirements as a *float* (i.e., 8 bytes instead of 4 bytes). As such, the range of values is much larger (often some value to the 308th power.) However, Arduino C makes no distinction between a *float* and a *double*. Both data types are treated equally in Arduino C.

Floating Point Precision

The *precision* of a number refers to *the number of significant digits* you can expect for that number. In Arduino C, the highest precision you can expect for a floating point value is 7 digits of precision. What this means is that even though you can represent a floating point number with 38 digits, only the first 7 are significant. The remaining 31 digits are the computer's best guess as to what the digits should be. Given that fact, it seems misleading that *PI* is defined the way it is. For all practical purposes, *PI* could be defined as

```
#define PI 3.141592
```

and forget the rest of the digits because the computer won't be able to represent those digits in any math operation with greater precision than six or seven digits. However, if you're just going to display *pi* and not manipulate it in any way, then *PI* gives you that constant with considerable precision.

■ **Note**   In some Arduino literature, you will see variables defined using *uint8_t*, *uint16_t*, or perhaps other terms that are similar. These constants are used to help define the data type for the underlying C++ compiler. It's pretty easy to figure out what they mean. For example, *uint8_t* translates to an *unsigned int* comprised of 8 bits. (The *_t* element helps to mark it as a data type.) Unless stated otherwise, we use the standard C data types presented in Table 3-1.

The string Data Type

A *string* is a sequence of ASCII characters treated as a single entity. In other words, it's a string of characters. The string data type may be implemented two different ways. The first we shall discuss is to define the string as a character array. An *array* is nothing more than a grouping of one or more elements of a data type and each of those elements share a common name. (We will cover arrays in detail in Chapter 5.) In this case, you can define a string as

```
char myString[15];
```

which allocates enough memory space for a string with 14 characters in it. Note that the base data type for a string is an array of *chars*.

Wait a minute.... Why 14 characters and not 15?

The reason is because C needs to append a null character (`'\0'`) to the end of the character array for the compiler to use the *char* array as a *string* data type. The compiler uses this null byte to mark the end of the string. Therefore, any *string* variable is limited to the number that appears within the brackets minus 1. In our example, we have set aside enough memory for 15 characters. Because the last of the characters must be used by the *string* termination byte (i.e., the null character, `'\0'`), we can only use 14 characters for the actual string data. Keep in mind, if you forget the null termination character, `'\0'`, for the string, don't be surprised when your code seems to be marching through memory without stopping.

Arduino C is smart enough to know when to add the null termination byte in many cases. For example, all of the following are valid ways to define and initialize a *string* variable using a character array.

```
char name[] = "Jane";
char name[5] = "Jane";
char name[100] = "Jane";
char name[4] = "Jane";   // Uh-oh!.
```

In the first example, note how the brackets following the variable name are empty (e.g., *name[]*). The reason is because we decided to let the compiler figure out how many bytes of storage are needed based on the number of characters appearing between the double quote marks on the right side of the assignment operator. Since the name Jane has 4 characters, the compiler sets aside 5 bytes of storage to make sure there's enough for the name plus the null termination character.

The second form simply has the statement hard-code the 5 bytes that are needed. The last form reserves 100 bytes of storage, where the first four contain the characters for "Jane" and the 5th character is the null character (\0) that terminates the string. This third form would allow you to expand *name[]* up to 99 characters in length at some other point in the program, if needed. (You know why it's 99 characters.) In the last example, there is no room for the null termination character, so the compiler complains that the string is too long.

So, which is the "best" option to use? Personally, I like the first statement where the size is missing between the array brackets. There are two reasons for my choice. First, the compiler is *really* good at counting—even better than me, especially when I'm tired. Second, if I find out Jane actually prefers to be called Janie, I only have to edit her name, not the array size. Still, because all three forms work, your needs and preferences will dictate the form you choose. Keep in mind, however, the third form can be very wasteful of precious bytes of memory.

You can also initialize a string on a character-by-character basis, if you wish. In that case, surround each character with a single quote mark, each character separated from the next by a comma. (*Single quote marks are used to denote a single character constant. Double quotes are used for a sequence of characters, or a string, as seen earlier.*) Take a look at this example:

```
char name[] = { 'J', 'a',  'n', 'e', '\0'};
char name[5] = { 'J', 'a',  'n', 'e', '\0'};
char name[] = { 'J', 'a',  'n', 'e'};
char name[5] = { 'J', 'a',  'n', 'e'};
```

Notice that the compiler is smart enough to know the null termination character must be added, even if you don't explicitly write it in the initializer list. Also notice that when you initialize a character array on a character basis, the initializer list starts with an opening brace ({) and terminates the list with a closing brace (}). The characters within the list are surrounded by single quote marks, each separated from the other by a comma.

String Data Type

The *String* data type is different than the string data type that is built up from the *char* data type. (Note the uppercase letter S for this data type.) The String data type is actually a C++ class that is built up from the *string* data type but is treated as an object rather than a simple character array. What this means is that you have a lot of built-in functionality with the *String* data type that you would have to code yourself with the *string* data type. For example, suppose you have a sequence of characters that you read from a sensor into a *String* variable named *myData*. Further suppose you need to convert them all to uppercase letters.

If you defined *myData* as a *String* object, you could perform the conversion simply as

```
myData = myData.ToUpperCase();
```

and you're done! The reason this works is because, within the *String* object is a method that contains the code to do the conversion for you. (Recall that C++ refers to functions that are buried in the class as a method.) You simply define the variable as:

```
String myData = String(100);
```

This defines a *String* named *myData* with enough space for 99 characters. To use a method that is built into a class, follow the variable name you've given the class with a period (called the *dot operator*) followed by the method you wish to call. For example:

```
myData = myData.ToLowerCase();
```

Such functionality is common with programming languages like C++, C#, and Java that support the object-oriented programming (OOP) paradigm. (Chapter 14 presents a quick overview of OOP.) While Arduino C is not an OOP language, it is nice that you can use some OOP features. Table 3-3 shows some of the methods that are available when you use *String* objects.

Table 3-3. Built-in String Functions

Function	Purpose
String()	Define a *String* object
charAt()	Access a character at a specified index
compareTo()	Compare two *Strings*
concat()	Append one *String* to another *String*
endsWith()	Get the last character in the string
equals()	Compare two *Strings*

(continued)

Table 3-3. (*continued*)

Function	Purpose
equalsIgnoreCase()	Compare two *Strings*, but ignore case differences
getBytes()	Copies a String into a *byte* array
indexOf()	Get the index of a specified character
lastIndexOf()	Get the index of the last occurrence of a specified character
length()	The number of characters in the string, excluding the null character
replace()	Replace one given character with another given character
setCharAt()	Change the character at a specific index
startsWith()	Does one string begin with a specified sequence of characters
substring()	Find a substring within a *String*
toCharArray()	Change from *String* to character array
toLowerCase()	Change all characters to lowercase
toUpperCase()	Change all characters to uppercase
trim()	Remove all whitespace characters from a *String*

While we're not ready to use all of these functions now, they are presented here for completeness. We will use some of them in later chapters.

Which Is Better: String or strings Built from char Arrays?

Listing 3-1 shows a program that uses two *String* data type variables and adds them together to form a new *String*, and then displays it on the *Serial* monitor.

Listing 3-1. A Program to Concatenate Strings

```
void setup() {
  // put your setup code here, to run once:
  Serial.begin(115200);
  String firstName = "Jack ";
  String lastName = "Purdum";
  String fullName = firstName + lastName;
  Serial.println(fullName);
}
void loop() {}
```

The program does its job and uses 3626 bytes of memory when using a *String* class object.

Now let's write a program that uses character arrays instead of the *String* class object. The code appears in Listing 3-2.

Listing 3-2. A Program to Concatenate Character Arrays

```
void setup() {
  // put your setup code here, to run once:
  Serial.begin(115200);

  char myName[12] = "Jack ";
  char lastName[] = "Purdum";
  strcat(myName, lastName);   // A standard library function to concatenate
                              // character arrays  Serial.println(myName);
}
void loop() {}
```

The program shown in Listing 3-2 displays the same results, but only uses 2044 bytes of memory. Given how scarce memory is in the μc world, most programmers do not use the *String* class for processing string data. True, the *String* class is convenient, but at a price of increasing memory demands by over 40 percent seems too expensive. For that reason, we concentrate on string data that is built from *char* arrays.

The void Data Type

Programmers argue whether the *void* data type is really a data type at all. The term *void* really means the absence of a useful data type. One use for the *void* keyword is when it is used with functions to show that a function does not return a useful value. For example, if you look at the ASCII table program, both the *setup()* and *loop()* functions are defined as:

```
void setup() {
      // the setup code body
}

void loop() {
      // the loop code body
}
```

The use of *void* here means that no data is returned from either of these two functions. Using our backpack analogy, *void* means that the function puts nothing in the backpack before it shows you the back door of the black box. You are returning to the caller with an empty backpack. As such, there is no reason for code to be generated to unpack your backpack upon return from a *void* function, since there is nothing useful inside your backpack.

Another use of *void* is to say that no information is passed in the form of parameters to the function. This means that you can leave your backpack on the porch when you call a function, because nothing's stuffed into it anyway. In other words, you could write the two functions as

```
void setup(void) {
      // the setup code body
}

void loop(void) {
      // the loop code body
}
```

and the program would compile and run exactly as before. That is, "empty" parentheses means the function is defined with a *void* argument list. Most programmers who use Arduino C do not use the keyword *void* between the opening and closing parentheses of a function. Personally, I like the use of *void* in this context, as it serves to confirm that no information is being passed into the black box from the outside world. I will admit, however, that I am likely a crowd of one who likes this convention.

The array Data Type

Virtually all of the basic data types support arrays of those types. An *array* is little more than *a collection of identical data types that share a common variable name*. You've already seen examples of character arrays. The following statements show some other array definitions:

```
int myData[15];
long yourWorkDay[7];
float temp[200];
```

Each of these statements defines an array of a specific type. Suppose we use the following data definition:

```
int val[4];
```

Let's further assume that the compiler places the array starting with memory address 500. You can envision an array like the one shown in Figure 3-3.

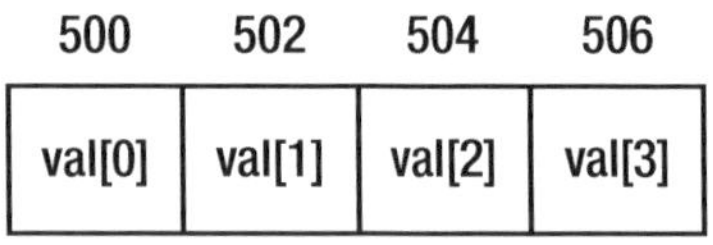

500	502	504	506
val[0]	val[1]	val[2]	val[3]

Figure 3-3. *How an array of ints looks in memory*

Because each element of the array uses an "*int*-sized" chunk of memory, which we know from Table 3-1 is 2 bytes, you can see that the first element of the array, *val[0]*, uses locations 500 and 501. The second element of the array (*val[1]*) uses memory locations 502 and 503, and so on. There are a number of things we can generalize from Figure 3-3.

Array Generalizations

- The number of array "units" are called *array elements*. The array definition, like *int val[4]*, tells us that the compiler creates the array with 4 array elements.

- An *array index* tells us which element of the array is being referenced.

- Array elements always begin their index with 0, not 1. That is, the first element in the array is *val[0]*, not *val[1]*. Sometimes you will hear this fact referred to as *zero-based indexing*.

- Because array elements are numbered starting with 0, we can derive the *N – 1 Rule*: The highest valid array index is always 1 less than the number of elements in the array. In the case of *int val[4]*, the number of elements is 4, but the highest valid array index is 3 (see Figure 3-3).

- Trying to index into an array using an index higher than dictated by the N – 1 Rule may appear to work, but often results in spectacular program failure.

I will postpone additional details about arrays until later chapters. If we need any specifics before that chapter, I will be sure to point them out.

Defining vs. Declaring Variables

Most programmers use the terms "define" and "declare" as if they were the same. *They are not!* If you learn nothing else in this book, please let it be that defining a variable and declaring a variable are entirely different animals. To illustrate this difference, let's take a simple definition of an integer variable named *val*:

```
int val;
```

Although this may seem like an innocuous statement, there is a lot of stuff going on behind your back. Let's walk through what's actually going on. While I've taken a few liberties to make things easier to understand, the basics described here are essentially what actually happens.

Language Errors

First, when the compiler sees this statement, the first thing it does is check the statement for errors. There are basically three types of program errors: syntax errors, semantic errors, and logic errors. A *logic error* usually means you've implemented an algorithm badly. This type of error usually manifests itself with a program that compiles without error, but gives the wrong results. A *syntax error* occurs whenever you write a program expression that does not follow the rules of the language being used. A *semantic error* occurs when you follow the rules of the language, but use the wrong context. For example, English grammar rules say a sentence needs a noun and a verb. The sentence "The dog meowed." follows the syntax rules, but it breaks the semantic rules because dogs don't meow. If the compiler detects either type of error, you get one of those ugly orange error messages displayed at the bottom of the IDE. However, since our statement is correct, the compiler then moves to the next phase of the compile process.

Symbol Tables

The next step causes the compiler to scan its symbol table to see if *val* has already been defined in the program. Table 3-4 shows a simplified symbol table. (My software company produced C compilers and our symbol table had just under two dozen columns in the symbol table. The ellipsis (…) is used to denote the added complexity one would actually find in a real symbol table.) Simply stated, a symbol table is a compiler construct that keeps track of the variables you've defined in a program.

Table 3-4. *A Simplified Symbol Table*

ID	Data type	Scope	lvalue	…
myData	*int*	0	600	…
x	*float*	0	610	…

What Table 3-4 shows is that two variables, *myData* and *x*, are already defined in the program. The ID column stands for Identifier and is the name for each defined variable. Often you will hear programmers use the term "identifier" instead of "variable name." Operationally, they are the same. You can see that *myData* is an *int* data type, whereas *x* is a *float*. Both variables have a scope level of 0 (an explanation of which I will defer for later.)

You can think of the first three columns as an attribute list for a variable. An *attribute list* is nothing more than terms that are used to describe something. For example, an attribute list for me might be: male, six-feet tall, and two years younger than dirt. The attribute list for *myData* is: an *int* data type, scope level 0, and an lvalue of 600. The lvalue column presents the memory address of where each variable resides in memory. Therefore, reading the attribute list for *myData* from the symbol table tells us that we can find the integer variable residing at memory location 600 in SRAM memory.

lvalues and rvalues

An *lvalue* refers to the memory location where a particular data item resides in memory. Therefore, *the lvalue for a data item is the memory location where that item is stored*. For lvalues to make sense, consider what happens after the compiler has determined that our statement to define *val* is syntactically correct. The next thing the compiler does is check to see if you have already defined a variable named *val*. If you had, there would already be an entry in the symbol table for *val*. If that were the case, the compiler would issue a "redeclaration error" for *val*. (As you will learn shortly, this error message should be "redefinition error".) Because there is no definition for *val* at this point, everything looks good so far.

So far, the symbol table now looks like Table 3-5.

Table 3-5. *The Symbol Table After Syntax Checking on val*

ID	Data type	Scope	lvalue	...
myData	*int*	0	600	
x	*float*	0	610	
val	*int*	0	???	

It is important to note that the lvalue for *val* is still unknown. That is, *val* doesn't have a dedicated place to live in memory yet.

Still, because there is no duplicate definition error, the compiler sends a message to the system's Memory Manager (MM). In essence, the compiler sends a message to the MM that says: "Hey, MM! It's me ... the compiler. My programmer needs 2 bytes of free memory. Can you fulfill my request?" At that point, the MM scans its list of available free memory, and likely finds two free bytes somewhere. We'll assume the free memory it finds resides at a starting memory address of 625. The MM returns a message to the compiler with the 625 memory address.

The compiler then issues a message: "Hey, Arduino! It's me ... the compiler. You can use the 2 bytes of free memory starting at memory address 625." At that point, the compiler changes Table 3-4 to look like Table 3-6.

Table 3-6. *The Symbol Table After Adding New Variable val*

ID	Data type	Scope	lvalue	...
myData	*int*	0	600	
x	*float*	0	610	
val	*int*	0	625	

Note what has happened here. We now have a memory address where the new variable *val* lives. You have *defined* variable *val* because it now has a known memory address, or lvalue. Therefore ...

- a data item is *defined* if and only if it has a known lvalue in the symbol table

- a data item is *declared* if it exists in the symbol table, but does not have an assigned lvalue

Memorize the difference between the two and don't be afraid to correct other programmers who mix up the two terms. The distinction is important, as you will find out later.

You will see an example of a data declaration later in the book. For now, however, keep in mind that a *data definition* means you can locate a variable using its lvalue. A data declaration is nothing more than an attribute list for a data item ... it has no lvalue. That is, data declarations for a data item tell you its ID, its type, and its scope level, but it does not yet exist in memory. Data declarations are used primarily for data type checking purposes.

We can depict the lvalue with the simple diagram shown in Figure 3-4, which reflects the state of the symbol table, as seen in Table 3-6. That is, *val* has been defined because it has a known lvalue (i.e., 625) and, therefore, *val* exists in memory starting at memory address 625. (The term *lvalue* comes from the old assembly language programming days and stood for "location value," or a reference to where a data item was stored in memory. Some students find it easier to remember "left value" since the lvalue forms the "left leg" of Figure 3-4.)

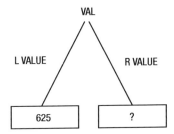

Figure 3-4. *An lvalue-rvalue diagram*

Notice that we have the rvalue marked with a question mark in Figure 3-4. The reason is because the rvalue is unknown at this moment in time. *The rvalue of a data item is what is stored at a data item's lvalue.* Because C is not required to initialize a non-*static* data item's rvalue to zero or any other particular value when it is defined, you should *always assume* that the rvalue of a data item contains whatever random bit pattern may exist at its lvalue until a value has explicitly been assigned into the data item. Because of this fact, we show the rvalue for *val* as a question mark: it contains whatever junk happens to be at its lvalue. (rvalue is also a hangover from assembly language programming days and stood for "register value". Again, some students think of it as "right value" since it forms the "right leg" in Figure 3-4.)

Also keep in mind that the lvalue is always the starting memory address for a data item. That is, *val* is stored at its lvalue, which is memory address 625. However, because *val* is an *int* data type, it actually uses 2 bytes of storage and occupies memory addresses 625 and 626.

Understanding an Assignment Statement

Suppose you want to assign the value 10 into *val* after it has been defined. The following is the statement to do that:

```
val = 10;
```

Again, this is a simple statement involving a single expression and the binary assignment operator. However, stop and think about what the compiler has to do to process the statement. First, the compiler must check the statement for syntax errors. No problem there. Next, the compiler must go to its symbol table to see if a variable named *val* exists. Again, everything looks fine because *val* is in the symbol table. Next, it makes sure *val* has a valid lvalue (memory address), which it does (i.e., memory address 625). If the lvalue column was empty (all rows in the lvalue column in the symbol table are initialized to null when the table is created because null is never a valid memory address), the compiler would know this is a data declaration, and the variable is not yet defined. It should be clear that a variable that is not defined cannot have a value assigned into it. However, since *val* has a valid lvalue (or memory address), the compiler can process the assignment statement.

To process the assignment statement, the compiler goes to the data item's lvalue in memory and copies the value on the right-hand side of the assignment statement (i.e., 10) into the 2 bytes of memory at the lvalue memory location. It knows it must use 2 bytes of memory because of the *int* designation in the second column of the symbol table (see Table 3-6). This means that the rvalue of *val* is changed from a random bit pattern in memory to 10. This is shown in Figure 3-5. If you could look at memory locations 625 and 626, you would see 00001010 00000000. (Most PCs store the low byte first and the high byte second at the memory locations. The end result is the same: the value 10 is stored at the lvalue 625. Sometimes at cocktail parties you'll hear people discussing the "Endian" problem. Simply stated, it refers to whether the low or high byte comes first in memory. For details, see http:\\en.wikipedia.org/wiki/Endianness.)

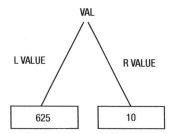

Figure 3-5. *The lvalue-rvalue diagram after processing the assignment statement*

Note that any time your program needs to use the data stored in *val*, it uses *val*'s lvalue to go to that memory address and fetch "*int* bytes" of data (each *int* is 2 bytes) from that memory location. (I've taken some liberties here, because the actual processing takes place on your μc board, not the PC, and the storage locations are known by the time you are ready to run the program. Still, the simplification presented here should help you understand how variables and memory relate in a program.)

The Bucket Analogy

Understanding lvalues and rvalues is so important to a true understanding of C that I developed the Bucket Analogy to make it easy to remember the details about lvalues and rvalues. Suppose you have various buckets lying around. Each bucket is just big enough to hold a specific number of bytes of data. Some buckets can only hold 1 byte of data, whereas others can hold 2 bytes. Still others can hold 4 bytes, and so on. Using Table 3-1, you can see that a 1-byte bucket could hold a *byte, char, unsigned char,* or *boolean* data item. A 2-byte bucket could be used to hold an *int, unsigned int,* or a *word*. A 4-byte bucket could be used for a *long, unsigned long, float,* or *double*. Let's further assume you have a whole room filled with these various sized buckets.

Now consider the following two program statements:

```
int val;
val = 10;
```

These are the same statements we discussed earlier. The first statement fills in the symbol table information, as we discussed earlier, and is shown in the last line of Table 3-6. In the first statement, the word *int* tells us the type of data and *val* tells us its name. You will also hear the word *int* as it's used here referred to as a *type specifier*. Likewise, you may hear the term *identifier* used instead of term *variable name*. Potato, paataahto....

In the Bucket Analogy, the type specifier in the first statement can be thought of as determining the size of the bucket needed to hold the relevant data. From Table 3-1, you know that an *int* requires a 2-byte bucket to hold its data. The lvalue for *val* tells you where that bucket is located in memory. As we saw earlier, the second program statement

```
val = 10;
```

means that we go to *val*'s bucket located at memory address 625 and pour 2 bytes of data into the bucket with the data arranged in such a pattern as to form the value 10. This can be seen in Figure 3-6. The Bucket Analogy tells you that the bucket's size is determined by the variable's type specifier (e.g., *int*), the location of the bucket is its lvalue (e.g., 625), and if you peek inside the bucket, you see its rvalue (e.g., 10).

Figure 3-6 also shows a 1-byte bucket stored at memory location 700 with the character 'A' stored in it. The bucket stored at memory address 700 is only half as big as the bucket used to store *val*. The bucket is smaller because it only takes 1 byte to store a *char* data type.

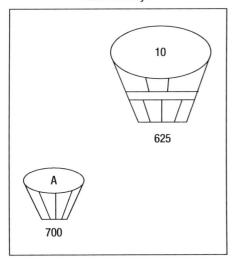

Figure 3-6. *The Bucket Analogy for val*

The Bucket Analogy provides the following three conclusions:

- The size of a bucket depends upon the type specifier for the data type being stored

- Where the bucket is stored in memory is the data item's lvalue

- The contents of the bucket is the data item's rvalue

Any time you use a variable in a program, you are probably locating a specific bucket using its lvalue and using the contents of that bucket (i.e., its rvalue) in some expression.

Now consider the three statements in the following code fragment:

```
int val = 10;
int sum;

sum = val;
```

It should be clear that the last statement must use lvalues and rvalues to resolve the assignment expression used in the statement. Let's walk through the process.

In the previous program statement, the compiler goes to the symbol table and finds the lvalue for *val*. The compiler uses the memory address (*val*'s lvalue) to fetch *val*'s 2-byte bucket. Peeking into the bucket, we can see the rvalue of 10.

Next, the compiler the looks up *sum*'s lvalue, goes to that memory address, and fetches its bucket. Now that both buckets (i.e., operands) are available, the assignment operator causes the compiler to pour the 2 bytes of *val*'s bucket into *sum*'s bucket. The assignment process, therefore, replaces whatever may have been in *sum*'s bucket with the contents of *val*'s bucket.

There's an important lesson here: all simple assignment statements copy the contents of the bucket on the right side of the assignment operator into the bucket of the operand on the left side of the assignment operator. It should also be obvious that *all simple assignment statements copy the right operand's rvalue into the left operand's rvalue*. By thinking in terms of rvalues and lvalues, you will develop a more robust understanding of C.

Using the cast Operator

Consider the following statements:

```
int val = 65;
char  letter;

letter = val;
```

The first two statements define buckets for *val* and *letter*, and place them in memory at (we assume) locations 625 and 700, respectively. Figure 3-6 shows where the buckets are, but *val* now has the number 65 stored in it. Therefore, *val*'s lvalue is 625 with an rvalue of 65 and *letter* has an lvalue of 700 with an rvalue of the random bit pattern that existed when it was defined. Now consider the last expression:

```
letter = val;
```

Simply stated, this statement grabs the *val* bucket and tries to pour 2 bytes of data into *letter*'s 1-byte bucket! Not good. Doing this runs the risk of spilling 1 byte of information, because *letter*'s bucket is too small to hold all of *val*'s data. One byte of potentially valuable information is going to dribble onto the floor. Even worse, the Arduino C compiler does not even complain about the data dribble! It merrily makes the assignment and moves on. As a result, *letter* could contain some bogus value that could cause you problems in your program later on. Clearly, this was just a bad design by the programmer, who should have known better than to try and shove a 2-byte *int* into a 1-byte *char*.

Why didn't the compiler complain about the type specifier mismatch? The reason is because the C++ compiler is configured to not issue certain error messages and warnings. The error and warning messages are suppressed because new programmers are often intimidated by too many error messages. If you wish to see these messages, you can alter your IDE preferences (File ➤ Preferences) and set the "Show verbose output during:" option by checking the "compilation" check box.

As it turns out, and as you saw in Table 3-1, a *char* is capable of holding the value 65 without overflow. Therefore, our assignment of the *int* into the *char* doesn't cause a problem … in this case.

However, suppose *val* was initialized to 300 instead of 65. Now the value cannot be stored in a *char* because the value is too large for a single byte. The compiler still won't complain, even though the value cannot be represented with a *char*. Even so, 1 byte of data is going to be slopped on the floor during the assignment.

The Cast Rule

The *Cast Rule* is simple: whenever an assignment expression has a larger data type being assigned into a smaller data type, use the cast operator.

So, what is the cast operator? Consider the following example:

```
int val;
long bigVal =25000;

val = bigVal;
```

Once again, the statement has a larger data type (a 4-byte *long*) being assigned into a smaller data type (a 2-byte *int*). This assignment runs the risk of losing 2 bytes of information. However, in this case, the value 25000 can safely be stored in both a *long* and an *int*, so no data loss occurs. However, you should still apply the Cast Rule, as follows:

```
val  = (int) bigVal;
```

The preceding cast operator is (*int*). In other words, the cast operator is nothing more than two parentheses surrounding the destination data type. Because you want to cast a *long* to an *int*, you surround the destination data type (*int*) with a set of parentheses. In other words, to use a cast, surround the destination data type with parentheses, and then place the cast in front of the variable that is the source data type (e.g., the *long*). The data type of the cast operator (i.e., *int*) must match the data type that is to receive the results of the cast (*val* is an *int*). That is, if you are assigning a value into an *int*, the cast must also be an *int*. Again, the cast operator must be placed immediately in front of the data item whose rvalue is to be cast into the new data type. In this example, the *(int)* cast must appear immediately before *bigVal*. The cast has the effect of acting like a funnel that compresses the data so that it fits into the smaller data type.

Silent Casts

Suppose later in the program code we see something like this:

```
bigVal = val;
```

Does this need a cast? Technically, no, it does not. The reason a cast is not needed in this example is because you're trying to pour the contents of a 2-byte bucket into a 4-byte bucket. Because the destination bucket is bigger than the source bucket, there's no risk of spilling data on the floor. I have not found any compiler that complains about this type of mismatched data assignment, even though the code is implicitly casting (i.e., changing) an *int* to a *long*. In other words, the compiler is casting the data without telling you about it. This is called a *silent cast* because there is no indication that the cast is taking place.

I hate silent casts.

The reason I hate silent casts is because they almost always come back at some point in the program to bite you in the butt. As a result, you should *always use a cast when you use an assignment statement between two different data types*. Even though it is not strictly necessary, you should rewrite the preceding statement as:

```
bigVal = (long) val;
```

If nothing else, the cast documents that you really did want to force the data of an *int* into a *long*.

The Arduino compiler doesn't complain about either noisy or silent casts, which, to me at least, is a bug for the "noisy" cast. To be on the safe side, always use the cast operator when performing an assignment expression involving two different data types. It will save you time in the long run and your instructor will be impressed that you truly understand what's going on with such expressions.

There are other expressions where a cast should be used, but I discuss those in later chapters after you have a little more experience under your belt.

Summary

You've covered a lot of important concepts in this chapter and I implore you not to read further until you completely understand the concepts presented in this chapter. One of the major tripping points for C students is the concept of pointers. (Pointers are an advanced topic and are not covered until Chapter 8.) However, if you *really* do understand lvalues, rvalues, and the Bucket Analogy, you will sail through the concept of pointers without so much as a hiccup. The benefits associated with really understanding the concepts in this chapter are not limited to just pointers. Many other programming concepts are also based on a good understanding of the concepts presented in this chapter. Invest the time to truly learn these concepts now. It will pay huge benefits later on.

EXERCISES

1. Which of the following variable names are valid and which ones would draw a syntax error?

bigFeet	your Feet	switch	12Meters
_SystemVal	-Negative	NoGood	realGood

    Answer: *your Feet* is not valid because it has a space character in its name. *switch* is invalid because it is a C keyword. *12Meters* is invalid because it starts with a digit character. *-Negative* is invalid because it starts with a math operator. All the rest are acceptable.

2. How do you pronounce the word "*char*" as in

    ```
    char c;
    ```

    Answer: This is probably not the most important question to ask, but one I still do get asked. Some pronounce it like "char" as in "charcoal" or to "char" a steak. Others pronounce it as "care" as is "caretaker." There is no right or wrong answer. It just depends upon whether you identify with something that is burnt and ugly or someone who lovingly takes care of puppies. I'll let you guess which one I prefer.

3. Suppose you have a *char* variable. Write the binary values for 32, 72, 111, 128.

    Answers:

    ```
    32  =  00100000
    72  =  01001000
    111 = 01101111
    128 = ?
    ```

    You can't represent 128 with a signed *char* because the max value is 127. If you set the high bit, the interpretation is the value −1, not 128.

4. Suppose you're at a cocktail party and someone asks you what "precision" means in Arduino C. What's your answer?

    Answer: *Precision* refers to the number of significant digits a floating number has. In Arduino C, the numeric range for floating point numbers is fairly large … up to 38 digits. However, only the first 6 (sometimes 7, but don't count on it) digits are significant. All the remaining digits are the computer's best guess as to their value.

5. What's the difference between the *string* and *String* data types?

    Answer: The *string* data type is made up of nothing more than an array of *char* data. The *String* data type subsumes the *string* data type, but adds a number of methods that can be used with the *String* data type (e.g., see Table 3-3). It's not too much of a stretch to think of the *String* data type as a shell—or wrapper—that encompasses *string* but also has other methods defined within it. (*String* uses OOP methods.) The good news is the added functionality that *String* brings to the party. The bad news is that the extra functionality means more memory resources are chewed up, even if you don't use that extra functionality. Because resources are so scarce with μcs, we avoid using the *String* data type.

6. What's an lvalue? What's an rvalue?

    Answer: An lvalue is a location in memory where a data item resides. An rvalue is the value of that data item.

7. Relate lvalues and rvalues to the Bucket Analogy.

    Answer: Think of the bucket as something that can hold data. The size of the bucket depends upon the number of bytes of data the bucket needs to hold (e.g., 1 byte for a *char*, 2 bytes for an *int*, 4 bytes for a *float*, etc.). It is the data item's type specifier that determines the size of the bucket. When you define a variable, as in

    ```
    int k = 25;
    ```

    the type specifier, *int,* determines you need a 2-byte bucket; the lvalue is where you place the bucket in computer memory; and the rvalue tells you the value that you see when you peek into the bucket (i.e., 25).

8. What's wrong with the following statements and how do you fix them?

```
int val;
double x = 1000.0;
val = x;
```

Answer: The last statement is an assignment statement, so you are taking the rvalue of *x* and copying it into the rvalue of *val*. Using the Bucket Analogy, you are pouring the contents of a 4-byte bucket into a 2-byte bucket, so the potential exists for losing data. You fix this by using a cast operator, as in

```
val = (int) x;
```

The cast has the effect of skimming off 2 bytes of "unused" water and just assigning the meaningful data (i.e., 1000) into *val*. Alas, it's up to you to know the max value the *int* can hold before the "skimming" process starts throwing the kids out with the bath water.

Keep in mind that the Arduino compiler does allow silent casts, and these are almost never a good idea. As a rule, always use a cast when you use the assignment operator with differing data types.

CHAPTER 4

Decision Making in C

The real power of a μc is its ability to read data, make a decision based on that data, and then take the appropriate action(s). Stated differently, a μc has the ability to make decisions based upon the information provided to it from the "outside" world via various input devices. In this chapter, you will learn the various expressions that enable your program to make decisions based upon the state of some set of data.

Relational Operators

As you might guess, a decision is often based upon comparing the values of two or more pieces of data. You make such decisions all the time, probably without thinking much about the process that is involved in making the decision. The phone rings and you get up to answer it. Implicitly, you made a decision whether to answer the call or not. Further, that decision involved comparing the expected benefits from answering the call (e.g., it might be someone you want to talk with) versus the expected costs of not answering the call (i.e., I may miss out on talking to someone important). Some decisions are better than others. Indeed, the definition of a dilemma is when you have two or more choices and they are all bad.

Table 4-1 presents the relational operators available to you in Arduino C. The relational operators form the basis of all decision making in C. All the operators in the table are *binary operators*, which means each relational operator requires two operands.

Table 4-1. Relational Operators

Operator	Interpretation
>	Greater than
>=	Greater than or equal to
<	Less than
<=	Less than or equal to
==	Equal to
!=	Not equal to

The result of all relational operations is either logic *true* (non-zero) or logic *false* (zero). For example:

```
5 > 4    // Logic true; 5 is greater than 4
5 < 4    // logic false; 5 is not less than 4
5 == 4   // logic false; 5 is not equal to 4
5 != 4   // logic true; 5 is not equal to 4
```

© Jack Purdum 2015
J. Purdum, *Beginning C for Arduino, Second Edition*: Learn C Programming for the Arduino, DOI 10.1007/978-1-4842-0940-0_4

Clearly, you can also use variables in the expressions. If $a = 5$ and $b = 4$, then:

```
a > b    // Logic true
a < b    // logic false
a == b   // logic false
a != b   // logic true
```

These expressions are exactly the same as the previous set, only we substituted variable names for the numeric constants. Now let's see how to use the relational operators with some C statements.

In a computer program, unless the central processing unit (CPU) is told to do otherwise, the CPU processes the source code program instructions in a linear, top-to-bottom manner. That is, program execution starts at whatever is designated as the starting point for the program and plows through the source code from that point to the next statement until all of the statements have been processed.

The if Statement

In an Arduino C program, the program starting point is the function named *setup()*. The program processes all of the statements in the *setup()* function block, starting with the first statement and marches through the statements from statement 1 to statement 2 to statement 3 ... until it reaches the closing parentheses of the *setup()* function block. You can, however, alter this linear processing flow by using an *if* statement.

The syntax for an *if* statement is as follows:

```
if (expression1)
{          // Start of if statement block
           // execute this if statement block only if expression1 is true
}                         // End of if statement block

// statements following the if statement block
```

An *if* statement block consists of the *if* keyword followed by a set of opening and closing parentheses. Within those parentheses is an expression that evaluates to either logic *true* or logic *false*. After the closing parenthesis of the *if* test expression is an opening brace character ({). The opening brace marks the start of the *if* statement block. The opening brace is followed by one or more program statements, called the *if statement block*, that are to be executed if the *if* test is logic *true*. Almost every programmer on the planet indents the statements within the *if* statement block one tab stop. The *if* block statements are then followed by a closing brace (}), which marks the end of the *if* statement block.

▓ **Note**   You can change the indent size using the IDE Edit menu and clicking the Increase Indent or Decrease Indent option. If the indent space is too large, some of the source code disappears off the right edge of the screen. To see the end of a long source code line means you may have to use the horizontal scroll bar. If the indent is too small, it's harder to see the statement block controlled by the *if* statement. You can experiment and find out what works for you. Personally, I prefer an indent of two spaces. It's enough of an indent to see the statement blocks, but it's small enough to minimize the number of statements that need the horizontal scroll bar. If you can't decide, you can let the IDE decide for you. The menu sequence Tools ➤ Auto Format (or Ctrl+T) will automatically format your code using the default formatting. If you modify the indent amount, the auto format uses your settings for formatting the source code.

What if Expression1 Is Logic True?

Consider the following code fragment:

```
int b = 10;

// some more program statements…

if (b < 20) {
    b = doSomethingNeat();      // Do this is b is less than 20
}
doSomethingElse(b);
```

The code fragment begins by defining an integer variable named *b* and initializing it to 10. Then some unspecified statements are executed followed by an *if* test. If *b* has remained unchanged by the unknown statements, its value is still 10. Because *b* is less than 20, the expression is logic *true*, the *if* statement block is executed, and function *doSomethingNeat()* is called. Evidently, the *doSomethingNeat()* function has an *int* function type specifier. This means that just before you leave the function, the *doSomethingNeat()* function code places an *int* value in your backpack and, when program control returns back to the *if* statement block, the code opens your backpack, takes out the *int*, and assigns it into *b* . Then the statement following the *if* statement block is executed, which means *doSomethingElse(b)* is called.

What if Expression1 Is Logic False?

If the *if* test on expression1 is false, the *if* statement block is skipped and the call to *doSomethingNeat()* is *not* made. Therefore, after a false expression1 test, the next statement to be executed by the program is *doSomethingElse(b)*. You can see the path of program execution more clearly in Figure 4-1. A logic *true* result of the relational test causes program flow to execute the statement(s) inside the *if* statement block. If the relational test result is logic *false*, the *if* statement block is skipped and the program resumes execution at the first statement following the closing brace of the *if* statement block. As you can see, a decision has been made in the program based upon the program's data.

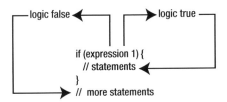

Figure 4-1. *Execution paths for if test*

One more thing: you *will* make the following mistake somewhere down the road:

```
if (val = 10)
{

    size = 10;

}
```

Note that the relational test (*expression1*) expects a true or false result. In this case, however, we used a single equal sign (i.e., the assignment operator) by mistake for the relational expression rather than the proper "is equal to" operator (==). *This means the code performs an assignment statement, not a relational test.* This is what I call a *Flat Forehead Mistake* (FFM). You know, the kind of mistake where you slam the heel of your hand into your forehead while muttering: "How could I make such a stupid mistake!" Relax. All good programmers have a slightly-flattened forehead and you should expect your fair share of such hammerings. The good news is that, although you might make a FFM mistake a second time, you'll find the error more quickly the second time. Anytime you end up in an *if* statement's statement block when you know you shouldn't be there, check for this type of error. It's pretty easy to forget the second equal sign character.

Braces or No Braces?

When the *if* statement block consists of a single program statement, the braces defining the statement block are optional. For example:

```
if (b == 10)
    b = doSomethingNeat();
doSomethingElse();
```

works exactly the same as it did before. If the two versions behave the same, why the extra keystrokes?

There are several reasons why you should *always* use braces for *if* statement blocks. First, always using braces adds consistency to your coding style, and that's a good thing. Second, adding the braces delineates the *if* statement and makes it stand out more while you're reading the code. Finally, while you may think only one statement is needed right now, subsequent testing and debugging may show you need to add another statement to the statement block. If that's true, you *must* add the braces. If you don't always add braces you get something like the following:

```
if (b == 10)
    b = doSomethingNeat();
    doBackupNow();
doSomethingElse();
```

The indenting suggests the programmer wanted to call both *doSomethingNeat()* and *doBackupNow()* only when b equals 10. However, the way the code is written, the call to *doBackupNow()* is always called because what the programmer actually has written is:

```
if (b == 10) {
    b = doSomethingNeat();
}
    doBackupNow();
doSomethingElse();
```

Always remember that the *if* statement block without braces default to a single statement being controlled by the *if* test. My suggestion: always use braces to delineate the *if* statement block even when it's not required. That way you lessen the chances that it will appear the code has a mind of its own.

A Modified Blink Program

Let's write a program that uses the example Blink program from the IDE as its starting point, but makes some modifications to it. The original Blink program (File ➤ Examples ➤ Basics ➤ Blink) blinks the Arduino's onboard LED. The program we're developing uses two external LEDs, two resistors, and a few breadboard jumper wires. The circuit is designed to light one of the LEDs for one second (just like the original Blink program), and then turn it off and then turn the other LED on. The circuit is shown in Figure 4-2.

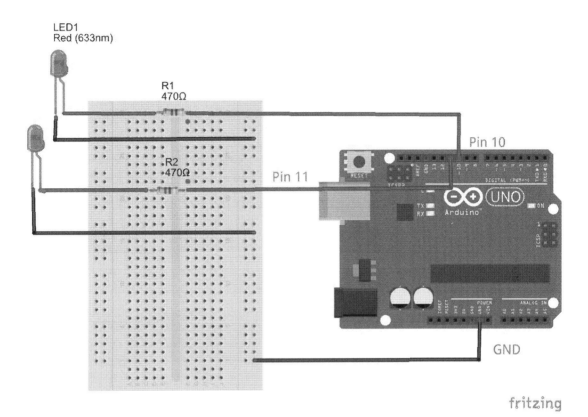

Figure 4-2. *An alternating LED Blink program*

The Circuit

The circuit involves connecting one wire from digital I/O pin 10 on the Arduino to a 470 ohm resistor. The other end of the resistor is connected to the anode (long) leg of the LED. The cathode end of the LED is connected to the Arduino ground (GND) pin. Note how we have connected a wire from the Arduino GND pin to the ground rail of the prototyping board. The term *rail* refers to any row of pins that are all connected together. In Figure 4-2, all of the connection points of the right-most pin column of the breadboard are connected together. Because we have connected this common column of connection points to ground, we call it the "ground rail". If you wanted to, you could connect a wire from the +5V pin on the Arduino board to the second right hand pin column and create a +5V rail. (The breadboard shown in Figure 4-2 is symmetrical in that you could have used the leftmost two columns for the same purpose.) Many breadboards mark these rails with a minus sign for the ground rail and a plus sign for the positive voltage rail. Some manufacturers may also use the color red to mark the positive voltage rail and black from the ground rail. The ground rail serves as a common ground for both LEDs.

As a general rule, most circuits that use jumper wires like you see in Figure 4-2 use black wires to denote a GND connection and red wires for positive voltage connections. Obviously this is not a rule etched in stone, but one that can help when debugging a circuit.

Circuit Resistor Values

So, what should the value be for each of the resistors? It really depends upon the specific LEDs you are using. The maximum load on an Arduino I/O pin should never exceed 40mA (milliamperes), but I prefer to think of 20mA as the maximum current. The max current rating on my LEDs is 50mA, so they fall well within the I/O pin rating. *Ohms Law* states that *volts = amps × ohms*. You can rearrange the terms and state

```
Resistance = Volts / Amps
```

because the Arduino board operates with 5 volts and the maximum amperage is 20 milliamps (or .020 amps), the resistance value turns out to be 250 ohms. (These calculations do not take into account the forward voltage of the LED, which results in less current. This errs on the safe side for the LED.) However, that resistance is running the Arduino I/O pin at my maximum current rating, which may not be such a great idea. As a result, I increased my resistor values to 470 ohms. You can always start with a higher resistance value and see what works. Decreasing the resistance value will increase the brightness of the LED. Drop the resistance too far and the LED will do its imitation of a Supernova, thus creating a small void in the universe ... not good. Increase the resistance too much and it will be extremely dim. Obviously, it makes more sense to err on the high side. For most LEDs, resistor values between 150 and 1000 ohms will work just fine. The schematic for the circuit is shown in Figure 4-3.

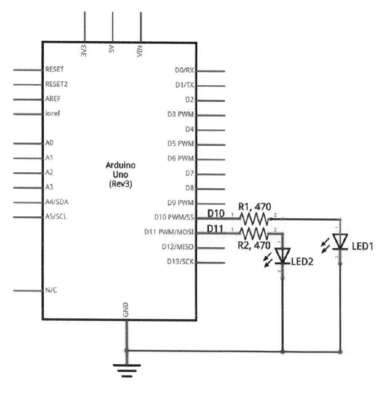

Figure 4-3. *Schematic for alternate Blink program*

The polarity of the LED does matter as you can see in the circuit diagram in Figure 4-3. While there are exceptions, the negative (*cathode*) terminal for most LEDs is shorter than the *anode* and usually has a flat edge on the plastic lens just above the cathode. The good news is that, even if you do get the leads reversed, the worst thing that (usually) happens is that the LED does not light. The circuit can be seen in Figure 4-4.

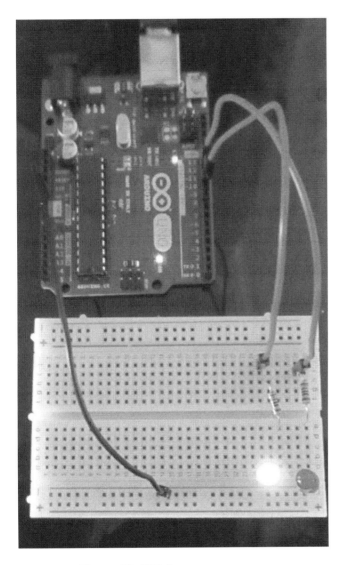

Figure 4-4. The modified Blink program

The Modified Blink Program

Now let's look at the program code. Listing 4-1 presents the source code for our modified Blink program. The first two lines define *int* variables named *LED1* and *LED2*. However, notice the *const* keyword that appears immediately before the *int* keyword.

const Keyword

The *const* keyword is what is called a *data type modifier*. In this particular case, the *const* keyword is used to modify the *int* type *specifier*. The use of the *const* data type modifier means that any variable defined with the *const* data type modifier cannot change that variable's initialized value during the course of program execution. In our program, this means that *LED1* and *LED2* have the values 10 and 11, respectively, the entire time the program runs and those values are etched in stone. If you tried to assign a new value to a *const* variable after its definition, like this:

```
LED1 = 8;
```

the compiler would issue an error message like this:

```
error: assignment of read-only variable 'LED1'
```

This says that *LED1* is a read-only variable (i.e., a constant) and cannot be changed.

Why use a *const* variable? Perhaps the most important reason is because we have wired the circuitry to use those particular LEDs using those specific pins. If we change those pin assignments, the program isn't going to work correctly. The *const* specifier means you cannot inadvertently change those pin assignments in the program as it executes.

Another reason for using *const* data definitions is because they can lend clarity to your code. For example, we could have written the statement to turn on an LED with the statement:

```
digitalWrite(10, 1);
```

But, which statement would you prefer to read when you're trying to figure out what the code does: the preceding statement or the following statement:

```
digitalWrite(LED1, HIGH);
```

Anything you can do to make your code easier to read is a good thing. Using the keyword *const* (when appropriate) is one of those good things because you have given the LED pin a name and it cannot be changed as the program runs. (We don't like magic numbers, right?)

We can make some *const* generalizations:

- Use *const* anytime you define a data item that you do not want to change during program execution.

- The keyword *const* appears immediately before the data type specifier (i.e., *const* is used before the *int* keyword).

- The variable being defined must include the value of the constant at the point of its definition (i.e., the data definition must have an assignment operator ('=') as part of the data definition).

- By convention, variables defined with the *const* data type modifier are often written with all uppercase letters.

While the last generalization is not etched in stone, using all caps for the variable name makes it easy to remember that it is a defined program constant.

Listing 4-1. Modified Blink Code

```
/*
  Alternate Blink
  Turns on one LED on for one second while the other is off, then
  reverses the LEDs for 1 second, repeatedly.
  Dr. Purdum, 11/13/2014
  */
// Given each LED pin a name and don't let it be changed by the program:
const int LED1 = 10;
const int LED2 = 11;

// the setup routine runs once when you press reset:
void setup() {
  // initialize the digital pins as an output.
  pinMode(LED1, OUTPUT);
  pinMode(LED2, OUTPUT);
}

// the loop routine runs over and over again forever:
void loop() {
  digitalWrite(LED1, HIGH);    // turn LED on (HIGH is the voltage level = 5V = ON)
  digitalWrite(LED2, LOW);     // turn LED off by making the voltage LOW (= 0V = OFF)
  delay(1000);                 // wait for a second
  digitalWrite(LED1, LOW);     // turn the LED off by making the voltage LOW
  digitalWrite(LED2, HIGH);    // turn LED on (HIGH is the voltage level)
  delay(1000);                 // wait for a second
}
```

After the LED data definitions, the code calls the *setup()* function which is responsible for actually starting the program to run. That is, *setup()* performs the Initialization Step in our program. All the *setup()* function does is initialize the two input/output (or I/O, since they can be used for either) pins to serve as output pins via the calls to *pinMode()*. By using *pinMode()* to set the pins in their OUTPUT state, when one of these pins is called using the *digitalWrite()* function, the pin's state is set to +5 volts when the pin mode is HIGH. If the pin's mode is LOW, the voltage is driven to 0 volts on the pin, thus turning it off.

Note how the two statements set the environment for the way the Arduino pins behave in the program ... exactly what we would expect an Initialization Step to do. Also note that *pinMode()* needs to know which pin to use and what to change it to (INPUT or OUTPUT). So, out comes your backpack and you stuff it with the appropriate pin number and pin state before each call to *pinMode()*. Once the two pin modes are set in the *setup()* function, the program automatically proceeds to the *loop()* code.

The *loop()* function statement block begins with a call to *digitalWrite()* for *LED1*, setting that pin to the HIGH (i.e., voltage on) value. (More work for your backpack.) Next, another call to *digitalWrite()* is made, but this time for *LED2* with the mode set to LOW. The *digitalWrite()* call to *LED1* has the effect of turning *LED1* on. The second call statement to *digitalWrite()* has the effect of turning *LED2* off. Note that all these calls make your backpack pretty busy.

After the two *digitalWrite()* calls, the *delay(1000)* call is made which causes the program to pause for 1 second. (The *delay()* function expects your backpack to be stuffed with a value measured in milliseconds; 1000 milliseconds is 1 second.) After the one second delay, the same sequence of *digitalWrite()* calls are made, only the pin state in these calls is reversed, after which the program is again paused for one second. If you study this code, you should be able to convince yourself that this sequencing causes the two LEDs to blink back and forth once every second. This process continues forever, or until the power is removed or a component in the system fails.

I encourage you to put this circuit together and run the program. If you have one of the Arduino Starter Kits mentioned in Chapter 1, it will take you just a couple of minutes to build the circuit. Getting down and dirty with the hardware and fiddling around with the software is the *only* way to really learn this stuff.

Software Modifications to the Alternate Blink Program

Now let's modify the program to use *if* statement blocks. The only statement block that is affected is the *loop()* function block. The modified code is presented in Listing 4-2.

Listing 4-2. The Modified Blink Program Using if Statements

```
/*
  Alternate Blink
  Turns on one LED on for one second while the other is off, then reverses the
  LEDs for 1 second, repeatedly.

  Dr. Purdum, Dec. 15, 2014
  */

  // Give each LED a name:
const int LED1 = 10;
const int LED2 = 11;
long counter = 0;

// the setup routine runs once when you press reset or apply power:
void setup() {
  pinMode(LED1, OUTPUT);
  pinMode(LED2, OUTPUT);
}

// the loop routine runs over and over again forever:
void loop() {
  if (counter % 2 == 1) {
    digitalWrite(LED1, LOW);      // turn LED off by making the voltage LOW
    digitalWrite(LED2, HIGH);     // turn LED on (HIGH is the voltage level)
    delay(1000);                  // wait for a second
  }
  if (counter % 2 == 0) {
    digitalWrite(LED1, HIGH);     // turn LED on (HIGH is the voltage level)
    digitalWrite(LED2, LOW);      // turn LED off by making the voltage LOW
    delay(1000);                  // wait for a second
  }
  counter = counter + 1;
}
```

where the new variable, *counter*, is a *long* data type that is initialized to 0 and defined just after the data definitions for LED1 and LED2 near the top of the source code file. (You can load the Blink source code using the File ➤ Examples ➤ Basics ➤ Blink from the IDE. You can then examine the complete source code file.) Let's look at the code.

The conditional expression of the *if* statement compares 0 to the following subexpression:

```
counter % 2
```

The subexpression takes the current value of counter and, using the modulo operator (%), performs a modulus 2 operation on it. The percent sign (%) is called the *modulo* (or *modulus*) *operator and yields the remainder after division*. Because a modulo operation returns the remainder after division, any number modulo 2 is the same as asking whether the number is odd or even. Consider the following:

```
1 % 2 = 1    // goes 0 times, with a remainder of 1 (it's odd)
2 % 2 = 0    // goes 1 time, with a remainder of 0 (it's even)
3 % 2 = 1    // goes 1 time, with a remainder of 1 (it's odd)
4 % 2 = 0    // goes 2 times, with a remainder of 0 (it's even)
5 % 2 = 1    // goes 2 times, with a remainder of 1 (it's odd)
```

and so on. Because counter is incremented by 1 (*counter* = *counter* + 1) each time we pass through the loop, the modulo test has the effect of toggling the LEDs on and off because the value of *counter % 2* alternates between 1 and 0. If you look at the first if statement block, the *if* expression using the modulo operator is going to alternate between 1 and 0. Since any non-zero value is treated as a logic *true* result, the first *if* statement block is executed on each alternate pass through *loop()*. If the first *if* statement expression is logic *true*, the second if statement test must be logic *false*. Could it also be true that each time counter is an odd number, the first *if* statement block is executed and the second *if* statement block is skipped? Think about it. With a little thought, you should be able to convince yourself that the new program in Listing 4-2 performs pretty much exactly as it did in Listing 4-1.

Alas, the modified code is a good example of *RDC ... Really Dumb Code*. Let's see why.

The if-else Statement Block

Think about the code in the previous section. If the first if test is logic *true*, the second if test must be logic *false*. Likewise, if the first if test is logic *false*, the second if test must be logic *true*. Yet, in either case, we evaluate an unnecessary if test on each pass through the loop. Clearly, if one if test is *true*, the other must be *false*. That is, we always perform two *if* tests on each pass through the loop when we should be able to only do one test. Do not proceed further until you understand what I've said here ... it's important.

C provides another form of the simple *if* statement called the *if-else* statement. The syntax for the *if-else* statement is:

```
if (expression evaluates to logic true) {
        // perform this statement block if logic true
} else {
        // perform this statement block otherwise
}
```

As you can see, the first statement block following the *if* test is executed if, and only if, the relational test is logic *true*. Otherwise, the else statement block is executed.

The *if-else* allows us to simplify our loop code somewhat by getting rid of an unnecessary *if* test, as can be seen in the following code fragment:

```
void loop() {
if (counter % 2 == 1) {     // Is it an odd number?
    digitalWrite(LED1, LOW);  // Yep...turn LED1 off (LOW)
    digitalWrite(LED2, HIGH); // turn the LED2 on (HIGH)
} else {                      // If it's not odd, it must be even...
    digitalWrite(LED1, HIGH); // turn LED1 on (HIGH)
    digitalWrite(LED2, LOW);  // turn LED2 off (LOW)
}
```

```
delay(1000);                  // wait for a second
counter = counter + 1;
}
```

Note how we were also able to get rid of one *delay()* call by using the *if-else* statement and use only one *if* test expression. The preceding code fragment is an example of SDC ... Sorta Dumb Code. The reason that this code is SDC is because we can simplify it a little bit more by defining two new variables names, *led1* and *led2*. These two new *int* variables are not constants as before (hence lowercase letters) but are just plain variables. Further, because the C language is case sensitive, there is no conflict between the names *LED1*, *LED2* and *led1*, *led2*. Because *led1* and *led2* can have differing values, we can simplify the code a little, as shown here:

```
void loop() {
if (counter % 2 == 1) {
    led1 = 11;                // LED on pin 11 will be lit
    led2 = 10;                // LED on pin 10 will go out
} else {
    led1 = 10;                // LED on pin 10 will be lit
    led2 = 11;                // LED on pin 11 will go out
}
digitalWrite(led1, HIGH);   // turn LED on (HIGH)
digitalWrite(led2, LOW);    // turn LED off (LOW)
delay(1000);       // wait for a second
counter = counter + 1;
}
```

In this case, we simply reverse the LED I/O pins based upon the *if* test and then make the call to *digitalWrite()*. The program, of course, still behaves as before. A partial advantage is that you only have to pack your backpack twice now, since we have removed one pair of calls to *digitalWrite()*. Try the code out and verify that I'm not pulling your leg.

There are several lessons to be learned here. First, a simple *if* test is good enough to make the program work, but an *if-else* actually often is more efficient because you can reduce the number of *if* test expressions. Second, the *if-else* statements can be reworked to make it easier to read and understand the code. This second lesson leads to a third lesson: There's more than one way to skin a cat. Just because you have a program working doesn't mean it's the most efficient way to write the code. When you're dealing with relatively small amounts of memory, even small adjustments to the code may mean the difference between having the program run or running out of memory.

If this code was turned in for a programming assignment, I would give the person a C. That is, it's average code that works and that is what I would expect from everyone in the class. You'll see how to elevate that grade later in the chapter.

Cascading if statements

Often a program requires specific actions to be taken when a specific value for a variable is read. For example, you might have a variable name *myDay* that can assume the values 1 (Sunday) through 7 (Saturday). The code might look like this:

```
int myDay;

                    // Some code that determines what day it is...
```

```
if (myDay == 1) {
        doSundayStuff();
}

if (myDay == 2) {
        doMondayStuff();
}

if (myDay ==3) {
        doTuesdayStuff();
}

if (myDay == 4) {
        doWednesdayStuff();
}

if (myDay == 5) {
        doThursdayStuff();
}

if (myDay == 6) {
        doFridayStuff();
}

if (myDay == 7) {
        doSaturdayStuff();
}
```

Any time you see a repeating sequence like this, you need to scratch your head and ask: Is this good code? Short answer: No. In fact, this is yet another example of RDC. The reason is because the way it is presently written, the program often executes a lot of unnecessary code. For example, suppose *myDay* equals 1 (Sunday), which means the first *if* test is true and we call *doSundayStuff()*. The problem is that the program then proceeds to perform six more unnecessary *if* tests even though we know it's Sunday and none of the other six tests can be true. (On one consulting job, I saw this same type of code, but with 31 *if* tests because it was for the day of the month rather than the day of the week. One of the rare examples of IDC: Incredibly Dumb Code.)

So, how do you fix this RDC? C allows you to nest *if* statements within an *if* statement. For example:

```
if (myDay == 1) {
        doSundayStuff();
} else {
        if (myDay == 2) {
                doMondayStuff();
        } else {
                if (myDay == 3) {
                        doTuesdayStuff();
                } else {
                        // you get the idea...
                }
        }
}
```

If you follow the logic, when *myDay* equals 1, *doSundayStuff()* is called and all of the rest of the *if* tests are skipped because the first *else* statement block is never executed if the first relational test is true. If the first *else* statement block is skipped, all of the subsequent *if* and *else* statement blocks are also skipped. This is called a *cascading if* statement block. The style convention with cascading *if* statements is to indent each *if* test to make it easier to read and reinforce that you are looking at a cascading *if* statement. Try different values for *myDay* until you are convinced that the unnecessary *if* blocks are, in fact, skipped.

Personally, I'm not a big fan of cascading *if* statements and avoid them when it makes sense to do so. The main reason is because a long cascade can get to the point where you have to horizontally scroll the source code window to see the code. Also, if the day happens to be Saturday (i.e., the last day in the cascading *if* block to be tested), you still end up performing 7 *if* tests on *myDay*, which seems wasteful. Finally, I just find it hard to read cascading *if* blocks. It would be a lot more efficient if we could just perform the test once and then jump to the appropriate statement. Fortunately, that's exactly how the *switch* statement works. However, before I discuss the *switch* statement, let's consider an easier way to increment or decrement a variable.

The Increment and Decrement Operators

In our discussion of the *loop()* function, the last line in the code fragment was this:

```
counter = counter + 1;
```

This statement simply takes the rvalue of counter, increments it by 1, and assigns the new value back into the rvalue of counter. In other words, the statement is an increment operation on counter. This is such a common operation in programming that C includes a special operator called the increment operator that is designed specifically to increment a variable.

Two Types of Increment Operators (++)

There are two flavors for the increment operator: pre-increment and post-increment. The pre-increment operator is written:

```
++counter;      // pre-increment
```

Note that the increment operator (++) appears *before* the variable name. The interpretation is that the rvalue of the variable (*counter*) is fetched, its value incremented and then used in whatever expression in which it happens to appear.

The post-increment operator is written:

```
counter++;      // post-increment
```

Notice that the ++ symbol appears *after* the variable name with the post-increment operator. In this case, the rvalue of the variable (*counter*) is fetched and used in the expression, and then incremented.

You're probably saying, "So what?" Consider the following code fragment:

```
int c = 5;
int k;

k = ++c;        // pre-increment
```

What's the value of *k*? Is *k* equal to 5 or 6? Because this is a pre-increment operator, the rvalue of *c* (5) is fetched, its rvalue is incremented to 6, and then the value is assigned into the rvalue of *k*. So *k* is now equal to 6.

Now consider if the last statement instead was written:

```
k = c++;        // post-increment
```

In this instance, the rvalue of *c* (5) is fetched, that rvalue is then assigned into k, and then variable *c* is incremented. In this case, *k* equals 5, not 6 as before, but *c* is still equal to 6.

The increment rules are simple: a *pre-increment operator increments the rvalue before it is used* in an expression while a *post-increment operator uses the rvalue in the expression and then increments the rvalue*. Keep this distinction buried in your mind because, if you don't, a bug is going to bite you in the butt down the road and the forest-for-the-trees problem makes it hard to see this kind of bug.

Two Flavors of the Decrement Operator(--)

As you might guess, the decrement operator (--) is similar to the increment operator, but is used to decrease the rvalue of a variable by 1. That is,

```
counter = counter - 1;
```

could be written as

```
counter--;
```

because the decrement operator appears after the variable name, is it a post-decrement operation. Because there is no other expression to evaluate (such as an assignment operator), you could also write the statement as:

```
--counter;
```

This is a *pre-decrement* operator. Again, you can use pre- or post-decrement operators in this statement because no other subexpression needs to be processed. Either way, *counter*'s rvalue is decremented before the next program statement is executed.

Suppose that *c* is 6 when the following expression is executed. What's the value of *k* when the statement is finished executing?

```
k = --c;
```

The statement causes the rvalue of c to be fetched, its rvalue is immediately decremented to 5, and that value is *then* assigned into *k*, leaving both variables *c* and *k* with the value of 5.

Now consider a similar statement, but using the post-decrement operator. If *c* is 6

```
k = c--;
```

the he statement causes the rvalue of *c* to be fetched and its rvalue (6) assigned into *k*, and then its rvalue is decremented. As a result, *k* equals 6 but *c* equals 5.

Because the increment and decrement operators are *unary operators* (i.e., they only require one operand), when used by themselves in a statement, as in

```
c++;
++k;
```

you are free to use either the pre- or post-increment or decrement operator. However, when the pre- or post-operators are used as part of a larger expression, you need to pay attention to how the operators are used.

Precedence of Operators

Because we have added several new operators, let's update our precedence table. In fact, we're going to add all of the C operators even though you haven't studied all of them. The complete list of precedence operators is shown in Table 4-2.

Table 4-2. *Precedence of Operators Table*

Level	Operators
1	()　[] → . (dot)
2	!　~　++　--　+ (unary) -(unary) * (indirection) & (address of) (cast) `sizeof`
3	* (multiplication) /　%
4	+ (binary) − (binary)
5	<<　>>
6	<　<=　>　>=
7	==　!=
8	& (bitwise AND)
9	^
10		
11	&&
12			
13	?:
14	=　+=　-=　*=　/=　%=　&=　^=　|=　<<=　>>=
15	, (comma)

While the precedence table looks like a lot to memorize ... it is! For that reason, I suggest that you write this page number on the inside of the back cover page of this book because you will be referring to this page often as you start writing your own programs. With a little practice, you'll find yourself using the table less and less. However, I've been writing C code for over 35 years and I still need to refer to the precedence table. For now, just write this page number inside the back cover page for easy reference. (I will discuss the operators as we encounter them throughout the text.)

The switch statement

The *switch* statement is another control keyword and has the following syntax:

```
switch (expression1) {  // opening brace for switch statement block
      case 1:
            // statements to execute when expression1 is 1
            break;
```

```
        case 2:
                // statements to execute when expression1 is 2
                break;
        case 3:
                // statements to execute when expression1 is 3
                break;

        // more case statements as needed

        default:
                // execute if expression1 doesn't have a "case value"
                break;
}       // closing brace for switch statement block
// All break statements send program control here
```

Using the *myDay* example from the nested *if* discussion, each *case* statement block would correspond to a day of the week. The last *case* statement block would then be for *case 7*. If *expression1* somehow had a value other than 1 through 7, the *default* statement block is executed, perhaps issuing some kind of error message or condition (e.g., a red LED turns on). In other words, *if a value for expression1 does not match any case value, the default statement block is executed.* Notice that any *break* statement sends program control to the same place: the first statement following the closing brace of the *switch*. You can think of the *default* statement block as a catchall for any value that doesn't have a corresponding *case* value for its statement block.

```
switch (myDay) {  // Start of switch statement block
  case 1:
    doSundayStuff();
    break;
  case 2:
    doMondayStuff();
    break;
  case 3:
    doTuesdayStuff();
    break;
  case 4:
    doWednesdayStuff();
    break;
  case 5:
    doThursdayStuff();
    break;
  case 6:
    doFridaytuff();
    break;
  case 7:
    doSaturdayStuff();
    break;
  default:
    Serial.println("Somethings went terribly wrong...shouldn't be here");
    break;
}     // End of switch statement block
// This is where control goes after any break statement
```

The *expression1* that controls the *switch* must evaluate to an integral data type. That is, *expression1* could be a *byte*, *char*, *int*, or *long* (including their unsigned counterparts), it cannot be a floating point type (float or double) nor can it be a reference data type (e.g., array, string, or String). Although Arduino C also accepts a *boolean* data type for expression1, that seems suspect to me and I wouldn't suggest using it. After all, a *boolean* is either true or false so an *if-else* statement block would work.

Note that braces are not used to delineate a *case* statement block. Within the *switch* statement, *case* statement blocks begin with the colon character (:) and extend through the *break* statement. The *break* statement is required at the end of each *case* statement block.

So, where does program control go once it processes a *break* statement? A *break* statement causes program control to jump to the first statement *following* the closing brace of the *switch* statement. In the preceding syntax guide, control is sent to whatever statement happens to be where the last comment is. This is the next statement after the *switch* appears in the source code.

If you forget the *break* statement for a given *case*, program execution "falls through" to the next *case* statement. This can be a potential source of errors in your programs. However, there are also times when two *case* values may need to execute the same program statements. In those situations, the "*case* fall through" can actually simplify the code.

For example, consider Listing 4-3. In this program we use the *Serial* object to ask the user to enter a letter between A and F, perhaps representing a course grade. The *available()* method of the *Serial* object is only greater than 0 when the user has typed in a letter on the *Serial* monitor. (Make sure you set the *Serial* monitor to use "No line ending" in the text box at the bottom of the monitor and the baud rate is 9600.) When the user does enter a letter, we convert it to upper case by the call to *toupper()*, after throwing the letter c in our backpack, and then reassign it back into c for the *switch* statement block. Note how letters 'B' or 'C' generate the same message. This illustrates a *case* "fall through."

Listing 4-3. A switch Example

```
void setup() {
  // put your setup code here, to run once:
  Serial.begin(9600);
  Serial.println("Enter a letter A - F:");
}

void loop() {
  char c;

  while (true) {
    if (Serial.available() > 0) {
      c = Serial.read();
      c = toupper(c);        // Make it upper case
      switch (c) {
        case 'A':
          Serial.println("Great job");
          break;
        case 'B':            // Note fall-through here...
        case 'C':
          Serial.println("You passed");
          break;
        case 'D':
          Serial.println("You're on the edge");
          break;
        case 'F':
          Serial.println("See you again next semester.");
```

```
            break;
        default:
          Serial.println("You can't even follow instructions?");
          break;
      }
    }
  }
}
```

If you look at case 'B', you can see that we omitted the *break* statement, which means program control "falls through" *case* 'B' into *case* 'C'. In this example, that's what we wished to do. However, most of the time you will have a matching *case-break* for each state you need to control. The *default* statement is a catchall for bad input.

A switch Variation, the Ellipsis Operator (...)

There will be times when you need a more broad type of *switch* fall-through. For example, it's pretty common to assign grades such that 0 to 59 is an F, 60 to 69 is a D, 70 to 79 is a C, and so on. In this situation, we want a fall-through that is broader than a single letter. In this situation, we can use the ellipsis operator. The ellipsis operator allows us to state a range of values for the variable that is *expression1*. The following code fragment shows how this works:

```
char letterGrade;
int grade;
// some code that gives grade a value between 0 and 100
switch (grade) {
    case 0...59:
        letterGrade = 'F';
        break;
    case 60...69:
        letterGrade = 'D';
        break;
    case 70...79:
        letterGrade = 'C';
        break;
    case 80...89:
        letterGrade = 'B';
        break;
    case 90...100:
        letterGrade = 'A';
        break;
    default:
        Serial.println("Should never see this.");
    break;
}
```

In the code fragment, note how the *ellipsis operator* (which is simply three periods placed in a row) allows us to construct ranges of values for *grade* and react accordingly. It is important to note that you *must* have a space before the first period and after the last period of the ellipsis operator. Otherwise you will get an error message, probably saying something about a bogus floating point value. Obviously, you could write the code as a cascading *if* statement, but I think the *switch* with the ellipsis is a little easier to read.

Note that this use of the ellipsis operator is an extension that is built into the GCC compiler ... it is *not* part of the C standard. However, you can use it in your Arduino programs.

Just make sure your code does what you design.

Which to Use: Cascading if-else or switch?

I prefer the *switch* statement for several reasons. First, even following normal coding style conventions, it's pretty rare that you have to scroll the source code window horizontally like you may have to do with a long cascading *if-else* block. Second, the *switch-case* statements actually result in a jump table, which means there are no false *if* tests being evaluated like there can be with a cascading *if* statement block. (A jump table in this context is little more than a list of memory addresses where code execution should continue.) Finally, and this is subjective, I find it much easier to read a *switch* statement block than a cascading *if* block. While there may be situations where a cascading *if* has to be used, the *switch* is almost always a better choice.

The goto Statement

The *goto* statement can also be used to direct program control to some point in the program other than the next statement. However, teaching you how to use the *goto* statement is the same as teaching you how to grow warts on your kids. Using a *goto* in your code is ugly and reflects bad coding style. If you really want to learn about the *goto* statement, someone else will have to teach you.

Getting Rid of Magic Numbers

Now let's see how you can raise your grade for the modified Blink program. If you look back to Listing 4-1, you find the statements:

```
const int LED1 = 10;
const int LED2 = 11;
```

If you were a beginning μc programmer, would the numbers 10 and 11 make any sense to you? I don't think so. As a result, I call these "magic numbers" because they are constants in the program that have no apparent meaning in and of themselves.

What if I added a few lines and changed the code to:

```
#define IOPIN10  10
#define IOPIN11  11

const int LED1 = IOPIN10;
const int LED2 = IOPIN11;
```

Now the data definitions for *LED1* and *LED2* as least give me some idea of what the numeric values 10 and 11 mean in the program, plus I think it makes the purpose of *LED1* and *LED2* a little clearer.

The C Preprocessor

When the compiler takes over and starts compiling your program code, you can think of it actually making two passes through the source code. On the first pass, the compiler looks for directives that it must process before it can actually start compiling your program code. These directives are called *preprocessor directives* because they must be "preprocessed" before the compiler can do its thing. Table 4-3 presents the some of the commonly used preprocessor directives for Arduino C. (Chapter 11 contains more detail on the preprocessor.)

Table 4-3. *Arduino C Preprocessor Directives*

Directive	Action
#define NAME value	Ascribes the identifier *NAME* to the constant *value.*
#undef NAME	Removes *NAME* from the list of defined constants
#line lineNumberValue "filename.ino"	Allows the compiler to refer to any line numbers in the file named *filename. ino* to be referenced as line *lineNumberValue* from this point on by the compiler. Normally used in debugging. This is not in the Arduino C reference material, but the compiler recognizes it.

#if definedConstant expression operand	Conditional compilation. Example:
	
	```#if LED == 12```
	``` #define VOLTS 5```
	```#endif```
	
	This is not in the Arduino C reference material, but the compiler recognizes it.

#if defined NAME // statement(s) #endif	Allows for conditional compilation of statements if NAME is defined. The statement block ends with *#endif.* This is not in the Arduino C reference material, but the compiler recognizes it and most libraries use it.
#if !defined NAME // statement(s) #endif	Same as *#if* defined, but processes a statement block only if *NAME* is not defined. This is not in the Arduino C reference material, but the compiler recognizes it.
#ifdef	Same as *#if* defined. This is not in the Arduino C reference material, but the compiler recognizes it.
#ifndef	Same as *#if !defined.* This is not in the Arduino C reference material, but the compiler recognizes it.

#else	Can be used with *#if* like as *if-else* statement, but to control compiled statements. Example:
	
	```#if defined ATMEGA2560```
	``` #define BUFFER 64```
	```#else```
	``` #define BUFFER 32```
	```#endif```
	
	This is not in the Arduino C reference material, but the compiler recognizes it.

#elif	Used with *#if* for cascading *#if*s.
#include "filename.xxx"	Opens the file named *filename.xxx* and reads the contents of the file into the program source code. Usually, if double quotes surround the file name, the search for the file is in the currently active directory. If angle brackets are used (*<filename.xxx>*), the search begins in some implementation-defined manner. This is not in the Arduino C reference material, but the compiler recognizes it.

Note that *preprocessor directives are really not statements since they are not terminated with a semicolon.* Because of this, they must be written as shown in the examples that follow.

The Arduino Language Reference (using Help ➤ Reference from within the IDE or http://arduino.cc/it/Reference/HomePage online) states that only *#define* and *#include* are supported. However, using those preprocessor directives presented in Table 4-3 did not draw compilation errors with the Arduino 1.6.0 compiler. Since the Arduino IDE compiler is derived from the Open Source C++ compiler (GCC), you can expect the directives to be supported.

The important thing to notice here is that the *#define* preprocessor directive gives you a way to define a constant in a more meaningful way than does *const*. (Also, because a *#define* does not actually define a variable with a lvalue, it uses less SRAM memory.)

So what? Well, let's see another benefit that *#define* brings to the party. Suppose you have the following statements in a program you wrote:

```
int minCarFine = 125;
int minTruckFine = 125;
int minMotorcycleFine = 125;
```

Now suppose your state legislature passes a law such that the minimum truck fine is now $150. There is a terrific temptation to do a global search for 125 and replace with 150. This is a train wreck waiting to happen. For example, if your code has a constant 8125, it automatically would be changed to 8150 with a global search and replace; probably not what you intended to do.

Suppose instead you wrote:

```
#define MINCARFINE 125
#define MINTRUCKFINE 125
#define MINCYCLEFINE 125

int minCarFine = MINCARFINE;
int minTruckFine = MINTRUCKFINE;
int minMotorcycleFine = MINCYCLEFINE;
```

The first good thing is the magic numbers are gone from the statements in the source code because you have given them a name. Second, the source code is actually easier to read than before. Third, if the politicians do change the fines, you can go to one spot in the program, make the following change:

```
#define MINTRUCKFINE 150
```

and recompile the program and all the instances where the truck fine is used are correctly changed to the new value. No error-prone search and replace. The compiler does all the work for you. Good stuff.

One more thing about preprocessor directives that you need to keep in mind. That is, any *#define* is a *textual substitution in the source code* … nothing else. As such, all *#defines* are a typeless data declaration: they do not have an lvalue in the symbol table nor is their data type checked. Indeed, once the preprocessor pass in finished, none of the *#define*'s exist anymore. They have all been substituted with their appropriate text. Therefore, suppose you do something silly like:

```
#define VALUE   3.333
// some code
int myValue = VALUE;     //Oops! Integers can't have a decimal point
```

The last statement is trying to place a floating point number into an *int*. Clearly, this is probably not what the programmer intended, but the Arduino C compiler doesn't complain. The compiler simply truncates VALUE to 3 for *myValue*. The compiler can do this because it has no idea of the data type associated with VALUE … VALUE is typeless.

Heads or Tails

Let's write a program that uses our current two LED breadboard circuit to simulate tossing a coin. To do this, let's begin the exercise by using the Five Program Steps for our design.

Initialization Step

Recall that the Initialization Step is used to establish the environment in which we want the program to run. Because we wish to use our two LEDs from the previous program, we need to initialize the I/O pins that control the LEDs. We also know that we need to generate a series of random numbers for use in the program. Where are those random numbers going to come from?

Any time you need a value or an object for use in a program, the first thing you should do is see if someone else has already created code for that object. The first place to check is the Arduino Language Reference. Sure enough, it appears that there is a random number generator available. Upon inspection, we see a function named *randomSeed()* as well as *random()*. Further reading tells us that *random()* produces a series of pseudo random numbers.

Pseudo random numbers?

What this means is that, while the values of the series of numbers is randomly distributed, you will get the identical sequence of values each time you use *random()*. While this can be great while debugging a program, it's clearly not what we want when we are finished testing the program. Reading the *randomSeed()* documentation we find out that we can "seed" the random number generator with a unique value at the outset and *random()* then generates a unique set of random numbers for that seed value. Therefore, it seems appropriate that we use *randomSeed()* in the Initialization Step.

We also need some working variables to store various values in the program.

Input Step

In this step we need to gather all of the data necessary to solve the task at hand. The only data that the program uses is the random number produced by the random number generator.

Process Step

Our program needs to inspect the random number value and determine if it is a heads or a tails. The random number generator produces numeric values, not heads or tails. Also, the type of data that is returned from the random number generator is a *long*. Because there is no "heads" or "tails" data type, we need to invent our own. Since a coin toss has a binary result (i.e., there are only two states possible: heads or tails), we can view the random number as an odd or even result. You already know that a number modulo 2 yields either 1 or 0 as the result, depending on whether the number is odd or even. Perfect! We'll treat odd numbers as a head and even numbers as a tail.

Output Step

As it turns out, the Output (or Display) Step is the most complicated step. The process is not difficult, just busy. Our goal is to light one LED when the number is odd (i.e., a head) and the other LED when the number is even (i.e., a tail.) It would seem, therefore, that we should turn both LEDs off for a second or so and then turn the appropriate LED on for a few seconds based on the random number that was generated. Then we should repeat the process over and over.

Termination Step

Because we aren't doing anything fancy and the program is designed to run forever (or until the power is removed or something fails), there is no Termination Step.

Now, load the IDE and write your version of the code *before* you look at the code presented in Listing 4-4. You will learn twice as much doing it yourself than you will looking at my code. Plus, you may have a better way to write the code. Give it a try.

Listing 4-4. The HeadsOrTails Program Code

```
/*
  Heads or Tails
  Turns on an LED which represents head or tails. The LED
  remains on for about 3 seconds and the cycle repeats.

   Dr. Purdum, Nov 12, 2014
 */


#define HEADIOPIN       11        // Which I/O pins are we using?
#define TAILIOPIN       10

#define PAUSE           50        // How long to delay?

int headsCounter;                 // Heads/tails counters
int tailsCounter;

long loopCounter;
long randomNumber = OL;           // 'L' tells compiler it's a long data type,
                                  // not an int.

// the setup routine runs once when you press reset:
void setup() {
  Serial.begin(115200);
  headsCounter = 0;
  tailsCounter = 0;
  loopCounter = 0;

  pinMode(HEADIOPIN, OUTPUT);
  pinMode(TAILIOPIN, OUTPUT);
  randomSeed(analogRead(A0));                 // This seeds the random number generator
}

void loop() {

  randomNumber = generateRandomNumber();
  digitalWrite(HEADIOPIN, LOW);               // Turn both LED's off
  digitalWrite(TAILIOPIN, LOW);

  delay(PAUSE);                               // Let them see both are off for a time slice

  if (randomNumber % 2 == 1) {                // Treat odd numbers as a head
    digitalWrite(HEADIOPIN, HIGH);
    headsCounter++;
```

```
  } else {
    digitalWrite(TAILIOPIN, HIGH);       // Even numbers are a tail
    tailsCounter++;
  }
  loopCounter++;
  if (loopCounter % 100 == 0) {          // See how things are every 100 flips
    Serial.print("After ");
    Serial.print(loopCounter);
    Serial.print(" coin flips, heads = ");
    Serial.print(headsCounter);
    Serial.print(" and tails = ");
    Serial.println(tailsCounter);
  }
  delay(PAUSE);                          // Pause for 3 seconds
}

long generateRandomNumber()
{
  return random(0, 1000000);             // Random numbers between 0 and one million
}
```

We begin the program with a series of *#defines* and data definitions:

```
#define HEADIOPIN   11
#define TAILIOPIN   10
#define PAUSE       50

int headsCounter;                        // Heads/tails counters
int tailsCounter;

long loopCounter;
long randomNumber = 0L;                  // 'L' tells compiler it's a long data type,
                                         // not an int.
```

Note that the *#define*'s remove many of the magic numbers in the program and make the code more readable. If we want to change the pause between coin tosses, all we need do is change its *#define* and recompile the program. (Of course, you have to upload the compiled code to the µc again, too.)

Next, we run the *setup()* code. Most of the Initialization Step code has been discussed before. However, the statement

```
randomSeed(analogRead(A0)); // This seeds the random number generator
```

is new. The function call to *RandomSeed()* seeds the random number generator using the value returned by a call to *analogRead(A0)* as the seed value. You can read the complete documentation for the *analogRead()* function online at the reference URL mentioned earlier or directly from the IDE (Help → Reference). However, basically, the function reads the voltage on pin 0 and maps it to a value between 0 and 1023. Whatever that value is (and it changes constantly due to electrical noise on the unconnected pin), it is used to seed the random number generator. Having done that, we're ready for the Input and Process Steps as presented in the *loop()* function.

▨ **Note**   Unconnected pins are not always a good thing. Recently I was working on an RF circuit involving a rotary encoder. I neglected to connect the encoder switch pin properly to the circuit and left it in a "floating" (unconnected) condition. As my hand got closer to the encoder to turn it, the value on the floating pin spit out a series of apparently random values that I was monitoring on the *Serial* monitor. Tying the pin to +5 volts through a pull-up resistor solved the problem; a classic RDC move on my part. Moral: If a pin seems to have a mind of its own and you don't want random values appearing on it, check to make sure you didn't leave it floating in the circuit.

In the *loop()* function, *generateRandomNumber()* is called which returns a number between 0 and 1000000. (I go into detail about writing your own functions in Chapter 6. For now, just trust me on this one.) Upon returning for the function call, our backpack is opened and a *long* value is taken out and assigned into *randomNumber*. Next, the two calls to *digitalWrite()* turn off both LEDs and call *delay()* so that we can observe that they are turned off. (It's okay to use *delay()* because we aren't doing any interrupts or time-sensitive processes.) We then use the modulo operator as before to determine if the random number is heads or tails.

The *if* statement again uses the modulo operator to determine if we have tested any multiple of 100 coin flips yet. If the *loopCounter* equals an even multiple of 100, the remainder is 0 and the *if* statement block is executed. The block simply displays the two counters for heads and tails for the total number of coin flips. Notice the *Serial* method used in the last *println()* statement has an "*ln*" at the end of it. This causes the next displayed line to appear on a new line.

You might also like to know that after 50,000 flips, my program produced 25,050 heads and 24,950 tails. In theory, it should be 25,000 for each, but these numbers suggest that Arduino C has a pretty good random number generator.

Summary

In this chapter, you learned various ways to make a decision in your program code. Each method has its own advantages and disadvantages. With experience, you'll get a feel for which decision test is the best one for the task at hand. You also learned a number of style conventions (e.g., using braces even when a single *if* statement may not require it). Style considerations may seem silly to you at the moment, but if you work in a commercial environment (or plan to do so), coding style becomes very important when a different set of eyes has to view your code. Pick a style and use it consistently. It will make your code easier to read and debug. Finally, I showed you how you can use some of the preprocessor directives to 1) make your code easier to read and debug by removing magic numbers from your code, and 2) make changing constants at some point in the future less error-prone.

EXERCISES

1. What's wrong with the following code?

```
if (random())
{
    x = 50;
}
```

Answer: the *random()* function returns a random number as a *long* data type. The *if* statement expects the value between the parentheses (expression1) to be a Boolean value, true or false, but the value is a *long*. This is a *semantic error*. That is, the code is syntactically correct, but the expression is used in the wrong context. The compiler should at least give a warning here, but it does not. Moral: Just because the compiler lets you get away with something doesn't always mean it's right.

2. Are there any errors in the following code?

```
if (j = k)
{
    doStuff();
} else {
    doOtherStuff();
}
```

Answer: Rather than using the test for equality in the *if* test expression, a single equal sign is used instead. This will not draw an error message from the compiler because, again, the syntax is correct. However, the programmer likely wanted to perform a relational test between variables *j* and *k (i.e., ==)*, not an assignment.

3. What happens when you run an LED without a resistor in the circuit?

Answer: You may get lucky and nothing happens. However, if you are using an LED with a max current rating of less than 20mA, you could burn out the LED. If the current rating for the LED is much above 40mA, you could burn out the μc board. Either way, the odds of something good happening are stacked against you. Moral of the story: Use an LED with a resistor having a value of 150–1000 ohms. Side observation: blue or white smoke coming from a component cannot be put back into that component.

4. Modify the HeadsOrTails program so that it reports back to your PC how many heads and tails were sensed during a given number of "coin tosses".

Answer: You can use the code in Listing 4-3 as the base code, but modify the last *if* statement block that uses the modulo operator to:

```
if ( (headCount + tailCount)  ==  desiredNumberOfFlips) {It is
assumed that you have a long variable named desiredNumberOfFlips
and that it has been set in setup() to the appropriate value.
```

5. Why is a *switch* statement block better than a cascading *if* block?

Answer: First, long cascading *if* blocks may force you to use horizontal scrolling to view all of the code. Second, if you have, say, 10 *if* statements in the block and the 10th *if* statement is currently the one that needs to be executed, you will have to evaluate 9 false expressions before you get to the one needed. Third, a *switch* builds a jump table so one evaluation at the top of the *switch* causes the code to jump to the proper *case*, thus avoiding unnecessary tests. Finally, most programmers find it easier to read a *switch* block than a cascading *if* block.

6. Design a circuit that accepts digit characters from the *Serial* keyboard and interprets the number so that 1 is Sunday, 2 is Monday, and so on. Based on the number entered, you light a LED associated with that day of the week. You should use digital

pins 4–10 for the LEDS. Keep in mind that people do make mistakes when entering data. Listing 4-3 shows you how to read the *Serial* monitor for keystrokes.

Answer: There are so many ways to code this that there is no single answer. However, it is really little more than wiring up additional LEDs like you see in Figure 4-3. I would suggest you use a *switch* block to control the LEDs.

7. If you press the number 5 on your keyboard in the *Serial* monitor and click the Send button, what does the following code do?

```
char c;
int num;

if (Serial.available() > 0) {
  c = Serial.read();                    // This fetches the '5'
  // some code to make sure it was a digit character...
  num = (int) (c -'0');
}
```

Answer: I'm not going to tell you. Type the code in, get it working, and then explain to your best friend what it does in a way that they can understand. If you can teach it, you understand it. Hint: There's a difference between digit characters typed on a keyboard and numeric values. For additional help, look up "ASCII Table".

CHAPTER 5

■ ■ ■

Program Loops in C

One of the things computers can do more efficiently than humans is repetitive tasks. People get bored, and when that happens, their attention drifts and errors creep into the task at hand. Computers have the attention span of a gnat (i.e., none), so they are great at performing repetitive tasks. Unless a μc loses power or a component fails, they will loop forever, unless instructed to do otherwise.

In this chapter, you will learn

- What makes a "good" program loop

- How to use a *for* loop

- How to use the *while* statement

- How to use a *do-while* statement and its differences

- Infinite loops

- The *break* and *continue* keywords

You have already used program loops in every program that we've discussed via the *loop()* function that is present in every Arduino program. In this chapter, however, we will flesh out the details of program loops.

The Characteristics of Well-Behaved Loops

Most program loops are written to terminate at some point. However, other loops, like the *loop()* function, are written to run forever. Indeed, to stop most μc programs requires removing power from the board, uploading a new program, or pressing the reset button on the board to stop the current program from running.

In the sections that follow, we will forget about the *loop()* function that is automatically included with each new program and its infinite execution sequence. Instead, we want to look at loops that you control with your own code. With that in mind, let's examine the three conditions that constitute a well-behaved loop.

Condition 1: Initialization of Loop Control Variable

As used here, a *loop* is simply the execution of one or more program statements, and upon reaching the last statement of the sequence, the program goes back to the first statement and repeats the execution sequence. *A well-behaved loop always initializes one or more variables to a known program state before the loop statements begin execution.* Usually, the value of one variable is used to control the number of iterations that are made through the statement loop. The initialization condition often involves setting the control variable to 0. This places the loop control variable in a known state. That is, the rvalue of the loop control variable is a known value.

© Jack Purdum 2015

J. Purdum, *Beginning C for Arduino, Second Edition*: Learn C Programming for the Arduino, DOI 10.1007/978-1-4842-0940-0_5

Some programmers "know" that a specific compiler initializes the rvalue of the variable to zero (or *null*, if it is a reference type variable). However, there is nothing in the ANSI C standard that requires the compiler to initialize all variables to 0 or *null*. Indeed, even *null* can be redefined by the compiler vendor to whatever makes sense for their particular processor. As a result, the best assumption you can make about the rvalue of a freshly defined variable is that it contains whatever random bit pattern (i.e., junk) happened to exist at that particular variable's lvalue. Assuming a variable is initialized automatically to some known state is just not a good programming habit.

Condition 2: Loop Control Test

The second condition of a well-behaved loop is that a test is performed to see if another iteration through the loop statements is needed. Usually, this test involves a relational operator and the loop control variable. The outcome of the relational test determines if another pass is made through the statements controlled by the loop.

Condition 3: Changing the Loop Control Variable's State

The third condition of a well-behaved loop is that the variable or expression controlling the loop must change state. If the control variable did not change state during the processing of the loop statements, the loop executes forever. That is, the outcome of the test in Condition 2 would never change, which means the loop would run forever. Loops that run forever are called *infinite loops*. Recall that the Arduino *loop()* function is designed to do just that—run forever. However, that may not be the desired case for the code you are writing inside the *loop()* function.

With these three conditions in mind, let's examine the *for* loop control structure.

Using a for Loop

The general syntax structure of a *for* loop is as follows:

```
for (expression1; expression2; expression3) {
        // for loop statement body
}
// the first statement following the for loop structure
```

The *for* loop consists of the *for* keyword, followed by an opening parenthesis character ('('). After the opening parenthesis come three expressions, each of which is separated from the other by a semicolon. The third expression is followed by a closing parenthesis character ('(') which is immediately followed by an (optional) opening brace. After the opening brace, there is one or more program statements that are to be controlled by the *for* loop. These program statements are often referred to as the *body of the for loop*. After the statements in the body, there is a closing brace, which marks the end of the *for* loop structure.

In the loop structure, *expression1* usually initializes the variable that controls the loop. However, since *expression1* can have a comma-separated list of subexpressions, we can't say *expression1* always initializes a loop control variable. (You will see an example of this in the next paragraph.) *expression2* performs some form of logical test to determine if another pass through the loop body is warranted. *expression3* is usually responsible for changing the state of the loop control variable, but is not required to do so. (In fact, you could move *expression3* into the loop body if you wanted to, but that's not the conventional style.). Figure 5-1 shows the program flow of the *for* loop.

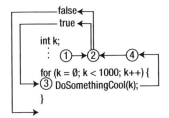

Figure 5-1. *The program flow using a for loop*

To summarize, loop expressions of a well-behaved loop perform the following tasks:

- *expression1*: Usually initializes a loop counter

- *expression2*: Usually performs a relational test

- *expression3*: Usually responsible for changing loop the counter (changes state)

Although there are exceptions to each of these expression summaries, they are the most common.

In Figure 5-1, the *for* loop begins with the definition of variable *k*, followed (perhaps) by some additional statements. Then the *for* loop is entered, *expression1*, or *k* = 0, is processed. Because that expression is normally followed by a semicolon, *expression1* is a complete statement.

Note that *expression1* can have a comma-delimited list of subexpressions. For example, you may see something like this:

```
for (k = 0, j = 1; k < 1000; k++) {
```

where *j* is initialized to 1 as part of *expression1*. I'm not a fan of using a comma and a second (or more) subexpressions. I think the code is more readable if only the controlling loop variable is initialized in *expression1*. You can always initialize *j* just before the *for* loop.

You can also move the definition and initialization of variable *k* into *expression1*, as in:

```
for (int k = 0; k < 1000; k++) {
```

Note that, in this example, variable *k* is defined and initialized as part of *expression1*. I'm not a big fan of this variant either. Also, if the definition of *k* is part of *expression1*, that variable is removed from the symbol table when the closing brace of the *for* loop is reached. If you need to use *k* after the loop finishes, defining the variable as part of *expression1* is simply not going to work.

Once *expression1* is processed, control passes to *expression2*, or *k* < 1000 in Figure 5-1. (Note that program control does not return to *expression1* again as part of the *for* statement block ... it's done for the day.) What happens next depends on the outcome of *expression2*. If *expression2* evaluates to logic *true*, control is passed to the statements in the loop body, or point 3 in Figure 5-1. If *expression2* is *true* and after the statements in the loop body are processed, control is passed to *expression3* (point 4 in Figure 5-1) for evaluation. If *expression2* evaluates to logic *false*, the *for* loop ends and control passes to the first statement following the closing brace of the *for* loop statement block.

Usually, *expression3* is used to change the state of the variable that controls the loop iterations, or variable *k* in our example. You can also have a comma-delimited list of subexpressions, as in:

```
for (k = 0; k < 1000; k++, j--) {
```

Once again, I'm not a big fan of complex expressions in the *for* loop expressions. Personally, I'd push the decrement of *j* back into the loop body's statement block. I don't have a strong theoretical argument for this predilection; it's just the way I do things.

After *expression3* is processed, control passes back to *expression2* to test whether another pass through the loop should be made. The path now taken again depends upon the outcome of the evaluation of *expression2*. If the expression evaluates to logic *true*, the loop body statements are executed again. If the statement evaluates to logic *false*, the *for* loop ends and control is sent to the first statement following the closing brace of the *for* statement block.

Program to Show Expression Evaluation

We can write a short program that shows the order in which the *for* loop expressions are evaluated. The displayed results you see on the *Serial* monitor reflect what is shown in Figure 5-1. The source code appears in Listing 5-1.

Listing 5-1. Demonstrate Loop Evaluation

```
void setup() {
  int k;

  Serial.begin(9600);

  for (k = 0, Serial.print("Exp1 k = "), Serial.println(k);  // Expression 1
       Serial.print("Exp2 k = "), Serial.println(k), k < 10; // Expression 2
       k++, Serial.print("Exp3 k = "),  Serial.println(k)) { // Expression 3

    Serial.print("In loop body, k squared = ");   // for Loop statement body
    Serial.println(k * k);
    delay(1000);
  }
}

void loop() {}
```

I should point out that this is a pretty ugly program and uses programming structures that I would normally not use. However, it does show the sequence in which the three expressions are evaluated. Figure 5-2 shows a sample run of the program. If you look at the first line in Figure 5-2, you can see that the first expression is *expression1*. If you look at the rest of the table, you can see that *expression1* is never visited again. After all, once *k* is initialized to zero, it doesn't need to be reinitialized.

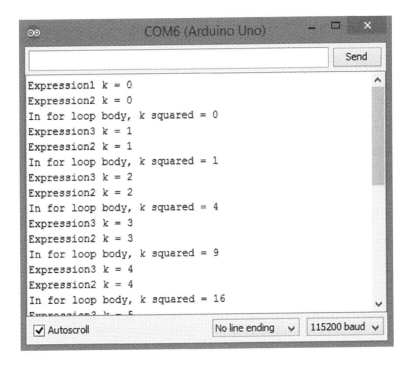

Figure 5-2. *Output from Listing 5-1*

The second line shows that *expression2* is visited next. Because *k* is less than 10, that expression evaluates to logic *true*, and the *for* loop body is executed. The loop body simply uses the *Serial* object to display the square of the current value of *k*. The output is line 3 in Figure 5-2.

Now note how we immediately branch to *expression3* to change the state of the loop counter (i.e., *k*++). Once the loop counter is changed (i.e., the loop state changes), the code immediately evaluates *expression2* (i.e., *k* < 10) again to see if another pass through the loop is needed. Because *k* is less than 10, another pass through the loop is made. If you follow the output shown in Figure 5-2, you should be able to convince yourself of the expression evaluations up to the point where the loop state dictates that the loop should end.

Listing 5-2 shows a little more practical use of a *for* loop.

Listing 5-2. Table of Squares

```
#define MAXLOOP 10

void setup() {
  int squares[MAXLOOP];
  int counter;

  Serial.begin(9600);
  // Construct the list
  for (counter = 0; counter < MAXLOOP; counter++) {
    squares[counter] = counter * counter;
  }
```

```
  // Display the list
  for (counter = 0; counter < MAXLOOP; counter++) {
    Serial.println(squares[counter]);
  }
}

void loop() {
}
```

The code begins with a *#define* that is used to set the array size. *MAXLOOP* is also used to control *expression2* in the loop tests. In *setup()*, the statement *int squares[MAXLOOP];* defines an array named *squares[]*, which is used to hold the list of squared values. The *Serial* object is initialized and the first *for* loop is entered. *expression1* initializes *counter* to 0, since that is the variable that controls the state of the loop. Because *counter* is 0 on the first pass through the loop, *expression2* (*counter* < *MAXLOOP*) is logic *true*, causing the code in the *for* loop statement block to be executed.

There is only one statement in the *for* statement block. The multiplication operator (*) takes the current value of *counter* (i.e., 0), squares it (also 0), and then assigns that value into the first element (*squares[0]*) of the *squares[]* array. After the assignment, control goes to *expression3* and increments the variable that controls the loop (*counter++*). Note that this changes the state of the loop since *counter* controls the number of passes being made through the loop.

After *expression3* is executed, control immediately goes to *expression2* for re-evaluation. Because *expression2* is still logic *true* (*counter* is now 1, which is less than *MAXLOOP*), the *for* statement body is again executed. This process repeats up to the point where the counter has been incremented to 10. At that point, *expression2* is no longer true, and the first *for* loop terminates.

The first statement following the first *for* loop is the start of the second *for* loop. You should be able to walk yourself through that code, step by step, on you own. (Don't just say: "Yeah, I can do that." Do it!)

Most *for* loops behave in a manner similar to that shown in Listing 5-2. Make sure that you are comfortable with how that code works before moving on. As a small test, read the code in Listing 5-3 and describe to yourself what it does and what the Five Program Steps are in the program.

Listing 5-3. A for Loop Test Program

```
#define LED 13

void setup() {
  // put your setup code here, to run once:
  pinMode(LED, OUTPUT);
}

void loop() {
  // put your main code here, to run repeatedly:
  int counter;

  for (counter = 0; counter < 1000; counter++) {
    if (counter % 2 == 0) {
      digitalWrite(LED, HIGH);
    } else {
      digitalWrite(LED, LOW);
    }
    delay(500);
  }
}
```

To make sure that your assessment of the code in Listing 5-3 is correct, type the code into your Arduino and run it. Did it do what you expected? If not, you should explain to yourself why it performed otherwise. It's a good learning experience.

When to Use a *for* Loop

C provides you with several loop flavors, so how do you know which one to select? For the moment, let's just make a simple generalization and say: If you know how many passes are to be made through the loop before the loop begins execution, a *for* loop is usually a good choice.

Another thing you'll like about *for* loops is that all three conditions for a well-behaved loop can be found within the parentheses of the *for* loop. *expression1* usually is used to initialize the variable that controls the loop. *expression2* usually involves a test that results in logic *true* or *false*, which determines whether another pass should be made through the loop. Finally, *expression3* usually changes the state of the loop control variable. The syntax structure of the *for* loop makes room for all of the expressions to be in one place, almost forcing you to write a well-behaved loop.

I'll have more to say about this topic after all loop structures have been discussed.

The while Loop

The second type of loop structure we examine is the *while* loop. The following is the syntax of the *while* loop:

```
while (expression2) {
    // Statements in the loop body
}    // End of while statement block
```

Notice that only *expression2*, the expression that tests whether another pass through the loop statement body is needed, appears as an integral part of the *while* loop syntax. Obviously, you can still write a well-behaved *while* loop; it's just that the syntax structure doesn't really confront you with the three conditions the way the *for* loop syntax structure does. Indeed, any *for* loop can easily be written as a *while* loop.

Let's rewrite the *for* loop from Listing 5-2 as a *while* loop:

```
// some additional statements
counter = 0;                     // This is expression1
while (counter < MAXLOOP) {      // This is expression2
   squares[counter] = counter * counter;
   counter++;                    // This is expression3
}                                // End of the while loop
```

Notice the placement of the well-behaved loop expressions.

- The first condition of a well-behaved loop states that the loop control variable must be initialized to some known state. With a *while* loop, this initialization step must be done *before* you enter the *while* loop because it is not part of the loop syntax itself. This is why we have the statement *counter* = 0 just before entering the *while* loop.

- The second condition of a well-behaved loop is that some form of logical test must be performed on whatever variable controls the loop (i.e., *counter*). The *while* loop does have *expression2* as part of its syntax structure, as can be seen by the expression that appears within the parentheses that follow the *while* keyword. The expression *counter* < *MAXLOOP* in our example is *expression2* for a well-behaved loop.

- The third condition of a well-behaved loop is that the state of the variable controlling the loop must change. There is nothing that is integral to the *while* loop syntax that forces you to write, or even think about, *expression3*. You must supply some statement *within* the statements of the *while* loop body that changes the state of whatever variable controls the *while* loop. In our example, the statement *counter++* becomes *expression3*.

You should be able to convince yourself that the example *while* loop presented earlier is functionally equivalent to the code depicted in Listing 5-2 using the *for* loop structure. The only real difference between *for* and *while* loops is that the syntax structure of a *while* loop is a little less "in your face" about the expressions necessary to write a well-behaved loop. If you tuck away that fact into the back of your mind, you'll have fewer FFM experiences.

When to Use a while Loop

If you can write a *while* loop pretty much the same as a *for* loop, which one should you use? Indeed, if they are functionally the same, why even have a *while* loop? That's sorta like asking why have both a tack hammer and a sledge hammer in your arsenal of tools. While you could drive tacks with a sledge hammer, the tack hammer makes certain tasks a little easier. The same is true with loops: one may be better-suited to a specific job than another.

Although there are few hard-and-fast rules in programming, we can offer a few guidelines for your loop choice decision. As a general rule, if you must perform a task a specific number of times, a *for* loop is often the preferred choice. For example, suppose you're writing a piece of software that must cycle through all of the lights in the building at the end of each business day and turn off any lights that are still on. If there are, say, 1,500 lights in the building, you know your program code must visit each of those lights to perform its task. Because the task must be performed a known number of times, most programmers would probably write the code using a *for* loop.

Now suppose you are writing a program that must search through an inventory list of an unknown number of parts looking for a specific part number. Perhaps the list contains new items that have just been added and perhaps some out-of-date items. We are sure, however, that the part number is in the list. When that part number is found, you want to exit the loop and use the information associated with the part for some additional purpose (e.g., filling an invoice). In this case, you don't need to examine every part in the list; you want to quit the search once you've found the part for which you are looking. Most programmers code such tasks as a *while* loop. The *while* loop idiom becomes the solution for a "search until" type of problem. The main reason is that even though there may be a known maximum number of items to examine (i.e., *expression2*), once you find what you're looking for, you bail out of the loop—you do not visit every item. The program presented in Listing 5-4 illustrates a *while* type of loop.

Listing 5-4. Using a while Loop to Find a Target Value

```
int searchList[200];

void setup() {
  int index;
  int target = 5343;                     // Part number to find

  Serial.begin(115200);

  memset(searchList, 0, sizeof(searchList)); // Clear the array

  searchList[160] = target;              // Our target
```

```
  index = 0;                              // Expression1 of well-behaved loop

  while (true) {                          // Expression2 of well-behaved loop
    if (searchList[index] == target) {
      break;
    }
    index++;                              // Expression3 of well-behaved loop
  }

  Serial.print("Found target at index = ");  // Display result
  Serial.println(index);
}

void loop() {

}
```

The code in Listing 5-4 is pretty short, but it has a lot of useful items in it. The first thing we do is define an array of 200 *ints* named *searchList[]*. Because we have placed the definition of *searchList[]* outside either the *setup()* or *loop()* functions, it is said to have *global scope*. We discuss the concept of scope in a later chapter. For now, just think of scope as the life and visibility of *searchList[]*. That is, the *searchList[]* array can be accessed anywhere in the current source file of the program. As a rule, data items with global scope are automatically initialized by the compiler to 0. This means that each of the 200 *ints* in the *searchList[]* array have the value of 0 when the definition of the array is finished. Personally, I just don't make that assumption. Because of my distrust of global initializations, I do it myself, as you'll see in a moment.

After *searchList[]* is defined, execution enters the *setup()* function, where we define a couple of *int* working variables, including one named *target* that we initialize to the rvalue of 5343. We also create a *Serial* object so we can use the *Serial* monitor to display our program output. Next, we call the *memset()* function after filling our backpack with three pieces of information (i.e., function arguments):

- the name of array we want to initialize

- the value we want to initialize the memory to (i.e., 0)

- the number of bytes we want to initialize

The *memset()* function is often a piece of hand-tweaked assembly language code that the compiler people designed to initialize a block of memory to a specific value. (The *memset()* function is part of the collection of function libraries that come with the Arduino IDE.) The three function arguments we stuffed into our backpack provide the function with the information it needs to set the memory block (i.e., the *searchList[]* array) to a specific value (i.e., 0). However, we have not seen the *sizeof()* operator before.

The sizeof() Operator

The *sizeof()* operator looks like a function call, but it isn't. Instead, *sizeof() is an operator that returns the number of bytes allocated for a data item.* Because we have placed the name of the *searchList* array within the parentheses of the *sizeof()* operator, evaluating that expression returns the number 400.

400? Why 400?

The reason is because *searchList[]* is an array of 200 *ints*. Therefore, because each element in the array is an *int* and each *int* requires 2 bytes of memory, the total number of bytes is 200 * 2, or 400 bytes of memory.

The next question you should be asking yourself is: How does the compiler know where those 400 bytes are in memory? This is worth remembering: in C, *anytime an array name is used by itself, it is viewed by the compiler as the lvalue of the array.* For example, if our definition of *searchList[]* caused the compiler to locate the array at memory location 300, the lvalue of the *searchList[]* array is 300. Therefore, from the compiler's point of view, the call to *memset()*

```
memset(searchList, 0, sizeof(searchList));  // Clear the array
```

actually looks like

```
memset(300, 0, 400);                        // Clear the array
```

which says: "Go to memory location 300 and set the next 400 bytes of memory to zero." The value 400, remember, is derived from the data type and size of the array (i.e., 200 elements at 2 bytes for each element).

Could you initialize the *searchList[]* array to 0 some other way? Sure! You could use something like the following code fragment:

```
for (index = 0; index < 200; index++) {
    searchListing[index] = 0;
}
```

The next question, however, is: Why would you? The *memset()* function is going to be at least as fast as your *for* loop and is just sitting there waiting for you to use it … plus, it's already been tested and debugged. Why reinvent the wheel?

After the call to *memset()*, the code sets element 160 of the *searchList[]* array to the target value of 5343. This means that *searchList[160]* equals 5343, while all the other 199 values have been set to 0 by the call to *memset()*.

The next statement sets *index* to 0, which is really *expression1* of a well-behaved loop. Note that, unlike the *for* loop syntax, a *while* loop has *expression1* set before you enter the loop code. An *if* statement checks to see if the array element the code is presently examining (i.e., *searchList[index]*) is equal to *target*. If we are looking at one of the elements whose value is 0, the *if* test fails (logic *false*) and the code in the *if* statement block is skipped. This means that *index* is post-incremented (*index++*, which is *expression3*) and the code goes back up to the top of the *while* loop to check *expression2*. However, because we wrote the *while* loop's *expression2* as *(true)*, the program enters the *while* loop's statement block and once again evaluates the *if* expression. This process repeats up to the point where *index* equals 160.

Eventually, *index* is incremented to equal 160. At that point, the *if* test becomes logic *true* and we execute the code in the *if* statement block. Because the only statement in the *if* statement block is a *break* statement, program control immediately breaks out of the *while* loop and executes the first statement following the closing brace of the *while* statement block. (The behavior of the *break* statement is similar to what you saw with the *switch* statement in Chapter 4.) In our program, the *break* sends program control to the first line after the *while* loop, which does a call to the *Serial* object to display a message and the value of *index* where the match was found. Obviously, the value of index is 160.

You could rewrite the *while* loop program in Listing 5-3 as a *for* loop if you wanted to and it could be made to function exactly the same way. However, the purpose of the program is easily satisfied with a *while* loop, so that's what we used.

The do-while Loop

The third type of loop structure is the *do-while* loop. The syntax is as follows:

```
do {
        // Loop body statements
} while (expression2);
```

As with the *while* loop, only the second condition (*expression2*) is an integral part of the loop structure. It is your responsibility to supply the missing two expressions of a well-behaved loop. Also, even though this form of loop structure is similar to a *while* loop, it has one major difference: with a *do-while* loop, you are guaranteed that the loop body statements are executed at least one time. Consider the following code fragment for a standard *while* loop:

```
int k = 1001;
while (k < 1000) {
      DoSomethingCool(k);
      k++;
}
```

When program control first enters the *while* loop, the test on *k* fails because *k* was initialized to1001. Because *expression2* is logic *false* (*k* is not less than 1000), the loop body statement to call *DoSomethingCool()* is never executed. (You could write a *for* loop that initializes *k* to 1001 and get the same result, right?)

Now let's rewrite the code as a *do-while* loop:

```
int k = 1001;
do {
      DoSomethingCool(k);
      k++;
} while (k < 1000);
```

In this case, the call to *DoSomethingCool()* is made even though *k* is initialized (*expression1*) to the same value as in the *while* loop fragment.

Why a do-while is Different from a while Loop

Therefore, the same conditions for *expression1* cause different results, depending on whether you use a *while* or a *do-while* loop structure. The difference is because *expression2* performs its test at the bottom of the *while* loop after the statements in the loop body have been executed at least one time. The moral of the story is: it is possible to never execute the statements in the loop body with either the *while* or *for* loops structures. However, you are guaranteed that at least one pass through the loop body statements is made with a *do-while* loop. You will likely find that you use the *do-while* loop variant much less frequently than the other two loop structures. Still, it's another tool to add to your tool belt.

The break and continue Keywords

The *break* and *continue* keywords are often used within loop structures. Simply stated, a *break* statement sends program control to the statement that immediately follows the closing brace of the enclosing statement body. (The enclosing statement body doesn't have to be a loop structure, it can also be a *switch* statement block.) The *continue* statement immediately sends program control to the test conditions of the loop (i.e., *expression2*) for this pass through the loop. That is, any statements contained in the loop following the *continue* statement in the statement block are skipped when the *continue* statement executes.

The break Statement

An example may help you see how the *break* statement works. Suppose you have a situation where you monitor the temperature of 200 vats filled with chemicals. When you find one that has reached a specified temperature, you exit the loop and call a method that adds another ingredient to that vat. How might you code such an algorithm? Consider the following code fragment:

```
#define MAXVATCOUNT 200
#define GOALTEMPERATURE 160
// Some statements and setup()
int vatTemperature;
int counter = 0;
loop() {
        while (counter < MAXVATCOUNT) {
                vatTemperature = ReadVatTemp(counter);
                if (vatTemperature >= GOALTEMPERATURE) {
                        break;
                }
                counter++;
                if (counter == MAXVATCOUNT) // Reset so we stay in loop
                        counter = 0;
        }
        AddChemicals(counter);
        if (counter < MAXVATCOUNT) {
                counter++;
        } else {
                counter = 0;              // Just in case this is the last vat
        }
}
```

Now walk through the code, concentrating on the *while* loop. Because *counter* is initialized to 0, the *while* test is true (*counter* is less than or equal to 200) so the code calls *ReadVatTemp(counter)*, which reads the temperature for vat number 0. That temperature is then assigned into *vatTemperature*. Let's assume that the temperature is 150 degrees. The *if* test will fail, causing *counter* to be incremented by 1 (*counter* now equals 1). The program then uses an *if* statement to test whether *counter* is less than *MAXVATCOUNT*. Because the outcome of the *if* test is *false* (i.e., *counter* is not equal to *MAXVATCOUNT*), *counter* remains unchanged, and control is passed back to the *while* loop test *expression2* (i.e., *counter < MAXVATCOUNT*). Because *counter* is still less than *MAXVATCOUNT*, the process repeats.

Let's suppose the first 50 vats don't have the required temperature. However, vat number 51 does return a temperature that is equal to *GOALTEMPERATURE*. Because the two temperatures are equal, the *break* statement is executed. Because a *break* statement causes program control to be transferred to the first statement following the closing brace of the loop structure, *AddChemicals(counter)* is called and the chemicals are added to vat number 51 (the rvalue stored in *counter*). The code must then increment *counter*. (Otherwise we might "double-add" chemicals to the same vat. We assume that the vat has enough time before the loop revisits the vat for the reaction to have changed the temperature.) Because these statements are contained within the *loop()* function, program control is transferred back to the top of the loop body and the *while* statement is again tested using the new value for *counter*.

It should be clear that the *break* statement is used to exit a loop before the test in *expression2* would terminate the loop. It should also be pointed out that the *break* statement only breaks out of the loop containing the *break* statement. If you are using nested loops, it may take multiple *break* statements to completely exit all loops.

The continue Statement

Can you rewrite the preceding *break* code example to use a *continue* statement? Consider the following:

```
#define MAXVATCOUNT 200
#define GOALTEMPERATURE 160
// Some statements...including setup() code
int vatTemperature;
int counter = 0;
loop() {
        while (counter <= MAXVATCOUNT) {
                vatTemperature = ReadVatTemp(counter);
                if (vatTemperature < GOALTEMPERATURE) {// Big difference
                        counter++;
                        if (counter > MAXVATCOUNT)
                                counter = 0;
                        continue;
                }
                AddChemicals(counter);
                if (counter < MAXVATCOUNT) {
                        counter++;
                } else {
                        counter = 0;                    // Just in case this is the last vat
                }
        }
}
```

If you walk through the code, you should be able to convince yourself that the program behaves much the same way it did before, but using a *continue* statement instead of a *break*. Note how the program control flow is slightly different now. If the vat temperature is less than the goal temperature, the *continue* statement executes, which sends control to *expression2* of the *while* statement, thus ignoring all of the statements that follow the *continue* statement. The same caveat applies to *continue* statements within nested loops. The *continue* statement sends control to the expression for the loop containing the *continue* statement. Although you won't use the *continue* statement that often, sometimes it offers a clean alternative for coding a loop.

A Complete Code Example

Let's reuse the circuit you used from Chapter 4 for the Heads or Tails program (see Figure 4-2). However, this time let's use the random number generator and look for a specific value to be produced. When the desired value is found, the code should light the "found it" LED for one second, send a message to the PC via the *Serial* monitor, and report the value of the loop counter. However, each time we cycle through the positive values for the *int* variable that is controlling the loop, we should light the other LED for one second and send a message back to the PC to show how many times we have recycled the *int*. (Recycling the *int* is explained in a bit.)

Recall that the random number generator returns a *long* data type, which means there are several billion possible return values from the random number generator. That could mean a long time between LED flashes. Rather than growing a beard while we wait, let's limit the range of the random number generator to values between 0 to 5000.

Given all this information, how should you start coding the solution? You start with the Five Program Steps.

Step 1. Initialization

We need to set up the I/O pins and the baud rate for the *serial* communication back to the PC, establish a target numeric value, define our working variables, and seed the random number generator.

Step 2. Input

The input process is fairly simple: it's the value returned from a call to the random number generator.

Step 3. Process

In this case, all we need do is check to see if the data from the random number generator is equal to our target value. If the value is equal to our target value, we need to prepare to turn on the "found it" LED. We also need to increment our pass counter variable and see if it is still positive. If not, we need to get ready to flash the recycle LED.

Step 4. Output

If a match was found, we need to turn on the "found it" LED for one second. We also need to output a message to the PC with the current value of the counter variable. If the counter variable went negative, we need to turn on the recycle LED for one second and send a message to the host PC.

Step 5. Termination

Let's put in a termination condition. If the recycle LED has "flipped" five times, let's shut the program down. The *Serial* monitor will tell us when the program ends.

You should try to write the code yourself at this point. You have enough knowledge under your belt to get the job done. It would be a cop-out to just read the following code and move on. You will learn *much* more, however, if you try to write the code first.

Listing 5-5. Random Number Match

```
// define the pins to be used.
#define MAX 5000L
#define MIN 0L
#define TARGETVALUE 2500L

#define MAXRECYCLES 5
#define FOUNDITIOPIN   10        // Use the green LED
#define RECYCLEIOPIN   11        // Use the red LED
#define PAUSE 1000

int foundIt = FOUNDITIOPIN;
int recycle = RECYCLEIOPIN;
long randomNumber;
int recycleCounter = 0;
int counter = 0;
```

```
void setup() {

  Serial.begin(9600);
  pinMode(foundIt, OUTPUT);
  pinMode(recycle, OUTPUT);
  randomSeed(analogRead(A0));            // This seeds the random number generator
}

void loop() {

  while (counter != -1) {                // Check for negative values
    randomNumber = generateRandomNumber();
    if (randomNumber == TARGETVALUE) {
      Serial.print("Counter = ");
      Serial.print(counter, DEC);
      Serial.print("  recycleCounter = ");
      Serial.println(recycleCounter, DEC);
      digitalWrite(foundIt, HIGH);
      delay(PAUSE);
      digitalWrite(foundIt, LOW);
    }

    counter++;
    if (counter < 0) {                   // We've overflowed an int
      counter = 0;
      recycleCounter++;
      Serial.print("recycleCounter = ");
      Serial.println(recycleCounter, DEC);
      digitalWrite(recycle, HIGH);
      delay(PAUSE);
      digitalWrite(recycle, LOW);
    }

    if (recycleCounter == MAXRECYCLES) {
      FakeAnEnd();                       // End program
    }
  }
}

long generateRandomNumber()
{
  return random(MIN, MAX);               // Generate random numbers 0 and 5000
}

void FakeAnEnd() {                       // Fake the end of the program
  while (true) {
    ;
  }
}
```

You should feel fairly comfortable when looking at the code. The *setup()* function initializes the baud rate for communicating with the host PC. The I/O pins are set and the random number generator is seeded.

111

Inside the *loop()* function, the *while* loop tests to see if *counter* is negative; *counter* is an *int*, so if the current value is 32,767 and it is incremented one more time, the value "rolls over" because the high bit (or the sign bit) changes to a 1, which is interpreted as a negative number. This is what is meant by "recycling the *int*".

Because *counter* is initialized to 0 when the program starts, the first *while* test is logic *true* and we enter the loop statement body. The code then calls the random number generator and checks the value against the target value. If they match, an appropriate message is sent to the PC over the serial link and the "found it" LED is lit for one second. If no match is found, *counter* is incremented. The *if* test then checks to see if *counter* "rolled over" to a negative value. If it did, *counter* is reset to 0, the *recycleCounter* is incremented, a message is sent to the PC, and the recycle LED is lit for a second.

Finally, the code then checks to see if the *recycleCounter* equals the maximum number of recycles we wish to run (i.e., equal to *MAXRECYCLES*). If so, the call to *FakeAnEnd()* makes it look like the program ends. What actually happens is we create a *while* loop that has no *expression1* or *expression3*. If you think about it, a loop that is missing those expressions results in an infinite loop because the state of the loop never changes. An *infinite loop, therefore,* is a loop that never ends. Because there are no statements in the infinite loop, it appears that the program has ended. However, what is really happening is that we are spinning around in a tight *while* loop doing nothing.

Listing 5-5 Is SDC

The code in Listing 5-5 is Sorta Dumb Code (SDC) for several reasons, even though it does perform as designed. First, look closely at the code and ask yourself: Does the *while* test ever have a chance to see a negative value for *counter*? The answer is No. The reason why the *while* statement never sees a negative value is because we check for that possibility within the *while* loop code itself, and change it to 0 if it is negative. Therefore, you might as well replace the *while* test with

```
while (true) {
```

which sets up an infinite loop for the *while* test. This is a more honest statement than the phony test Listing 5-5 uses. (If something is always true, why waste the resources to test it?) The fact that we've created an infinite loop won't be a problem because we use *FakeAnEnd()* to terminate the program anyway. Think about it.

Secondly, any time you see a repeating code pattern, try to think of ways to simplify it. In our case, the statements

```
digitalWrite(foundIt, HIGH);
delay(PAUSE);
digitalWrite(foundIt, LOW);
```

and

```
digitalWrite(recycle, HIGH);
delay(PAUSE);
digitalWrite(recycle, LOW);
```

are almost the same. Why not replace these statements with

```
ToggleLED(foundIt, PAUSE);
```

and

```
ToggleLED(recycle, PAUSE);
```

and write the following new function:

```
void ToggleLED(int whichLED, int howLong) {
    digitalWrite(whichLED, HIGH);
    delay(howLong);
    digitalWrite(whichLED, LOW);
}
```

While these are minor changes, they do remove some clutter from the loop body and make it a little easier to read. (A more detailed discussion of writing functions is presented in Chapter 6. However, the function discussed here is a pretty simple improvement to identify and a simple function to write.)

The process of simplifying or "cleaning up" the code is called *refactoring*. While refactoring in this case may save a few bytes of memory and add the time overhead of a function call, these impacts are quite small. Is it worth it? To me, yes, it is. Anytime I can do anything that makes the code easier to read with little or no performance or resource penalty, I make the change. Sometimes I feel that in the rush to get something to work, I cobble the code together with bailing wire and chewing gum. Refactoring simply allows me to go back and reexamine the code so I can remove the bailing wire and chewing gum. Indeed, just *thinking* about future code refactoring will make you a better programmer as you write the code.

Getting Rid of a Magic Number

The code fragment we used to discuss the *sizeof()* operator, however, should have caused your brain to itch a little. Why? One reason is because the *for* loop had a "magic number" (200) in it:

```
for (index = 0; index < 200; index++) {
```

Suppose you increase the list size 200 to 210 elements. Now you have to plow through all of the source code looking for each occurrence of 200 and change it to 210. As I mentioned in an earlier chapter, this is a very error-prone process.

What if we rewrote the *for* loop as the following?

```
for (index = 0; index < sizeof(searchList) / sizeof(searchList[0]); index++) {
```

Given what you know about the *sizeof()* operator, the statement resolves to

```
for (index = 0; index < 400 / 2; index++) {
```

which reduces to:

```
for (index = 0; index < 200; index++) {
```

Recall that *sizeof()* returns a byte count of a specific data item, so the expression *sizeof(searchList)* returns 400, as you saw earlier. Likewise, the expression *sizeof(searchList[0])* returns the size of a single element of the *searchList[]* array, or 2 bytes for each *int* element.

So, what is the advantage of using the *sizeof()* form in the *for* loop? Well, if you increase the size of the array to 210, the expression factors out to:

```
for (index = 0; index < 420 / 2; index++) {
for (index = 0; index < 210; index++) {
```

Now that you have removed the magic number and replaced it with the *sizeof()* expressions, if you change the array size, recompiling the code automatically changes to the new array size for you! No error-prone process to wade through.

A Macro for an Array Size

This array size calculation using *sizeof()* is so useful that programmers often create what is called a *parameterized macro* definition for it. Recall that a *#define* is a preprocessor directive that causes a textual substitution in the source code. Suppose you write this at the top of your program source code:

```
#define ArrayElementSize(x)   (sizeof(x) / sizeof(x[0]))
```

Now further suppose you write the *for* loop like this:

```
for (index = 0; index < ArrayElementSize(searchList); index++) {
```

When the preprocessor pass finishes making its pass over your source code, the preceding statement becomes this:

```
for (index = 0; index < sizeof(searchList) / sizeof(searchList[0]); index++) {
```

Look familiar? Note how the *x* in the macro is replaced by the array name *searchList[]* after the preprocessor does its magic. The parameterized macro named *ArrayElementSize()* allows you to pass a parameter (i.e., the name of the array) to the macro, which can then determine the element count for the array. Shazam! Less work for you to do and no magic numbers to boot!

Loops and Coding Style

The question of coding style relative to program loops really boils down to a few simple questions. First, if a loop only controls a single statement, braces are *not* necessary to mark the start and end of the loop statement body. So the question becomes one that we first asked when you studied *if* statements: If the braces are not necessary, should I bother using them?

Yes ... next question.

Okay, rather than a flippant answer, the reason is because, more often than not, you will end up adding one or more statements to the loop statement body, thus forcing you to add the braces anyway. This is particularly true of debugging statements that use *Serial.print()* to examine the values of variables. Always adding the braces also lends consistency to your code, and that's almost always a good thing. Finally, the braces make it easy to see the start and end of a statement block.

One mistake you will make is forgetting to have a matching closing brace. This happens most often when you have a large number of program statements being controlled by the loop. You can always tell which is the matching brace by placing the cursor immediately to the right of a brace. The IDE will highlight the other brace that goes with the block defined by the brace. This works for both opening and closing braces.

The second question is: Should I place the opening brace of the loop statement body on the same line as the loop keyword (e.g., *for, while*) or should I drop it down to the next line? That is, should you use

```
for (k = 0; k < 1000; k++) {     // brace on same line
```

or

```
for (k = 0; k < 1000; k++)
{                                // brace on new line
```

114

Actually, I prefer to leave the opening brace on the same line as the loop keyword because that lets me see one more line of source code without having to scroll the display. Also, that was the "K&R" style back in the Dark Ages when I first started using C. However, some IDEs, like Visual Studio, default to placing the brace on the next line below the first letter of the loop keyword. Also, there are a lot of programmers who prefer the brace on a new line because it makes it easier to see the statement block. If you work in a corporate environment, you may not have a choice and have to use the style dictated by the shop. If you do have a choice, whatever style you select, use it consistently.

Third, I don't think I've ever seen a competent programmer who does not indent the statements within the loop body one tab stop. This is one of those situations where, if you see someone jump off a bridge, you *should* follow suit and jump off, too. Always indent the statements within a loop statement body (and *if* and *switch* statement blocks, too!) It makes them stand out and easier to read, and "easier to read" means less time spent debugging. If you're lazy, you can always use Ctrl+T (or Tools ➤ Auto Format) and let the IDE format your code.

Finally, sometimes you read code where there is a very long loop body with a ton of statements within the loop body. In those cases, you might see something like this:

```
while (k < MAXCOUNT) {
        // a bunch of loops statements
}                                      // End: while (k < MAXCOUNT)
```

The intent of the comment at the end of the closing loop brace is to help find where the loop statements start and end. I rarely do this, but perhaps I should. However, as mentioned earlier, if you place the cursor immediately after the closing brace of a loop, the Arduino IDE "boxes" the matching opening brace up at the top of the loop. Because of this, and even though the comment is laudable, I usually don't bother adding such comments.

Portability and Extensibility

Often you hear programmers talk about writing "portable code." Writing portable code is a goal that good programmers try to fulfill. Simply stated, *portable code* refers to *program source code that can be moved from one programming environment and successfully recompiled in a different programming environment with no changes to the source code*. It would be like taking a program written for the Arduino IDE and successfully recompiling it without change in the Visual Studio IDE.

Why is writing portable code so hard? There are a bunch of reasons. First, it's pretty unlikely that all of the functions you find in the Arduino IDE are the same as those in the Visual Studio (or NetBeans, or Enterprise, etc.) IDE. For example, *pinMode()* doesn't even exist in Visual Studio's IDE. Still, if you stick with functions that are part of the Standard C library for most of your code (e.g., like *memset()*), chances are pretty good that the Visual Studio C compiler also has those library functions, too.

Another portability problem is data type sizes. For example, suppose you are writing hourly temperature data to an SD card. Further suppose you need to know the number of bytes written to the file each day. You could write it as something like

```
bytesWritten = 48;
```

because you know each *int* takes 2 bytes for the Arduino IDE, so 24 * 2 equals 48. Well, there you go again—using those stupid magic numbers! If you decide at some later date that you need to write the data every 30 minutes, you're back to the search-and-replace issues again.

Instead, you write this:

```
#define SAMPLESPERDAY    24
bytesWritten = SAMPLESPERDAY * 2;
```

Better, but still SDC. What if you move from the Arduino to a bigger microcontroller that uses 4-byte *ints*, like the netDuino does? Now you are not using enough bytes for the data. So you modify the preprocessor statements again to:

```
#define SAMPLESPERDAY    24
bytesWritten = SAMPLESPERDAY * sizeof(int);
```

Now you have *bytesWritten* coded in such a way that it is portable between the Arduino and the netDuino, even though their *int* sizes are different. Writing code with the idea of portability in the back of your head is always a good thing.

Okay, so what does *extensible code* mean? Code is *extensible* if it *can accommodate different sized data sets without changes to the source code*. In other words, if you are writing code to work with a company's inventory list of 1000 items, extensible code means that you could take the same code and easily implement it for another company that has an inventory list with 5,000,000 items in it. Extensible code is desirable, especially in a business environment, because the software can grow painlessly with the company's growth.

Often code fails (and extensibility ends) at what are called *boundary conditions*. For example, if your inventory list has up to 1000 items in it, the boundary conditions are 0 and 1000. Boundary conditions set the limits for many program structures, like *for, while,* and *do-while* loops. Program bugs love to hide in boundary conditions. For example, beginning programmers might write this:

```
for (i = 1; i = 1000; i++) {
   if (target == inventoryList[i])
      break;
   // more code...
}
```

There are a number of problems here. First, arrays start with 0, not 1, so the lower boundary condition (i.e., 0) never gets used. Second, *expression2* in the *for* loop should be a relational test, not an assignment operator, so that's going to cause problems. Third, if they replace the assignment operator (=) with the test for equality (==), the code may die an spectacular death because the *if* test expression becomes *i ==inventoryList[1000]* at the upper boundary, even though there are only 0–999 valid inventory indexes.

Once again, getting rid of magic numbers is the first step to making the code extensible. Defining your arrays like this

```
#define MAXINVENTORY 1000
// more code...
int inventoryList[MAXINVENTORY];
```

makes it easier to extend the program without using error-prone processes like global search-and-replace.

Finally, think before you write. A few minutes defining the Five Program Steps for a given problem is a minimal preparation step to writing a new program. Thinking and preparation makes writing programs easier—and easier usually means more enjoyable.

Summary

Because of the way Arduino C uses the *loop()* function in all its programs, you have been using loops since you ran your very first program. However, this chapter has introduced you to program loops in a more formal way, plus making you aware that there are several different loop structures. You should now be comfortable using *for, while,* and *do-while* loops in your programs. You should also understand what the necessary and sufficient conditions are for a well-behaved program loop.

Take some time to invent a few loop programs of your own. If you can tie the code to a circuit, so much the better. You will always learn more if you try to create your own code.

EXERCISES
---

1. Look at the following code fragment:

    ```
    int k;
    for (k = 0; k < 1000; k++) {
               k = DoSomethingCool(k);
    }
    ```

    What happens if the function *DoSomethingCool()* ends up decrementing *k* before it passes the value back to the *for* loop statement body?

    Answer: If the function decrements *k*, on the first pass the value assigned into *k* by *DoSomethingCool()* is –1. That value is then passed to *expression3 (k++)*, which increments *k* to 0. Control then passes to *expression2*, which checks to see if *k* is less than 1000. Because *k* is now 0 again, the call to *DoSomethingCool()* is called again, which assigns –1 into *k* … again. Clearly, this ends up in an infinite loop.

2. What happens in the following code fragment?

    ```
    #define EVER ;; // Just two semicolons...

    // Some statements

    for (EVER) {
        // Do some statements here
     }
    // The rest of the program
    ```

    Answer: Know what? I'm not going to tell you. Instead, create a small program with this code in the *loop()* function and make the following changes:

    ```
    for (EVER) {
        Serial.println("Pass... ");
    }
    ```

    And then look on the Arduino IDE monitor (Ctrl+Shift+M) to see what happens. Try to explain what you see.

3. Suppose you want to find a part that has the numeric ID number 1000 out of an inventory that has 500,000 items. Although all part numbers are present in the inventory list, they are not necessarily in sorted order. (That is, you can't assume that part number 1000 is the 1000th item in the inventory list.) Write a code fragment for the loop to look for the part number?

    Answer: Did you write code similar to the following?

    ```
    #define INVENTORYCOUNT 500000

    int counter = 0;
    ```

```
int partLocated;
int targetPart;
targetPart = PartToLookFor();  // Assume this sets k = 1000
while (counter <=  INVENTORYCOUNT) {
        partLocated = NextPartNumber(counter);
        if (partLocated ==  targetPart)
             break;
      counter++;
}
```

If you did, ask yourself this: What is the size of the inventory count and what is the maximum number that can be expressed with an *int?* Look at Table 3-1 and fix the problem.

4. In the most general terms possible, when would you use the various loop structures?

Answer: Use the *for* loop when you must execute the loop body a known number of times. Use a *while* loop when you are looking for a particular value in a list of possible values. Use a *do-while* loop when you must execute the statements in the loop body at least one time while searching a list.

5. What is refactoring?

Answer: Refactoring is the process of looking for ways to simplify and "clean up" your code. Some of the biggest benefits of refactoring are to make the code more readable and perhaps more efficient by removing duplicate or redundant code. You can find more details at http://c2.com/cgi/wiki?WhatIsRefactoring.

6. Which loop coding style do you prefer and why?

Answer: There is no answer. It will depend upon how you feel about style or whether you even have a choice. Your style may be dictated by company guidelines.

7. Remember the TV show *Knight Rider?* The car named Kitt has a series of lights that would sequence on and off, from left to right. Using Figure 4-2 as a guide, add 5 or 6 more LEDs to the circuit. Now figure out the code to make the LEDs flash in a sequence similar to Kitt's lights.

Answer: I'm not going to show you the code, just give you some hints.

```
int leds[] = {4, 5, 6, 7, 8, 9, 10};  // These LEDs are wired to pins 4-10.

void setup() {

  int i;

  for (i = 0; i < sizeof(leds) / sizeof(leds[0]); i++) {
    pinMode(leds[i], OUTPUT);       // Initialize LEDs for output
  }
}

void loop() {
  // you're on your own...
}
```

CHAPTER 6

■ ■ ■

Functions in C

You already know what a function is, but let's give it a formal definition. A *function* is a *body of code designed to solve a particular task*. You should think of a function as a black box, the contents of which are unknown to you. All you care about is that it addresses some task to be accomplished in your program. Hundreds of functions are available for you to use in various function libraries. A *function library* is simply a collection of functions that share a common area of interest (e.g., the Math and Time functions in Arduino C.) However, many vendors have added new libraries of their own to support products and add-ons that they sell for the Arduino family. Functions make your life easier because you can stand on the shoulders of those who came before you. You can use their code rather than writing, testing, and debugging the code yourself.

In this chapter you will learn

- The various components that make up a C function

- What function arguments are

- What function parameters are

- How data is passed between your program and a function

- Which design considerations are important when designing a function

- What "pass-by-value" means

- What a program stack is and how it is used with functions

- What a function signature is

- What an overloaded function is

There is a lot of information packed into this chapter. Take your time and think about what you are reading ... functions are a basic building block of all C programs.

The backbone of C is its robust library of functions. In fact, C is one of the few languages that doesn't have any I/O capability built into the language. Initially, ANSI C only had 32 keywords; Arduino C has slightly less. Contrast those keyword counts with a language like Visual Basic with over 170 keywords and you may wonder how you can do anything with C. Actually, C purposely was designed to be a crisp language with a minimal number of keywords. Rather than bloat the language with a high keyword count, C pushes many standard language tasks off into its standard function library. The neat part about this approach is that you are not constrained by the way the language does things. If you don't like the way the existing library routines do things, you are free to write your own replacement. Later on in this chapter, we will write a replacement for the standard library routine that determines if a specified year is a leap year. While I may think my *IsLeapYear()* function is better than yours, you are free to disagree and write your own replacement. Such a design philosophy makes it easy to modify or extend the language as you see fit.

© Jack Purdum 2015
J. Purdum, *Beginning C for Arduino, Second Edition*: Learn C Programming
for the Arduino, DOI 10.1007/978-1-4842-0940-0_6

The Anatomy of a Function

Later in this chapter you will write a short program that asks the user to enter a year, and the program informs the user if the year entered is a leap year. In doing this, you will write a function named *IsLeapYear()* that tests whether a given year is, in fact, a leap year.

Let's take a look at the general structure of a C function, as shown in Figure 6-1.

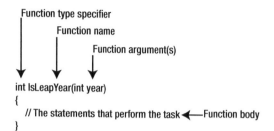

```
int IsLeapYear(int year)
{
    // The statements that perform the task ◄——Function body
}
```

Figure 6-1. *Parts of a function*

Function Type Specifier

First, the function type specifier appears at the start of the function definition. In our example, we want the function to return an integer value. For my specific purposes, I want the function to return the *int* value 1 if it is a leap year, and 0 if it is not. Most leap year functions return a Boolean value that is logic *true* if it is a leap year, and logic *false* if not. *The purpose of a function type specifier is to define the type of data that is returned when the function is called.* Recalling our backpack analogy, the function type specifier tells you the type of data the function code placed in your backpack just before you left the function and returned to the caller. The type of data returned from the function can be whatever data type you wish it to be (e.g., *float, long, char, byte*, etc.), depending on how you write your function's code. If no value is returned from the function, the type specifier must use the *void* keyword for the function type specifier.

■ **Note** Just because the function places a piece of data in your backpack to haul back to the caller does not force the caller to actually use that data. Indeed, each of the *Serial.print()* methods you have used in previous programs returned a count of the number of characters printed, but we have yet to actually use that information. Each function description should tell you the function type specifier, and, hence, what's in your backpack when you leave the function.

Function Name

The second part of a function is the name of the function. Function names follow the same naming rules you use for variable names. Most library functions start with a lowercase letter, although that is not a requirement of the language. Personally, I tend to start the name of functions that I write with an uppercase letter so that I know that I wrote the function and it did not come from a library of functions written by someone else. Again, this is not a naming rule, simply a style convention I tend to follow. That way, if something in the code isn't working correctly and I see an uppercase function name, I know that I wrote that code and it may contain the error. (Chances are pretty slim that an error exists in public library functions.)

Good Names, Bad Names

The choice of a function name does matter. Good function names tell you *what* the function does, but not *how* it does it. For example, suppose you need to search a list of data to find a particular value. There are many different ways to organize and search the list of data (e.g., sort into ascending order, create a binary tree, use hash codes, etc.) You decide to sort the data and then search the list using a binary search algorithm. You name the function *DoBinarySearch()*. Now fast-forward a few months, you now have learned how to use hash codes, and you discover that the hash algorithm will significantly improve the performance of your program. You write the function and name it *DoHashSearch()*. Now you have to go back through your source code and change all instances of *DoBinarySearch()* to *DoHashSearch()*. True, you could just change the code in the *DoBinarySearch()* to implement the hash code algorithm, but that seems a little deceptive. Also, if someone else has to look at your code, they read it expecting to find a binary search algorithm and end up scratching their head because they are reading a hash code algorithm.

A better name for the function would be *FindListItem()*. The reason it's a better name is because it tells the user of the function *what* the function does, not *how* it's done. If you decide to implement a different algorithm at some later date, you can do so with a clear conscience because the function name says nothing about how things are done. A function should be a black box in that it tells you what it does, but provides no details on its implementation.

Some of you are saying: "But major language and compiler vendors do have functions named *ShellSort()*, *QuickSort()*, and other algorithm-specific names." True, but you want your functions to be *task-specific*, not *algorithm-specific*. If you are working with a language that offers you a choice, great! However, I would still write my own function, as in:

```
int FindListItem(int list[], int target)
{
    ShellSort(list);              // Sort the data
    return FindItem(list, target); // Find the item
}
```

In this case, you've wrapped the details of *how* the sort is done in a function that says *what* is to be done. If you decide later than some other algorithm works better, it is very easy to make the change and you don't have to lie about the implementation. Even better, the person using your code doesn't have to do a search-and-replace in their program. A simple recompile and your new algorithm is in the program!

Function Arguments

After the function name comes an opening parenthesis followed by zero or more function arguments. *Function arguments are used to pass data to the function that it may need to perform its task.* In earlier chapters, we used the analogy of stuffing data into your backpack prior to calling the function. Those pieces of data were function arguments. Multiple function arguments are delineated with commas between arguments. You often hear programmers refer to function arguments as an *argument list*. The argument list ends with a closing parenthesis.

As mentioned before, you can think of a function as a black box with a front door, back door, and no windows. (What goes on inside the black box, stays inside the black box ... no peeking as to its implementation.) Program control enters the front door carrying a backpack with any data in it that the function needs to perform its task. The contents of the backpack are the function arguments. Some functions, like the *setup()* and *loop()* functions you've seen in every program, do not need outside help to do their thing. In these cases, the function has a *void* argument list and the backpack is empty. (Indeed, you can write the word *void* as the argument list for both *setup()* and *loop()*, recompile the program, and the compiler is completely happy with the changes.)

After the function does its thing, the backpack emerges from the back door. The content of the backpack is the data produced by the function. The type of data that is stuffed into the backpack is dictated by the function type specifier of the function. If the backpack is empty, the type specifier for the function is *void.* If, for example, the backpack contains a floating point number when control exits the back door, the function type specifier for that function must be either *float* or *double,* depending upon the type of data the programmer who wrote the function decides is needed.

For example, consider the following:

```
int buyNails;
int nailsPerFoot;
int numberOfFeet;
                        // some more code...
buyNails = NailsNeeded(nailsPerFoot, numberOfFeet);
```

The *NailsNeeded()* function has two arguments, *nailsPerFoot* and *numberOfFeet.* In this example, the argument list for the backpack is stuffed with the value of these two *int* rvalues and control is sent to the *NailsNeeded()* function. Once inside the function's front door, program code removes the two *int*s, does some form of calculation, places a count of the nails needed as an *int* into the backpack, and sends control back to the caller. Upon return from the function, the content of the backpack is then dumped into the rvalue of the variable named *buyNails.* Stated differently, the content of the backpack becomes the rvalue of *buyNails.* One of the advantages of function arguments is that the compiler can check to ensure that you are passing the correct type of data to the function. For example, if you tried to make the call to the standard library function named *bit()* using this

```
bit(2.33);
```

the compiler complains because it knows that the argument to the function cannot be a floating point number. Catching this kind of mismatch between the type of data being sent to a function and the data type that the function expects is one form of *type checking.* The compiler also performs type checking on the value returned from a function ... sort of. Suppose you want to square the value 10,000. You could write

```
int val = pow(10000, 2);        //WRONG!
```

and the compiler doesn't complain. However, this code is wrong on several levels. First, *pow()* returns a floating point number and the code is trying to jam a 4-byte *float* into a 2-byte *int* bucket. Second, the numeric value computed by *pow()* in this example would overflow the maximum value an *int* can hold. (*INT_MAX* is a *#define*'d constant for the maximum value of an *int.* You can use this constant in your code for range checking.). Third, the arguments to *pow()* are floating point numbers, so a decimal point is needed to ensure the compiler processes the arguments correctly. The call should be this:

```
float val = pow(10000.0, 2.0);
```

The lesson here is that the Arduino C compiler performs some type checking, but some errors can slip through the cracks. If a function is returning bogus values, make sure you're passing data to the function that is consistent with its argument list. Also, make sure that the return value matches the variable type you are using to hold the return value.

You can get more help from the compiler when tracking down bugs of this nature. Go to the File ➤ Preferences menu option and check the box that tells the compiler to issue "verbose" messages during compilation. These verbose messages often are helpful when tracking down some types of program errors. When the verbose mode is turned on, you will also get processing messages (displayed with white lettering) that simply detail normal compile processes. The list can be quite long and scroll out of view. However, compiler warnings are displayed in orange lettering and you can scroll back through the messages and read those that are of interest to you. Personally, I find the additional messages distracting, so I leave the preferences without using the verbose mode.

Function Signatures and Function Prototypes

The function type specifier, the function name, and the function's argument list are collectively called the *function signature*. The function signature for my leap year function is:

```
int IsLeapYear(int year)        // Function signature
```

If you add a semicolon on the end of the function signature,

```
int IsLeapYear(int year);       // Function prototype... note semicolon at end
```

The function signature becomes a *function prototype*. Function prototypes are used by the compiler to check to see if you spelled the function name correctly, if you are passing it the correct data types to the function, and if you are using any return value correctly. Because this information is used for type checking, function prototypes usually appear at the top of the source code file so that the compiler reads them before you actually use them. This allows the compiler to place the information about the function in the symbol table, thus creating an attribute list for the function that can be used for type checking.

▓ **Note**   The Arduino compiler maintains an internal list of function prototypes for the standard library function and creates *ad hoc* prototypes for the functions you write. If your project has two or more source code files, you would normally create a header file for those additional source code files. Header files are used to pass information to the compiler that it needs to properly process your program. For example, if you added a source code file named *MyFunctions.cpp* (it's a C++ file), you would also create a header file named *MyFunctions.h*, which would contain the function prototypes (and other information) for all of the functions defined in the *MyFunctions.cpp* source code file. Then, at the top of your *.ino* project file, the first line would be

```
#include "MyFunctions.h"
```

which tells the compiler to read that header file so it can do function type checking on your new functions. I will have more to say about this in Chapter 11.

One more thing: there is no code generated with a function prototype. That is, the actual code for the function appears elsewhere, either in a library or later in your code. As such, no actual program memory is allocated for a function prototype. This means there is no lvalue for the function prototype in the symbol table. Only the function's attribute list as constructed from the function signature is in the symbol table. Because there is no lvalue, function prototypes are data declarations, not data definitions.

Finally, if you know a function's signature or its prototype, you know the information necessary to use the function. You also know what type of data is returned from the function. What you don't know from either of these things is how the function is implemented, which is as it should be. What happens inside the black box stays inside the black box.

Function Body

The *function body* begins with the opening brace ({) that follows the closing parenthesis of the argument list and extends to the closing brace (}) of the function. Stated differently, the function body starts at the point where the function signature ends. All of the statements between these two characters comprise the function body. Obviously, the statements in the function body determine how the function is implemented.

If the function type specifier is anything other than *void*, at least one of the statements in the function body must contain the keyword *return*. For example:

```
int VolumeOfCube(int width, int length, int height)
{
    int volume;
    volume = width * length * height;
    return volume;
}
```

In this example, the function type specifier is an *int*, so the function must have a *return* statement in it. If you forgot the statement

```
    return volume;
```

the compiler should issue an error message. You can think of the *return* statement as an instruction telling the compiler what to put into your backpack. If the function type specifier is *void*, there is no need to place anything in the backpack. Otherwise, there needs to be a *return* statement telling the compiler what data type to put in the backpack and return back to the caller.

Note that experienced C programmers tend to make their code as short as possible. As a result, programmers often would write the code as

```
int VolumeOfCube(int width, int length, int height)
{
    return width * length * height;
}
```

which removes the temporary variable *volume*.

Unfortunately, the Arduino C compiler lets you get a little lazy about return values. For example, if you wrote

```
int myFunction(int a)
{
    int temp = a;
}
```

the compiler should complain that you are not returning a value from the function, even though you used the *int* type specifier. Alas, unless you have the verbose compiler messages turned on, the compiler is mute about this error. This can be nettlesome if you did something like

```
int number = myFunction(10);
```

because some kind of indeterminate junk is going to be assigned into *number*. Debugging this type of error can be frustrating because the code looks so simple and you're getting no debugging hints from the compiler. Just keep in mind: when the compiler seems to be executing code that isn't there, it isn't.

The compiler is doing exactly what you told it to do. It's just not being real helpful in telling you what you meant to do isn't what it *is* doing.

On a more positive note, if you change the function type specifier from *int* to *void*

```
void myFunction(int a)
{
        int temp = a;
}
```

and then try to do something silly like

```
int number = myFunction(10);
```

which tries to assign "nothing" (i.e., void) into number, the compiler issues an error message stating

```
void value not ignored as it ought to be
```

which is at least helpful in finding the error.

Overloaded Functions

Whenever a function shares a common name, but has two or more different signatures, it is called an *overloaded function*. In most cases, it is the argument list that differs across signatures. (Technically, the C programming language does not allow overloaded functions, whereas C++ does. Because the Arduino C compiler is built upon the GCC compiler, Arduino C does permit overloaded functions. This is a good thing!) Often, two signatures are used when a default value doesn't solve the task at hand. For example, in Chapter 5, Listing 5-4 uses the *random()* function, passing in lower and upper bound values for the random number:

```
randomNumber = random(MIN, MAX);
```

However, if we look at the documentation for *random()*, we see that we could have used

```
random(201);
```

because the function has an overloaded function signature with a single argument in its argument list.

Another example is

```
Serial.print(val);
```

which you have used in other programs. However, if you want to display *val* in hexadecimal instead of decimal, you could use:

```
Serial.print(val, HEX);
```

Clearly, the *print()* method for the *Serial* object is overloaded because the same method name has two (actually, more than two) function signatures.

Overloaded functions add a degree of consistency (i.e., using the same name) in a programming situation where there is a small nuance of difference in what the function needs to perform its task. Overloaded functions are not difficult to understand, but you do need to consult the documentation for any functions you are not familiar with, simply because they well may be overloaded. If they are overloaded, it simply means you have more choices in the way you go about solving a problem. I will have more to say about overloaded functions in later chapters.

What Makes a "Good" Function

I've already touched on some of the things that are part of a good function definition, but let's consider those conditions in a little more depth.

Good Functions Use Task-Oriented Names

A good function name is a description of what the function does. Usually, a function is designed to solve some particular problem or task. If so, the function name should reflect what the function does. Often the function name is action-oriented, such as *GetThis()*, *DoThat()*, *SetBit()*, *ReadIOBit()*, and so forth. Such names reflect the nature of the task at hand, *not* how that task is accomplished.

As mentioned earlier, function names should reflect *what* is to be done, not *how* it is done. The exception is when you are writing a function that specifies the way something must be done (e.g., *BubbleSort()*, *ShellSort()*, *CreateLinkedList()*, etc.) Such method-oriented names are fine if a task requires that the problem be solved a specific way. For example, suppose you need to search a 100,000-word document for a specific phase. One way is a brute force approach where you just plow through the file looking for the phrase. You might name that function *BruteForceSearch()*. A more sophisticated algorithm uses a Boyer-Moore algorithm, suggesting you name the function *BoyerMooreSearch()*. Clearly, method-named functions require you to suggest the underlying method or algorithm being used. However, more often than not, you will be creating task-oriented functions. Using task-oriented function names makes it easier for you to change the underlying algorithm without breaking existing code.

Good Functions Are Cohesive

A cohesive function is a function that is designed to accomplish a single task. Chances are, if you can't explain to someone what a function does in two sentences or less, the function is too complicated and is not cohesive. In such cases, redesign the function and break it into smaller tasks and make each of those smaller tasks a function.

I mentioned that students often want to build a Swiss Army knife function—a function that is designed to address multiple tasks at once, and, inevitably, doing none of them well. Also, such multiuse functions require more control code in them to pick between the options. More code almost always means more time writing, testing, and debugging the code. Also, by breaking the tasks down into simpler multiple functions, you increase the odds that you can reuse those functions in other programs.

How do you know when a function lacks cohesion? First, the two-sentence rule is a good start in deciding if the function attempts to do too much. Another tip-off is when you see an argument list with three or more arguments. Usually, a single-task function doesn't need all that much help in terms of data from the outside world. Small backpacks are a good thing. When you see a long argument list, you should step back and ask yourself if the function is cohesive.

Good Functions Avoid Coupling

Coupling refers to the need for one function to depend upon the results of another function to perform its task. For example, earlier I mentioned a function named *FindListItem()* and suggested:

```
int FindListItem(int list[], int target)
{
        ShellSort(list);                    // Sort the data
        return FindItem(list, target);      // Find the item
}
```

This is really not a good function because it has two tasks:

- Sorting the data

- Finding the item in the sorted list

It would be better to remove the *ShellSort()* function call out of the *FindListItem()* function, and move the *FindItem()* function code into the *FindListItem()* function body. You could then toss the *FindItem()* function away. The *FindListItem()* is no longer coupled to (or depends upon) the *ShellSort()* function to perform its task. The function is also more cohesive now because it no longer is required to perform two tasks. True, to have the code behave as before, you would need to have two calls:

```
ShellSort(list);
FindListItem(list, target);
```

However, in my mind, this divide-and-conquer approach is a good thing. If I later discover a new function is more efficient at sorting the list (e.g., *SuperfastSort()*), I can replace the *ShellSort()* call with *SuperfastSort()*. If we had the old form where the sort process is buried within the function, we're stuck with *ShellSort()*. This is especially true for function libraries where you may not have access to the source code for the library.

There are situations where you cannot totally avoid some level of coupling. If your program has to write to a data file, you need to open the file first. If you're reading a sensor, there may be a sequence of tasks that must be performed in a specific order for the sensor to do its job. For example, if you need to read a line of text from a data file, it is better to have separate *Open()*, *Read()*, and *Close()* functions than to bury the *Open()* and *Close()* functions within a *Read()* function. That way, you can still have a cohesive function with minimal coupling.

Writing Your Own Functions

What is the first step you should do when writing your own functions? The first step should be to determine if someone else has already written the function. A good place to start your search is `http://arduino. cc/it/Reference/Librarie` and `http://playground.arduino.cc`. Reading about existing libraries may even provide new insight into solving old problems. A Google search may also be a productive area of investigation. If you purchase a shield or some other hardware-specific board, you should also see if their web site hosts source code from their customers. Many do and some of the code is very good. Lesson number one is: *Don't write code if you don't have to.*

Assuming you can't find an existing function that fulfills your needs, then it is time to consider designing your own function. For this example, you are going to design and write a function that determines if a given year is a leap year or not. For the existing libraries I could find, their leap year function returns a Boolean value of *true* if it is a leap year, or *false* if it is not a leap year. Although I could make do with those existing functions, it doesn't behave the way I want to use it. (We'll set the function design goals in a few moments.) So, let's make a small trip to the drawing board.

Function Design Considerations

Clearly, you need to design the function to accomplish a single (cohesive) task. Figure 6-1 provides a useful roadmap for starting our design. Let's examine the pieces of the function signature presented in Figure 6-1 from a design perspective.

Function Type Specifier

First, what data type do we want the function to return? While the leap year function for most language libraries (C, Java, C++, Visual Basic, C#) return a Boolean, we want ours to return an *int*. Why an *int* data type for the return value instead of a Boolean? The reason is because the most common use for a leap year calculation is to determine how many days there are in February for a given year. Perhaps the day makes a difference in a billing cycle, interest payment, or some other calculation. Whatever the reason, if you use a "standard" leap year calculation, you need code that looks something like the following:

```
// some SDC code... at least for my purposes
int daysInFeb;
if (IsLeapYear(year) == true)
        daysInFeb = 29;
else
        daysInFeb = 28;
```

This code is SDC for the task we have specified, so we might refactor it by initializing *daysInFeb* and remove the *else* clause:

```
// still some SDC code...
int daysInFeb = 28;
if (IsLeapYear(year) == true)
   daysInFeb = 29;
```

The problem is that we still need the *if* statement to set the proper number of days in February. However, if you write the function to return 1 (as an *int*) if it is a leap year or 0 otherwise, then you can write:

```
// some PGC code...
int daysInFeb = 28 + IsLeapYear(year);
```

Given what we want the function to accomplish, this is *Pretty Good Code* (PGC) and is a good design for our solution. As a general rule, less code is good code as long as its intent remains clear and it accomplishes the task at hand.

Showoff Code

I just saw the following C statement online:

```
i=(i<<3) + (i<<1) + (*string - '0');
```

Essentially, what this does is take an ASCII digit code and multiply it by 10. While this is clever code, I would fire the guy who wrote it if he worked for me because it's "show-off code." Writing code like this is difficult for other programmers to decipher and just isn't worth the hassle it costs to suport it. If you are writing code for yourself and there's some huge performance gain by bit-shifting the data, perhaps then it's okay. However, chances are such code is really not necessary. Indeed, the compiler may well optimize the difference away.

Function Name

What's in a name? A lot! We've already stated that we want task-oriented names, not method-oriented names. We've already settled on a name. *IsLeapYear()* suggests that the function is going to address the task of finding out if a given year is a leap year. Will this cause a function name collision (i.e., two functions with

the same name) in your code? After all, this name is used in some other libraries and the function signature is the same. Even if you do happen to include a library with the same function name, the compiler gives precedence to the function whose source code is being compiled. Because you are supplying the source code for the function, name collision is not a problem. Also, our function type specifier is an *int*, whereas the standard library is a *boolean*, which means the signatures are different.

Argument List

Our function does need data from the "outside world" to accomplish its task. Specifically, the backpack needs to have an *int* data type that specifies the year stuffed into it before we call the function. Again, visualizing a function as a black box with a single entry and exit point is a good mental picture for the way a function should work. That is, after you write this function, handing the function to another programmer for use of your function should prompt only three questions from them:

- What task does this function perform?
- What data do I need to send to the function?
- What data do I get back from it?

If you've done your design work well, the function name answers the first question, the argument list answers the second question, and the function type specifier answers the third question. That is, the function signature fills the bill. When the day is done, a programmer using your code could care less how you write the code inside the function—as long as it accomplishes the task at hand with reasonable efficiency.

Function Body

The function body begins with the opening brace, followed by the statements that are necessary to accomplish the task at hand, followed by a closing brace. Because our type specifier returns an *int*, you immediately know that one of the statements must use the *return* keyword to send an *int* value back from the function.

If you think about it, the function argument list corresponds to the Input Step of the Five Program Steps you learned in Chapter 2. The function body reflects the Process Step since it contains the statements necessary to solve the task. What you need now is an algorithm that tells you how to determine if a year is a leap year.

You can Google "leap year" and find the algorithm for the leap year calculation. An *algorithm* is simply a step-by-step set of instructions for solving a problem. The leap year algorithm states: *If the year can be evenly divided by 4, but not by 100, it is a leap year. The exception occurs if the year is evenly divisible by 400, it is a leap year.*

Although you could write the code using a couple of nested *if* statements, C provides a less messy way of writing the code. To implement this algorithm, let's take a small detour and learn about the logical operators C provides to you and how you can use them.

Logical Operators

Logical operators allow you to combine logical expressions. The logical operators are presented in Table 6-1.

Table 6-1. *Logical Operators*

Operator	Meaning	Example
&&	Logical AND	*X && Y*
||	Logical OR	*X || Y*
!	Logical NOT	*!X*

The best way to illustrate the use of the logical operators is to first consider how they relate to a concept known as a truth table. *Truth tables* show all of the possible outcomes of a logical test using two expressions.

Logical AND Operator (&&)

The logical AND operator is formed by placing two & characters back-to-back with no space between them (&&). Consider the truth table for the logical AND operator, as shown in Table 6-2.

Table 6-2. *Logical AND (&&) Truth Table*

Expression1	Expression2	Expression1 && Expression2
TRUE	TRUE	TRUE
TRUE	FALSE	FALSE
FALSE	TRUE	FALSE
FALSE	FALSE	FALSE

Suppose you have variables *k* and *j*, and *k* equals 2 and *j* equals 3, then the statement

```
if (k == 2 && j == 3)
```

finds *expression1* (*k* == 2) is *true* and *expression2* (*j* == 3) is also *true*. Looking in Table 6-2, because both expressions within the *if* statement are true, the logical AND of the two expression is *true*. However, using the same values for *k* and *j*, the following statement

```
if (k == 9 && j == 3)
```

results in *expression1* being *false* (*k* is not equal to 9), which corresponds to the third row in Table 6-2 (i.e., False-True for the expressions) yielding a *false* condition for controlling the outcome of the *if* statement. As you can see from Table 6-2, a logical AND operation only yields a logic *true* result when both expressions are *true*. All other combinations are logic *false*.

In complex expressions, you may have multiple logical operators being used. (You will write one later in this chapter.) If that's the case, you also need to know where the logical operators fit in with respect to operator precedence. Table 4-2 from Chapter 4 (the page number of which you wrote on the back cover of this book, right?) shows that the logical AND and OR operators have precedence levels of 10 and 11 in Table 4-2, respectively. As you can see from Table 6-1, the NOT operator is a unary operator and from Table 4-2 you can see it has a relatively high precedence level of 2. You can use the precedence table to resolve complex statements.

Logical OR (||)

The logical OR operator is formed by placing two vertical bars—also called *pipe* (|) characters—back-to-back with no space between them (||). The truth table for the logical OR operator is shown in Table 6-3.

Table 6-3. *Logical OR (||)*

Expression1	Expression2	Expression1 || Expression2
TRUE	TRUE	TRUE
TRUE	FALSE	TRUE
FALSE	TRUE	TRUE
FALSE	FALSE	FALSE

Once again, suppose you have variables k and j, and k equals 2 and j equals 3, then the OR expression in the following

```
if (k == 2 || j == 3)
```

is logic *true*. However, it is also *true* that

```
if (k == 9 || j == 3)
```

results in logic *true* for the OR expression when it was logic *false* for the AND operator. A logic OR is only *false* when *both* expressions are *false*. As long as at least one expression is *true*, the outcome is *true*. In fact, if the first evaluated expression in an OR statement is logic *true*, the code will not even bother evaluating the next part of the OR statement. This is called *short-circuit expression evaluation* and allows the compiler to perform a small code optimization.

Logical NOT (!)

The logical NOT operator is the exclamation point (!). Because the logical NOT operator is a unary operator, its truth table is a little simpler, as shown in Table 6-4.

Table 6-4. *Logical NOT (!)*

Expression1	! Expression1
TRUE	FALSE
FALSE	TRUE

As you can see in Table 6-4, all the NOT operator does is invert, or toggle, the logic of the expression. For example, suppose k equals 2 again. Then

```
if (! k == 2)
```

is logic *false*. Because *expression1* is *true* (*k* does equal 2), Table 6-4 shows that the result of the logical NOT operator is logic *false*. I surround the expression in a NOT operation with parentheses, as in

```
if (! (k == 2) )
```

because the test for equality operator (==) has a lower precedence than the NOT operator. Also, the parentheses makes it more clear what the intent of the expression is.

Writing Your Own Function

Now that you understand the logical operators, let's write the body of our function. Repeating our leap year algorithm … *if the year can be evenly divided by 4, but not by 100, it is a leap year. The exception occurs if the year is evenly divisible by 400, it is a leap year.*

Let's break this down, part by part.

First, the statement: "If the year can be evenly divided by 4" means that dividing the year by 4 should not produce a remainder after division. This is precisely what the modulo operator (%) is intended for: it returns the remainder after integer division. You can write this element of the algorithm as the logical expression:

```
(year % 4 == 0)
```

Second, the statement: "but not by 100" is actually saying: "but the year is not evenly divisible by 100." Again, the modulo operator (%) is designed for this type of operation, so you can write the expression as:

```
(year % 100 != 0)
```

Taken together, if both of these expressions are *true*, the year is a leap year. Therefore, you can write the two expressions as:

```
(year % 4 == 0) && (year % 100 != 0)
```

If these two expressions are *true*, it is a leap year. This complex expression corresponds to the first row in Table 6-2. You are not done, however, because of the "exception" stated in the algorithm.

The third expression is: "The exception occurs if the year is evenly divisible by 400, it is a leap year." You can write this expression as:

```
(year % 400 == 0)
```

The algorithm states that, regardless of the other two expressions, if this expression is *true*, it is a leap year. Therefore, if the complex expression

```
(year % 4 == 0) && (year % 100 != 0)
```

is *true*, or if the simple expression

```
(year % 400 == 0)
```

is *true*, the year is a leap year. Clearly, this is a situation where the OR operator is needed for the exception.

Now that you have broken the algorithm down into its component expressions, you can write the test on *year* to determine if the year is a leap year. The complete *if* test becomes:

```
if (year % 4 == 0 && year % 100 != 0 || year % 400 == 0) {
        return 1;        // It is a leap year
} else {
        return 0;        // not a leap year
}
```

If you read the preceding *if* expression, you literally end up restating the leap year algorithm. Now let's take all the pieces/parts and fit them into a function.

The IsLeapYear() Function and Coding Style

No doubt you can take things from here and finish writing the leap year function. However, let me suggest that the coding style that you use does make a difference. Although there are no coding style "rules" for functions, the function style shown in Listing 6-1 has served me well over the years.

Listing 6-1. The IsLeapYear() Function

```
/*****
    Purpose: Determine if a given year is a leap year

    Parameters:
      int year          The year to test

    Return value:
      int               1 if the year is a leap year, 0 otherwise
*****/
int IsLeapYear(int year)
{
        if (year % 4 == 0 && year % 100 != 0 || year % 400 == 0) {
                return 1;        // It is a leap year
        } else {
                return 0;        // not a leap year
        }
}
```

This style starts the function definition with the documentation for the function using a multiline opening comment sequence of characters (/*) followed by four more asterisks. The next line defines the task that this particular function is supposed to address. The next statement (or statements if the function has more parameters) tells the nature of the data that is being passed into the function. If you enter the black box with an empty backpack, you should still have a parameters section. In that case, however, you just specify *void* for the parameter list.

Arguments vs. Parameters

Note that I specifically use the term parameters here, but arguments elsewhere. When you call the *IsLeapYear()* function, you determine which variable has its value sent to the function. You might, for example, have an array of integer values, each of which represents a year. You may decide that *year[3]* has its value passed into the *IsLeapYear()* function. That is, you get to decide which argument gets passed (e.g., *IsLeapYear(year[3])*) to the function.

Now look at things from the *IsLeapYear()* perspective. It has no choice about the data: the value to be used is "dictated" to it … that value is handed to the function (in a backpack shoved through the front door!) and it has no choice in the matter. Therefore, think of an argument as a choice that the programmer makes as to the value that gets sent to the function. Think of a parameter as a value that is forced into the code … there is no choice in the matter from the function's point of view.

After the parameter list comes the Return value element of the function documentation. Clearly, the value returned from the function is dictated by the function type specifier. However, the documentation should state the interpretation of that value. In our case, a value of 1 means the year passed to the function is a leap year, and 0 means the year is not a leap year.

Following the return value comes a series of four asterisks and a closing multiline comment character pair, *****/. This sequence is used to delineate the end of the function documentation comment. The next line is the beginning of the function definition and starts with the function type specifier (*int*), and is followed by the function signature (*IsLeapYear(int year)*). The next line is the opening brace of the function body, followed by the statement(s) that comprise the function body, followed by the closing brace of the function body.

Why Use a Specific Function Style?

Once again, C could care less about the coding style you use, so why use this style? For almost 20 years I owned a software company that produced C programming tools and I insisted that every function a programmer wrote followed this style … *exactly*. If I found code that didn't use this style, that programmer had to buy lunch on Friday for all the other programmers. It didn't take long for new programmers to learn the coding style rules.

The reason for following these coding style rules was because it lent itself to creating a self-documenting programmer's manual. Early in the company's history, I wrote a program that would search through all the C source code files looking for the /***** character sequence. Once that sequence was found, I knew that everything from that point until the program read the *****/ character sequence was the documentation comment for that function. The program then copied the complete comment, plus the line following the ending comment sequence (i.e., the function signature), into a simple text file. The program also wrote the source file name (e.g., *date.c*) and the line number where the function started in the source file.

After all the source files were read, the program sorted the functions by name and printed out the text file. The resulting printout then contained a complete list of all the functions that were available in the function library arranged in alphabetical order, including the source file name and line number.

Had a consistent style not been used by the programmers, this type of manual would be much more difficult to produce and the process would have been less automated. Also, using a consistent style makes it easier for programmers to read each other's code. Even if you are just writing code for yourself, a consistent style will still make it easier for you to read your own code, especially six months down the road. For those of us who can't remember what they had for breakfast, this programming consistency is a real plus. Whatever style you end up using, make sure you use it consistently. It will make life easier for you in the long run.

Leap Year Calculation Program

The code in Listing 6-2 presents a complete program designed to take input from the user and determine if the year entered is a leap year or not. The *setup()* function simply establishes the communications rate for the *Serial* object and initializes the serial buffer. You can think of the serial buffer as a small (64-byte) section of memory devoted to storing data from the serial port.

In the *loop()* function, the call to the *Serial.available()* function returns the number of data bytes that are currently in the serial buffer. If any data is available, several working variables are defined and the program calls *ReadLine()*.

Listing 6-2. Leap Year Program

```
/**
  Program: find out if the user typed in a leap year. The code assumes
    the user is not an idiot and only types in numbers that are a valid
    year.

  Author: Dr. Purdum, Nov. 17, 2014
**/

#define MAXCHARS 10

void setup()
{
  Serial.begin(9600);
}

void loop()
{
  if (Serial.available() > 0) {
    int bufferCount;
    int year;
    char myData[MAXCHARS + 1];          // Save room for null

    bufferCount = ReadLine(myData);
    year = atoi(myData);                // Convert to int
    Serial.print("Year: ");
    Serial.print(year);
    Serial.print(" is ");
    if (IsLeapYear(year) == 0) {
      Serial.print("not ");
    }
    Serial.println("a leap year");
  }
}

/*****
  Purpose: Determine if a given year is a leap year

  Parameters:
    int yr              The year to test

  Return value:
    int                 1 if the year is a leap year, 0 otherwise
*****/
int IsLeapYear(int yr)
{
  if (yr % 4 == 0 && yr % 100 != 0 || yr % 400 == 0) {
    return 1;   // It is a leap year
  } else {
```

```
        return 0;    // not a leap year
    }
}


/*****
   Purpose: Read data from serial port until a newline character is read ('\n')

   Parameters:
     char str[]    character array that will be treated as a null-terminated string
   Return value:
     int           the number of characters read for the string

   CAUTION:  This method will sit here forever if no input is read from the serial port
and no newline character is entered.
****/
int ReadLine(char str[])
{
    char c;
    int index = 0;

    while (true) {
      if (Serial.available() > 0) {
        index = Serial.readBytesUntil('\n', str,  MAXCHARS);
        str[index] = '\0';  // null termination character
        break;
      }
    }
    return index;
}
```

The code for the *ReadLine()* appears near the bottom of Listing 6-2. Although the *ReadLine()* code has some SDC elements in it, it's good enough for our purposes here. The code uses an infinite *while* loop to wait for a character to appear in the serial buffer. When that happens, the call to *Serial.readBytesUntil()* is made. (Notice how library functions use a lowercase letter for the start of the method name, while my functions all start with an uppercase letter. Most Arduino libraries use the objected-oriented syntax of an uppercase class name (e.g., *Serial*) followed by a lowercase method name (e.g., *read()*) with a dot operator separating the two names.)

The first argument in the *readBytesUntil()* method is a *newline character* ('\n'), which is C's abbreviation for pressing the Enter key). The purpose of the newline character is to terminate the input stream to the *Serial* object. The second argument dictates where the *Serial* object is to place the characters that are read from the *Serial* monitor. The third argument sets the limit to the number of characters that are to be read. This limit ensures that we don't "overflow" the character string where we are storing the characters. In other words, the three arguments say: "Read characters from the *Serial* object into *str[]* until you read a newline character, up to a max of MAXCHARS." Note that the drop-down box at the bottom of Figure 6-2 has the Newline option selected. This means that when you click the Send button (or press Enter), the newline character is appended to whatever has been typed in the input text box. This ensures that the newline character is present for *readBytesUntil()* to terminate reading characters.

The *readBytesUntil()* method returns the number of characters read, which we assign into *index*. When the newline character is read, that character is *not* placed into the character array. Instead, the newline character is replaced with a null character ('\0') and placed into the array using *index* to determine where to place the null. Therefore, the character array can now be treated as a string variable by the rest of the program.

Upon return from *ReadLine()*, the code calls the standard library routine *atoi()* (ASCII to integer) to convert the contents of the string variable to an integer variable named *year*. The call to *IsLeapYear()* then determines whether the year is a leap year or not.

Figure 6-2 shows what the *Serial* monitor looks like as the program runs. (You can activate the serial monitor using the Tools ➤ *Serial* Monitor menu sequence, or by using the Ctrl+Shift+M key sequence, remember?)

Figure 6-2. *Using the serial monitor*

To supply the year to be tested, place the cursor in the text box at the top of the serial monitor dialog box and type in the year to test. Click the Send button (or press Enter) to transfer the data to the serial buffer on the µc board. The call to *IsLeapYear()* then causes the appropriate message to be sent back to the PC, as shown in Figure 6-2. (Make sure you see the Newline choice in the drop-down list box at the bottom of the monitor.)

There are a few things going on in the program that I will defer until the next chapter. However, it is important that you understand the mechanism the function uses to pass data into and back from a function.

Passing Data into and Back from a Function

Understanding how data is passed back and forth between a function and the main program is important. Up to this point, we have been using our backpack analogy to explain how data is passed to and returned from a function. What follows is a simplified description of how things work when functions have arguments being passed into them and values being passed back from them. While I've taken a few liberties, the concepts are true.

Consider the following line from Listing 6-2.

```
if (IsLeapYear(year)) {
```

In this instance, the function call to *IsLeapYear()* becomes *expression1* for the *if* statement. Let's see how this works.

Pass-by-Value

The first thing to notice is that the variable name *year* is passed to the *IsLeapYear()* function. This is an example of what is known as *pass-by-value*. When data is passed to a function using the pass-by-value mechanism, it is the rvalue of the variable that is sent to the function, not the variable itself. In other words, a temporary copy of the value of *year* (i.e., its rvalue) is copied and used in the call to *IsLeapYear()*. For purposes of discussion, let's assume that *year* equals 2012.

The mechanism for getting the value 2012 to the code for the *IsLeapYear()* function is called the stack. The *stack* is a small section of memory that is organized like a plate dispenser at a salad bar. If the stack is empty, it looks like Figure 6-3, where *TOS* stands for *Top Of Stack* and *BOS* stands for *Bottom Of Stack*. If the stack is empty, it's like a salad bar with no salad plates and looks like Figure 6-3. (I've taken some liberties with the ordering of stack arguments, but the concepts are viable.)

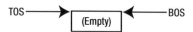

Figure 6-3. *The program stack when empty*

Note that the TOS and BOS are equal ... they have the same address in memory because the stack is empty.

Now suppose we push a memory address onto the stack. Let's further assume all memory addresses for the μc board are 4-byte values. Suppose we push a memory address (40,000) onto the stack; the stack now looks like Figure 6-4. Pushing the memory address onto the stack causes the BOS to sink downward by 4 bytes, as illustrated in Figure 6-4. That is, the BOS sinks down four places to make way for the 4-byte memory address (40,000), while the TOS remains constant. Let's further assume that the memory address 40,000 represents the memory address that holds the next program instruction that is to be executed after returning from the *IsLeapYear()* function call. (The ATMega2560, for example, has 256,000 bytes of memory.)

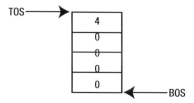

Figure 6-4. *The program stack with a memory address on the stack*

So, how do we get the copy of the value of *year* to the function? As you might guess, we push a copy of *year*'s rvalue onto the stack. Because *year* is an *int*, the copy of that value (2012) requires two bytes of storage. This changes our picture of the stack to that shown in Figure 6-5. (The dividing line is a little heavier to show the delineation between the two data items.)

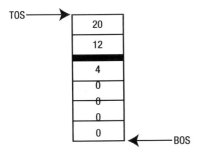

Figure 6-5. *The program stack after pushing on the value of year*

When the stack reaches this state, the program transfers control to the *IsLeapYear()* function code. (The compiler knows exactly where to jump in memory to start executing the function code. That is, *IsLeapYear()* has an lvalue just like every other data object in the program.) You can think of the stack as the backpack that shows up with data from the outside world.

The signature for *IsLeapYear()* tells the function code how the data from the outside world is packed into the backpack. That is,

```
int IsLeapYear(int yr)
```

causes the code to first look for the *int* data that is stored on the stack. It knows an *int* is on the stack because the parameter list (*int yr*) tells it what has been placed on the stack. Because each *int* requires 2 bytes of storage, the function code goes to the memory address held at the TOS, grabs 2 bytes of data (i.e., 2012) and copies it into the rvalue for the temporary variable *yr*. After the assignment of 2012 into *yr* takes place, the TOS is adjusted to reflect that two bytes that have been popped off the stack. Like the salad bar plates, the TOS pops up to reflect that two plates that have been removed. This means the stack once again looks like Figure 6-4.

Now the function's statement body code is executed. Because 2012 is a leap year, the outcome of the *if* statement is that the function must return the value 1 to the caller. To do that, the code pops off the next 4 bytes from the stack, which is the return address where the program is to resume execution after the call to *IsLeapYear()* is completed (i.e., memory address 40,000). That memory address is popped off into the program instruction pointer. You can think of the *program instruction pointer* as a program director that tells the program where to find the instruction for the next program statement. Once 40,000 is popped off into the instruction pointer, the code places the 2-byte return value of 1 on the stack. Now the stack looks like Figure 6-6.

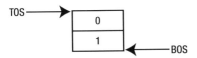

Figure 6-6. *The stack after the return value is pushed onto the stack*

Because the year 2012 is a leap year, the value 1 is pushed onto the stack. The function's type specifier tells us that the return value is an *int*, so 2 bytes of stack space are required. In other words, the backpack now holds the value 1 inside of it stored as an *int*.

Because the instruction pointer holds the memory location of where the next program instruction resides, the program branches back to the statement:

```
if (IsLeapYear(year)) {
```

However, because the code is now executing the instruction *after* the call to *IsLeapYear()*, the statement appears as though it is written as:

```
if (1) {
```

The reason the code appears this way is because the call to *IsLeapYear()* has been completed and the return value (i.e., 1) has been determined by the function's statement block code. The *IsLeapYear()* function's type specifier tells us that an *int* is sitting on the stack (i.e., is in the backpack). That is, the contents of the backpack has been popped off the stack as an *int* and becomes *expression1* for the *if* statement. Because a non-zero value is interpreted as logic *true*, the program sends a message back to the PC over the serial link and informs the user that 2012 is a leap year.

While all of this pushing and popping data onto and off the stack may seem like an H-bomb to kill an ant, it is important that you understand how data is passed to and returned back from a function call. It is also important to note that it is a *copy* of *year's* rvalue in the *loop()* function that is sent to *IsLeapYear()*, not its lvalue. This is what is meant by pass-by-value. Because *IsLeapYear()* has no clue where *year* is stored in memory, there is no way that *IsLeapYear()* can change the rvalue of *year* itself. *Pass-by-value means that only the rvalue of an argument is sent to a function, not its lvalue. And as long as the lvalue remains unknown to IsLeapYear(), there is no way that the function can accidentally change the value of year back in loop().* Pass-by-value is a mechanism (i.e., encapsulation) that attempts to protect the original data from contamination by outside agents.

Summary

This chapter discussed many different aspects of designing, writing, and using functions in your programs. Functions are important because they are the building blocks of all C programs. By following the design and construction techniques discussed in this chapter, subsequent program development should become easier as you gain experience and reuse functions from previous projects. When it comes to writing functions in C, investing a little design time now can pay huge benefits down the road. Again, take your time and let the information in this chapter sink in well. Life gets easier if you do.

EXERCISES

1. What is a function?

   Answer: A function is a piece of code that is designed to perform a single task.

2. If you had to guess, what is the most common mistake beginning programmers make when writing a C function?

   Answer: Beginning C programmers try to make the function a Swiss Army knife. That is, they try to make the function do more than a single task. The result is a function that is far too complex and one that is less likely to be reusable in other programs.

3. What is a function signature?

   Answer: A function signature is everything from the function type specifier through the closing parenthesis. Therefore, the function signature includes the function type specifier, the function name, and its parameter list.

4. What does function overloading mean?

   Answer: Function overloading occurs when two functions share the same name but have different signatures. For example, *Serial.write(name)* displays the content of variable *name* on the output device. *Serial.write(name, 4)*, however, only displays the first four characters of *name*. Both flavors share the same function name, but have different signatures. It is the different signatures that allow the compiler to figure out which flavor of the function to use.

5. What is a function type specifier?

   Answer: A function type specifier appears immediately in front of a function signature and specifies the type of data that is returned from the function.

6. Can a function return more than one value?

   Answer: No.

7. Name three things you should strive for when writing your own functions.

   Answer: First, select a name that tells what the function does, not how you do it. A function is a black box with front and back doors and no windows. The user has no reason to peek inside and see how you are solving the task. Second, the function should be cohesive. It should be designed to solve one task and do it well. No Swiss Army knives. Finally, functions should stand alone. That is, as much as possible, they should not rely on the results of some other function(s). The function should not be coupled to some other function.

8. Explain cohesion and coupling as they apply to functions.

   Answer: Cohesion refers to a clear statement of a function's task. The description of a cohesive function should be possible in a sentence or two. Coupling refers the need of one function to use the results of another function. If two function are coupled, that means the results of one function depends upon another function. Ideally, there should be no coupling between functions.

CHAPTER 7

Storage Classes and Scope

This chapter examines the various ways that data are made available to your programs by examining how and where that data is stored. The concepts presented in this chapter are important because inadvertent access to a program's data is a frequent source of program bugs. As a general rule, you want to restrict the access to a piece of data as much as possible. That way, inadvertent changes to the data are less likely, resulting in programs that have fewer bugs.

Hiding Your Program Data

What's the big deal about hiding data in a program? After all, if you hide the data "completely," nothing could ever change the data and the state of the program would never change, rendering the program pretty much useless. On the other hand, giving free access to the data by every element in the program makes it very difficult to determine who changed what. As a result, when a bogus value for a variable shows up, you don't know where to start looking or who to blame for the bogus value. That is, debugging a program becomes more difficult. Therefore, the issue becomes one of balance: you restrict access to the data as much as possible while still letting those program elements that need access to the data have that access.

The process of restricting access to data is called *encapsulation*. Simply stated, *encapsulation means restricting the access to a data item*. You encapsulate the data in your program for the same reason medieval kings kept their daughters in the castle tower ... to keep people from messing around with them.

Given that encapsulation is desirable, what are your options for restricting access to the data? Surprisingly, there are quite a few options available to you. Most of these options are based upon the concept of scope. The *scope of a data object refers to its visibility and lifetime in a program*. The understanding of scope becomes clear when discussed by example.

The Three Scope Levels

There are three levels of scope available in a C program. The first, and "loosest," most generous scope level, is global scope. A data item defined with *global scope is accessible from the point of definition of the data item to the end of the file in which it is defined*. Data items with global scope are the least virtuous types of data since anyone in the source code file can have his way with them.

The second type of scope is function block scope. A data item with *function block scope* has its scope extend from the point of definition of the data item to the closing brace of the function block in which it is defined. Because function block data hides itself from all other parts of the program, other than the function where it lives, it is considered reasonably virtuous.

© Jack Purdum 2015
J. Purdum, *Beginning C for Arduino, Second Edition*: Learn C Programming
for the Arduino, DOI 10.1007/978-1-4842-0940-0_7

The third type of scope is *statement block scope*. A data item with *statement block scope extends from the point of definition of the data item to the closing brace of the statement block in which it is defined*. Because its scope is restricted to a single statement block, its virtuosity is considered to be two steps short of sainthood.

Let's consider each of these three scope levels in detail, starting with the most restrictive.

Statement Block Scope

The most restrictive (virtuous?) level of scope is the statement block scope level. Consider the following code fragment:

```
if (x < MAXVAL) {          // start of if statement block
      int temp;            // temp's scope starts after this line
      temp = x * 100;
}                          // temp goes out of scope here
```

Note how the variable named *temp* is defined within the *if* statement block. From the program's point of view, *temp* comes into existence the instant it becomes defined. That is, *temp* begins its existence when the semicolon of the *int temp;* statement is read. The next statement simply multiplies whatever *x* is by 100 and shoves its rvalue into *temp*. So far, nothing is done with the result stored in *temp*. When the closing brace of the *if* statement block is reached, *temp* "goes out of scope"... it dies and is no longer available to the program.

Let's write a complete program so we can see how statement block scope works. Consider Listing 7-1.

Listing 7-1. Statement Block Scope Program

```
/**
   Program: Demonstrate the concept of statement block scope

   Author: Dr. Purdum, Sept. 19, 2014
**/
#define MAXVAL 1000

int k = 0;

void setup()
{
  int x = 5;
  Serial.begin(9600);

  if (x < MAXVAL) {
   int temp;
   temp = x * 100;
   }
  Serial.print("The value of temp is: ");
  Serial.println(temp);
}

void loop()
{
}
```

If you try to compile and run this code, the compiler issues the following error message:

```
StatementBlockScopeProgram.ino: In function 'void setup()':
StatementBlockScopeProgram.ino:21: error: 'temp' was not
declared in this scope
```

So, what's the problem? There are two problems, actually. As the error message points out, line 21 is the offending line, and refers to the statement:

```
Serial.print(temp);
```

The error message tells you that *temp* is "not declared in this scope." Stated differently, *temp* is "out of scope." What does that mean?

What Does Out of Scope Mean?

The problem is that you have defined *temp* to have statement block scope. Statement block scope means that the data item exists from the point of its definition to the end of the statement block in which it is defined. This means that temp "lives" or is "usable" from the point of its definition to the closing brace of the *if* statement block. Once the closing brace of the *if* statement is reached, *temp* is removed from the symbol table: *temp* is dead and no longer lives … it is "out of scope." Because it is out of scope, it no longer has an lvalue in the symbol table, so you can no longer access or use it. Listing 7-2 shows what the statement block scope for temp looks like.

Listing 7-2. Statement Block Scope for Temp

```
void setup()
{
  int x = 5;

  Serial.begin(9600);

  if (x < MAXVAL) {
    int temp;  // Scope for temp starts here
    temp = x * 100;
  }              // ...and temp scope ends here.
  Serial.print("The value of temp is: ");
  Serial.println(temp);
}
```

In Listing 7-2, the shaded area defines the statement block scope for variable *temp* and extends from the end of the statement that defines *temp* to the closing brace of the *if* statement block. Variable *temp* may be used anywhere within the shaded area because it is "in scope." Anywhere outside that shaded area, however, variable *temp* doesn't even exist. Outside the shared area in Listing 7-2, variable *temp* is no longer in the symbol table … it is out of scope … it is invisible … it is dead. As such, trying to use *temp* several lines after it has gone out of scope must draw an error message from the compiler … which it did.

The second problem with the error message is that it assumes that the terms define and declare are synonymous. They are not! You will see more evidence that they are different terms later in this chapter.

Why Use Statement Block Scope?

Given that variable *temp* is in scope for such a short time, why use it?

First, in a code example that is as trivial as this one, there is no reason to use statement block scope. However, if the statement block is more complex, statement block scope does afford protection from the programmer trying to use that variable outside of its statement block. That is, the programmer is encapsulating and protecting the data at its most restrictive level.

Second, once a variable goes out of scope, it should free up any resources tied to that variable, hence increasing the amount of available SRAM memory. Initially, the thought was that because variables are stored in SRAM memory, which is a scarce commodity, limiting the scope of a variable would help with managing that scarce memory. While this could be important given the limited amount of memory most μc boards have, experiments done by the author suggests that the storage used by the variable is *not* immediately reclaimed when the variable goes out of scope. In other words, statement block scope variables do not appear to be more memory efficient than other scope levels. However, the concepts associated with statement block scope still apply. Perhaps future compiler refinements will make better use of memory reuse and garbage collection. Meanwhile, it doesn't hurt to keep the scope of a variable as limited as possible.

It appears, therefore, that the real reason for using statement block scope is to limit access to the variable from other parts of the program. As a general observation, you probably won't use statement block scope as much as you will function block scope.

Function Block Scope

A variable that has *function block scope* has life and visibility from the point of its definition to the end of the function in which it is defined. The shaded areas in Listing 7-3 illustrate local scope for variable *x*. (You may hear function block scope called *local scope*, too.)

Listing 7-3. Listing Block Scope for Variable x

```
int k;
void setup()
{
  int x = 5;    // Scope for x starts here...
  Serial.begin(9600);

  if (x < MAXVAL) {
    int temp;   // Scope for temp starts here
    temp = x * 100;
  }             // ...and temp scope ends here.
  Serial.print("The value of temp is: ");
  Serial.println(temp);
}               // ...and x scope ends here.
```

A variable with local scope has visibility and life that extends from its point of definition to the closing brace of the function in which it is defined. In Listing 7-3, variable *x* is in scope from its definition to the closing brace of the *setup()* function. This means that any program statement within the shaded area of Listing 7-3 has access to variable *x*. Anything outside the shaded area knows nothing about *x*.

Function block scoped variables are quite common in C programs. Indeed, function block scope is consistent with viewing a function as a black box. Nothing outside of the function has a clue about the data defined within the black box. Function block scope offers a degree of encapsulation, but is not so restrictive as to render the variable useless. (Statement block scope is so restrictive that it finds limited use. It would likely be more popular if it truly always saves memory resources.) As you learned in Chapter 6, functions are task-oriented pieces of code and function block scoped variables work in concert to solve a particular task. When their work is done (i.e., the function block code has been executed), the variables within that function cease to exist as far as the rest of the program is concerned.

What would happen if you moved the definition of *x* as shown in the following code fragment? (Note how we have moved the definition of *x* to the bottom of the function.) When you try to compile this variation of Listing 7-1,

```
void setup()
{
  Serial.begin(9600);

  if (x < MAXVAL) {
   int temp;
   temp = x * 100;
  }
  Serial.print("The value of temp is: ");
  Serial.println(temp);
  int x = 5;                    // New definition point...
}
```

the compiler issues the following error message:

```
StatementBlockScopeProgram.ino: In function 'void setup()':
StatementBlockScopeProgram.ino:15:7: error: 'x' was not declared in this scope
```

What went wrong? The problem is that variable *x* doesn't come into scope until it is defined at the bottom of the *loop()* function. However, the program code attempts to access *x* before its definition takes place. This is one reason that most programmers place the data definitions used within a function immediately after the opening brace for the function body.

Name Collisions and Scope

What happens if you define a variable named *temp* in *setup()* but also have another variable named *temp* in *setup()*, but within the *if* statement block? Won't the two variables "collide" because they have the same name? There is no name collision because the first *temp* is defined within the *if* statement block (statement block scope) and the second *temp* is defined outside the *if* statement and has function block scope. In fact, if you had the following code fragment in your program:

```
if (x < MAXVAL) {
 int temp;
```

```
 temp = x * 100;
}
int temp;
```

the second definition of *temp* does not generate a duplicate definition error because the *temp* defined within the *if* statement block has died before the second definition of *temp* takes place.

To drive the idea home that function block scope is different than statement block scope, make the following changes to Listing 7-1.

```
#define MAXVAL 1000

void setup()
{
  int x = 5;
  Serial.begin(9600);
  if (x < MAXVAL) {
    int temp;

    temp = x * 100;
    Serial.print("The lvalue for temp is: ");
    Serial.println((long) &temp);
    Serial.print("The rvalue for temp is: ");
    Serial.println((long) temp);
  }
  int temp;

  Serial.print("The lvalue for 2nd temp is: ");
  Serial.println((long) &temp);
  Serial.print("The rvalue for temp is: ");
  Serial.println((long) temp);
}
```

The following statement:

```
Serial.println((long) &temp);
```

uses the "address of" operator (&), which causes the code to display the lvalue of a variable, rather than its rvalue. (You will learn more about the address of operator in Chapter 8.) If you run the program, the serial monitor should look similar to Figure 7-1.

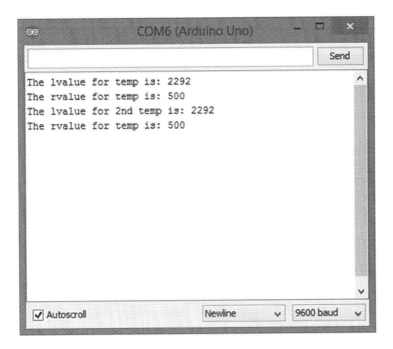

The lvalue for temp is: 2292
The rvalue for temp is: 500
The lvalue for 2nd temp is: 2292
The rvalue for temp is: 500

Figure 7-1. *The lvalues for temp*

The output in Figure 7-1 was very surprising to me! When I ran this code using Arduino 1.0.5 of the IDE, the memory address for the *temp* defined with the *if* statement block scope was 2292, but the *temp* defined with function block scope was stored at memory address 2294. Clearly, with that version of the compiler, the two variables had different lvalues even though they shared the same name.

However, when I compiled the same code under IDE 1.5.8, the results shown in Figure 7-1 are displayed. What this output means is that the compiler is smart enough now to optimize the second memory allocation for *temp* away and just "reuse" the old allocation for *temp*. (Release 1.6 is also different than what's shown in Figure 7-1.) Because ANSI does not require the compiler to initialize variables defined with either function or block scope, the "new" *temp* retains the "old" *temp*'s value! Still, the fact that there are two

```
int temp;
```

definition statements in *setup()*, but they don't produce a "duplicate definition" error, shows that they are actually different variables from the compiler's point of view. This is true because their scope levels are different.

If two variables share the same name at the same scope level, you will get an error message. For example, if you modified the code to the following (read the program comments closely):

```
#define MAXVAL 1000
void setup()
{
  int x = 5;
  int temp;      // definition of temp with function block scope

  if (x < MAXVAL) {
    int temp;    // definition of temp statement block scope
```

149

```
    temp = x * 100;
    Serial.print("The lvalue for temp is: ");
    Serial.println((long) &temp);
  }
  int temp;      // oh-oh...definition of temp with function block          // scope...again

  Serial.print("The lvalue for 2nd temp is: ");
  Serial.println((long) &temp);
}
```

The compiler issues the following error message:

```
StatementBlockScopeProgram.ino:12:6: error: 'int temp'
previously declared here
Error compiling.
```

Because you now have two definitions of *temp* at the same scope level (i.e., function block scope within the same function), the compiler must issue an error message.

Global Scope

From time to time, you need a variable that is accessible by all functions within the entire program's source code file. If you have a piece of data that must be available everywhere in the program, that variable could be defined with global scope. A variable has *global scope if the data item is defined outside of a function block in the current source code file.* Look at Listing 7-1. Near the top of the listing you can see variable *k* defined as:

```
int k;
```

Note that *k* is defined outside of the *setup()* and *loop()* function blocks. In this case, the scope for variable *k* extends from its point of definition to the end of the source code file. The global scope for *k* is the shaded area in Listing 7-4. This means that any statement that appears after the definition of *k* has access to *k*; *k* is "globally" accessible to all functions and statement blocks within the source file.

Listing 7-4. Global Scope for Variable k

```
/**
  Program: Demonstrate the concept of statement block scope

  Author: Dr. Purdum, Dec. 18, 2014
**/
#define MAXVAL 1000

int k = 0;    // Scope for k starts here...
void setup()
{
  int x = 5;

  Serial.begin(9600);
```

```
   if (x < MAXVAL) {
     int temp;
     temp = x * 100;
     }
   Serial.print("The value of temp is: ");
   Serial.println(temp);
}
void loop()
{
}   // Scope for k ends here...
```

The good news is that you now have a variable that all of the functions in the file can access. This makes it easy to use the value of *k* within each function in the source code file. The bad news is that you now have a variable that all of the functions in the file can access. That is, we have thrown the idea of encapsulation out the window because everything in the source file has access to *k*. This is kind of like locking the princess in the castle keep and then handing out copies of her room key to every knight in the realm. Every element (knight) in the program can mess around with *k* (Princess Kay). If something goes amiss with *k*, it's now more difficult to determine the cause of the problem because access to *k* is no longer restricted.

Trade-offs

Obviously, there's a trade-off here. Do you use more restrictive definitions (i.e., use statement or function block scope) to protect your variables and pass the variable as a function argument, or do you use global definitions to make it easier to share data between functions? The answer is: It depends. If you have a variable named *port* defined in *loop()* and you've written a function named *SetPort()* that needs access to *port*, your code needs to make *port* available to the *SetPort()* function. If you move the definition of *port* outside of *loop()* and let it have global scope, *SetPort()* now has full access to *port*. However, giving *port* global scope is not an ideal solution because you are no longer encapsulating and protecting the variable from contamination by forces outside of *loop()*. Global scope means the data is exposed to any evildoers that might exist in the program, and if they do something nasty to *port*, where do you start looking for the culprit?

However, alternatives do exist. The obvious alternative is to keep the definition of *port* inside *loop()*, thus giving it function scope, but pass *port* as a function argument to *SetPort()*. Now *SetPort(port)* can use the value of *port*, but still afford it an enhanced level of protection. If something strange now happens to *port*, at least you have a reduced number of places where *port* went south to the function where it is defined.

Global Scope and Name Conflicts

Again using Listing 7-4 as a point of discussion, suppose you define a variable named *k* inside the *loop()* function. Because the global scope of *k* includes *loop()* (see Listing 7-4), won't the two variables have a name collision?

Nope.

The reason is because the syntax rules for C state that *the variable with the most restrictive scope level prevails in situations where they are both in scope*. In our example, because the *k* defined within *loop()* has a more restrictive function block scope level than the *k* with global scope, the function block scope variable prevails over the global scope *k* when execution is taking place within *loop()*. If you were silly enough to define yet another *k* variable within the *if* statement block, that *k* would prevail when the program is executing the *if* statement block, even though the other two *k* variables are in scope.

Of course, having two *k* variables defined in the same program—even at different scope levels—is reason enough for you to be tarred and feathered. The rule for defining two different variables using the same name in a program is simple: Don't.

Scope and Storage Classes

Arduino C recognizes four storage classes: *auto, register, static,* and *extern.* All four are keywords in Arduino C and cannot be used as variable names. If you try to define variables named as follows:

```
int register;    // Bad names...
int auto;
```

the compiler issues an error message stating:

```
error: declaration does not declare anything
```

Because these keywords are storage classes for variables, the compiler is expecting the name of the variable to appear before it reads the semicolon. Clearly, the compiler recognizes both as keywords but will not let you use them as a variable name.

Now, let's see how these storage classes work in a program.

The auto Storage Class

The *auto* storage class is the default storage class for variables with function block scope. You can also define *auto* variables with statement block scope, as in

```
auto int temp;
for (auto int k; k < MAXVAL; k++)
```

and the compiler accepts the syntax without error. The actual impact of using an *auto* storage class in Arduino C appears to make no difference to the generated code, and, therefore, relegates itself to a documentation feature. The author has not seen the *auto* keyword used in published code for years, although there may be some examples. (No doubt someone will write an article now that uses the *auto* keyword!) Personally, it doesn't seem worth the effort to use the *auto* keyword.

The register Storage Class

The *register* storage class is used to inform the compiler that the data item should be stored in a μc register rather than in memory. The idea is that such a data definition would optimize the generated code for speed by keeping the variable in a register. The use of the keyword *register* is a *suggestion* to the compiler's code generator, not an edict. That is, the code generator makes the final decision about the fate of a variable defined with the *register* storage class. The syntax is:

```
register int myVal;
```

The compiler is pretty smart anyway and makes heavy use of its register set, so it seems unlikely that using the *register* storage class in a data definition is going to make much difference. (If you're really into this kind of thing, look at the documentation for the avr-objdump.exe program in the Tools directory for dumping object files and allowing you to inspect the generated code. Using that tool is beyond the scope of this book.)

As a general rule, the compiler is pretty smart without our help, so there is probably little to be gained by telling it that it should use a *register* for a particular variable.

The static Storage Class

As you know, variables with function or statement block scope die when you exit the function in which they are defined. This means that each time the function is called, a new set of these variables is created. This also means that any values for the variables in the function from the previous execution of the function's code are lost.

There are, however, situations where it would be nice if you could preserve the value of a variable between function calls. For example, you might like to maintain a count of the number of times a particular function is executed. That goal is not possible with variables defined with the default (*auto*) storage class because they are re-created each time the function is called. Obviously, one solution is to move the variable of interest out of the function and define it with global scope. While this solves the lost-value problem, you are exposing the variable to the room key issues of data privacy. The *static* storage class solves this problem in a more elegant way.

Consider the program in Listing 7-5.

Listing 7-5. Using the static Storage Class

```
void setup() {
  Serial.begin(9600);
}

void loop() {
  while (true) {
    Serial.println(MyCounter());
  }
}

int MyCounter()
{
    int counter = 0;
    // do some stuff...
    return ++counter;
}
```

Study the code before reading on. What do you expect the *Serial.println(MyCounter())* statement to print? If you said 0, you get a C. If you said 1, you get an A. Note that variable counter uses the default (*auto*) storage class. Therefore, counter is set to 0 each time the *while* loop in the *loop()* function causes the *MyCounter()* function to be called. Because we use the pre-increment operator on *counter* in the *MyCounter()* function, its value is incremented to 1 *before* the value is returned to *loop()*. That's why its value is 1 instead of 0 on each pass through the loop. No matter what, the value seen in *loop()* remains 1 forever.

Now add the *static* keyword at the start of the definition of *counter*, like this:

```
static int counter = 0;
```

and recompile, upload, and run the program. What happens to the program output? (You're going to have to type in the code and run it to find out. It's good practice.)

The Effect of the static Storage Class

Using the *static* storage class specifier causes the compiler to generate code that preserves the value of *counter* between function calls to *MyCounter()*. First, the data definition of *counter* is not executed each time the function is called. In fact, *counter* is not generated using the stack mechanism you studied in Chapter 6. Rather, *counter* is created when the program first begins execution and is allocated in such a way (i.e., in a piece of memory devoted to global-type data storage called the heap) that its current value is maintained throughout the program's execution. The compiler takes care of these details for you. The end result, however, is that you have a variable that can maintain its value between function calls without exposing it outside of the function in which it is defined using global scope. In other words, the *static* storage class allows you to encapsulate a variable, but still allow it to retain its value between function calls. It's a have-your-cake-and-eat-it-too kind of thing.

If you need to set the starting value of a static variable to something other than 0, the data definition *must* specify that starting value. For example, if you need the starting value to be 10, the definition must be:

```
static int counter = 10;
```

You can only set the initialized value for a *static* variable at its point of definition. By default, *static* variables are initialized to 0. While that may seem to make the statement that initializes the counter to 0 unnecessary, you should *never* assume compiler behavior if you don't have to. It almost never pays to be lazy. Explicitly initialize the variable yourself. If nothing else, it documents your intention.

The extern Storage Class

Consider the short program presented in Listing 7-6.

Listing 7-6. Short Program with Error

```
void setup() {
  // put your setup code here, to run once:
  Serial.begin(9600);
}

void loop() {
  number *= number;
  Serial.println(number);
}
```

Type the code in and try to compile it. Obviously, the program won't compile because there is no definition for *number* in the source code.

Adding a Second Source Code File to a Project

If you look closely at Figure 1-5 in Chapter 1, on the upper-right edge of the screen just below the icon that looks like a magnifying glass is a downward-pointing triangle. Click that triangle. You should see a small menu similar to that shown in Figure 7-2. When you see that menu, click the New Tab option. Your display will change to look like Figure 7-3.

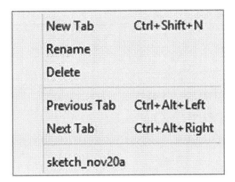

Figure 7-2. The "triangle" menu

Figure 7-3. Giving the new program tab a name

155

Notice that near the bottom of the source code window there is a text box for entering a name for the new program tab that's about to be created. I named mine *myExternPage*. Now click OK; the IDE looks like Figure 7-4. Notice how there is a new source code tab in the source code window named *myExternPage*. Also notice that I have added the definition for *number* in this new source code tab.

Figure 7-4. IDE with new source code tab

It's important to note that by creating a new source code tab in the IDE, you are also creating a new disk file for the project that uses the same name as the tab name you gave it. This new source code file appears under the sketch name for the project being developed. As you can see at the top of Figure 7-4, I've named this sketch *ExternTestCode*. Because this also becomes the directory where the source code for the sketch is located, the new *myExternPage* file also appears in that directory. Both source code files carry the "ino" secondary file name.

Using the extern Keyword

Now click the first tab and add the following line at the very top of the file. (We are giving *number* global scope.)

```
extern int number;
```

The keyword *extern* is a storage class modifier that tells the compiler that the variable is defined in a different source code file (i.e., it's defined in *myExternPage.ino*) but let me use it in this file (i.e., *ExternTestCode.ino*) as an *int* variable. Because the variable named *number* is defined in the second source code file, it has an lvalue assigned when that code file is compiled. Therefore, the keyword *extern* means the file is defined in another file, so its lvalue is not known in this file. Therefore, the statement

```
extern int number;
```

is a data declaration, not a data definition. In Chapter 3 I said that data declarations form an attribute list, but do not allocate memory for the variable. In terms of the symbol table, the *extern* declaration statement tells us the variable's ID, its data type, and its scope level. We do, therefore, have a complete attribute list with enough detail to allow us to use it in this file even though it is defined in a different file. The statement cannot, however, tell us its lvalue because the variable is defined in another file.

You're probably thinking: "Wait a minute! We must know the lvalue of a variable to be able to use it, but you're telling us we don't know the lvalue. How can that work?"

I can explain with a simplified explanation of the compile process itself. When the compiler begins the task of generating the code for the file with the *extern* keyword in it, any point where the compiler needs to supply the lvalue for *number*, it instead leaves two question marks because it doesn't know the lvalue for *number* at this point in the compile process. (It doesn't really do this, but it works for my explanation.) Now the compiler opens the second source code file and finds the *definition* for *number*. It can now fill in the lvalue for *number* in the symbol table.

One of the last steps in creating an executable program (collectively all of this is called the *build process*) is the *linker* pass. It is the linker's responsibility to fill in any missing lvalues that may have been created during the compile process. The linker is going to find the two question marks for the missing lvalue for *number* in the first source code file. However, a quick peek in the symbol table for *number* locates the lvalue and the linker overwrites the two question marks with the lvalue for *number*. Now the code in the first source code file knows where the variable defined in the second source code file lives, and all is right with the world.

By the way, the linker does the same thing for all of the library files you might use (e.g., the code for the *Serial* object). After all, there has to be lvalues for library functions, too. Think about it. (If you'd like more information about the build process, see http://arduino.cc/en/Hacking/BuildProcess.)

Why a New Source Code File?

Sometimes a project gets to the point where it makes sense to split the source code into two or more source code files. Sometimes you may want to split the file simply because it's getting too long and you're tired of scrolling from top to bottom in such a long file. Perhaps you split the files such that those functions that are concerned with the Input Step are in one source file, while functions dealing with the Process Step are in another source file. It may even make sense to have a third source code file for the Display Step. The *extern* keyword, in many cases, makes it possible to split source files.

Function Prototypes

Suppose you have a statement in *loop()* that calls our *IsLeapYear()* function that we developed in Chapter 6. Further suppose that we placed the actual code for the function in a second file in the project. This means we want to use the function in file 1, but have defined it in file 2. How can you solve this problem?

If you place the following near the top of the first source file before *setup()*:

```
int IsLeapYear(int yr); // This is a function prototype for IsLeapYear()
```

you are giving the compiler enough information to use *IsLeapYear()* in the program. This statement is called a *function prototype*. A function prototype is a data *declaration* that tells the compiler the specifics it needs to know in order to let you use the function in the current source file. More specifically, *a function prototype allows the compiler to create an attribute list for the data object and stuff it into the symbol table*. However, because the actual code for the data object *IsLeapyear()* is in another file, it cannot fill in the lvalue for the object. This is why function prototypes are data *declarations*, not data definitions.

Back in Chapter 4, I pointed out that many programmers use the terms "define" and "declare" as though they are synonyms. We could agree with them, but then we'd both be wrong. Each has a very specific meaning. A data declaration is simply an attribute list for a variable ... memory is not allocated for a data declaration. This means a data declaration has an empty lvalue column in the symbol table. What a function prototype does is say: "Okay, compiler, I don't know where this data object is going to end up in memory (lvalue = ?), but here's enough information for you to use the object in this source code file." When all of the source files have been compiled and the pieces are all pulled together (this is the job of the linker), only then does *IsLeapYear()* have a known lvalue.

Whenever you need to access a variable in one file but it is actually defined in a different file, use the *extern* keyword. The *extern* keyword in front of what would otherwise be a data definition turns it into a data declaration. The *extern* access specifier simply tells the compiler: "Hey! This variable is not defined in this file. However, use this statement so you can create an attribute list for the variable so I can use it in this file." In a real sense, therefore, the *extern* keyword serves the same purpose for variables as a function prototype does for functions. That is, *extern* allows you to create a data declaration for a variable that is defined in some other file.

#include Preprocessor Directive

As your gain experience using C, you will move to more complex programs. For example, you may want to add a 16×2 LCD display to your project. If you do, you will likely need to access the Liquid Crystal Display library that is available with the Arduino IDE. Once again, there are literally hundreds of libraries available for the Arduino, and there is no reason for you to reinvent the wheel. Always search for a library before you start writing one. Chances are pretty good that someone has already done a good chunk of the work for you.

If you were developing a program to use the LiquidCrystal library, the first place you would want to look for help on using the library is in the

```
libraries\LiquidCrystal\Examples
```

directory off the Arduino main directory. The Examples subdirectory would give you several sample sketches that use the library. This is a great way to learn how to use the library properly.

If you load one of these example sketch files, you will see that they begin with the line:

```
#include <LiquidCrystal.h>
```

This is an example of the *#include* preprocessor directive. This directive tells the C preprocessor to find a file named *LiquidCrystal.h*, open it, and *read its contents into the current source code file at this point in the program*. Files that end in ".h" are called *header files*. Therefore, *LiquidCrystal.h* is the header file for the LiquidCrystal library. (You can find this header file at `libraries\LiquidCrystal\src`.)

Okay … so what?

Well, if you open the header file, you will discover it is packed with all kinds of information that the LiquidCrystal library needs to do its job. If you look about halfway down the file, you'll find the following lines:

```
void clear();
void home();

void noDisplay();
void display();
void noBlink();
void blink();
void noCursor();
void cursor();
void scrollDisplayLeft();
void scrollDisplayRight();
void leftToRight();
void rightToLeft();
void autoscroll();
void noAutoscroll();

void createChar(uint8_t, uint8_t[]);
void setCursor(uint8_t, uint8_t);
```

What do these lines look like to you? That's right! They are function prototypes for the functions that are available to you in the LiquidCrystal library. (Actually, because these are written as part of the LiquidCrystal C++ class, they are really *class method prototypes*, not function prototypes.) Note how *setCursor()* uses two *unsigned* 8-bit *ints* as its function arguments. Could those be row-column coordinates?

A common #include Idiom

At the top of the *LiquidCrystal.h* header file are the lines:

```
#ifndef LiquidCrystal_h
#define LiquidCrystal_h
```

These two lines say: "If the symbolic constant *LiquidCrystal_h* (note the underscore) is not yet defined in this sketch, *#define* it now." However, if you look at the very last line in the file, it is this:

```
#endif
```

Think about what this means. If the symbolic constant *LiquidCrystal_h* is already defined at this point, the entire contents of the head file is ignored. Why would you want to do that? Actually, a complete explanation is given in Chapter 14. However, I can give a quick answer here: the reason is to avoid duplicate definition errors. Header files may contain data definitions in them. If we didn't have a mechanism to detect that they have already been defined, the compiler would issue a bunch of duplicate definition errors. By using the *#ifndef* preprocessor directive at the top of the header file, we avoid reading the file twice.

Good coding practices say we should never read the same header file twice—but hiccups happen. This technique simply prevents the hiccup from causing a problem.

Where Are the Header Files Stored?

Actually, there are two flavors for using the *#include* preprocessor directive. In the one presented earlier,

```
#include <LiquidCrystal.h>
```

note how the header file name is surrounded by angle brackets (<>). When angle brackets are used around the header file name, the compiler looks in the default file include directory for the header file. In this case, the compiler looks in the LiquidCrystal\src directory.

However, as you gain experience in writing code, you may well wish to write your own header files for a sketch. In that case, you would use the following:

```
#include "MyHeaderFile.h"
```

The *double quote marks* tell the compiler to look for the header file in the current sketch directory where you are writing the program. If the compiler cannot find the header file there, it would next look in the default (angle brackets) header file directory. By using the appropriate characters surrounding the header file name, you can tell the compiler where to find the necessary header file.

The volatile keyword

Although rarely used, I should mention the *volatile* keyword at this point. The *volatile* keyword is a variable *qualifier* rather than a storage class or access specifier. The syntax for using it is:

```
volatile int lastTestValue;
```

volatile is a directive to the compiler that says this particular variable must be loaded from memory any time the code references it. Often, when code is using a variable, that variable's rvalue is already in an Atmel temporary register so there is no need to reload it again from memory. This results in a small performance boost because a trip to memory to reload the value is bypassed. Optimizing compilers do this kind of thing all the time.

While this optimization is a good thing most of the time, there are times when the value stored in memory can get out of sync with the value held in a register. This kind of problem is most likely to occur when Interrupt Service Routines (ISRs) are being used in the program. (There is an example involving interrupts in Chapter 13.) By using the *volatile* qualifier, you are telling the compiler to refetch the rvalue of the variable (just in case it was cached) anytime the program uses that variable. This decreases the chance that the rvalue for the variable is out of sync.

Summary

You've covered a lot of ground in this chapter. The concept of scope is more important than many programmers realize because it has the potential for making your programs easier to read and debug. You should also appreciate what function prototypes bring to the party, especially when you split source code files. As you begin writing nontrivial programs, it makes sense to split the source code into different files. If nothing else, it makes scrolling through a source file a little quicker than it might be otherwise. Hopefully, this chapter also makes it clear that there is a very real difference between the terms *define* and *declare*.

I encourage you to create a program of your own that has two (or more) source files and uses the *extern* keyword to communicate data between the two files. The only way to learn this stuff is to jump in the mud and start slogging around in it.

EXERCISES

1. What are the scope levels in C?

   Answer: There are three scope levels in C: statement block, local (function), and global.

2. Why is it usually a good thing to avoid using the global storage class?

   Answer: The global storage class means that the data item is exposed for use to every data object in the file, from its point of definition to the end of the file. This is bad because it makes it more difficult to determine where erroneous values creep in when the variable has an improper test value. Global scope defeats the benefits of encapsulation.

3. What are the C storage classes?

   Answer: The storage classes are: *auto*, *register*, *static*, and *extern*.

4. Suppose integer variable *myDay* is globally defined in one file, but you need to access it in a different source file. What do you need to do to have access to *myDay*?

   Answer: You need to have a variable declaration for *myDay* in source files where it is not defined. You do this by using the statement:

   ```
   extern int myDay;
   ```

5. What is the default scope level for a function?

   Answer: All functions in C have global scope.

6. What is the default storage class for a library function.

   Answer: *extern*. Think about it.

7. What would happen to our *IsLeapYear()* function if some idiot passed it a "negative year"?

   Answer: Actually, the function still provides the correct answer. However, it might be a good idea to filter out negative years before the calculation. How would you do this? (Hint: Check out the *abs()* standard library function.)

8. Often external devices send messages to the Arduino over the *Serial* object or some other communication link (e.g., Wi-Fi). Usually, these messages come in as a sequence of characters, like 70.0,95,15:00. Perhaps this message conveys the message: "The temperature is 70 degrees with 95 percent humidity at 3PM." How would you extract this information and display it on the Serial monitor? I'll give you a starting place and the answer doesn't need to use the *loop()* function. Hint: you will likely want to use the standard library function *atoi()* to help you.

```
      void setup() {
        char message[] = "70.0,95,15:00";

        int index;
        int holdIndex = 0;
        int temperature;
        int humidity;

        // You need to provide the Process Step

        Serial.print("The temperature is = ");
        Serial.print(temperature);
        Serial.print(" with humidity =  ");
        Serial.print(humidity);
        Serial.print("at ");
        Serial.print(&message[holdIndex]);
      }
```

Answer: This is not a trivial program. If you got yours working, you are really doing well!

```
      void setup() {
        char message[] = "70.0,95,15:00";

        int index;
        int holdIndex = 0;
        int temperature;
        int humidity;

        Serial.begin(9600);

        index = FindCharacter(message, ',');
        if (index > 0) {                     // Found a comma
           message[index] = '\0';            // Make it a string
           temperature = atoi(message);
           holdIndex += index + 1;           // Look past the null for next pass
        }
        index = FindCharacter(message + holdIndex, ','); // Really
        passing message[5]
        if (index > 0) {                     // Found a comma
           message[index] = '\0';            // Make it a string
           humidity = atoi(&message[holdIndex]);
           holdIndex += index + 1;
        }
        Serial.print("The temperature is = ");
        Serial.print(temperature);
        Serial.print(" with humidity = ");
        Serial.print(humidity);
```

```
  Serial.print(" at ");
  Serial.print(&message[holdIndex]);
}
void loop(){}


/*****
 This method looks for a specific character in a string

 Parameter list:
   char msg[]     an array of characters, null terminated
   char c         the char to find

 return value:
   int            the position in the string where found or
                  0 if no match
*****/
int FindCharacter(char msg[], char c)
{
 int i = 0;

 while (msg) {
  if (msg[i] == c) {
    return i;
  } else {
    i++;
  }
 }
 return 0;
}
```

The key is the *FindCharacter()* function, which marches through the input string looking for the comma character. When it finds one, it returns the index number of the position in the string where the comma appears. This is assigned into *index* upon return from the function. With the input string of *"70.0,95,15:00"*, index equals 4. The code then writes a null character at that position, so the string now looks like: *"70.0NULL95,15:00"*. The *atoi()* function converts the substring "70.0" to an *int* value and assigns it into *temperature*.

Note how the next call to *FindCharacter()* uses *message + holdIndex* as the string argument. This is the same as passing in *message[5]*, or "95,15:00" as the start of the string because we added 1 to *holdIndex* in the *if* statement block. You should convince yourself that the after the second call to *FindCharacter()*, the *Serial.println()* for the time simply display the "tail" of the string.

There are more efficient ways of writing this program, but we can't use those techniques until after we understand something about C pointers.

CHAPTER 8

Introduction to Pointers

One of the most powerful features of the C programming language is pointers. While many of the features of any programming language have the power for you to shoot yourself in the foot, pointers give you the power to blow your entire leg off. Because of the raw power of pointers, many popular languages either don't support pointers at all (e.g., Java) or only let you use them in a very limited way (e.g., C#). Personally, most people go wrong using pointers because they don't really understand what pointers are or what they do. Fortunately, you've been introduced to programming in a way that will make understanding pointers a snap. With that understanding comes faster, more efficient C programs. Let's jump right in!

Defining a Pointer

Because a pointer is a different type of data than anything you've studied thus far, the syntax necessary to define a pointer must also be different. Figure 8-1 shows the syntax for a pointer definition.

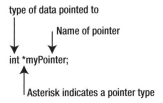

Figure 8-1. *Pointer syntax*

Figure 8-1 shows that there are three basic components to a pointer definition:

- The type of data that this pointer is associated with
- An asterisk to mark this variable as a pointer instead of a "regular" variable
- The name of the pointer

Let's examine each of these three elements in detail and see what they mean. However, we will do that examination in reverse order of importance. You'll understand why I chose this order shortly.

© Jack Purdum 2015
J. Purdum, *Beginning C for Arduino, Second Edition*: Learn C Programming for the Arduino, DOI 10.1007/978-1-4842-0940-0_8

Pointer Name

Pointer variables have the same naming rules as do all other variables in C. In other words, you can give them any valid C variable name you wish, but because pointers are different, it's worthwhile giving them a name that jogs your memory that they are a pointer. Clearly, *myPointer* would do this, but the more common convention is to begin the pointer variable name with *ptr*. Some sample pointer names might be:

```
ptrMyQuizScores
ptrNameptrPuppy
ptrStateCapital
ptrSisters
```

Again, it's not imperative that you begin pointer variables with *ptr*, but it doesn't hurt to let everyone know that this is a pointer variable. You could, for example, store nitroglycerin in little celluloid spheres, but then naming each one "ping pong ball" is probably not a good idea. Likewise, it is not a good idea to give pointer variables a generic C variable name. Define your pointers in a way that tells the person reading the code that they are looking at a pointer.

Asterisk (*)

The asterisk is used in the pointer definition to inform the compiler that this is a pointer variable rather than a regular data type. After all, if you left the asterisk out of the pointer definition, it would look like any other data definition. Placing the asterisk in the definition marks the variable as a pointer and allows the compiler to treat the variable differently than it would otherwise. I will explain the difference later in this chapter.

Note that C doesn't really care about the precise position of the asterisk, as long as it appears after the type specifier for the pointer and before the name of the pointer. Note the following asterisk placements:

```
int*  ptrTemp;        // Immediately after the type specifier
int   * ptrHumidity;  // Floating between type specifier and name
int   *ptrDewPoint;   // Immediately before the name
```

C doesn't really care which form you use. Personally, I kinda like the last version that ties the asterisk and the pointer name closely together. There is no theoretical reason for my preference. It's how I learned how to define pointers almost 40 years ago. It's an old-dog-new-trick thing with me.

When you get to the end of the chapter, write some sample sketches and get some experience with pointers trying out the various definition styles. Then pick a style you like and use it from then on. A consistent coding style really does make it easier to read and debug program source code.

Pointer Type Specifiers and Pointer Scalars

From an operational point of view, *the data type specifier for the pointer is the most critical part of the definition*. In Figure 8-1, the *int* type specifier tells the compiler that this pointer will only be used with *int* data types. While the syntax rules allow you to use an *int* pointer with a different type of data, doing so usually results in a disaster. For example, all of the following are valid pointer definitions:

```
int *ptrSheepCount;
char *ptrFirstName;
long *ptrBigVal;
float *ptrYardsOfCloth;
```

CHAPTER 8 ▩ INTRODUCTION TO POINTERS

In these examples, each pointer is defined to point to a different type of data. That is, *the pointer's type specifier is dictated by the type of data with which the pointer will be used.* The rule is simple:

The pointer's type specifier dictates the type of data to be used with that pointer.

Pointing one type of pointer to a different type of data is a train wreck waiting to happen. To make things even worse, it may *appear* that using a mismatched pointer is working in the program. Trust me ... using pointers the wrong way will eventually result in a spectacular failure.

Okay, so pointer type specifiers are important. The real question is: Why are pointer-type specifiers so important? The reason is because pointers use the pointer type specifier in order to read/write the data correctly.

Pointer Scalars

Consider the following two pointer definitions:

```
char *ptrLetter;
int *ptrNumber;
```

Both of these statements define a pointer variable, but the type specifiers for each pointer tell you that they are to be used with different data types. When the compiler sees these two definitions, it places the two definitions in the symbol table and allocates memory for each. If you look back at the simplified symbol table shown in Chapter 3, Figure 3-4, the Data Type column for these pointer definitions would be an asterisk. One of the columns I didn't show in the table is labeled Scalar. When compiling definitions of pointers, the compiler does fill in the Scalar column of the symbol table. For *ptrLetter* the scalar would be 1. For *ptrNumber* the scalar would be 2.

So, what determines the scalar size? The *scalar size is exactly the same as the Byte Length* as seen in Table 3-1. Whatever the storage requirements are for a given data type, that's its scalar size. If a *char* requires 1 byte of memory to store it, that's its scalar. If a *float* takes 4 bytes of memory to store it, its scalar is 4. Even better, however, is that you can create your own custom data types and pointers can also be used with those new data types. (I'll cover those concepts in Chapter 10.)

When the compiler finishes processing the preceding two pointer definitions, memory might look something like Figure 8-2. If you look carefully at Figure 8-2, you can see that *each pointer uses 2 bytes of storage.*

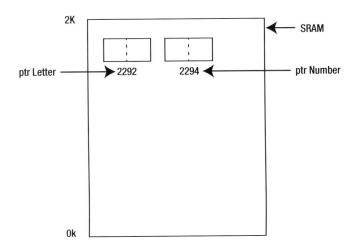

Figure 8-2. Memory map after pointer definitions

That's odd.

Whenever we defined data types before, a *char* data type used one byte and an *int* used two bytes. Yet, the pointer definition shows that each pointer requires the same amount of storage; 2 bytes. Why? The reason is because the rvalue of a valid pointer variable is always one of two things: a memory address or *null*.

If a pointer variable has an rvalue that is equal to *null*, that means that the pointer is not safe to use. That is, a *null* pointer points to garbage and should not be used. *A useful, or valid, pointer variable always has an rvalue that is a valid memory address*. If your μc board has 2K of SRAM memory and you have a *Serial.print()* statement that says its rvalue is 3000, stand back, cuz your program is about to go supernova! I explain why a little later in this chapter.

Why All Arduino Pointers Use Two Bytes for Storage

As you know, the Arduino family of μc boards has three types of memory associated with them. The first is program (or flash) memory and it is in this section of memory into which your programs are loaded. This program memory is nonvolatile. That is, when power is removed from the board, your program memory remains intact. The second type of memory is SRAM, or static random-access memory. The variables that you use in your program are stored in SRAM memory. SRAM memory is volatile memory, which means that once power is removed from the board, the content of this section of memory is lost. The last type of memory is Electrically Erasable Programmable Read-Only Memory (EEPROM). EEPROM memory is also nonvolatile, which means that it can also retain its values even when power is removed.

You learned in Chapter 7 that as your program runs, variables come into scope and go out of scope depending upon what the code requires. These variables are stored in SRAM, which you can think of as being organized like the stack we discussed in Chapter 7. Because the amount of SRAM is less than 65K (i.e., 2^{16}, or the maximum value for a two-byte unsigned integer), it only takes two bytes to store a memory address for the program's data. Unlike a PC that may have gigabytes of memory and hence must use 4-byte memory addresses, your μc board can use 2-byte pointers because of the relatively small amount of SRAM available. (There are chips available that can address larger memory sizes and hence use 4-byte pointers. Diligent's chipKit Max32, for example, has 512K of flash and 128K of SRAM. Because these memory sizes are greater than 65K, it uses 4-byte pointers.) In other words, *pointer variables are always allocated enough storage to hold a valid memory address*. As mentioned earlier, all (properly initialized) pointers can have only two types of rvalues:

- a memory address

- *null*

Okay, but where does this scalar thingy come in? Consider Figure 8-3; note how the *char* pointer is designed with a scalar of 1 byte, enabling it to "see" a *char* data type. It is the pointer's type specifier that permits the pointer to work correctly with its designated data type. You know that an *int* data type requires two bytes of storage. This means that the *int* pointer has a scalar of two bytes so it can "see" an *int* data type correctly. If you define a pointer using the *long* type specifier, its scalar would be 4 bytes. If you look back at Table 3-1, the middle column of that table (i.e., Byte Length) tells you the scalars for the different data types. You can conclude, therefore, that *the scalar value for a specific pointer is equal to the number of bytes required to store that data type in memory*. In all cases, however, the pointer still only requires two bytes for storage for an Arduino.

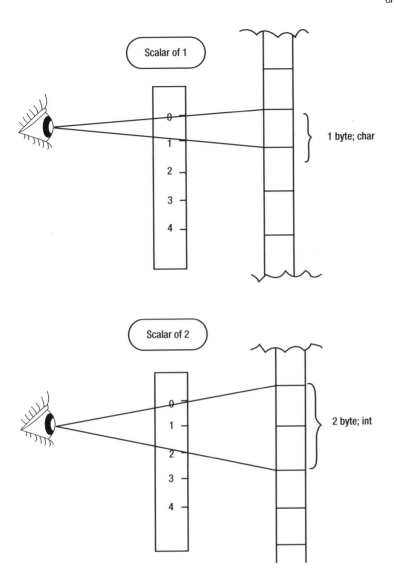

Figure 8-3. *Pointer scalars*

A valid question you might be asking yourself at this point is: What do pointers bring to the table to make them worthwhile? Before we can answer that question completely, you need to understand how to initialize a pointer.

Pointer Initialization

The instant after you define a pointer, you should think of it as being unusable. That is, after the compiler processes the following statement

```
int *ptrNumber;
```

you have an *int* pointer that has a garbage rvalue. Suppose the compiler ends up placing the pointer at memory address 2294 (see Figure 8-2). All you can count on is that *ptrNumber* has an lvalue of 2294 and its rvalue is whatever pattern of bits just happened to exist for those 2 bytes beginning at memory location 2294. That is, the rvalue of *ptrNumber* is garbage. If you're worried about the random junk the pointer contains, you could define and initialize the pointer as part of its definition, as in:

```
int *ptrNumber = NULL;
```

This statement makes it clear that the pointer does not *point to* valid data and that it should not be used. Quite honestly, while this may be a good coding practice, most C programmers don't initialize their pointers to *null*. If you wish to define a pointer and initialize it to *null* using the symbolic constant *NULL*, you need to add the following statement at the top of the source code file:

```
#include <stdio.h>
```

This header file contains a definition of the symbolic constant *NULL*. The default header file directory for the Arduino compiler is wherever you installed your Arduino IDE followed by the path name:

```
hardware\tools\avr\avr\include
```

If you look in the *stdio.h* header file (or any of the other header files stored in the *include* directory), you are going to see some pretty cool, albeit intimidating, code. A complete understanding of all that you find there is beyond the scope of this book. However, if you're really interested, simply copy the statement of interest into the Google search engine and read what the sources have to say.

Now that you know how to define a pointer and what its scalar is used for, let's actually try to use a pointer. First, suppose you have the following three statements in a program:

```
int a;
int b = 5;
a = b;
```

The last statement actually does more work that you may think. Simplifying the compile process a bit, the statement says: "Go to *b*'s lvalue and make a copy the rvalue you find there (i.e., 5). Now go to the symbol table and look up *a*'s lvalue. Go to *a*'s lvalue and copy the rvalue of *b* into the rvalue for *a*." Simply stated, *most (non-pointer) assignment statements simply copy the rvalue of one variable into the rvalue of another variable.*

Not so for pointer assignments.

Using the Address-Of Operator

Recall that a pointer should only hold a valid memory address or *null*. This means that the rvalue of pointer variables don't hold "normal" rvalues. Any pointer that is useful *must* hold a memory address. So how do we assign a memory address into a pointer. Simple! You use the *address-of* operator. *The address-of operator* (&) *says that you wish to use the lvalue of the variable, not its rvalue.* Read that last sentence over about a dozen times until it is etched in your brain.

Suppose you have the following code fragment in a program:

```
int number = 5;
int *ptrNumber;
```

Let's further assume that *number* has an lvalue of 2292 and the lvalue for *ptrNumber* is 2294 (like in Figure 8-2). You initialized *number* with an rvalue of 5, but you didn't initialize *ptrNumber*, so it contains garbage at this point in the program. Now, let's add another statement:

```
int number = 5;
int *ptrNumber;

ptrNumber = &number;
```

The purpose of the address-of operator (&) is to tell the compiler: "Don't do the standard rvalue-to-rvalue assignment in this statement. Instead, take the address (lvalue) of *number* (2292) and copy it into the rvalue for *ptrNumber*."

As before, read the previous sentence about 10 times and think about what it is saying. It is saying that the rvalue of *ptrNumber* is now the lvalue of *number*. Reread and think again....

First, *ptrNumber* now has an rvalue that holds the memory address (lvalue) of *number*. This is exactly what *ptrNumber* should hold: The memory address, or lvalue, of the *int* variable named *number*. This relationship can be seen in Figure 8-4. Notice that after the pointer assignment takes place, the address-of operator caused the lvalue of *number* to be copied into the rvalue of *ptrNumber*. That is, you have initialized *ptrNumber* so it now "points to" *number*. Think about what this means. *Because ptrNumber now knows the memory address where number lives in memory, ptrNumber has full access to number's data (i.e., its rvalue).* If *ptrNumber* has the right scalar value, which it does (*ptrNumber* is an *int* pointer and now points to the *int* named *number*), you can use *ptrNumber* to change the rvalue of *number*!

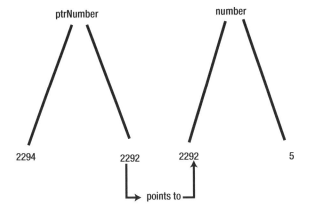

Figure 8-4. *The rvalues and lvalues for ptrNumber and number*

The Indirection Operator (*)

If you wish to use a pointer to change the rvalue of the variable it points to, you use the indirection operator, which is the asterisk operator. Makes sense: we are going to use a pointer to indirectly change the value of another variable.

Wait a minute! The indirection operator is the same character as the multiplication operator. Why doesn't the compiler throw a fit? The reason is because the compiler knows which operator to use based on the context in which you are using it. The multiplication operator requires two operands to work properly (e.g., operand1 * operand2). As you will see shortly, the indirection operator is a unary operator and only requires one operand. Therefore, the compiler knows from the context in which the asterisk is used as to which type of code to generate.

I have talked about *syntax errors*, which occur when you don't obey the rules of the language. I also mentioned earlier that *semantic errors* occur when you use the language in the wrong context. (I used the example of an English sentence, where I said: "The dog meowed." The sentence has a noun and a verb as the rules of English require, but the context is wrong. This would be a semantic error.)

The syntax rule for the indirection operator is:

```
*variableID = expression1;
```

For example:

```
*ptrNumber = 10;
```

The indirection operator is the asterisk. You can verbalize the preceding statement as: "Get the rvalue of *ptrNumber* (2292), go to that memory address, and copy the value 10 into *int* bytes of memory at that address." Notice the importance of the pointer's type specifier. It tells the compiler to convert the number 10 into scalar bytes (i.e., an *int*) of data (i.e., 2 bytes) and then copy those bytes into memory address 2292. The result after the statement is finished is that *number* now equals 10. You have "indirectly" changed the value of *number* using a pointer variable.

Imagine the kind of mischief that might result if you defined *ptrNumber* to be a *char* pointer rather than an *int* pointer. In that case, the assignment statement using the indirection operator would convert the value 10 into a 1-byte value and assign it into memory address for *number*. The value for would now only be "half right" because the second byte of *number* would contain whatever random junk just happened to be in memory at that address.

The lesson is simple: don't mix apples and oranges. If you want to use indirection to change an *int*, you must use a pointer that was defined with the *int* type specifier. Otherwise, all bets are off and you're on your own when it comes to debugging your program. (Actually, the Arduino compiler does a pretty good job of catching this type of error and issues an error message telling you it cannot convert one type of pointer into another type of pointer. It's even better, however, if you don't get caught doing this kind of thing in the first place!)

Using Indirection

Let's write a short program that shows the use of pointers. The source code appears in Listing 8-1.

Listing 8-1. A Simple Pointer Program

```
/*
  Purpose: Simple program to demonstrate using a pointer

  Dr. Purdum, Nov 22, 2014
 */
#include <stdio.h>
int counter = 0;

void setup() {
  int number = 5;
  int *ptrNumber;

  Serial.begin(115200);
  Serial.print("The lvalue for ptrNumber is: ");
  Serial.print((long) &ptrNumber, DEC);
  Serial.print(" and the rvalue is ");
  Serial.println((long) ptrNumber, DEC);
```

```
  //=== Put new statements here!

  Serial.print("The lvalue for number is: ");
  Serial.print((long) &number, DEC);
  Serial.print(" and has an rvalue of ");
  Serial.println((int) number, DEC);
}
void loop() {}
```

The code in Listing 8-1 simply displays information about *ptrNumber* and *number* on your PC using the *Serial* object. The program output when I ran the program on my PC is shown in Figure 8-5. For my machine, it shows that *ptrNumber* is stored at memory address 8690 has an rvalue of 168. The rvalue of 168 is the result of the random bits that happen to be stored in the two bytes starting at memory address 8690. If you had defined *ptrNumber* using the syntax

```
int *ptrNumber = NULL;
```

the rvalue of *ptrNumber* would be displayed as 0. For my computer, the lvalue for variable *number* was 8692 with an rvalue of 5. You may have different values for everything except the rvalue of *number* should still be 5 on your machine.

Now let's add two new statements to the program shown in Listing 8-1 and rerun it. The statements are:

```
ptrNumber = &number;
*ptrNumber = 10;
```

You should place these statements in Listing 8-1 where you find the comment:

```
  //=== Put new statements here!
```

Now recompile, upload, and run the new version of the program. Notice that the rvalue of *number* now displays as 10 rather than 5. The reason is because the first of the two new statements initializes *ptrNumber* to point to *number* using the address-of operator. Next, you used the indirection operator to assign the value of 10 into *number*.

Using the Indirection Operator in an Assignment

You can also use a pointer variable in an assignment. For example, add a new data definition for variable *k* near the top of the *setup()* function:

```
int k;
```

Now add the following new lines of code immediately after the last two lines you just added, so it looks like this

```
ptrNumber = &number;
*ptrNumber = 10;
k = *ptrNumber;
```

and add some code so you can see the value of *k* after the new statements:

```
Serial.print("The lvalue for k: ");
Serial.print((long) &k, DEC);
```

```
Serial.print(" and has an rvalue of ");
Serial.println(k, DEC);
```

When you run this version of the program, the output looks like that shown in Figure 8-5. Notice that the code uses indirection to assign the value 10 into variable *k*. As before, the indirection operator (*) instructs the code to go to the address pointed to by *ptrNumber* (the lvalue of *number*), fetch *int* bytes of data (i.e., 2 bytes holding the value 10), and copy those 2 bytes into the rvalue of *k*. As a result, the rvalue for both *number* and *k* are the same.

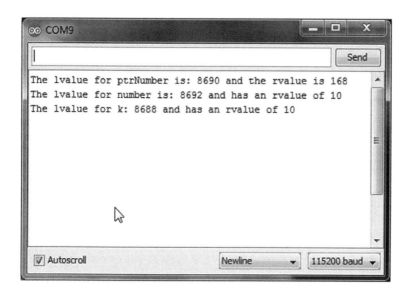

Figure 8-5. *Using the indirection operator in an assignment statement*

Surely you were paying close enough attention to Figure 8-5 to notice that the lvalues for *ptrNumber*, *number*, and *k* are different than shown in Figure 8-4. What happened? While you were nodding off, I switch Arduino boards from an UNO with 2K of SRAM to an Arduino 2560 with 8K of SRAM ... just to see if you're paying attention. As a result, the stack addresses are much larger than on the UNO with its smaller SRAM. If you add another *Serial.println()* statement after *ptrNumber* has been initialized to point to *number*, however, you would still find that its (garbage) lvalue changes from the 168 shown in Figure 8-5 to the lvalue of *number* (i.e., 8692). It's still quite likely that your actual numbers will be different, depending on the board you are using.

While we're here, look at the lvalues for the variables. Now look at the order in which they are defined in Listing 8-1: *number* is first to be defined (8692), *ptrNumber* is next (8690), and *k* is last (8988). Could it be that the compiler uses the stack mechanism discussed in Chapter 7 to allocate memory for these variables? Think about it.

Summary of Pointer Rules

Let's take a moment and review the various rules you need to follow when using pointers. A pointer variable must be defined using an asterisk in the definition, such as

```
int *ptr;
```

which defines a pointer that will be used with an *int* variable. The scalar of the pointer is determined at the time the pointer variable is defined. The pointer's type specifier determines the scalar. The scalar is used to determine how many bytes are to be manipulated by the pointer.

- A pointer never points to anything useful until it is initialized. The address-of operator is used to initialize a pointer with the lvalue of what is being pointed to:

```
ptr = &myVariable;
```

- The address-of operator (&) causes the lvalue of the variable (*myVariable*) to be fetched, and that value is then assigned to the rvalue of the pointer variable (*ptr*).

- After a pointer is initialized, you can use indirection to change the rvalue of the variable being pointed to. Therefore, the statements

```
int myVariable;
int *ptr;
ptr = &myVariable;
*ptr = 10;
```

have the effect of assigning the value 10 into *myVariable* using the indirection operator (*) and *ptr*.

You can also read the value being pointed to using the indirection operator, as in the statement:

```
Serial.print(*ptr);
```

This statement would print the value 10 on the serial display device.

Why Are Pointers Useful?

In Chapter 6 you saw that functions cannot change the value of an argument passed to it because, by default, function arguments are pass-by-value data items. That is, temporary copies of the arguments are passed to the function, not the arguments themselves. This also means that the function knows nothing about the lvalues of the actual variables being used; only their rvalues. Because the arguments are copies, the lvalue of the original variable is not available, which means a function cannot change the value of the original variable being passed to it in your backpack.

However, what if you need the function to change the value of the argument? This is often the case when you need to change two or more values in the function code. True, you can return one value from the function, but you want the function to change more than one value. No problem, use a pointer.

For example, suppose you have a temperature sensor that reads the temperature every hour and records the value in an array named *temps[]*. At the end of the day, you want to read the 24 values and record the minimum and maximum temperatures for the day. Something like the following code fragment would do the job. The source code is found in Listing 8-2.

Listing 8-2. Minimum and Maximum Temperature Program

```
/*
  Purpose: find the minimum and maximum values of an array of
  data values

  Dr. Purdum, Nov. 22, 2014
  */
```

```
#include <stdio.h>
#define READINGSPERDAY 24
#define VERYHIGHTEMPERATURE 200
#define VERYLOWTEMPERATURE -200


int todaysReadings[] = {62, 64, 65, 68, 70, 70, 71, 72, 74, 75, 76, 78,
                        79, 79, 78, 73, 70, 70, 69, 68, 64, 63, 61, 59};

void setup() {
  int lowTemp;
  int hiTemp;
  int retVal;

  Serial.begin(115200);

  Serial.println("=== Before function call:");
  Serial.print("The lvalue for lowTemp is: ");
  Serial.print((long) &lowTemp, DEC);
  Serial.print(" and the rvalue is ");
  Serial.println((long) lowTemp, DEC);
  Serial.print("The lvalue for hiTemp is: ");
  Serial.print((long) &hiTemp, DEC);
  Serial.print(" and the rvalue is ");
  Serial.println((long) hiTemp, DEC);

  retVal = CalculateMinMax(todaysReadings, &lowTemp, &hiTemp);

  Serial.println("=== After the function call:");
  Serial.print("The lvalue for lowTemp is: ");
  Serial.print((long) &lowTemp, DEC);
  Serial.print(" and the rvalue is ");
  Serial.println((long) lowTemp, DEC);
  Serial.print("The lvalue for hiTemp is: ");
  Serial.print((long) &hiTemp, DEC);
  Serial.print(" and the rvalue is ");
  Serial.println((long) hiTemp, DEC);
  Serial.println("\n");
}
void loop() {}

/*****
      Purpose: Get the daily temperature reading (READINGSPERDAY) and set the minimum
               and maximum temperatures for the day.

      Parameter list:
        int temps[]        the array of temperatures
            int            *minTemppointer to the minimum temperature value
            int            *maxTemppointer to the maximum temperature value

      Return value:
            int            the number of readings processed
*****/
```

176

```
int CalculateMinMax(int temps[], int *minTemp, int *maxTemp)
{
    int j;
    *minTemp = VERYHIGHTEMPERATURE ; // Make the min temp ridiculously high
    *maxTemp = VERYLOWTEMPERATURE;    // Make the max temp ridiculously low
    for (j = 0; j < READINGSPERDAY; j++) {
        if (temps[j] >= *maxTemp) {
            *maxTemp = temps[j];
        }
        if (temps[j] <= *minTemp) {
            *minTemp = temps[j];
        }
    }
    return j;
}
```

The *CalculateMinMax()* function has three parameters: An *int* array of temperature readings and two *int* pointers that store the minimum and maximum temperatures for the data passed to the function.

Now note how the function is called from within the *setup*( ) function:

```
retVal = CalculateMinMax(temps, &lowTemp, &hiTemp);
```

The first argument is the *temps[]* array that holds the 24 temperature readings. It is important to note that when you use an array name "by itself" (*temps*, no array brackets after it), you are referencing the lvalue of the array. This is because arrays are reference types rather than value types. In fact, you can write the function declaration for *CalculateMinMax()* as either the way it is shown in Listing 8-2 (note the use of brackets for *temps* in the first instance, but not the second as shown by the shaded areas):

```
int CalculateMinMax(int temps[], int *minTemp, int *maxTemp)
```

or as

```
int CalculateMinMax(int *temps, int *minTemp, int *maxTemp)
```

The interpretation of *temps* in either signature is the same to the compiler … it's an lvalue. The reason is because the call to *CalculateMinMax()* uses the name of the array by itself without brackets, which evaluates to the lvalue of the array....

Going back to the function call to *CalculateMinMax()* in *setup()*, notice that the next two arguments after *temps[]* are the *int* variables *minTemp* and *maxTemp*. Because you want the function to permanently change these values within the function, the function needs to know where these variables live in memory. This means you must send the lvalue for both variables to the *CalculateMinMax()* function. *Passing the lvalue instead of the rvalue changes the default argument behavior for a variable from pass-by-value to pass-by-reference. Placing the address-of operator (&) before the variable names switches the two variables from pass-by-value to pass-by-reference.*

If you think about it, the call in *setup()*

```
retVal = CalculateMinMax(temps, &lowTemp, &hiTemp);
```

has the effect of making the function signature to behave as though it were written as:

```
int CalculateMinMax(int temps[], int *minTemp = &lowTemp, int *maxTemp = &hiTemp)
```

177

Breaking out the last two parameters from the signature should look familiar:

```
int *minTemp = &lowTemp;
int *maxTemp = &hiTemp;
```

These two statements are the syntax you would use to initialize two pointers to the *lowTemp* and *hiTemp* variables back in *setup()*. In other words, pass-by-reference using the address-of operator (&) back in *setup()* has exactly the same effect as initializing the two parameters in *CalculateMinMax()* as pointers to *int* variables. A sample run of the code in Listing 8-2 is shown in Figure 8-6.

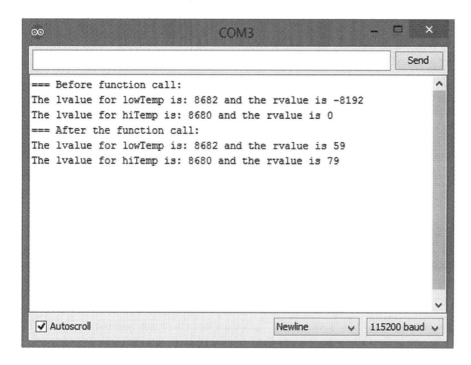

Figure 8-6. *Sample run of the MinMaxTemperature program*

In Figure 8-6, you can see that the lvalue for *lowTemp* is 8682 and *hiTemp* is 8680. (Why are the lvalues two bytes apart? Answer: Because *int*s use two bytes of storage.) You can also see that the rvalues for the two variables are different because they reflect whatever random bit pattern existed at those memory addresses when the program began execution. After the call to *CalculateMinMax()*, you can see their lvalues are still the same, but the temperatures have been assigned to the proper values by the function. Clearly, this means you were able to change the variables back in *setup()* using pointer indirection even though both variables are out of scope within *CalculateMinMax()*. This would not be possible without using pointers. Take a little time to study Listing 8-2 to be sure you understand how pointers allow you to change rvalues for variables that are out of scope.

The program shows another advantage of pointers. Recall that using an array name by itself as a function argument is the same as passing the lvalue for that array to the function. Suppose the array of temperatures was for ten days instead of one day. If the compiler could not simply pass the array name, it would have to use the stack mechanism discussed in Chapter 7 and push 240 *int* values onto the stack, thus consuming 480 bytes of stack space. Also, those same 480 bytes would have to be popped back off the stack by the code in the function. These pushing and popping instructions take time to say nothing about chewing up a huge chunk of SRAM in the process. By using call-by-reference, you can use arrays as if they were pointers and save both time and memory in the process.

Modified Blink Program

Let's take the Blink program that is distributed with the IDE and modify it to use a pointer. This is a contrived example, but it may help you to see what's going on when you use a pointer. The code is presented in Listing 8-3.

Listing 8-3. Modified Blink Program

```
/*
  Blink  by Scott Fitzgerald

  Modified by:
  Dr. Purdum, 12/19/2014
 */


#define LED    13

// the setup function runs once when you press reset or power the board
void setup() {
  // initialize digital pin 13 as an output.
  pinMode(LED, OUTPUT);
}

/*****
   Purpose: To blink the onboard LED using a pointer

   Parameter List:
     int pinthe pin attached to the LED
     int *whichStatea pointer to the state variable back in loop()
   Return value:
     n/a
*****/
void  BlinkLED(int pin, int *whichState)
{
  digitalWrite(pin, *whichState);     // turn the LED on (HIGH is the voltage level)
  delay(1000);                        // wait for a second
  *whichState = !(*whichState);       // Change state
}

void loop() {
  static int state = HIGH;     // State of LED
  BlinkLED(LED, &state);       // Call function
 }
```

Most of the code should look pretty familiar to you. In *loop()*, we define *state* with the *int* type specifier, but also use the *static* storage specifier. This means that the first line of code in *loop()* is only evaluated once. It is not processed on each pass through *loop()*. The code then calls *BlinkLED()*, which is a simple function to perform a d*igitalWrite()* of the LED pin. However, note that we are sending the lvalue of *state* to the function, not a copy of *state*'s value. This means we are using pass-by-reference, not pass-by-value. As such, we define the second parameter to *BlinkLED()* as a pointer, since we have an lvalue, not an rvalue. Anytime we need *state*'s rvalue in *BlinkLED()*, we'll need to use the indirection operator (*). Because we initialized *state* to HIGH when we defined it, the first call to *BlinkLED()* turns the LED on.

In the function call to *BlinkLED()*, the code turns on the LED and then executes the statement:

```
*whichState = !(*whichState);  // Change state
```

What? Anytime you see a "busy" statement like this used in an assignment, just break it down to its simplest form. Because the expression on the right side of the assignment statement must be resolved first, and parentheses force us to evaluate whatever is contain within them first because parentheses have the highest precedence of all operators, we evaluate *whichState* first. We know the state is *HIGH* because this is our first pass through *loop()*. Therefore, *whichState* causes us to use indirection to fetch variable *state*, which is currently HIGH. Next we evaluate the NOT operator, which means the right-hand expression becomes NOT HIGH. The expression NOT HIGH evaluates to LOW. This means that the value LOW is assigned into *whichState* using indirection. However, since *whichState* is a pointer to *state* back in *loop()*, it is the value of *state* that actually gets changed by the assignment statement in *BlinkLED()*.

Why did we have to use the parentheses in the pointer assignment in the *BlinkLED()* function? Actually, we don't. If you look at the Precedence Table in Chapter 4, you will find that the NOT and indirection operators have the same precedence level. Whenever there are ties in precedence, most of the operators are *left-associative*, which means the tie is evaluated in the expression by reading the operators from left to right. In our statement, the result is the same. So, why did I use the parentheses if they are not required? The reason is because it better documents what my intention is for the statement. Once again, it makes it easier to understand what the expression does and that's a good thing.

I urge you to type this short program in and study the code until you are sure you understand what's going on. It will pay benefits down the road.

Pointers and Arrays

As you may have guessed, there is an intimate relationship between pointers and arrays. Listing 8-4 shows a simple program that displays the content of a character array.

Listing 8-4. Display Character Array

```
/*
  Purpose: Display a character array using array indexes

  Dr. Purdum, Nov 22, 2014
  */

void setup() {
  char greet[6];
  int i;

  Serial.begin(9600);

  greet[0] = 'H';   // Initialize the array with some characters
  greet[1] = 'e';   // the slow way...
  greet[2] = 'l';
  greet[3] = 'l';
  greet[4] = 'o';
  greet[5] = '\0';  // null termination character
```

```
   for (i = 0; i < 5; i++) {
      Serial.print(greet[i]);    // Change this statement
   }
}
void loop() {}
```

When you run this program, the output is simply "Hello". To do that, you used the array indexes to march through the character string. Now change the statement in the *for* loop of Listing 8-4 to

```
Serial.print(*(greet + i));
```

and compile, upload, and run the program. What happens to the output? Absolutely nothing. The program still displays "Hello".

Now try changing the same statement to:

```
Serial.print(*(greet + i * sizeof(char)));
```

Does the output change? Nope, it's still the same. The reason is because each variation makes use of the fact that using *an array name by itself is the same as using the lvalue of the array.*

Consider Figure 8-7.

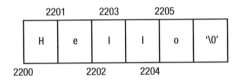

Figure 8-7. *The greet[] array in memory*

Assume that the *greet* array is stored starting with memory address 2200 (i.e., its lvalue is 2200). Now look at the statement:

```
Serial.print(*(greet + i));
```

On the first pass through the loop, because *i* is 0, the statement resolves to:

```
Serial.print(*(greet + 0));
Serial.print(*(2200 + 0));
Serial.print(*(2200));
```

The indirection operator simply says to go to memory address 2200 and fetch the character found there. This is the letter H. On the second pass through the *for* loop, the statement resolves to

```
Serial.print(*(greet + 1));
Serial.print(*(2200 + 1));
Serial.print(*(2201));
```

and the indirection operator fetches the letter e. The process repeats until the loop ends, at which time the word Hello is on the display.

The second variation of the statement is:

```
Serial.print(*(greet + i * sizeof(char)));
```

The *sizeof()* operator returns the number of bytes required to store the data type enclosed by its parentheses. From Table 3-1 you know that a *char* requires 1 byte for storage in memory. Therefore, the statement resolves to

```
Serial.print(*(greet + i * 1));
Serial.print(*(greet + 0 * 1));
Serial.print(*(2200 + 0));
Serial.print(*(2200));
```

and the H is displayed. For the second pass, the statement resolves to:

```
Serial.print(*(greet + i * 1));
Serial.print(*(greet + 1 * 1));
Serial.print(*(2200 + 1));
Serial.print(*(2201));
```

and the e is displayed. You should be able to figure out the rest of the sequence.

This exercise should convince you that using the array name *greet* is the same as the lvalue of the *greet[]* array. Now add the following pointer definition to *setup()* and change the *for* statement, as shown in the following code fragment:

```
void setup() {
  char greet[6];
  char *ptr;
  int i;

  Serial.begin(9600);
  greet[0] = 'H';
  greet[1] = 'e';
  greet[2] = 'l';
  greet[3] = 'l';
  greet[4] = 'o';
  greet[5] = '\0';

  ptr = greet;              // Initialize the pointer
  for (i = 0; i < 5; i++) {
    Serial.print(*ptr++);   // Change this statement...
  }
}
```

Once again, the program behaves exactly as before. The statement

```
ptr = greet;
```

takes the lvalue of *greet* and places it into the rvalue of *ptr*. To the compiler, because the name of an array is the same as the lvalue of the array, you don't need to use the address-of operator (&) as you did with the temperature variables in Listing 8-2. (In fact, if you did try to use the address-of operator, the compiler issues an error message.) The statement essentially does exactly the same thing as shown in Figure 8-4. It initializes *ptr* to point to the *greet[]* array. In the *for* loop, the statement

```
Serial.print(*ptr++);    // Change this line in 8.5 in for loop
```

uses the indirection operator (*) to fetch the content of *ptr* and display it. Since *ptr* equals 2200, the letter H is displayed. Because you used a post-increment operator on *ptr*, on the next pass through the loop, the indirection is performed on memory address 2201 and the letter e is displayed. As you can see, all three variations of the program produce the same results.

Let's make another modification:

```
while (*ptr) {            // This replaces the for loop
  Serial.print(*ptr++);   // Change this line in 8.5 in for loop
}
```

Now what happens? In this case, the *while* expression fetches what *ptr* points to (H), and if it is non-zero, it executes the *Serial.print()* call. This continues until the *ptr* points to the *null* at the end of the array. Because this evaluates to logic false, the loop ends. In other words, it works exactly at before.

What would happen if you completely got rid of the *for* loop and just used the statement:

```
Serial.print(greet);
```

Once again, the program works exactly the same as before. The reason is because now we are treating the character array as a *string* data type. (Do not confuse "string" with "String". The uppercase S refers to the *String* class while a lowercase s refers to a string built up from a character array.) By terminating the sequence of characters with the *null* termination character ('\0') as you did when the string was initialized, you can treat the character array as a string. That is, the *serial.print()* function gets the lvalue of the *greet[]* array, but can process it as though it is a string because of the *null* termination character. If you forget to add the *null* character to the *greet[]*, no problem. The *Serial.print()* function will just keep spinning through memory displaying whatever junk it finds until it reads a byte with the value 0. Comment out the last initialization byte and give it a try. My program only displayed about three bytes of junk before it stopped printing. Your results may be different.

Note the number of different ways that C allows you to accomplish the same task; in this case, printing out a short message. So, which is the "best" way to work with a string? As it turns out, the compiler is smart enough to generate virtually the same code whether you use pointer notation (*ptr*) or array notation (*greet[]*). If you are interviewing for a job or pontificating at a cocktail party, you'd probably use pointer notation. If you're writing code for a programmer who is still has his training wheels strapped on, use the array notation. Some shops have standards about such things and you may not have a choice. If you do have a choice, use whatever makes the most sense to you.

The Importance of Scalars

Let's make some minor changes to the program shown in Listing 8-5. However, notice that *greet[]* is now an *int* array, not a *char* array, and it initialized with numbers rather than characters.

Listing 8-5. Using an int Array

```
/*
  Purpose: Display an int array using array indexes

  Dr. Purdum, Mar. 11, 2015
*/
```

```
void setup() {
  Serial.begin(9600);

  int greet[6];  // Notice this is an int now
  int *ptr;      // ...as is this
  int i;

  greet[0] = 0;  // Numbers now...
  greet[1] = 1;
  greet[2] = 2;
  greet[3] = 3;
  greet[4] = 4;
  greet[5] = 5;

Serial.print("Using 'Serial.print(greet[i]);'   ");
  for (i = 0; i < 5; i++) {
     Serial.print(greet[i]);       //  Flavor #1
  }
Serial.println();

Serial.print("Using 'Serial.print(*(greet + i));'   ");
  for (i = 0; i < 5; i++) {
     Serial.print(*(greet + i)); //  Flavor #2
  }
Serial.println();

Serial.print("Using 'Serial.print(*ptr++);'   ");
  ptr = greet;
  for (i = 0; i < 5; i++) {
     Serial.print(*ptr++);        //  Flavor #3
  }
}
void loop() {}
```

If you run the program, it displays 01234. (*Expression2* of the *for* loop prevents the last element from being displayed.) If we look at the memory map for the integer version of greet, it has changed to that shown in Figure 8-8.

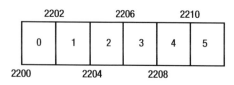

Figure 8-8. *The greet[] array in memory when stored as an int*

Notice how the offset from the greet lvalue (2200) is always *two bytes* now rather than one. Obviously, this is because an *int* takes twice as much storage as a *char*. However, how does the math work out for the statement within the *for* loop:

```
Serial.print(greet[i]);
```

184

This seems like it should resolve as

```
Serial.print(greet[i]);
Serial.print(greet + i);
Serial.print(2200 + 0);
Serial.print(2200);
```

which does align with the first number in the array. But, what happens on the next pass when $i = 1$?

```
Serial.print(greet[i]);
Serial.print(greet + 1);
Serial.print(2200 + 1);
Serial.print(2201);  // Uh-oh?
```

This is *not* the lvalue for the second value in the array. What went wrong?

Actually, nothing went wrong, because that's not how the compiler does the offset math. Any time the compiler calculates an offset from an array's base lvalue, *it scales the offset by the scalar for the data type.* To prove this, try the second variation you tried, but for an *int.*

```
Serial.print(*(greet + i));    // New line for Listing 8-5
                               which acts like it is written:
Serial.print(*(greet + i * scaler);
Serial.print(*(greet + i * sizeof(int)));
Serial.print(*(greet + i * 2);
Serial.print(*(2200 + 1 * 2);
Serial.print(*(2202));         // Taa-daa! The lvalue when i = 1
```

This works just fine, since 2202 is the lvalue for the second element of the array.

If you try the pointer version using the statement

```
Serial.print(*ptr++);
```

it also works just fine because *all pointer math is also scaled to fit the underlying data type.* In this case, any increment increases the offset by 2 because the scalar is 2 (each *int* requires two bytes of memory). You can alter the data type use in the program and you'll find the compiler adjusts the scalar for you automatically.

Pass-by-Value vs. Pass-by-Reference

We want to prove that there is a difference between pass-by-value and pass-by-reference. Consider the program in Listing 8-6.

Listing 8-6. Pass-by-Value

```
void setup() {
  // put your setup code here, to run once:
  Serial.begin(9600);
  int number = 10;

  Serial.print("lvalue for number is ");
  Serial.print((int) &number);
  Serial.print(" rvalue for number is ");
```

```
    Serial.println(number);
    SquareIt(number);
    Serial.print("After call: rvalue for number is ");
    Serial.println(number);
}

void loop() {}

void SquareIt(int temp)
{
    Serial.print("In SquareIt(), lvalue for temp is ");
    Serial.print((int) &temp);
    Serial.print("  rvalue for temp is ");
    Serial.println(temp);
    temp *= temp;
    Serial.print("The new rvalue for temp is ");
    Serial.println(temp);
}
```

When you run this program, the output is as shown in Figure 8-9. Note that the lvalue of number in *setup()* is 8694 and its rvalue is 10. (We have to cast &*number* to an *int* because the *Serial.print()* method doesn't know how to print a memory address.)

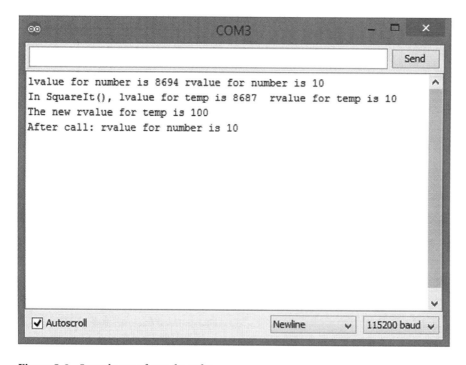

Figure 8-9. *Sample run of pass-by-value*

The code then calls the *SquareIt()* function, passing *number* to the function using the stack mechanism (i.e., backpack) discussed in Chapter 6. Inside the *SquareIt()* function, we display the lvalue of *temp*, the variable that received the copy of number from *setup()*. Clearly, because the lvalue of *temp* is 8687 while the lvalue of *number* back in *setup()* is 8694, they are two totally different variables. We know this because their lvalues are different even though their rvalues are the same ... they live in different parts of memory. The code then squares *temp* and shows its value is 100. Upon return from *SquareIt()*, we display the rvalue of *number* again to show that it is still 10, not 100. Clearly, we are passing a value to the function, not the variable itself.

Now, let's make a few changes to Listing 8-5 to make it pass-by-reference. Change the following statement in *setup()* from:

```
SquareIt(number);
```

to

```
SquareIt(&number);
```

Note how we have changed it to pass the lvalue of number by using the address-of (&) operator instead of the rvalue of *number*. We changed the *SquareIt()* function enough; I'll just present it here.

```
void SquareIt(int *temp)
{
  Serial.print("In SquareIt(), lvalue for temp is ");
  Serial.print((int) &temp);
  Serial.print("  rvalue for temp is ");
  Serial.println((int) temp);
  *temp = *temp * *temp;
  Serial.print("The new rvalue for temp is ");
  Serial.println(*temp);
}
```

After you make the changes to the source code, recompile, upload, and run the program. The output is shown in Figure 8-8. Note that the lvalue of number in *setup()* is still 8694 and its rvalue is 10.

The code then uses the address-of operator (&) before the argument *number* when it calls the *SquareIt()* function. This means we are sending the lvalue of *number* to the function, *not* a copy of its rvalue. In other words, even though *number*'s scope is limited to the *setup()* function, *SquareIt()* now knows where *number* lives in memory. Think about what this means. We have "hidden" *number* within *setup()* but have made it "indirectly" available to *SquareIt()* because we can use that lvalue as a pointer. We have encapsulated *number* in *setup()*, but made *number* available to *SquareIt()* by using pass-by-reference. Reread this paragraph until it makes sense.

We can prove all of this just by looking at Figure 8-8. Inside *SquareIt()*, we can see that temp lives at memory address 8687. The rvalue for temp is 8694.

Wait a minute! On my system, the lvalue of *number* is 8694 and the rvalue for *temp* is 8694. This is similar to what you saw in Figure 8-4! Just substitute *temp* for *ptrNumber* and change the lvalue/rvalue pairs and you have a picture of how things are now in *SquareIt()*. To get *number*'s rvalue, we have to use the indirection operator (*) on *temp* to get the value of *number* (10) as it appears in *setup()*. Then we execute the statement:

```
*temp = *temp * *temp;
```

What the ... ?? This makes sense if we break it down like the compiler would:

```
*temp = *temp * *temp;
*temp = (*temp) * (*temp);
```

```
*temp = 10 * 10;
*temp = 100;
```

What does this mean? Because *temp* is a pointer to an *int*, the statement sends control to the memory address stored in *temp*'s rvalue (8694), makes a two-byte *int* with a value of 100, and shoves that new value into the two bytes starting at address 8694. This means we have changed the rvalue of *number* that "lives" (i.e., has scope) back in *setup()*. The final call to *Serial.print()* back in *setup()* proves that *number* has been permanently changed by the call to *SquareIt()*. Study the output shown in Figure 8-10 and then think about it. How cool is that!

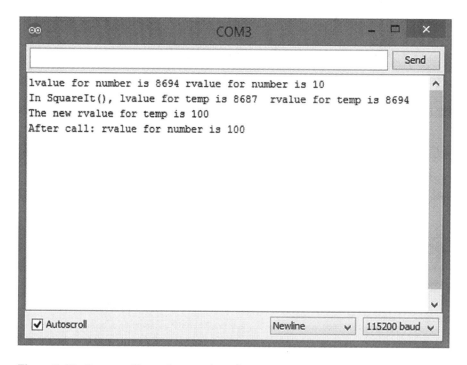

Figure 8-10. Program illustrating pass-by-reference

Your Turn

Now it's your turn to provide a solution to a programming problem. Here's the problem.

Using the two-LED circuit from Chapter 4, Figure 4-1, write a program that calls a function named *GetInput()* to acquire a single-digit number from the user via the *Serial* monitor. The numeric value from the user has the following interpretation:

```
0 = no LEDs lit
1 = LED1 lit
2 = LED2 lit
3 = both LED1 and LED2 lit
```

Any other entry by the user (i.e., "bad input") should keep the LEDs in whatever their current state is. *GetInput()* has a function type specifier of int and the only two values to be returned are 0 on "bad input" or

1 on "good input". Another function named *LightLEDs()* is used to turn the two LEDs on /off according to the value entered by the user. Other than *setup()* and *loop()*, you can only use the two new functions mentioned earlier. You are free to use any of the standard library functions.

At this point, I really hope you would sit down and try to draw up a program design of your own. If you do, you will learn much more than if you just read what follows. Give it a shot.

One Approach

Of course, the place to start is with Step 1 of the Five Program Steps. Step 1 is the Initialization Step, so what needs to be initialized? Well, since we are collecting input from the *Serial* monitor, we need to initialize the *Serial* object. Because there are two LEDs that are going to be used as indicators, we need to use *pinMode()* to set their state to be OUTPUT.

Step 2 is the Input Step, and we know that we will be using the *Serial* monitor to get input from the user in a function that is to be named *GetInput()*. Simple enough. However, what is not simple is how to get the information from the *GetInput()* function back to the caller. It's a problem because the only thing that can be returned from the function is a 0 or 1 to indicate that a "good" or a "bad" value was entered by the user. That doesn't leave us a means to return what the user entered (0 through 3 on "good" input) for subsequent steps.

Wait a minute! What if I pass a pointer to the *GetInput()* function as a function argument and let the user input set the value of the pointer in the function? That should work.

Step 3 is the Process Step, which in this case is to get the input from the user and determine which LEDs should be turned on (or off). Once we have determined the state the LEDs should have, Step 4, the Display Step, uses the *LightLEDs()* to display the LEDs.

We will assume that there is no Step 5, Termination Step, but rather the program will repeat itself to allow the user to enter another input value. Therefore, this will be our first program that actually uses the *loop()* function. At this point I hope you try to write your own solution before reading this one.

One Solution

First, consider the Initialization Step, as shown in the following code fragment:

```
#define LED1 11 // Which I/O pins are we using
#define LED2 10

void setup() {
  Serial.begin(9600);// Serial object set with "No Line Ending"

  pinMode(LED1, OUTPUT);
  pinMode(LED2, OUTPUT);
}
```

We define two symbolic constants for the LEDs and the pins associated with each. Why not use pins 0 and 1 instead of 10 and 11? The reason is because pins 0 and 1 are used to transmit and receive data by the USB connection. While you still could use pins 0 and 1 with artful programming that avoid RX/TX issues with the USB, why bother? We have plenty of unused pins, so it's easier to use other pins. (We also avoid using pins 2 and 3, since they are the only external interrupt pins many of the Arduino boards make available.) Once the pins are chosen, we use them for the necessary initialization code to *setup()*. The three statements simply activate the *Serial* object and perform the two *pinMode()* function calls to set the LEDs for OUTPUT.

Next, let's look at the *loop()* function. As you know, the *loop()* function creates an infinite loop that never ends, unless power is removed, the board is reset, or there is a component failure. The following code fragment presents our *loop()* function code:

```
void loop() {
  int goodBadFlag;  // Was the input good or bad?
  int LEDValue;

  Serial.println();
  goodBadFlag = GetInput(&LEDValue);
  Serial.print("flag = ");
  Serial.print(goodBadFlag);
  Serial.print("   LEDValue = ");
  Serial.print(LEDValue);
  LightLEDs(LEDValue);
}
```

The function body begins with the definition of two working variables. There are several calls to *Serial. print()* that serve as debug code to help you see what's going on. Using the *Serial* object is a common means for debugging (correcting) the program code. When you have the program fully debugged, removing the *Serial* object calls will decrease the code size.

Ignoring the *Serial* function calls, the first call is to *GetInput()*, which is used to retrieve input from the user. The function code is as follows:

```
/*****
  This function is used to get a numeric value from the user via the
  Serial monitor. Valid input are the values 0 - 3.

  Argument list:
      int *whichthe value entered by the user

  Return value:
      int   0 if the value is bad, 1 if good
*****/
int GetInput(int *which)
{
  char c;
  int temp = -1;
  *which = temp;
  while (true) {
   if (Serial.available() > 0) {
    c = Serial.read();
    if (isdigit(c)) {  // If they entered a digit character
     temp = c - '0';  // Subtract ASCII zero from the digit character
     if (temp >= 0 && temp < 4) {  // Is the value within range?
      *which = temp;
      return 1;// Yep, it's good
     }
    }
```

```
    return 0;   // If we get here, it's bad input
  }
 }
}
```

The function has a single argument, which is an *int* pointer named *which*. The code defines several working variables, setting *temp* equal to –1. The code then uses pointer indirection to also set *which* to –1. The code then creates an infinite *while* loop that waits for the user to supply some input from the *Serial* monitor. The statement

```
if (Serial.available() > 0) {
```

continually monitors the *Serial* input stream to see if the user has supplied any input. Suppose the user presses the 2 key and clicks the Send button on the *Serial* monitor. The call to *Serial.read()* immediately moves the digit character 2 into the *char* variable named *c*. The call to *isdigit()* using *c* as its argument is a standard library function that checks to see if the argument is a digit character. If *c* is not a digit character, zero is returned. If *c* is a digit character, non-zero is returned. Because we entered a "2" digit character, non-zero is returned and the *if* test is logic true.

Recall that when you touch a key on the keyboard, its corresponding ASCII code is sent to the computer. For the "2" digit character, the ASCII code is 50. The ASCII code for 0 (zero) is 48. Therefore, the statement

```
temp = c - '0';// Subtract ASCII zero from the digit character
```

actually resolves to:

```
temp = 50 - 48;
temp = 2;
```

The statement, therefore, is a quick and easy way to convert the ASCII code for a digit character into a "real" integer number that is assigned into *temp*. We then check *temp* to see if the value falls within our acceptable range of values (0 through 3, inclusive). If it is a valid *number* within our range, we use pointer indirection to assign *temp* into *which*. Because it is an acceptable value, we return the value of 1 from the function call to *GetInput()*. You should convince yourself that non-valid values or letters entered by the user end up returning 0 to the caller. Either way, program control returns to *loop()*.

Back in *loop()*, *goodBadFlag* is assigned the return value from the call to *GetInput()*. However, note that *LEDValue* has been changed by pointer indirection in *GetInput()* and now holds the value entered by the user is the number entered was valid. After the function call, there are a bunch of debug statements that use the *Serial* object to help you see what's going on.

The last statement in *loop()* is the call to *LightLEDs()* using *LEDValue* as its argument. The code fragment follows:

```
/*****
  This function is used to illuminate the correct combinations of LED
  according to the value of which

  Argument list:
      int combo key for lighting LEDs: 0=none, 1=LED1, 2=LED2, 3=both

  Return value:
      void
*****/
```

```
void LightLEDs(int combo)
{
switch(combo) {
case 0:              // both off
  digitalWrite(LED1, LOW);
  digitalWrite(LED2, LOW);
  break;
case 1:              // 1 on, 2 off
  digitalWrite(LED1, HIGH);
  digitalWrite(LED2, LOW);
  break;
case 2:              // 1 off, 2 on
  digitalWrite(LED1, LOW);
  digitalWrite(LED2, HIGH);
  break;
case 3:              // both on
  digitalWrite(LED1, HIGH);
  digitalWrite(LED2, HIGH);
  break;
default:
  Serial.println("Control should never get here");
  break;
  }
}
```

You should be able to convince yourself that, with the value of 2 entered by the user, *LED1* is turned off and *LED2* is turned on. The *default* case is simply a catchall if the user entered a non-valid number. You could, of course, use a series of nested *if* statements instead of the *switch*, but I think the *switch* is easier to read.

Debug Statements Using the Serial Object

Once you are convinced that the code is performing as wanted, you should remove the *Serial.print()* calls because they eat up memory that you may need for other uses. Perhaps the easiest way to do this is just to erase the statements from the code. While this works, what happens if you later unearth a bug and you need to put the debug statements back into the code? Well, you can always retype them back into the source code, but there's an easier way.

Suppose at the very top of the source code file I add a new line:

```
#define DEBUG
```

and I change the code in *loop()* to:

```
void loop() {
  int goodBadFlag;       // Was the input good or bad?
  int LEDValue;

#ifdef DEBUG             // NOTE
  Serial.println(" ");
#endif                   // ...end

  goodBadFlag = GetInput(&LEDValue);
```

```
#ifdef DEBUG                      // NOTE
  Serial.print("flag = ");
  Serial.print(goodBadFlag);
  Serial.print("   LEDValue = ");
  Serial.print(LEDValue);
#endif                            // ...end

  LightLEDs(LEDValue);
}
```

Note the *#ifdef DEBUG* preprocessor directives. What these tell the compiler is that, if *DEBUG* is defined in this file, include all the statements up to the *#endif* directive. If *DEBUG* is not defined in this file, do not compile any of the statements between the two directives into the program. You can add the same set to the *Serial.begin()* call in *setup()*. If you recompile the program, because we *#define*d *DEBUG* at the top of the file, all of the *Serial.print()* calls get compiled into the program.

Now, comment out the *#define DEBUG* directive at the top of the file, but leave the other preprocessor directives untouched and recompile the program. What happens? Because *DEBUG* is no longer defined in the file, none of the *Serial.print()* calls get compiled into the program. On my machine, the code size dropped from 2946 bytes to 2218 bytes by not including the debug code. If I need to reinstate the debug code later on, I just need to uncomment the *#define DEBUG* directive back in at the top of the source file. Kinda cool! You may hear this kind of debug code referred to as *scaffolding code* because it is used to surround the debug statements that serve as a safety net during the debug process, much like a scaffold protects the workers while building.

Summary

In this chapter you learned the hardest topic C can throw at you: pointers. You learned what pointers are and how to use the address-of and indirection operators to manipulate pointer data. You also learned how pointers are useful in overcoming local scope limitations when you want the function to permanently change a function argument. You also saw how pointers support the idea behind encapsulation because you can make local scope variables available to other non-local elements of the program. You also learned that pointers have a close relationship to the array data types. The sample programs in this chapter demonstrated that there are various ways to use pointers, but they are functionally equivalent.

There are a lot of new concepts in this chapter and you *must* master them before reading the next chapter. The next chapter adds more details about pointers and has a little more complexity. As such, it makes sense for you to spend enough time in this chapter before progressing to the next chapter. If you can do the exercises without error, you're ready to move on.

EXERCISES

1. What is a pointer?

    Answer: A pointer is a variable that, once initialized, has its rvalue initialized with the lvalue of another variable. Both the pointer and the matching variable must have the same data type specifier.

2. What does a pointer enable the programmer to do that might not be possible otherwise?

    Answer: Pointers allow functions to have direct access to data that would otherwise be out of scope. That is, pointers allow arguments to be passed by reference, thus giving a function the ability to permanently alter the rvalue of a variable that is not in scope. Pointers also allows arrays to be passed to functions in a more memory-efficient manner than pass-by-value would permit.

3. What does the address-of operator do and give an example?

    Answer: The address-of operator (&) gives the code access to the lvalue of a data item. It is normally used to initialize a pointer. A typical use might be:

    ```
    int val;
    int *ptr;

    ptr = &val;
    ```

    Variable *ptr* now holds the lvalue of *val* and can change it through the process of indirection.

4. What is the indirection operator (*) and what's its purpose? Give an example of how it might be used.

    Answer: The indirection operator is used by a pointer variable to access the rvalue of a different variable. To be used properly, the pointer must be initialized to point to the variable. For example:

    ```
    int val;
    int *ptr;
    ptr = &val;
    *ptr = 10;
    ```

    This code fragment uses indirection via *ptr* to change *val* to 10.

5. What is a pointer scalar and why is it important?

    Answer: A pointer scalar refers to the byte magnitude that pointer operations are scaled. For example, if a pointer to *char* is incremented, the offset from the lvalue is increased by 1 because that is the size of a pointer scalar for a *char* data type. However, if a pointer to *long* is incremented, the offset is adjusted by 4 because each *long* uses 4 bytes of storage.

    Suppose you needed to pass the value of the fifth element of an int array named *values* to a function named *func()*. How would you write the code?

    Answer:

    ```
    func(values[4]);
    ```

    The offset is 4 because of the N − 1 Rule for arrays. Bear in mind that this syntax is pass-by-value. That is, you are sending a copy of the value of the *values[]* array element to the function.

6. The *GetInput()* function listed earlier has a small hiccup in it. What happens if the user enters −2 for input. You can guard against negative numbers as input by only using the absolute value of the number entered by the user. Correct the *GetInput()* function so it doesn't accept negative numbers.

   Answer: You need to do this one by yourself. However, I will tell you that the standard library provides a function named *abs()*.

7. Take the code in Listing 8-4 and compile the program using the various pointer methods discussed in the text. Write down the one that uses the least amount of memory and try to explain why you think it uses the least memory.

   Answer: Interestingly, all have the same code size (1868 bytes) except for the version that uses the *while* loop (1852 bytes). This suggests that the compiler optimizes all the other forms to the same code. The *while* loop version does away with variable *i* and its manipulation in the program, which accounts for the difference.

CHAPTER 9

Using Pointers Effectively

This chapter is a continuation of Chapter 8. In that chapter, you learned what a pointer is and how to manipulate them in expressions. In this chapter, you will learn

- Valid pointer operations

- Pointer arithmetic

- Using pointers to functions

- The Right-Left Rule for deciphering complex data definitions

- Why using pointers can lead to more efficient code

When you have finished this chapter, you should be quite comfortable using pointers in your code.

Relational Operations and Test for Equality Using Pointers

Some C expressions make sense with almost any data type ... except pointers. A partial reason this is true is because a pointer can only have two types of rvalues: a memory address or NULL. Any other type of data is going to result in an error of some form. Because the rvalue for pointers is thus constrained, some operators simply don't make sense with pointers. Relational tests (e.g., >=, <=, >, and <) on pointers are acceptable only when both operands are pointers, and point to the same data. Therefore,

```
if (ptr1 < ptr2) {
    ...
}
```

is acceptable *only* if both pointers *ptr1* and *ptr2* point to the same object, but

```
if (ptr1 > 10) {
    ...
}
```

is not. This second form is unacceptable because the relational test is against a constant, not a pointer. You can use a cast to dispel the error message you get when using constants in pointer relational tests, but that's almost never a good idea. The reason it is not a good idea is because it is unlikely that testing against a specific numerical memory address almost never makes sense because an lvalue is not known until run time.

© Jack Purdum 2015
J. Purdum, *Beginning C for Arduino, Second Edition*: Learn C Programming
for the Arduino, DOI 10.1007/978-1-4842-0940-0_9

Pointer Comparisons Must Be Between Pointers to the Same Data

You should not perform relational operations on two pointers if they do not point to the same data object. If you think about it, such comparisons simply don't make sense. (An exception is checking a pointer to see if it is *null*.) The problem, however, is that the Arduino C compiler does not catch this type of error. Consider the following code fragment:

```
char *ptr1;
char *ptr2;
char array[50];
char name[10];

ptr1 = array;
ptr2 = name;
if (ptr1 > ptr2) { // Some RDC...
  //...
}
```

The *if* test on the pointers is nonsense and should be flagged as an error because you are comparing two pointers that point to different data objects. There is no way that two arrays occupy the same memory space. The Arduino C compiler, however, lets this code slide by. This can make debugging a pointer problem more difficult than it should be.

Pointer Arithmetic

Some forms of pointer arithmetic are allowed, others are not. Confusing them is simply begging the train to leave the rails. You performed pointer arithmetic in Chapter 8, but probably didn't think much about it. Now, let's dig in and look closely at what happens when you use pointers in your code. Consider the code in Listing 9-1.

Listing 9-1. Using Pointers

```
/*
  Purpose: Illustrate pointer arithmetic

  Dr. Purdum, Nov. 24, 2014
  */
#include <string.h>
void setup() {
  Serial.begin(9600);

  char buffer[50];
  char *ptr;
  int i;
  int length;

  strcpy(buffer, "When in the course of human events");
```

```
  ptr = buffer;
  length = strlen(buffer);              // How many chars in quote?
  Serial.print("The lvalue for ptr is: ");
  Serial.print((unsigned int)&ptr);
  Serial.print(" and the rvalue is ");
  Serial.println((unsigned int)ptr);
  while (*ptr) {
    Serial.print(*ptr++);
  }
}
void loop() { }
```

The first thing to notice is that we are including a header file named *string.h*. (Actually, you could leave this preprocessor directive out and the compiler still compiles the program without error.) If you read *string.h* with a text editor, you will find all kinds of functions designed to manipulate both strings and memory. (You should have looked at this header file as part of your reading of Chapter 6.) Most of the function declarations you find in that header file are part of the System V Standard C Library that's been around for decades. If you are interested in learning more about any given library function (e.g., *memcmp*), just Google the function name, and you will get more than enough information about the function.

(A *memcmp()* search turned up over 300,000 hits!) As stated before, search the libraries before writing your own functions. There's a good chance that what you need has already been written.

One of the function declarations you will find in the *string.h* header file is

```
extern char *strcpy(char *, const char *);
```

which copies the characters pointed to by the constant character pointer that is the second parameter into the character array pointed to by the first parameter. (When used in this context, *const* means that the function should not alter the data pointed to by the second parameter. Because *strcpy()* knows the lvalue of the second parameter, it *could* alter its contents. The *const* qualifier tells the compiler not to let that happen.) Therefore, the statement

```
strcpy(buffer, "When in the course of human events");
```

simply copies the quotation into *buffer*.

The statement

```
ptr = buffer;
```

simply initializes *ptr* to point to *buffer*. That is, it copies the lvalue of *buffer* into the rvalue of *ptr*. Remember that an array name by itself is the lvalue of the array (i.e., *buffer* is the same as &*buffer[0]*). Think about what's been said thus far until you're sure you understand what the last two sentences mean.

When you compile, upload, and run the program, your output for Listing 9-1 should look similar to that shown in Figure 9-1.

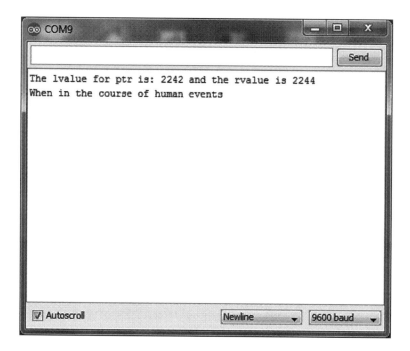

Figure 9-1. *Output from pointer arithmetic program*

You can tell from Figure 9-1 that *ptr* is stored at memory address 2242 and that *buffer* has an lvalue of 2244. The second line confirms that *ptr* does point to *buffer*. The code then enters a *while* loop to display the contents of *buffer*, using *ptr* to reference it. This is pretty much the same type of program you used in Chapter 8.

Now, add the following lines of code to the program in Listing 9-1, just before the closing brace of *setup()*:

```
for (i = 0; i < length; i++) {
  Serial.print(*(ptr + i));
}
```

Now run the program. The output when I ran the program is shown in Figure 9-2.

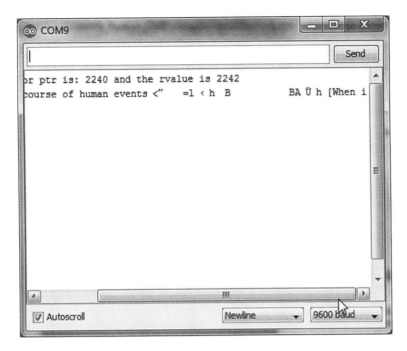

Figure 9-2. *Output from pointer arithmetic program with for loop added*

What? What's all of the garbage in Figure 9-2 that follows the word "events" all about? In other words, what is the following statement printing?

```
Serial.print(*(ptr + i));
```

This variation of the program using pointer arithmetic worked in the last chapter, but isn't working here. Why? To figure out the problem, look at the statement in Listing 9-1:

```
Serial.print(*ptr++);
```

This is controlled by the *while* loop. Now ask yourself: Why did the *while* loop terminate? The reason the *while* loop terminated is because *ptr* had been incremented so that it pointed to the *null* termination character for the quotation as stored in *buffer*. From the information in Listing 9-1 you know that *buffer* holds 34 characters plus one for the *null* character. When the *while* loop terminates, the rvalue for *ptr* must be 2277 (i.e., 2242 + 35) because you incremented *ptr* 35 times in the *while* loop. As a result, *ptr* no longer points to the start of the quote, but to its *null* termination character because you have been incrementing the rvalue of pointer in the *while* loop. After the *while* loop, the program code then falls into the new *for* loop that you just added, and the statement

```
Serial.print(*(ptr + i));
```

resolves to

```
Serial.print(*(2277 + 0));
```

which attempts to display whatever junk is stored in memory *after* the quotation has been stored in the *buffer* array! This is going to be whatever garbage happens to be in SRAM at the memory location, starting with 2277. Trust me, this is a Flat Forehead Mistake every C programmer has made at one time or another.

So, what's the fix? Very simple: reset the pointer any time you need to reuse it. In our case, add these lines before the new *for* loop code and run it again:

```
ptr = buffer;           // Reset the pointer back to buffer[0]...
Serial.println("");     // So the output prints on a new line
```

Now the output (as shown in Figure 9-3) is as expected.

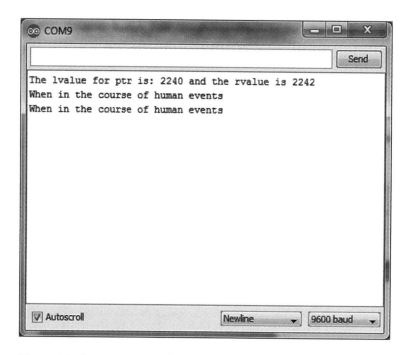

Figure 9-3. *Program output after resetting ptr*

Always remember: When you increment a pointer, it doesn't automatically reset itself.

The statement controlled by the new *for* loop

```
Serial.print(*(ptr + i));
```

shows how addition is one form of pointer arithmetic that is allowed. You learned in Chapter 8 that all pointer arithmetic is scaled to fit the data being pointed to. In this example, the scalar for a *char* data type is 1 byte, so each pass through the loop adds 1 to the rvalue of *ptr* and the code marches through the quotation. If *ptr* were pointing to *int* data, the expression

```
(ptr + i)
```

in the *Serial.print()* statement would add 2 to ptr on each pass because the scalar for an int is 2 bytes. Therefore, the arithmetic operation of pointer addition is permissible and is automatically scaled for the type of data being used.

Constant lvalues

You saw statements in Listing 9-1 that manipulated the pointer, as in

```
ptr = buffer;
```

and also the subexpression

```
ptr + i;
```

and both are perfectly acceptable expressions. The first statement simply initializes the pointer to point to the *buffer*, whereas the second statement increments (adds one scalar unit) to the pointer.

Now, using the variable named *buffer* from Listing 9-1, what happens when you try compiling the following statement?

```
buffer = buffer + 1;
```

The compiler gets a tad cranky and issues an error message. Why? Think about it.

You know that when an array name appears in a program statement by itself, it resolves to the lvalue of the array. Recall that it is the lvalue in the symbol table that allows the compiler to find where a data item resides in memory. The preceding statement, however, is attempting to change the lvalue by adding one to it. If the compiler allowed you to change the lvalue, there would be no way to find where that variable is stored in memory. Therefore, the compiler must issue an error message when any statement attempts to change the lvalue of a variable. You can add an offset to an lvalue to access the elements of an array, but you cannot directly change its lvalue. If you do try to change the lvalue of an array, you will get some form of error message telling you not to change "a constant lvalue." Pointers can change rvalues, not lvalues.

Two-Dimensional Arrays

Two-dimensional arrays are often used in programming to present tabular data. You might, for example, have a fire alarm system with 10 sensors per floor in a three-story building. You could organize those sensors as

```
int myFireSensors[3][10];
```

which could be used to store the current state of each sensor on all three floors. Obviously, you could also write the array as:

```
int myFireSensors[10][3];
```

Most programmers think of the organization for two-dimensional arrays in a row-column format, so this latter definition is "ten rows of sensors by three columns of floors." Which of the two forms is better? Doesn't matter. Pick one that makes sense to you and use it.

Let's write a short program that uses a two-dimensional array of characters. Although you could write the program as a simple array of Strings, we organize the data as *char*'s instead. The code is presented in Listing 9-2.

Listing 9-2. Using a Two-Dimensional Array of chars

```
/*
   Purpose: To illustrate the relationship between two-dimensional
     arrays and pointers.

   Dr. Purdum, December 20, 2014

   */
#define DAYSINWEEK 7
#define CHARSINDAY 10

static char days[DAYSINWEEK][CHARSINDAY] =
     {"Sunday", "Monday", "Tuesday","Wednesday",
      "Thursday", "Friday", "Saturday"};

void setup() {
  int i, j;
  Serial.begin(9600);    // Serial link to PC
  for (i = 0; i < DAYSINWEEK; i++) {
    Serial.print((int) &days[i][0]);  // Show the lvalue
    Serial.print(" ");
    for (j = 0; days[i][j]; j++) {
      Serial.print(days[i][j]);    // Show each char
    }
    Serial.println();
  }
}
void loop() {}
```

The character array is initialized by the statement:

```
static char days[DAYSINWEEK][CHARSINDAY] =
     {"Sunday", "Monday", "Tuesday","Wednesday",
      "Thursday", "Friday", "Saturday"};
```

The reason CHARSINDAY is set to 10 is because Wednesday is the longest day name, having nine characters. If you wish to view them as strings, you would need to define Wednesday with ten characters, or nine characters plus the *null* termination character. The result is a table with seven rows and ten columns of characters.

Why use the *static* storage modifier? Actually, the way the code is presented in Listing 9-2, the *static* modifier doesn't play much of a role in the way the data are handled by the compiler. The biggest difference is that the data are not allocated on the stack. (The *static* modifier changes where it gets allocated in SRAM memory.) If you run the program, the output should look similar to that shown in Figure 9-4. (I will have more to say about the *static* storage modifier in Chapter 14.)

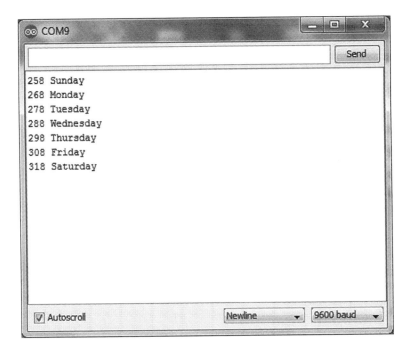

Figure 9-4. Two-dimensional program run

Another thing to keep in mind about data defined with the *static* storage modifier is that only a single instance of that data is ever defined, and it is defined at load time. For example, if you defined a *static* variable in a function that is called a thousand times, the *static* variable is only created once and that's when the program first starts. All thousand calls to the function share the same variable. That's why *static* data retain their values between function calls. Unlike variables that use the local storage class and are reallocated each time the function is called, *static* data hang around as long as the program is running.

In Listing 9-2, nested *for* loops are used to display the contents of the array. The first *Serial.print()* call in the code

```
Serial.print((int) &days[i][0]);  // Show the lvalue
```

uses the address of operator to display where this particular element of the *days[][]* array is stored in memory. The second *Serial.print()* call simply prints a blank space. The *j* loop code

```
  for (j = 0; days[i][j]; j++) {
    Serial.print(days[i][j]);    // Show one char
  }
  Serial.println();
}
```

then displays each element of the array by using the *i* and *j* indexes. Note how *expression2* of the *for* loop is written. Why does *expression2* eventually cause the *j for* loop to terminate? (Hint: think about the *null* termination character.)

If you look closely at Figure 9-4, you will notice that the lvalue for each row is exactly 10 bytes more than the previous element. Obviously, the rows are stored "back-to-back" in memory. In my own mind, I visualize such arrays simply as a long sequence of bytes. In this example, I visualize it as a sequence of 70 byte-sized blocks laid end to end. The second array dimension tells me how long each element is, or 10 bytes in this example. The first array dimension, 7, tells me where to "break" the blocks. Therefore, I mentally stack 7 chunks of memory one on top of the other, where each chunk is 10 bytes long. This forms a 7-row by 10-column table of characters.

Also notice that the lvalues have relatively low memory addresses compared to the lvalues in Figure 9-3. Why? The reason is because the variables in Figure 9-3 were allocated off the stack, while the lvalues for the *days[][]* array has the *static* storage class and is not allocated off the stack. Instead, a chunk of memory referred to as the *heap* is where *static* and global variables are allocated in SRAM. While I'm bending the facts a little, it's not too far off base to think of the stack as growing downward from the top of SRAM as local variables come into scope and variables allocated in the heap are found in low SRAM. If the two collide, you're out of memory.

A Small Improvement

Although the code in Listing 9-2 works as designed, you can make a minor change and get slightly better code. The improvement involves moving the *days[][]* array from its current global access location outside of any function to inside the *setup()* function. This move changes the access from global to local access, which affords the data an improved degree of privacy because nothing outside of *setup()* now has access to the array.

You might be thinking: "Wait a minute! In Chapter 7 you stated that local variables are allocated on the stack in SRAM. Doesn't this "improvement" increase the risk of running out of SRAM while the program runs?" To answer this question, move the definition of *days[][]* into the *setup()* function and recompile and run the program. What do you see?

Moving the *days[][]* array has no affect on the output of the program. Especially note that the lvalues do not change, which means the array hasn't moved. How's that possible now that *days[][]* is a local variable? The reason was just explained a few paragraphs ago. There is no change because data defined with the *static* storage specifier are always defined in the heap section of SRAM. Still, this second version of the program is better because you have restricted the access to the array by outside agents, yet haven't chewed up any more of the limited SRAM space. It is also important to know that, unlike local variables, *static* data are never reallocated once loaded. The *static* specifier assures you that the allocation only occurs once at load time.

How Many Dimensions?

Our sample program uses a two-dimensional array. Each dimension is called a *rank*, so Listing 9-2 uses a rank 2 array. So, how many ranks does Arduino C allow you to use? Well ... how many do you need? You might use a rank 3 array if you are doing 3D graphics, storing the coordinates for *x*, *y*, and *z*. If you're writing a game where those graphics change in relation to time, you might use a rank 4 array. I've tried to think of a rank 5 example and all I get is a headache. While I thought the old ANSI X3J11 spec stated a maximum rank of 256, I cannot find that limitation in print. I do know that the Arduino can compile a rank 5 array. I read where some theoretical physicists now believe there are 11 dimensions. If that makes sense to you, you probably don't need this book. I can't think of any reason to go beyond rank 4. If you need more, write the code and try to compile it. If it compiles, you should then send me a copy of the code ... I need a good example of a rank N program.

Two-Dimensional Arrays and Pointers

Can you rewrite the code in Listing 9-2 to use pointers? Sure, but it takes a little more thought. The modified code appears in Listing 9-3.

Listing 9-3. Modified Two-Dimensional Array Program to Use Pointers

```
/*
  Purpose: To illustrate the relationship between two-dimensional
    arrays and pointers.

    Dr. Purdum, December 21, 2014
  */
#define DAYSINWEEK 7
#define CHARSINDAY 10

void setup() {
  Serial.begin(9600);
}

void loop() {
  static char days[DAYSINWEEK][CHARSINDAY] =
      {"Sunday", "Monday", "Tuesday","Wednesday",
       "Thursday", "Friday", "Saturday"};

  int i, j;         // Note the dual definitions in one statement
  char *ptr, *base;  // Some programmers hate these. Your choice.

  base = days[0];    // Different for N-rank arrays where N > 1

  for (i = 0; i < DAYSINWEEK; i++) {
    ptr = base + (i * CHARSINDAY);
    Serial.print((int) ptr);       // Show the lvalue
    Serial.print(" ");
    for (j = 0; *ptr; j++) {
      Serial.print(*ptr++);        // Show one char
    }
    Serial.println();
  }
  Serial.flush();
  exit(0);
}
```

The first thing to notice is that there are two *char* pointer variables now, *ptr* and *base*. In the code, *ptr* is used to march through the character array, while *base* is used to keep track of where the array begins in memory. Recall from the previous program that when you ran the program back-to-back without resetting the pointer, random garbage ended up being displayed. The *base* pointer is used in Listing 9-3 to prevent the same problem.

The next difference is how the *base* character pointer is initialized to point to the array. The statement

```
base = days[0];
```

is necessary because this is a rank 2 array. A one dimensional array resolves to a pointer to *char*, so the name of the array *is* the lvalue for the array. However, with two-dimensional arrays, what you have is a pointer to an array, not a pointer to a pointer. For that reason, you need to show "rank - 1" array brackets. That is, if you have a rank 3 array, you would need to use *array[0][0]* in the pointer initialization. You could force the syntax using a cast, but that seems to be an artificial way to do it.

Inside the *for* loop controlled by variable *i*, the statement

```
ptr = base + (i * CHARSINDAY);
```

initializes *ptr* to point to the element of the array that you wish to display next. Looking at Figure 9-4, the *days[][]* array starts at memory address 258. Because you initialized *base* to point to the starting address of the first element of the array, *base* equals 258. So, on the first pass through the *i* loop, the expression resolves to

```
ptr = base + (i * CHARSINDAY);
ptr = 258 + (0 * 10);
ptr = 258 + 0;
ptr = 258;
```

which is exactly what we want. On the second pass through the *i* loop, *ptr* resolves to

```
ptr = base + (i * CHARSINDAY);
ptr = 258 + (1 * 10);
ptr = 258 + 10;
ptr = 268;
```

which agrees with the value displayed in Figure 9-4. You should be able to convince yourself that each pass through the *i* loop results in an lvalue for *ptr* that is 10 bytes larger than the previous value ... exactly as expected. Note that the base pointer is never changed. That's because all of the calculations are indexed from the beginning of the array.

Inside the *for* loop controlled by variable *j*, the statement

```
Serial.print(*ptr++);     // Show one char
```

simply causes the code to march through the array, displaying each character until the *null* termination character is read. When *ptr* has been incremented to the *null* termination character, *expression2* of the *for* loop terminates (the loop code interprets the *null* as a logic false condition), and the *j* loop ends. An end-of-line character is displayed, so the next display line appears on a new line. The program then increments variable *i* and the next pass through the *i* loop is made. The call to *Serial.flush()* makes sure that the *Serial* buffer is cleared and the call to *exit(0)* causes the program to end. These two statements are not used very often in Arduino programs, but does show how to terminate a program from within *loop()*.

Treating the Two-Dimensional Array of chars As a String

If you just want to print the contents of the array as strings, you can simplify the program even more. Remove the two *for* loops and replace them with the following single loop:

```
for (i = 0; i < DAYSINWEEK; i++) {
  Serial.println(days[i]);
}
```

If you compile and run this modified version of the program, the days of the week are displayed. How does that work? The operation of the program becomes clear when you realize (using the lvalues from Figure 9-4) where the starting bytes are located. That is, days[0][0] marks the "S" in "Sunday":

```
days[0][0] = "Sunday";        // lvalue = 258
days[1][0] = "Monday"         // lvalue = 268
days[2][0] = "Tuesday";       // lvalue = 278
// more elements...
```

Therefore, each time variable *i* is incremented by 1, the compiler adds an offset to the base index of the array name (258) that is equal to the size of the second element size for the array (i.e., 10) times its scalar size. For a character array, the scalar is 1, so the offset is always 10. This is why the lvalue that is used to display the string is always 10 larger than the previous address.

What if the array is defined as the following?

```
float myData[5][10];
```

What is the scalar for each increment of *i* in?

```
for (i = 0; i < 5; i++) {
  Serial.println(myData[i]);
}
```

Because the scalar for a *float* is 4, each increment on *i* advances the lvalue address by 40:

```
40 = sizeof(float) * second element size
40 = 4 * 10
40 = 40
```

As an exercise, you could change the code in Listing 9-3 to work with the *float* data type and display the lvalues to verify this conclusion is correct.

Pointers to Functions

You can call a function via a pointer in C. As you will see, this can be very useful when a set of known tasks must be performed based upon specific values. But first, let's see how to use a pointer to a function. Listing 9-4 shows the code for using a pointer to a function.

Listing 9-4. Using a Pointer to Function

```
/*
   Purpose: Show how to use a pointer to function

      Dr. Purdum, December 21, 2014
*/

void setup() {
  Serial.begin(9600);
}

void loop() {
  int number = 50;
  int (*funcPtr)(int n);   // This defines a pointer to function

  funcPtr = DisplayValue;  // This copies the lvalue of DisplayValue
  number = (*funcPtr)(number);
  Serial.print("After return from function, number = ");
  Serial.println(number);
  Serial.flush();
  exit(0);
}

int DisplayValue(int val)
{
  Serial.print("In function, val = ");
  Serial.println(val);
  return val * val;
}
```

Parts of Listing 9-4 look a little strange at first, but they do make sense. The first strange statement is:

```
int (*funcPtr)(int n);   // This defines a pointer to function
```

In the section titled "The Right-Left Rule" later in this chapter, you will learn a shortcut for deciphering complex data definitions. For now, however, this line simple states: "*funcPtr* is a pointer to a function that has a single *int* argument (*n*) and returns an *int* data type." If the function did not have an argument, the definition would change to:

```
int (*funcPtr)();   // This defines a pointer to function with no arguments
```

If the function takes two *float* arguments but doesn't return a value, the definition becomes:

```
void (*funcPtr)(float arg1, float arg2);   // Pointer to void function
```

As you can see, the type specifier for the function pointer is dictated by what the function's return value is. The name of the pointer, *funcPtr*, is preceded by the indirection operator so the compiler knows that a pointer is being defined. The surrounding parentheses mark the pointer as a pointer to function. The second set of parentheses groups the argument list for the function that will be pointed to.

You've probably already figured out the next statement:

```
funcPtr = DisplayValue;  // This copies the lvalue of DisplayValue
```

This statement copies the lvalue of the function into *funcPtr*. Just as a variable has a memory address where it resides in memory (i.e., its lvalue), so, too, does a function.

The next statement

```
number = (*funcPtr)(number)
```

calls the *DisplayValue()* function by using *funcPtr*, passing the value of *number* to the function. The function itself does little else than display the current value of the value passed to it. The function does, however, square *number* and send it back to the caller as the return value for the function call. The return value is then displayed to show that the number was, in fact, squared by the function. A sample run of the program is shown in Figure 9-5. As you can see in the figure, the number is squared during the function call and that value is returned to the caller. Again, we use the *Serial.flush()* and *exit(0)* calls to terminate the loop after one pass. You could, of course, just move the code into *setup()* and leave these two function calls out.

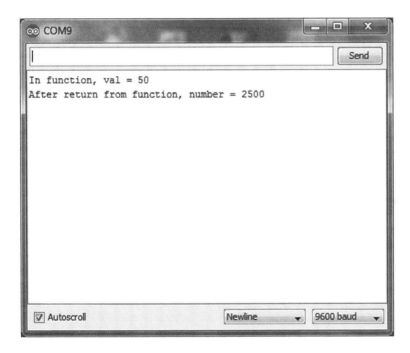

Figure 9-5. *Sample run of pointer to function program*

Arrays of Pointers to Functions

Arrays of pointers to function may sound complicated, but it really isn't. Indeed, arrays of function pointers is a very useful and efficient way to perform certain tasks. For example, suppose you have three processes that might be used depending upon the value returned from some other function call. Perhaps the function reads the temperature of a vat of candy. If the return value indicates the temperature is too low, a function to continue heating the candy is called. If the return value is too high, another function turns off the heat, but continues to stir the candy so it will cool. When the temperature is "just right," a third function is called that routes the candy to a series of molds. Listing 9-5 shows how you might simulate this process.

enum Data Type

Near the top of Listing 9-5 is a new data structure called an *enum* (i.e., enumerated) data type. The *enum* syntax is:

```
enum NameOfEnum {enumMember List};
```

The *NameOfEnum* is the name (or tag) you wish to use for the enumeration and it follows the normal variable naming rules. The *enumMemberList* is a comma-separated list of the enumerated values that you wish to use. By default, the list is assigned values starting with 0 and is incremented by 1 for each member. For example,

```
enum days {SUNDAY, MONDAY, TUESDAY, WEDNESDAY, THURSDAY, FRIDAY, SATURDAY};
```

would associate 0 with SUNDAY, 1 for MONDAY, and 6 for SATURDAY. You can override the default *enum* numbering by using explicit assignments, such as:

```
enum speeds {RESIDENTIAL = 35, STATEROAD = 55, FEDERALHIGHWAY = 70};
```

The member list names do not have to be in caps, but it is often done this way to reflect that the values are treated as constants in the program.

It is important to note that the preceding statements are *enum* data declarations, not *enum* definitions. To *define* an enumerated variable, you may use either of the following syntax forms:

```
enum days myDay;
enum SPEEDS {RESIDENTIAL = 35, STATEROAD = 55, FEDERALHIGHWAY = 70} mySpeed;
enum SPEEDS stateMax = STATEROAD;
```

The first statement assumes that an *enum* for *days* already has been declared in the code and defines an *enum* variable named *myDay*. The second form combines the declaration of the *enum* with the definition of a *SPEEDS enum* named *mySpeed*. Use whichever style you wish, but use it consistently. The last statement shows how to use the *enum* value in an assignment.

If you have this nagging sensation that *enum*'s seem to be the same as using a *#define*, you're almost right, but not quite. A *#define* is a textual substitution done during the preprocessor pass by the compiler. If you could look at the source code after the preprocessor pass, the tag associated with the *#define* is no longer present in the source code, only its associated value is present. As a result, there is no evidence of the *#define* in the symbol table, either. That is, there is no traceable lvalue.

The *enum* is different in that it does create a variable that you can track in the program. This can make debugging easier using *enum*'s than if *#define*'s are used. Also, some people are more comfortable with *enum*'s because it uses a more familiar syntax that ends with a semicolon statement termination character.

In Listing 9-5, an *enum* is used in conjunction with the candy vat temperatures. That is, *whichAction* can only assume the enumerated values of 0 (TOOCOLD), 1 (TOOHOT), or 2 (JUSTRIGHT). The code uses *whichAction* to index into the array of function pointers. The program is long enough that you might find it useful to load it into the IDE and scroll through the code as you read the narrative about the program.

Listing 9-5. Program Using an Array of Pointers to Functions

```
/*
  Purpose: illustrate how you can use an array of pointers to
    functions.

  Dr. Purdum, December 21, 2014
*/

enum temperatures {TOOCOLD, TOOHOT, JUSTRIGHT};
enum temperatures whichAction;

const int COLD = 235;
const int HOT = 260;

void setup() {
  Serial.begin(9600);         // Serial link to PC
  randomSeed(analogRead(0));  // Seed random number generator
}

void loop() {
  static void (*funcPtr[])() = {TurnUpTemp, TurnDownTemp, PourCandy};
  static int iterations = 0;
  int temp;

  temp = ReadVatTemp();
  whichAction = (enum temperatures) WhichOperation(temp);
  (*funcPtr[whichAction])();

  if (iterations++ > 10) {
    Serial.println("====================");
    Serial.flush();
    exit(0);
  }
}

/*****
  Purpose: return a value that determines whether to turn up heat, turn down heat, or if
    vat is ready. Pourable candy is between 235 and 260.

  Parameter list:
    int temp      the current vat temperature

  Return value:
    int            0 = temp too cold, 1 = temp too high, 2 = just right
*****/

int WhichOperation(int temp)
{
  Serial.print("temp is ");
  Serial.print(temp);
```

```
    if (temp < COLD) {
      return TOOCOLD;
    } else {
      if (temp > HOT) {
        return TOOHOT;
      } else
        return JUSTRIGHT;
    }
}

/*****
   Purpose: simulate reading a vat's temperature. Values are
     constrained between 100 and 325 degrees

   Parameter list:
     void

   Return value:
     int            the temperature
*****/
int ReadVatTemp()
{
  return random(100, 325);
}

void TurnUpTemp()
{
  Serial.println(" in TurnUpTemp()");
}

void TurnDownTemp()
{
  Serial.println(" in TurnDownTemp()");
}

void PourCandy()
{
  Serial.println(" in PourCandy()");
}
```

The *setup()* function establishes a serial link to the PC and the random number generator is seeded. Inside the *loop()* function, the statement

```
static void (*funcPtr[])() = {TurnUpTemp, TurnDownTemp, PourCandy};
```

is the heart of the program. This statement creates and initializes an array named *funcPtr* that is an array of pointers to functions.

As stated earlier, just like any other variable that is defined in a program, each function has an lvalue that marks where that function resides in memory. If something causes program control to branch to that memory location for the next program instruction, it is exactly the same as calling that function. In this particular example, *funcPtr[0]* holds the lvalue for the *TurnUpTemp()* function, *funcPtr[1]* holds the lvalue for the *TurnDownTemp()* function, and *funcPtr[2]* holds the lvalue for the *PourCandy()* function. As you can see in Listing 9-5, each of these functions simply displays a message saying that particular function was executed. This allows you to see which functions are visited as the program executes. Such "empty" functions are called *stubs* and are a commonly-used technique during the program development process. Figure 9-6 shows a sample run of the program. (Because the value for the temperature is generated randomly, it may take a while to see all three states appear on the *Serial* monitor.)

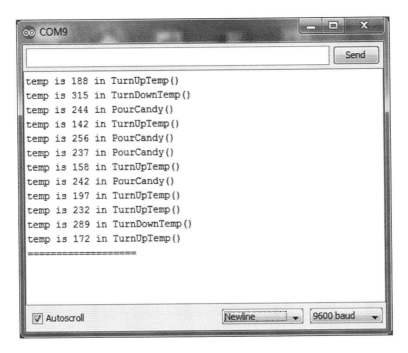

Figure 9-6. Sample run of the array of pointers to functions program

The heart of the program centers on the following three statements:

```
temp = ReadVatTemp();
whichAction = (enum temperatures) WhichOperation(temp);
(*funcPtr[whichAction])();
```

The first statement calls the *ReadVatTemp()* function. We've coded the function to return a random number between 100 and 350 degrees. (Actually, almost any candy that has a temperature of 350 degrees is pretty much a block of carbon by then.) The random number is then returned from the function call and assigned into *temp*.

The second statement takes the value of *temp* and passes it to *WhichOperation()* to determine if the temperature is too low, too high, or just right for pouring the candy into molds. The return value is then cast into the *enum* variable *whichAction* to determine which function should be called.

The third statement then calls the appropriate function by using *whichAction* as an index into the *funcPtr[]* array. Program control is then transferred to that function, which, in turn, displays its associated message. The dashed line is used to separate sets of runs should you press the μc board's reset button.

Arrays of pointers to functions takes a little getting used to, but offers an elegant solution to many programming problems that involve calling specific functions depending upon a certain value. Years ago I saw a C implementation of the game Monopoly, where each square on the board was associated with a particular function. Those functions were organized as an array of pointers to functions, which greatly simplified the coding for the game. Pointers to function are particularly useful with automated process control situations. Keep the pointer-to-function concept tucked away in the back of your mind. Often it is the perfect solution to a given programming task.

The Right-Left Rule

What went through your mind when you first saw the following statement?

```
static void (*funcPtr[])() = {TurnUpTemp, TurnDownTemp, PourCandy};
```

Statements like this are called *complex data definitions* because they involve more than a simple data type specifier and a variable name. Let's take this definition, remove the storage specifier (the initializer code that appears between the brackets), and just concentrate on what's left:

```
void (*funcPtr[3]) ();
```

(I used 3 for the array size because that's the number of functions that we wanted to use in Listing 9-5.) The question is: What does this definition do? Alternatively, how can you verbalize this definition? Actually, it's pretty simple when you use The Right-Left Rule that I developed over 30 years ago.

The Right-Left Rule says: locate the identifier in the definition (e.g., *funcPtr*) and then you spiral your way out of the definition in a right-to-left fashion. Figure 9-7 shows the steps to follow to verbalize the definition. Step 1 says to find the name of the data item. In Figure 9-7, you can see the name is *funcPtr*. Thus far, you can say: *funcPtr* is a ...

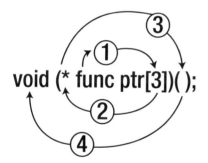

Figure 9-7. *Using the Right-Left Rule*

Now, look to the immediate right of the identifier. What you see is [3] in the data definition. Because you know that a bracket ([) introduces an array of some sort and that any number specifies the size of the array, you can now say: "*funcPtr* is an array of three ... ".

To find out what the array type is, you have to look to the left of the identifier to find out what the array is. As shown in Figure 9-7, step 2 moves you to the left, where you find an asterisk. Because an asterisk in a data definition is used with pointers, you can now say: " *funcPtr* is an array of three pointers to ... ".

To determine what the pointers point to, you need to move to the right again to see what the next attribute in the data definition is. What you actually see is the closing parenthesis. However, that is simply used to group the attributes surrounding the identifier. Since everything within the parentheses is already "used up," you must move to the right to find the next attribute. As shown in step 3 in Figure 9-7, you see a set of parentheses. In data definitions, parentheses are used to mark the argument list of a function. Therefore, you can now say: " *funcPtr* is an array of three pointers to functions ... ".

However, all function definitions must have a type specifier that tells what the function returns. To determine what the functions return, we need to move to the left in the data definition, as shown in step 4 of Figure 9-7. You can now say: "*funcPtr* is an array of three pointers to functions returning *void*."

If you look back to the right in the data definition after step 4, you see that there are no other attributes left for this data definition. Therefore, you can tell your friends that "*funcPtr* is an array of three pointers to functions that return *void*." You're done. Although people at cocktail parties won't seem too impressed by this skill, it will serve you well when you're trying to read some else's complex code.

Summary

Pointers are one of the most powerful features in the C language. Alas, pointers are also one of the most difficult concepts for beginning programmers to understand. Still, pointers offer you so much flexibility that they are well worth the effort it takes to master them. You should spend whatever time it takes to feel comfortable with the concepts presented in this chapter. The effort will pay back huge dividends in your programming endeavors.

EXERCISES

1. In Listing 9-1 if I changed *ptr* from a character pointer to an *int* pointer, and in the initialization statement I wrote,

   ```
   ptr = (int *) buffer;
   ```

   and then ran the program, what would you expect the output to look like and why?

   Answer: The output becomes

   ```
   We ntecus fhmneet
   ```

   plus a bunch of garbage. (Actually, casting to an *int* pointer would just show numeric values, not characters.) The reason is because the scalar for an *int* is twice as big as the scalar for a *char*, so every other letter in the quotation is printed. However, the *while* loop "skips over" the *null* termination character and displays junk until a *null* (zero) is finally read.

2. Why are pointer scalars important?

   Answer: Any pointer manipulation needs to know the type of data to which it points so the compiler can adjust the operation to fit the data. Incrementing a pointer, for example, must advance the pointer value by the scalar size of the object being pointed to, or disaster results.

3. When can you use two pointers in an arithmetic expression?

    Answer: Pointer arithmetic only makes sense when the pointers point to the same object.

4. If you define a pointer to a function, what is the rvalue of a properly initialized pointer to function?

    Answer: Just like any other pointer variable, it must hold an lvalue. In this case, it is the lvalue of where the function resides in memory.

5. What is the purpose of The Right-Left Rule?

    Answer: The purpose of The Right-Left Rule is to allow you to decipher complex data definitions.

6. Unwind and verbalize the following data definitions:

    ```
    int *ptr1[10];
    int (*ptr2)[10];
    int (*(*ptr3())[10])();
    int (*ptr4(int))();
    ```

    Answers:

    -   ptr1 is an array of 10 pointers to *int*.

    -   ptr2 is a pointer to an array of 10 *ints*.

    -   ptr3 is a function returning a pointer to an array of 10 pointers to functions that return *ints*.

    -   ptr4 is a function that takes an *int* argument and returns a pointer to a function that returns an *int*.

7. What is an *enum* and how is it different than a *#define*?

    Answer: An en*um* is a named constant, but persists after the preprocessor pass. Also, an *enum* is accessed using the dot operator.

CHAPTER 10

■ ■ ■

Structures, Unions, and Data Storage

This chapter takes a little deeper look at some of your options for storing data and in serial input/output (I/O) operations. You will also learn some new data structures that are available to you and how they can be used to advantage in your programs. More specifically, in this chapter you learn about

- The *struct* keyword
- The *union* keyword
- How to use EEPROM memory in your programs
- Other data storage options

As you saw in Table 1-1, µc boards have limited amounts of memory available to you. I've talked about flash and SRAM memory in previous chapters, but I haven't had too much to say about EEPROM memory. In this chapter, you will learn how to use EEPROM memory in your programs. However, before we dive into that topic, you need to take a little detour and learn about the *struct* keyword. After that, you will use a structure as an organizational object for storing data in EEPROM.

Structures

Not too long ago I was involved in a project that required storing information about people/companies who performed services for homes. The project was in Florida and it was mainly for people who lived in Florida on a part time basis. The project required storing a service company's ID number, name, password, and phone number. (Actually, more data was required, but this is good enough for our purposes.) From a data point of view, such disparate data poses a number of problems, not the least of which is how you "tie together" such differing data elements. You could define the data something like this:

```
int serviceID;
char serviceName[20];
char servicePW[10];
long servicePhone;
```

In this case, you try to link the data together by using the word "service" in the names of the data. Although better than nothing, such an approach doesn't really "tie" the data together and allow us to manipulate it as an integrated unit of information.

© Jack Purdum 2015
J. Purdum, *Beginning C for Arduino, Second Edition*: Learn C Programming
for the Arduino, DOI 10.1007/978-1-4842-0940-0_10

The problem of grouping dissimilar data items together is solved in C by using a structure. A *structure organizes different data items so they may be referenced by a single name*. A structure normally holds two or more data items, usually of differing data types.

Declaring a Structure

An example will help you to see how a structure is declared in C. Sticking with our service people example, you might declare the associated structure as follows:

```
struct servicePeople {
        int ID;
        char Name[20];
        char PW[10];
        long Phone;
};
```

Note that the preceding statements form a data *declaration* for a structure named *servicePeople*, but does not define a structure variable. A structure declaration is like a cake recipe: it tells you how to build a cake and what the cake should look like, but there's no cake to eat ... yet. The general syntax for a structure declaration is:

```
struct structureTag {
    // StructureMemberList
};
```

This syntax can be seen in Figure 10-1.

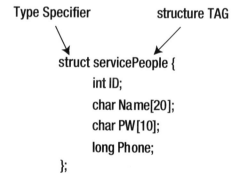

Figure 10-1. *The syntax for a structure declaration*

The declaration begins with the keyword *struct* as the data type specifier followed by the name, or structure tag, of the structure. *A structure tag identifies the structure that is being declared.* Structure tags follow the same naming rules as any other C variable. The structure tag is followed by an opening brace, followed by one or more variable definitions. Collectively, these variable definitions are called the *structure members*. After the list of structure members, there is a closing brace and then a semicolon. In our service example, the structure tag is *servicePeople* and it has four members. Therefore, the information stored in *ID*, *Name*, *PW*, and *Phone* are "tied together" under an umbrella structure tag named *servicePeople*.

It is imperative that you understand that the structure named *servicePeople* is a template, or cookie cutter, from which you can create a *servicePeople* data object. In other words, at this point, *servicePeople* is a data declaration ... no memory has been allocated yet for a single *servicePeople* variable. The structure declaration is like a set of blue prints for a house: It tells you the specifics about a house, but is not a house itself.

Defining a Structure

Obviously, you need to define a variable using this type of structure definition for the structure to be useful in a program. The syntax is:

```
struct structureTag structureVariableName;
```

To define a structure variable using our example, you would use:

```
struct servicePeople myServicePeople;
```

Figure 10-2 shows the structure definition. You now have defined a structure variable named *myServicePeople* that you can use in your program. The structure variable named *myServicePeople* now has an lvalue in the symbol table because memory has been allocated for it.

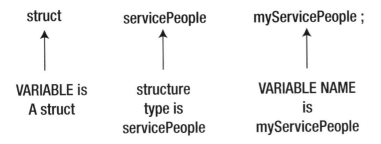

Figure 10-2. *Defining a structure variable named myServicePeople using the servicePeople structure tag*

An alternative way to define a structure is:

```
struct servicePeople {
        int ID;
        char Name[20];
        char PW[10];
        long Phone;
} myServicePeople;
```

In this case, the structure declaration and definition are combined into a single statement. That is, the definition of *myServicePeople* immediately follows the structure declaration, but is in a single statement.

You can, however, also define a structure variable without a structure tag, as in:

```
struct {
        int ID;
        char Name[20];
        char PW[10];
        long Phone;
} myServicePeople, yourServicePeople;
```

221

Notice that the structure tag (*servicePeople*) is missing. This is not a problem for the compiler because the data declaration and the data definition are combined into a single statement using the braces before the semicolon that ends the statement. In this example, the code defines two structure variables (*myServicePeople* and *yourServicePeople*) separated from each other by a comma. However, this latter form is less used because you may need to define another structure at some other point in the program and you would not have a structure tag available for the definition.

If you have 15 different companies performing services at your home, you can create an array of structures, as in:

```
struct servicePeople myServicePeople[15];
```

As you know, arrays are groupings of data that share the exact same data attribute. However, structures allow you to have arrays that may contain many different types of data in their member lists, thus creating a more complex data structure. This has led one of my colleagues (Kim Brand) to say that structures allow you to create "arrays for adults." Indeed, structures are similar to the object-oriented programming concept known as a class. The major difference, however, is that a class can also have functions (also called *methods*) defined within the class. Still, you will find that structures do provide a convenient way to organize dissimilar groups of data.

Accessing Structure Members

Now that you have all of your structure members tucked neatly away inside a structure, how do you access their data? Suppose you wish to retrieve the ID of a service person. If the data are stored in a structure variable named *myServicePeople*, the statement to fetch the ID is:

```
clientID = myServicePeople.ID;   // Retrieving structure data
```

In this example, the ID associated with the service person is copied into *clientID*. Obviously, it's a two-way street, so you could store a person's identification number in the structure, as in:

```
myServicePeople.ID = clientID;   // Setting structure data
```

Either form is a simple rvalue-to-rvalue assignment statement.

The Dot Operator

Notice that a period separates the structure name from the member's variable name. The period is called the *dot operator* and is used to denote accessing a member of the structure. You've studied the dot operator before when we talked about using the *Serial* object to print something in the *Serial* monitor using *Serial.print()*.

It may be useful for you to visualize a structure as a black box with a name on it. The name on the black box is the structure variable's name, like *myServicePeople*. Hidden inside the black box are the members of that structure. You cannot "see" those members because they are hidden from view by the black box structure itself. (Visually, think of the braces as creating a black box that surrounds the structure members.) However, there is a door in the black box. Think of the dot operator as the key that opens the door into the black box. Once you use the key (i.e., the dot operator), you have access to the members in the black box. Once inside the structure, all you need to do is specify the member you wish to use.

As shown earlier, if you are using the dot operator on the right side of the assignment operator, as in

```
clientID = myServicePeople.ID;   // Retrieving structure data
```

you are using the dot operator to fetch the data (i.e., its rvalue) of a particular member of the structure (i.e., *ID*) and then copy that data into the variable on the left side of the assignment operator (i.e., *clientID*). This also means that the state of the *myServicePeople* structure is unchanged after the statement is executed.

However, if the dot operator appears on the left side of the assignment operator, as in

```
myServicePeople.ID = clientID;  // Setting structure data
```

then the rvalue of *clientID* is copied into member *ID*'s rvalue of *myServicePeople* structure. Therefore, the state of *myServicePeople* is changed by the assignment statement because the rvalue of the *ID* member of the structure is changed.

Let's write a short program that uses structures and the dot operator. The code is shown in Listing 10-1.

Listing 10-1. Using the Dot Operator

```
/*
  Purpose: To show the use of the dot operator

  Dr. Purdum, December 21, 2014
*/

struct servicePeople {
  int ID;
  char Name[20];
  char PW[10];
  long Phone;
} myServicePeople, yourServicePeople;

void setup() {
  Serial.begin(9600);
  Serial.print("myServicePeople lvalue: ");
  Serial.print((int) &myServicePeople);
  Serial.print("  yourServicePeople lvalue: ");
  Serial.println((int) &yourServicePeople);

  yourServicePeople.ID = 205;                    // An assignment ...

  Serial.print("myServicePeople.ID rvalue: ");
  Serial.print(myServicePeople.ID);
  Serial.print("  yourServicePeople.ID rvalue: ");
  Serial.println(yourServicePeople.ID);

  myServicePeople = yourServicePeople;           // Copy entire structure

  Serial.println("\nAfter assignment:\n");
  Serial.print("myServicePeople.ID rvalue: ");
  Serial.print(myServicePeople.ID);
  Serial.print("  yourServicePeople.ID rvalue: ");
  Serial.println(yourServicePeople.ID);
  Serial.print("A servicePerson structure takes ");
  Serial.print(sizeof(servicePeople));
  Serial.println(" bytes of storage.");
}

void loop(){}
```

The code doesn't do much other than define two *servicePeople* structure variables named *myServicePeople* and *yourServicePeople*. The program uses several *Serial.print()* function calls to present information about the structure variables.

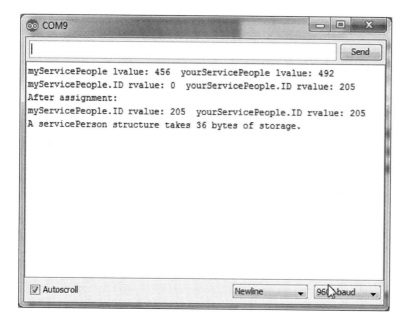

Figure 10-3. *Program output from Listing 10-1*

Escape Sequences

Note the statement in Listing 10-1:

```
Serial.println("\nAfter assignment:\n");
```

We haven't used this technique before, but it's worth knowing. The '\n' is called the *newline character* and causes the display device to advance to the next line. You could just add a couple of empty *Serial.println()* calls and do the same thing, but the use of the newline character is a little more efficient. If you look at the program output in Figure 10-3, you can see that we have an empty line before and after the string constant "After assignment:". The reason is because of the newline character. The reason for the backslash character (\) before the n is to inform the compiler that this is a special character and not the plain-old character n. If you leave the slash out, the string would look like "nAfter assignment:". This behavior applies to all of the sequences presented in Table 10-1.

Table 10-1 presents several escape sequences you may find useful.

Table 10-1. *ASCII Escape Sequences*

Escape Sequence	ASCII Value	Description
\a	7	Alarm, bell, buzzer
\b	8	Backspace
\f	12	Form feed
\n	10	Newline, line feed
\r	13	Carriage return
\t	9	Horizontal tab
\v	11	Vertical tab
\\	92	Backslash
\'	39	Single quote mark
\"	34	Double quote mark

Some escape sequences are rarely used on an Arduino (e.g., \v), but are presented for the sake of completeness. I urge you to write a simple program with a single string in it, try some of these escape sequences within the string, and see what they do on your *Serial* monitor.

Memory Requirements for a Structure

If you look closely at Figure 10-3, you can see that *myServicePeople* is stored at memory address 494 and *yourServicePeople* has an lvalue of 458. Hmm … 2 bytes for *ID*, 20 bytes for *Name*, 10 bytes for *PW*, and 4 bytes for *Phone* equals 36 (= 2 + 20 + 10 + 4). You can verify this by looking at the last line in Figure 10-3. Clearly, the lvalue for *myServicePeople* plus the structure storage requirement of 36 bytes equals the lvalue for *yourServicePeople* (494 = 458 + 36). Therefore, we know these two structure variables are stored back-to-back in flash memory. (This is an interesting fact, but I wouldn't always bet the farm on the compiler doing back-to-back memory allocations.)

The second line in Figure 10-3 shows that *myServicePeople.ID* has a value of 0, whereas *myServicePeople.ID* has the value of 205. This is exactly as it should be since the value 205 was assigned into the *ID* member of *yourServicePeople*.

The statement

```
myServicePeople = yourServicePeople;   // Copy the entire structure
```

copies the entire contents of the *yourServicePeople* structure variable into *myServicePeople*. By leaving out the dot operator that would pick a single member, this assignment copies the entire structure in a single statement. Because the compiler knows that each *servicePeople* variable uses 36 bytes of memory for storage, the compiler simply copies 36 bytes of data starting at memory address 458 (the lvalue of *yourServicePeople*) to memory address 494 (the lvalue of *myServicePeople*). As a result, the two structure variables now have the same rvalues for each of the structure members. The program displays the rvalues for the *ID* members for both variables on the next line of output. The last line in Figure 10-3 confirms that each structure variable requires 36 bytes of storage.

The code shows that although you could perform an assignment statement for each member of the two structures using the dot operator, it is much easier to simply copy the entire structure with an assignment statement.

Returning a Structure from a Function Call

Suppose you need to return a structure from a function call. How is that done? Listing 10-2 is almost identical to Listing 10-1 except for the lines marked with comments:

Listing 10-2. Modified Dot Operator Example

```
/*
  Purpose: To show the use of the dot operator

  Dr. Purdum, December 21, 2014
*/

struct servicePeople {
  int ID;
  char Name[20];
  char PW[10];
  long Phone;
} myServicePeople, yourServicePeople;

struct servicePeople SetPhoneNumber(struct servicePeople temp);   // New

void setup() {
  Serial.begin(9600);
  Serial.print("myServicePeople lvalue: ");
  Serial.print((int) &myServicePeople);
  Serial.print("  yourServicePeople lvalue: ");
  Serial.println((int) &yourServicePeople);
  yourServicePeople.ID = 205;
  Serial.print("myServicePeople.ID rvalue: ");
  Serial.print(myServicePeople.ID);
  Serial.print("  yourServicePeople.ID rvalue: ");
  Serial.println(yourServicePeople.ID);
  myServicePeople = SetPhoneNumber(yourServicePeople);   // Changed
  Serial.println("\nAfter assignment:\n");
  Serial.print("myServicePeople.ID rvalue: ");
  Serial.print(myServicePeople.ID);
  Serial.print("  yourServicePeople.ID rvalue: ");
  Serial.println(yourServicePeople.ID);
  Serial.print("A servicePerson structure takes ");
  Serial.print(sizeof(servicePeople));
  Serial.println(" bytes of storage.");
  Serial.print("myServicePeople.Phone rvalue: ");      // New
  Serial.print(myServicePeople.Phone);                 // New
}
void loop(){

}
// All lines below are new
struct servicePeople SetPhoneNumber(struct servicePeople temp)
{
  temp.Phone = 2345678;
  return temp;
}
```

The first new line is a function declaration at the top of the program. This is necessary for the compiler to know what *SetPhoneNumber()* takes for parameters and what its return value is. That is, the statement is a function prototype declaration that can be used for type checking. The next new line appears toward the middle of the listing and it is marked by the comment "Changed". In the following statement, the structure variable *yourServicePeople* is passed to the function:

```
myServicePeople = SetPhoneNumber(yourServicePeople);          // Changed
```

As you can see in Listing 10-2, the code for the new function sets the phone number for *temp* to 2345678. The code returns *temp* to the caller, which assigns the value of the structure into *myServicePeople*. The two new statements at the bottom of the *setup()* loop display the new phone number that has been copied into *myServicePeople.Phone*. Indeed, every member of the *myServicePeople* variable is the same as the *myServicePeople* variable ... sort of.

After the call to *SetPhoneNumber()*, you can see from the print statements that *myServicePeople.Phone* has been changed. But what about *yourServicePeople.Phone*? If you add a few more print statements, you will discover that *yourServicePeople.Phone* is 0. Why is that?

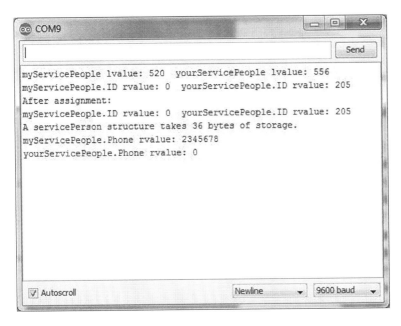

Figure 10-4. Returning a structure program output

Remember from our pointer discussions that, unless told to do otherwise, any value type that is passed to a function is a copy of that variable sent to the function, not the lvalue of the variable. Because a copy is sent, there is no way for the function to permanently alter the rvalue of the variable being passed. This conclusion holds for structures, too. The conclusion is always the same: functions cannot change the variables passed to it unless they have the variable's lvalue.

Structures can also be used to simplify passing arguments to functions. For example, perhaps a function needs to use the data stored in four sensors to decide whether to add a chemical to a vat. The signature for the function might be:

```
int AddChemical(int sensor1, int sensor2, int sensor3, int sensor4);
```

Instead, you could define a structure

```
struct sensors {
    int sensor1;
    int sensor2;
    int sensor3;
    int sensor4;
} vatSensors;
```

and then call the function using:

```
AddChemical(vatSensors);
```

This makes the function call a little less wordy. Also, if you later discover that some additional parameter needs to be added to the function call, it's pretty easy to change the structure declaration to add the new parameter. All of the calls to the function that use that structure could remain unchanged.

What if you need the function to permanently alter the value of *yourServicePeople.Phone*? That's the subject of the next section.

Using Structure Pointers

The old K&R (Kernighan and Ritchie, co-authors of the original book on C) version of C did not allow you to pass a structure to a function like you did in the last example. K&R C forced you to use a pointer to the structure when passing structures to functions. That limitation was removed with the adoption of the ANSI C standard (X3J11). When you passed the structure to the *SetPhoneNumber()* function in Listing 10-2, you used 38 bytes of stack space (36 for the structure and 2 for the return address) to do it. If you used a pointer, you could perform the same operation using only 4 bytes of stack space (2 for the pointer and 2 for the return address) and you could remove the assignment statement upon return from the function. Listing 10-3 is the same as Listing 10-2, except structure pointers are used.

Listing 10-3. Using a Pointer to Structure

```
/*
  Purpose: To show the use of pointers to structures

  Dr. Purdum, December 21, 2014
*/

struct servicePeople {
  int ID;
  char Name[20];
  char PW[10];
  long Phone;
} myServicePeople, yourServicePeople;

void SetPhoneNumber(struct servicePeople *temp);      // New signature declaration

void setup() {
  Serial.begin(9600);
  Serial.print("myServicePeople lvalue: ");
  Serial.print((int) &myServicePeople);
```

```
  Serial.print("  yourServicePeople lvalue: ");
  Serial.println((int) &yourServicePeople);
  yourServicePeople.ID = 205;
  Serial.print("myServicePeople.ID rvalue: ");
  Serial.print(myServicePeople.ID);
  Serial.print("  yourServicePeople.ID rvalue: ");
  Serial.println(yourServicePeople.ID);
  SetPhoneNumber(& myServicePeople);                        // Pass the lvalue
  Serial.println("After assignment:");
  Serial.print("myServicePeople.ID rvalue: ");
  Serial.print(myServicePeople.ID);
  Serial.print("  yourServicePeople.ID rvalue: ");
  Serial.println(yourServicePeople.ID);
  Serial.print("A servicePerson structure takes ");
  Serial.print(sizeof(servicePeople));
  Serial.println(" bytes of storage.");
  Serial.print("myServicePeople.Phone rvalue: ");          // New
  Serial.println(myServicePeople.Phone);                   // New
  Serial.print("yourServicePeople.Phone rvalue: ");
  Serial.println(yourServicePeople.Phone);
}
void loop(){
}

// Lines below are changed
void SetPhoneNumber(struct servicePeople *temp)            // Note pointer now used
{
  (*temp).Phone = 2345678;
}
```

Figure 10-5 shows a sample run of the program.

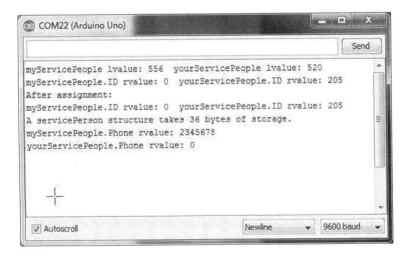

Figure 10-5. *Using pointer to structure*

There are a few minor changes between Listing 10-2 and 10-3. First, near the top of the listing the declaration for the *SetPhoneNumber()* is changed to reflect that the function now returns nothing (*void*) and that a pointer to structure is the parameter. Second, about midway in the listing you can see the call to the function has been changed to:

```
SetPhoneNumber(&myServicePeople);                    // Pass the lvalue
```

In the previous version, the return from the *SetPhoneNumber()* function call assigned the structure into *myServicePeople*. The code is now using a pointer to a structure as the argument, so you use the address-of operator (&) to pass the lvalue of *myServicePeople* to the function instead. Because the function now has direct access to *myServicePeople*, there is no need to return a structure from the function call and make the assignment into *myServicePeople* as there was in Listing 10-2.

The parameter passed to *SetPhoneNumber()* has been changed to a pointer

```
void SetPhoneNumber(struct servicePeople *temp)
```

which means that *temp* is a pointer to the *myServicePeople* structure.

The statement

```
(*temp).Phone = 2345678;
```

looks a little strange and needs some explanation. Because the dot operator has a higher precedence level than the indirection operator, you need to surround the indirection operator on *temp* with parentheses. The parentheses cause the compiler to fetch the lvalue of the *Phone* member of the structure and assign 2345678 into that address. This means that the statement changes the rvalue of *Phone* to 2345678. This is exactly what you want to do.

If you didn't use the parentheses to surround *temp*

```
*temp.Phone = 2345678;   // Wrong!
```

would instruct the compiler to fetch the rvalue of *Phone* and use it as an lvalue. Because the rvalue of Phone is 0, this would try to write 2345678 at memory address 0. This is another train wreck waiting to happen because Listing 10-5 tells you that the *myServicePeople* structure resides at memory address 558. A little quick math suggests that the *Phone* member of the structure can be found at memory address 590, not 0. Using an rvalue as an lvalue and writing data to an unknown memory address is almost never a good idea. Fortunately, the compiler catches this error if you tried to misuse the *temp* pointer.

The syntax used to access a structure member via a pointer is so common in C, a special operator was developed to simplify the statement from:

```
(*temp).Phone = 2345678;
```

to use the dereference operator (→) instead:

```
temp→Phone = 2345678;
```

The result is the same as the earlier version that used the parentheses and asterisk to change the phone number. You will likely see this shorter version more often.

Initializing a Structure

If you wish, you can initialize a structure variable at its point of definition, as in:

```
servicePeople myServicePeople = {
  101,                    // ID number
  "Kack's Lawn Service",  // Company name
  "Clowder",              // Password
  2345678,                // Phone number
};
```

The initialize value for each member is separated from the next by the comma operator. The preceding statements would cause the *myServicePeople* to be initialized with the values shown. Note that this form of initialization requires that the values align with the member definitions. This initialization obviously assumes that you have defined the *servicePeople* structure before the initialization statement block occurs in the code.

▓ **Note** By the way, while I was writing this section, I cut and paste the preceding definition from my word processing program into the Arduino IDE editor and compiled the program. I got an error message stating: "error: stray '\' in program". I'd be embarrassed to tell you how long it took me to overcome this forest-for-the-trees problem. As it turns out, if you paste quote marks from a text editor into the Arduino IDE source code window, it keeps the "left-leaning" and "right-leaning" double quote marks. However, if you erase those quotation marks and redo them inside the Arduino editor, the double quote marks are replaced with "vertical" quote marks and the quoted string changes color from black to light blue. The program then compiled without error. It was one of those old-dog-new-tricks thingies that ultimately led to a flat forehead moment....

Arrays of Structures

As you might guess, real life likely would have more than one service company tending to a home. It's not uncommon to have a pool company, a lawn company, a landscape company, and an "indoor" service company pay visits to a home. Clearly, an array of structures would be useful, since each element of the array could hold one service company.

Assuming the code has already declared the *servicePeople* structure, you could define an array of *servicePeople* as:

```
struct servicePeople myCompanies[10];
```

This would define an array named *myCompanies[]* that is capable of storing the necessary data for 10 *servicePeople* companies. If you want to assign the *ID* number 222 to the fifth company in the array, the statement is

```
myCompanies[4].ID  = 222;
```

would change the rvalue of *ID* for the fifth person in the *myCompanies[]* array. (Arrays are zero-based, right?)

After the array is defined, you can use regular assignment statements to set the values for the different elements of the array. However, if you wanted to initialize part of the array when it is defined, you might use:

```
struct servicePeople myCompanies[10] = {
    {1, "This is a dummy","admin", 5555555},
    {101, "Kacks Lawn Service", "Clowder", 2345678}
};
```

This code would initialize the first two elements of the array. (Strictly speaking, the *struct* keyword is not required in the preceding statement since the structure tag *servicePeople* identifies the structure provided you have declared the structure earlier in the program. However, the keyword does document that the code is using a structure.) The remainder of the array would have zero or *null* values stored for the rvalues of their members.

By the way, the data in this structure is likely not to change very often. Because the data are fairly stable, you could store the structure data in EEPROM memory, thus saving a few precious bytes of SRAM. More on this later in the chapter.

Unions

A *union* is a small chunk of memory that is set aside to hold differing data types. A *union* acts like a small buffer that is capable of holding a predefined type of data. For example, suppose you have a program that reads data from a series of different sensors. Some sensors return a *char*, others an *int*, whereas some return a *float* data type. Clearly, you could define temporary working variables, such as

```
char  tempChar;     // 1 bytes
int   tempInt;      // 2 bytes
float tempFloat;    // 4 bytes
```

and then assign the sensor readings into the appropriate variable. This approach uses 7 bytes of memory.
You could also use the following *union*:

```
union {
    char  tempChar;
    int   tempInt;
    float tempFloat;
} sensorReading;
```

You can also use a *union tag* in much the same manner that you did with structures. You could use

```
union sensorSystem {
    char  tempChar;
    int   tempInt;
    float tempFloat;
};
sensorSystem sensorReading;
```

which uses the *union* tag name *sensorSystem* to define the *union* type variable named *sensorReading*.
The *union* defined as *sensorReading* is big enough to hold any *one* of the three sensor types, *but only one at a time*. In other words, you can place a *float* into the *union* and then read it back, or you can place a *char* into the union and then read it back, or you can place an *int* into the *union* and then read it back, *BUT not*

all three at once! So, how much memory does *sensorReading* use? It uses 4 bytes rather than 7 like a structure would. Now, put the book down, leave the room, find a friend, and explain to them *why* this *union* only uses 4 bytes of memory. If you can do that, you already understand how a *union* works. If not, read on....

So, how do you use a *union*? For example, to place a *float* into the *union* and then read it back, you might use:

```
float currentFloatSensorReading = 51.25;
sensorReading.tempFloat = currentFloatSensorReading;     // move float into union
// some more code ...
currentFloatSensorReading = sensorReading.tempFloat;       // fetch int from union
```

Note how the dot operator is used to reference the appropriate union member. The dot operator works much the same as it did for structures. If you wish to read an *int* from the union, the statement might be:

```
currentIntSensorReading = sensorReading.tempInt;
```

The *union*, however, works differently that a structure. With a structure, the dot operator was followed by the structure <u>member</u> you wish to extract from the structure. With a *union*, the *dot operator separates you from the union member that tells you <u>how many bytes</u> to extract from the union*. This means you can do some really stupid stuff with a *union*. For example, consider:

```
float currentFloatSensorReading = 51.25;
sensorReading.tempFloat = currentFloatSensorReading;   // float into union
// some more code ...
currentFloatSensorReading = sensorReading.tempInt ;    // int from union
```

In this example, you put in a *float* value, but later extract the contents of the union as though it were an *int*. You are literally taking out "half a *float*" and thinking it's going to work as an *int*. Best case is that this causes a spectacular failure, making it easy to debug. Worst case is the value extracted from the *union* might be formed such that the value seems reasonable. The lesson is simple:

Whatever you put into the union should match what you take out of the union. It's your responsibility to keep track of things.

The advantage of a *union* is that you can move different types of data into and out of a single *union* variable. Also, the *union* only uses 4 bytes of memory whereas the discrete variables of a *struct* would use 7 bytes of memory. (A *union* is always allocated just enough memory to hold the largest data item that is a member of the *union*. Drawing on our Bucket Analogy, the compiler looks at all of the buckets associated with the *union*, grabs the biggest one, and that becomes the *union*'s bucket for all its members.) That's the good news. As mentioned earlier, the bad news is that the compiler assumes you are keeping track of what is currently in the *union*. Just remember, apples in, oranges out, almost always leads to unwanted surprises when you are using *union*s.

EEPROM Memory

In the previous sections of this chapter, you've discussed how to organize service company data into a *struct*. You then learned how to store that data in an array of structures. However, it doesn't do a whole lot of good if the company data disappears each time the power is removed from the μc board, either on purpose or by accident. In this section, you will learn one way to persist such data even if power is lost.

As you learned from Table 1-1, each Atmel-compatible μc board has a specific amount of flash, SRAM, and EEPROM memory available. Both the flash and EEPROM memory are nonvolatile, which means those types of memory do not lose their data when power is removed. You have also learned that data with global scope are allocated in SRAM memory with any initialized values copied from flash memory to SRAM. However, temporary data, like that we see passed as function arguments, are also chewing up SRAM space.

More bad news is that global data can be contaminated more easily than data with a more restrictive scope level (e.g., function scope). Because every element in the program has access to global data, it can be difficult to isolate the section of code that is contaminating the data. If you move the data inside a function body, scope is now limited, but the data are now allocated on the stack. Because there is less SRAM than flash memory and because SRAM is volatile memory, the array is not persisted when power is lost. One way to address this problem is to start using EEPROM memory.

Up to this point, our sample programs have not used EEPROM memory. It's not that we've avoided the stash of EEPROM memory. Rather, our programs have been so simple that we've never impinged on the memory limits so there was no need to use it. Also, we have kind of avoided using it because EEPROM memory is relatively slow.

Usually, EEPROM memory is used to store configuration data. The configuration data could be anything from terminal baud rates for I/O communications to data that is required to initialize program sensors. As I pointed out before, EEPROM has a finite number of erase/write cycles in which the EEPROM can reliably erase and write data. Although a million such cycles may be possible, most developers assume EEPROM develops a mind of its own after approximately 100,000 cycles. While that may sound like a lot of cycles, if you update a variable that is stored in EEPROM once every second, the program runs the chance of getting flaky in less than two days. Still, if the data is rarely changed, as is likely the case with our *servicePerson* array, EEPROM memory may be a viable alternative.

Using EEPROM

The Arduino IDE comes with an EEPROM library, which you can find in the Libraries directory where you installed your Arduino software. You should spend a little time reading up on the EEPROM library and its example code.

Data Logging

In the following discussion, our comments are directed to the "on board" EEPROM, and not any external EEPROM that may be sitting on a shield or other external device. EEPROM memory is not an optimal choice for data logging for several reasons. First, because EEPROM is fairly slow, it may not be able to keep up with whatever device is feeding it data. Second, data logging is usually a sequential process. This means maintaining a pointer to where the next byte of logged data it to be written. If this pointer is maintained in the EEPROM memory space, it can become unreliable because it may need to be updated (i.e., an erase/write cycle) fairly frequently. Also, the amount of EEPROM data is usually quite limited and there just may not be enough storage to be useful. Finally, EEPROM memory behaves like a *ring buffer*. That is, if your board has 512 bytes of EEPROM and you try to write to address 512 in EEPROM memory, it simply "wraps around" to EEPROM address 0 and writes the data. (The valid EEPROM addresses are 0 through 511, right?) Clearly, if you need whatever was stored at address 0, you have a problem. Because of these limitations, data logging programs frequently use an external device for storage of logging data.

For the moment, however, assume you have a very limited data set to preserve and you think EEPROM might be a good place to store it for now. Let's see how that might work. Instead of presenting a single long code listing, we are going to break it down so we can keep the relevant code visible while discussing that code. Also, the example is contrived because we start out with the data stored in SRAM memory and then move it to EEPROM memory. Clearly, this doesn't help solve a memory limitation problem. However, the example does show you a number of things you need to address when you use EEPROM memory.

Our design is to save the information on ten service companies that I mentioned earlier in this chapter. We want to keep information in the *servicePeople* structure, but store it in EEPROM. Listing 10-4 shows the global data definitions and declarations, the *setup()* loop code.

The first statement in Listing 10-4 is a *#include* preprocessor directive to read in the *EEPROM.h* header file. This file contains information the compiler needs to properly work with the EEPROM library. The *#define DEBUG* preprocessor directive is used to toggle debug print statements into and out of the code. You can see examples of this in the *setup()* loop. For example, the statements

```
#ifdef DEBUG
  Serial.print("EepromMax = ");
  Serial.println(eepromMax);
#endif
```

cause the *Serial.print()* statements to appear in the program only if *DEBUG* is defined for the program. (We have already covered the use of DEBUG.) Because the code does have a *#define DEBUG 1* preprocessor directive at the top of Listing 10-4, the print statements are compiled into the program. Recall that, if you comment out the *#define* DEBUG 1 directive, *DEBUG* is no longer defined and the *Serial.print()* statements are omitted from the program. Such code is commonly called *scaffold code*, because it is "toggled out" of the program after debugging is completed, much like scaffolding is removed once a building is finished.

Listing 10-4. The setup() Loop Code

```
/*
 Purpose: To write data to EEPROM memory.

 Dr. Purdum, December 22, 2014
 */
#include <EEPROM.h>
#define DEBUG 1          // We want to see debug print statements
                         // Comment out to avoid seeing print statements


const int MAXPEOPLE = 10;
struct servicePeople {  // Structure definition for servicePeople
  int ID;
  char Name[20];
  char PW[10];
  long Phone;
};

union servicePeopleUnion {              // A union definition for myUnion
  byte temp[sizeof(int)];
  int testID;
  struct servicePeople testServicePeople;
} myUnion;

servicePeople myPeople[MAXPEOPLE] = {    // company data for testing
  {0, "This is a dummy","admin",5555555},
  {101,"Kack Lawn Service","Clowder",2345678},
  {222,"Jane's Plants","Noah",4202513},
  {333,"Terrys Pool Service","Billings",4301016}
};
// function declarations:
void DataDump(struct servicePeople temp);
int FindEepromTop();
int ReadIntFlag();
```

```
void ReadOneRecord(int index);
void WriteFirstRecord();
void WriteOneRecord(int index);

int loopCounter = 0;          // Number of passes to make through loop
int initFlag = 0;             // Has the EEPROM been initialized?
struct servicePeople temp;    // A temporary structure

void setup()
{
  int eepromMax;
  int i;

  Serial.begin(9600);
  eepromMax = FindEepromTop();          // How much EEPROM?
#ifdef DEBUG
  Serial.print("EepromMax = ");
  Serial.println(eepromMax);
#endif
  initFlag = ReadIntFlag();  // Initialized?
  if (initFlag == 0) {
    for (i = 0; i < MAXPEOPLE; i++) {
        WriteOneRecord(i);
    }
  }
  initFlag = 1;  // Either way, EEPROM is initialized by now
}
```

▧ **Note** When you first get your Arduino board, the EEPROM is in a "fresh from the factory" condition. What this usually means is that all of the EEPROM memory bytes are initialized to 0xFF. Reading two of these bytes back to back gives 0xFFFF, which is –1 when those 2 bytes are read as an *int*. However, this is some RDC on my part, as I assumed that everyone was using an Arduino board that had never done anything with the EEPROM memory. To fix this, I added one line to *setup()*, immediately after the call to *ReadIntFlag()*. The code looks like this:

```
initFlag = ReadIntFlag();
// initFlag = -1;      // Remove comment at beginning of this
                       // line first time you run program.
if (initFlag < 0) {
  // Rest of code unchanged
```

By setting *initFlag* to –1, you force the code to initialize the EEPROM memory with the test values in the program. Once you have run the program, you can "recomment" the line back to the way it was.

Next, the code defines a *const* integer named *MAXPEOPLE* that is used to set the limit for the number of companies you will allow. You could use a *#define* instead, but this gives you an actual variable to work with if you wish. That is followed by a structure declaration for *servicePeople* and a *union* with a *union* tag of *servicePeopleUnion*. Although we don't really make much use of this *union*, it will at least let you see how a *union* is used.

The code then defines a *myPeople[]* array of *servicePeople* and initializes the array with four records. The first record is bogus. The sole purpose of this element of the array is to determine whether or not the array has been copied into EEPROM memory. If the *ID* member is 0, that means the array has not yet been copied into EEPROM memory. Actually, it is a good idea to copy the array into EEPROM regardless, since the code is within the *setup()* loop and hence actually part of the Initialization Step anyway. In fact, you could use the other three members of this element of the array for other purposes, as long as you are consistent with the data type of the member.

After the array is initialized, several function declarations are presented followed by definitions for several global variables. The code then finds the *setup()* loop. The first thing done is find the maximum amount of EEPROM memory that is available for the board. True, you know what this is for your board, but what if you change boards later? The code for the *FindEepromTop()* is presented in Listing 10-5. The code takes advantage of the fact that the amount of available EEPROM memory is held in an Arduino symbolic constant named *E2END*, and represents the largest valid address in EEPROM memory for the board being used. Adding 1 to that value returns the amount of EEPROM available.

Listing 10-5. Source Code for FindEepromTop()

```
/*****
  Purpose: Find out how much EEPROM this board has. I

  Parameter list:
    void

  Return value:
    int          the EEPROM size
*****/
int FindEepromTop()
{
   return E2END + 1;
}
```

If you try to write to an EEPROM address that is higher than the EEPROM that's available, the address pointer to the EEPROM wraps back to address 0. This can be a tricky bug to track if you don't realize what's happening. The reason is because, if you only have 512 bytes of EEPROM, the valid addresses are 0 through 511. Trying to write to address 512 "wraps around" back to the first memory address. There is no obvious indication that something went wrong. The EEPROM memory space, therefore, behaves as though it is a ring buffer.

Next, the code reads the first bytes of memory to see if the array has been copied to EEPROM. The code for the *ReadIntFlag()* is presented in Listing 10-6.

Listing 10-6. Source Code for ReadIntFlag()

```
/*****
  Purpose: This function reads the int-sized bytes of EEPROM and
          returns the integer found there.

  Parameter list:
    void

  Return value:
    int          0 if no records in EEPROM, 1 if there are
*****/
```

```
int ReadIntFlag()
{
  int i;

  for (i = 0; i < sizeof(int); i++) {
    myUnion.temp[i] = EEPROM.read(i);
  }
  return myUnion.testID;
}
```

The *ReadIntFlag()* shows how simple it is to read EEPROM memory. The EEPROM library that is distributed with the Arduino IDE only has two EEPROM functions: *read()* and *write()*, although the examples for the library also show how to clear EEPROM memory. (Coupled with the *FindEepromTop()* function presented in Listing 10-5, a *ClearEprom()* function could easily be added to the library.)

The *ReadIntFlag()* function is written so it works with differently sized *int* data types. The Diligent chipMax CPU, for example, uses a 4-byte *int*, whereas most Arduino boards are currently 2-byte *int*s. By using *sizeof(int)* to control the *for* loop, the code reads the necessary number of bytes to form an *int* into the *union*'s *temp[]* array for the board being used. (Note that we defined the *myUnion.temp[]* array using the same type of *sizeof(int)* expression.) Therefore, the *ReadIntFlag()* reads the proper number of bytes into the array regardless of the board you are using. When the *for* loop ends, the *temp[]* array *union* member holds the data needed to form an *int*. But here's the cool part: because *myUnion* can also hold an *int*, we use the statement

```
return myUnion.testID;
```

to return the *int* to the caller. This works because of the way a union works, as explained earlier. Treating those individual bytes simply as array elements rather than a specific data type allows us to abstract from the LittleEndian/BigEndian problem, which is a can of worms we don't need to discuss here. (If you wish to explore this issue further, simply Google endian problem.) Suffice it to say this approach is a good way to extract an *int* from EEPROM.

If *ReadIntFlag()* returns 0, you know that the *myPeople[]* structure array has not been read into EEPROM memory. As you can see in Listing 10-4, the code does return a value from the *ReadIntFlag()* function call. The *if* test avoids copying the data into EEPROM memory (perhaps for a second time). The code in Listing 10-4 simply copies the array to EEPROM via the call to *WriteOneRecord()*. The code for that function appears in Listing 10-7.

Listing 10-7. Source Code for WriteOneRecord()

```
/*****
  Purpose: This function writes one record from the myPeople[] array
           to EEPROM

  Parameter list:
    int index      The element of the myPeople[] array to write

  Return value:
    void
*****/
```

```
void WriteOneRecord(int index)
{
  byte *b;
  int i;
  int offset = index * sizeof(servicePeople);

  b = (byte *) &myPeople[index];    // Going to write this record
  for (i = 0; i < sizeof(servicePeople); i++) {
    EEPROM.write(i + offset, *b++);
  }
}
```

The *WriteOneRecord()* shows how to use the EEPROM *write()* function. The function accepts an index into the *myPeople[]* array as the only parameter to the function. The *byte* pointer, *b*, is initialized to point to the lvalue where this element of the *myPeople[]* array exists in SRAM memory. It does this by using the address-of operator. The variable *offset* is necessary to calculate the lvalue of where this particular element into which the *myPeople[]* array should be copied in EEPROM memory. The call to *EEPROM.write()* then writes each byte of the array element to EEPROM memory. The *expression2* of the *for* loop dictates how many bytes are written. The *sizeof(servicePeople)* expression, therefore, ensures that only 36 bytes are written to EEPROM memory. The call to *WriteOneRecord()* is called *MAXPEOPLE* times (i.e., 10) even though only the first four elements contain any useful data. Notice how *offset* makes sure the new data are copied to the correct lvalue in the EEPROM memory space. If this isn't clear, keep studying the code until it is. Take time to calculate the value for *offset* and it should make sense to you.

After the *for* loop finishes copying the data to the EEPROM memory space, the program falls into the *loop()* function for further processing. The code for the *loop()* function is shown in Listing 10-8. The first statement in the function defines and sets the *eepromIndex* variable to 1. This is done because you know the first record contains no useful information. Therefore, you are only interested in what follows the first record in the *myPeople[]* array.

Listing 10-8. Source Code for the loop() Function

```
void loo3p()
{
  static int eepromIndex = 1;   // Assume there are records

  loopCounter++;
  if (initFlag > 0) {  // There are records to read
    ReadOneRecord(eepromIndex++);
    if (myUnion.testServicePeople.ID != 0) { // Read some real data
      DataDump(myUnion.testServicePeople);
    }
  } else {
    eepromIndex++;        // Make sure loop can end with no records.
  }

#ifdef DEBUG
  Serial.println("==========");
#endif
  if (eepromIndex == MAXPEOPLE) {
    while(1);     // Just spin around here forever...
  }
}
```

There's not a whole lot going on in the *loop()* function. The variable *initFlag* tests to see if the data have been copied to the EEPROM memory space. Because this is the case, the program calls *ReadOneRecord (eepromIndex)* to read a record from EEPROM. The code for *ReadOneRecord()* is presented in Listing 10-9.

Listing 10-9. Source Code for ReadOneRecord()

```
/*****
   Purpose: This function reads one servicePerson record from
            EEPROM

   Parameter list:
      int index     The element of the myPerson[] array to read
                    from EEPROM

   Return value:
      void
*****/
void ReadOneRecord(int index)
{
  byte *bPtr;
  int i;
  int offset;

  offset = index * sizeof(servicePeople);      // must offset from 0 in EEPROM

  bPtr = (byte *) &myUnion.testServicePeople;  // where to put the data read

  for (i = 0; i < sizeof(temp); i++) {         // Loop through the bytes...
    *bPtr = EEPROM.read(offset + i);
    bPtr++;
  }
}
```

The code is very similar to Listing 10-7, only this time you are reading rather than writing, the data. Variable *offset* is necessary to place the byte pointer, *bPtr*, at the correct lvalue in the EEPROM memory space. Once *bPtr* is properly set, the code reads *sizeof(servicePerson)* bytes of data (36 bytes) from EEPROM into the *union myUnion*. Obviously, we want this data to be copied into the *servicePeople* structure of the *union*, which is why *bPtr* is set to the address of *myUnion.testServicePeople*. Notice how *offset* is used so the proper data are read.

Upon return from the call to *ReadOneRecord()*, the code checks to see if the *myUnion.testServicePeople. ID* is non-zero. If that is true, then the *DataDump()* function is called and...

Whoa! Back up the boat....

Why are there two dot operators in the statement?

```
if (myUnion.testServicePeople.ID != 0) { // Read some real data
```

Why not? This statement is a little like one of those Russian box-within-a-box-within-a-box thingies. As you know, a *union* is a data structure that is like a black box that needs a key (i.e., a dot operator) to "get inside" the *union* data structure. So, you pull that key out and open the *union* door and walk in. What do you see? First you see the *temp[]* array defined. Next, you see an *int* named *testID,* but then you see another black box named *testServicePeople.* You also know you need a different key (another dot operator) to get inside the *testServicePeople* structure. Therefore, to do anything useful with the contents of the *testServicePeople* structure means you need two sets of keys (dot operators) to get to the data that is obscured by two black boxes. This is why there are two dot operators ... you need one key to get inside the *myUnion* and a second key to examine the *testServicePeople* data structure to look at the structure member named *ID.*

There is no practical limit as to how many "boxes-within-boxes" levels can be used in a statement. Many years ago I worked with a (poorly designed) database structure that required 13 dot operations to get to the data I needed. Although this is an extreme (RDC) case, you should not go into cardiac arrest when you see a bunch of dot operators in a statement. Simply keep the black box concept in mind and pay attention to what data type you are entering with each key (dot operator) and you should have no difficulty figuring things out.

Eventually, the *DataDump()* function is called to display the data that was just read. The code is presented in Listing 10-10.

Listing 10-10. Source Code for DataDump()

```
/*****
  Purpose: Sends the data stored in parameter to the serial monitor

  Parameter list:
    struct servicePeople temp     // The data to be displayed

  Return value:
    void
*****/
void DataDump(struct servicePeople temp)
{

    Serial.println();
    Serial.print("ID = ");
    Serial.print(temp.ID);
    Serial.print("  Name = ");
    Serial.println(temp.Name);
    Serial.print("  PW = ");
    Serial.print(temp.PW);
    Serial.print("  Phone = ");
    Serial.println(temp.Phone);
}
```

As you can see, all the *DataDump()* function does is display the contents of the *myUnion. testServicePeople* structure that was just read from EEPROM memory. In a real application, the *myPeople[]* data would be used for some form of additional processing rather than just dumping to the serial device. Still, the program does show how to use EEPROM memory to store data that needs nonvolatile storage. A sample run of the program can be seen in Figure 10-6.

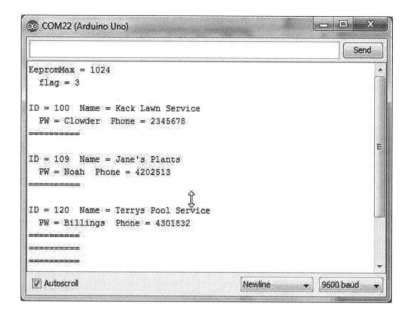

Figure 10-6. EEPROM program sample run

While EEPROM offers one way to persist data when the power is removed, the limited amount of EEPROM memory that is one your board simply may not be enough to meet your needs. If that's the case, what other options exist?

Other Storage Alternatives

There are a number of ways that you can increase the amount of data storage available for an Arduino-compatible board. Data logging, for example, is a common use for µc but an Arduino is likely going to need some help if large amounts of data are to be stored.

Shields

One inexpensive alternative is to add an EEPROM shield to your µc board. A *shield* is an additional board that can be attached to the µc board either directly plugging the shield into the Arduino board or an Arduino module connected through cabling. Several companies offer EEPROM shields that use the I2C Wire library to communicate with the main µc board. A 256K EEPROM shield can be found for less than $10. A quick search on the Internet should turn up several alternatives for you.

Another alternative is to use an SD (Secure Digital) card. Figure 10-7 shows an example. Figure 10-8 shows the same SD card inserted into the shield and the shield "stacked" onto an Arduino µc board.

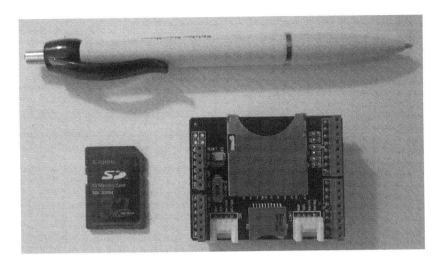

Figure 10-7. *An SD card and shield*

Figure 10-8. *Stacked SD shield and board. (Shield and μc board courtesy of Seeed Studio.)*

The stacking is made easy by vendors supplying Arduino-compatible boards where the pins align properly with the μc board. Note the header pins on the SD shield. This is done so you can stack yet another shield on top of the SD shield. These "Arduino Sandwiches" can go on as high as you want, provided you don't exceed the current limits of the Arduino. Figure 10-9 shows the pins for the SD shield shown in Figure 10-8, but from the underside of the shield. These are the pins that plug into the headers on the Arduino board.

Figure 10-9. *Pins for SD shield. (Photo courtesy of Seeed Studio.)*

Note that the pins on the SD shield pass through the board to the headers directly above the pins. This is what allows another shield to be stacked onto this shield. This makes increasing the functionality of a μc board quite easy.

The use of an SD shield increases the amount of storage available to the system significantly—into the gigabyte range. The board shown in Figures 10-8 and 10-9 supports both SD and micro SD cards and has UART, I2C, and SPI interfaces for increased flexibility. The vendor also has a format program (FAT16 or FAT32) and sample code that can be downloaded. Despite this feature set, the shield sells for less than $5. Because the SD storage medium is easily removed, subsequent processing of the data can be done on a regular PC if needed.

Whereas an SD library is shipped with the Arduino IDE, some SD vendors have boards that make use of more advanced features. Read the documentation for the SD library carefully as certain pins must be used for the library to work properly. Make sure you buy a card that is compatible with the Arduino SD library or that the vendor gives you a source for their library.

Other Uses for SD Storage

There are probably hundreds of projects you can think of that would benefit from additional storage. While additional EEPROM is one way to go, the addition of an SD shield offers the flexibility of removable storage. Figure 10-10 shows a GPS shield installed on a μc board. The wire with a "caramel" attached to it is the GPS antenna.

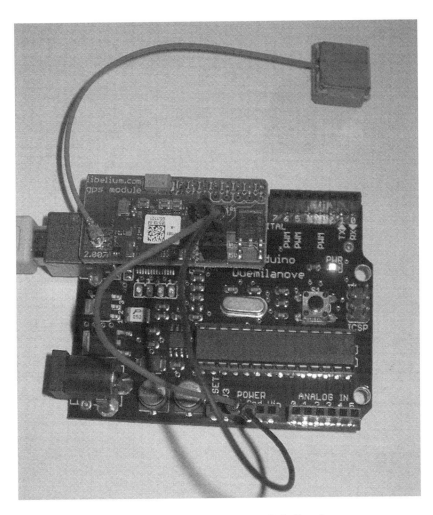

Figure 10-10. *A GPS shield. (GPS shield courtesy of Libelium.)*

It is possible to piggyback an SD shield and the GPS shield, add a 9V battery and then record the GPS data as you drive around town. Figure 10-11 shows the output using the Libelium software.

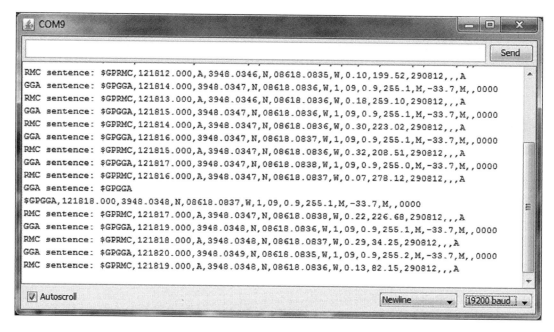

Figure 10-11. *Data from GPS shield viewed over a serial link*

There are several GPS libraries available plus new ones coming on line all the time. Again, Google is your friend and searching for the latest library is just an "Arduino GPS library" search away.

The output from that software is shown in Figure 10-12. Keep in mind that most Arduino libraries have an Examples subdirectory distributed with their libraries. These examples are a great way to learn how to use the library.

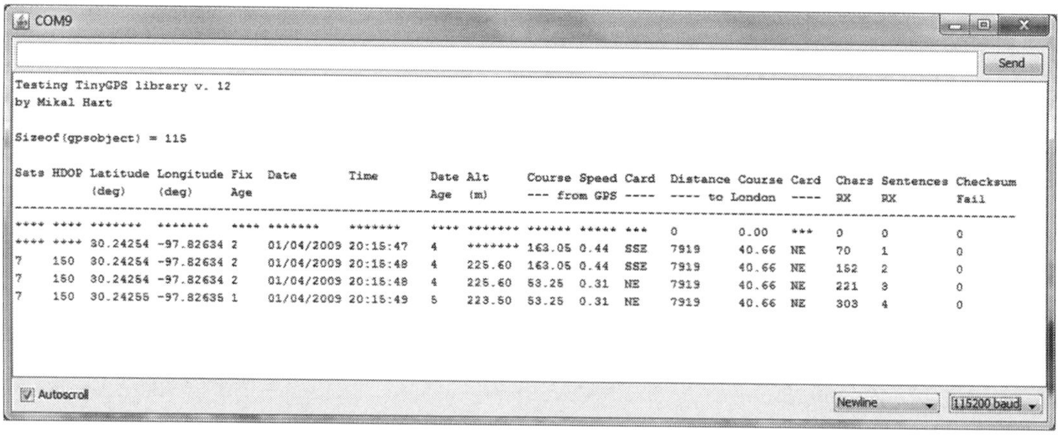

Figure 10-12. *GPS data using TinyGPS library*

Depending on the GPS sampling rate you select to write to the SD card, you can actually plot on a street map where you've been while recording the GPS data. If you ever wondered where your teenage son *really* went when he borrowed the family car, this might be your answer! A quick search on the Internet will likely produce lots of ideas for Arduino shields, including the GPS shield shown here. (More than 2 million hits occurred when I googled "Arduino GPS".

typedef

I should mention that C provides a way for you to create a new data type from existing data types. For example, in Chapter 13 we discuss interrupts and these are often associated with unsigned 8-bit variables. These 8-bit variables are tied to various Arduino pins and are collectively called a *port*. Although we could define a port as a *byte*, since a *byte* is an unsigned 8-bit data item, it would make more sense to call it a port. You can do this kind of thing with a *typedef*. The syntax would be:

```
typedef byte PORT;
PORT portC, portD;
```

Note that the *typedef* doesn't really "create" a new data type. Rather, it lets you rename the data type. *PORT* does not have to be in uppercase letters, but that is a convention that most programmers use. Also notice that the *typedef* is really a declaration in that it creates an attribute list for the "new" data type. The second statement actually defines two variables using the *typedef* attribute list for *PORT*. Proper use of *typedef*s can make your code more readable.

Another common use for a *typedef* is to use them with structures. For example, Listing 10-11 presents a short program showing how to use a *typedef*.

Listing 10-11. Using a typedef

```
typedef struct Students
{
   char name[20];
   int year;
   float gpa;
} STUDENTS;

void setup() {
  Serial.begin(115200);
  STUDENTS myClass[20];
  strcpy(myClass[0].name, "Jack Purdum");
  myClass[0].year = 3;
  myClass[0].gpa = 3.99;   // Never liked psychology

  Serial.print("Name: ");
  Serial.print(myClass[0].name);
  Serial.print("   Class: ");
  Serial.print(myClass[0].year);
  Serial.print("   gpa: ");
  Serial.println(myClass[0].gpa);
}

void loop() {
}
```

Note how the *typedef* encompasses the *struct* declaration. Also note how *Students* names the structure, whereas *STUDENTS* is the *typedef*.

Many programmers find that *typedef*s make it easier to read the code. My feeling is that it depends upon the complexity of the data's attribute list. In all honesty, I probably use *typedef*s less often than I should.

Another common use is to combine an *enum* with a *typedef*:

```
typedef enum {RESIDENTIAL = 35, STATEROAD = 55, FEDERALHIGHWAY = 70} SPEEDS;
SPEEDS myState = STATEROAD;
```

In this case, we have an *enum* list that we treat as a new data type using the *typedef* keyword with the identifier for the new data type stated at the end of the statement. This allows us to have a shorter definition of the *myState* variable. Some programmers append an underscore and a t (_t) to the end of the *typedef* identifier to make it clearer that this is a *typedef*. If you used this convention, the definition of *SPEEDS* would be written as *SPEEDS_t*. If you do prefer one style over the other, just make sure you use it consistently.

It may appear that a *typedef* is really little more than a *#define* in a different set of clothes. Well, not really. First, a *typedef* can only work within the confines of existing data types. You cannot, for example, use a *typedef* for a value. Second, a *#define* is processed by the preprocessor and involves a simple textual replacement in the source code. A *typedef* is processed by the compiler, and since it works with "real" data types, it persists after the compiler is finished.

Summary

In this chapter you learned how to organize dissimilar data using the *struct* keyword. You also saw how a *union* may be used as a small buffer space in your programs and how it may save you a few bytes of memory. You also learned how to read and write to EEPROM. Although EEPROM memory has some disadvantages, like relatively slow access and limited recycling, it is an effective way of storing configuration data or data that is not likely to change often. Finally, you saw how shields can be used to extend the functionality of a μc board, both in terms of storage (e.g., an SD shield) or features (e.g., a GPS shield). Always keep in mind that anytime you find yourself wishing the μc board had more of something (like memory) or you wish it could do some additional feature (like a little Internet searching), chances are you'll find a shield that can help solve your problem.

EXERCISES

1. In Listing 10-2, it was asserted that *yourServicePeople.Phone* was unchanged after the function call. Is this true? Prove it.

   Answer: Add these three lines to the bottom of the *setup()* loop:

   ```
   Serial.println();
   Serial.print("yourServicePeople.Phone rvalue: ");
   Serial.println(yourServicePeople.Phone);
   ```

   and recompile, upload, and run the program. You will see that the phone number member of *yourServicePeople.Phone* is unchanged and still has the value 0.

2. When discussing the section on arrays of structures, you saw the definition:

```
struct servicePeople myCompanies[10] = {
  {1, "This is a dummy","admin", 5555555},
  {101, "Kacks Lawn Service", "Clowder", 2345678}
};
```

Clearly, the *Name* member of the first element in this array suggests that the data is garbage. Why would someone "throw away" this first element?

Answer: You could use this first element to maintain a count of the number of valid elements in the array. In other words, the ID member of the first element of the array has the value 1 stored in it. This means that there is 1 company currently filled in for the array, even though the array is capable of holding 10 elements. You could access the data for the last valid data element using:

```
int index;
int validCompanyID;
index = myCompanies[0].ID;
validCompanyID = myCompanies[index].ID;
```

You can simplify this considerably by using:

```
int validCompanyID;
validCompanyID = myCompanies[myCompanies[0].ID].ID;
```

Think about it. You could also use this information to prevent a loop from reading garbage data.

3. The code in Listing 10-4 calls *WriteOneRecord()* ten times even though there are only four elements in the array that contain useful data. How could you avoid the redundant calls?

Answer: When the *myPeople[]* array is defined, 360 bytes of data (36 * *MAXPEOPLE*) are allocated to the array. Only the first 144 bytes (4 * 36) of the array contain information. Because this global data structure is defined with global scope, any uninitialized elements of the array are filled with 0s. However, EEPROM data that has never been written to is set to 0xFF (or −1 decimal). Therefore, you could modify the *for* loop in *setup()* to:

```
i = 0;
while (myPeople[i].ID != -1) {
        WriteOneRecord(i++);                 // Copy to EEPROM
}
```

4. The phone number displayed in Figure 10-6 is pretty lame. How would
    you spiff it up?

    Answer: If you add *#include <stdlib.h>* at the top of the program (so the program knows
    about the long-to-ASCII, *ltoa(),* function), and then add the following code to the top of the
    DataDump() function:

    ```
    char t[10];
    char buffer[10];
    ltoa(temp.Phone, t, 10);   // make long a char array

    strcpy(buffer, t);
    buffer[3] = '-';
    strncpy(&buffer[4], &t[3], 5);
    ```

    and then change the last *Serial.println()* to *Serial.println(buffer)*, the program
    displays the phone number with a hyphen between the exchange and the number
    (e.g., 234-5678). You should be able to figure out what the code does now.

5. What is a shield?

    Answer: In terms of Arduino boards, shields are small boards that usually piggyback directly
    onto the µc board. Each shield is designed to meet some specific need (i.e., more memory)
    or add a new feature (i.e., read GPS data). Most shields are surprisingly affordable.

6. If a statement contains more than one dot operator, what should you do?

    Answer: Just remember that the dot operator is like a key that lets you get inside a black
    box. Usually, multiple dot operators mean that you are accessing more than one *struct* or
    union. In OOP languages, like C++, the dot operator is often used to access the members
    and methods of a class. *Serial.print()* is an example of using the dot operator to access the
    print() method (i.e., function) of the *Serial* class. In fact, OOP constructs are little more than
    a *struct* with functions (i.e., methods) defined within them … something you can't do with
    straight C.

7. Given the code at the top of Listing 10-11

    ```
    typedef struct Students
    {
      char name[20];
      int year;
      float gpa;
    } STUDENTS;

    STUDENTS myClass[20];        // Make an array of them
    ```

    initialize the first three elements of *myClass[]* with data of your choice and then
    display the array.

Answer:

```
typedef struct Students
{
 char name[20];
 int year;
 float gpa;
} STUDENTS;

void setup() {
 int i;

 Serial.begin(9600);

 STUDENTS myClass[20] = {
  {"Katie Mohr", 4, 3.30},
  {"John Purdum", 1, 3.30},
  {"Jane Holcer", 2, 3.80}
 };

 for (i = 0; i < sizeof(myClass) / sizeof(myClass[0]); i++) {
  Serial.print("Name: ");
  Serial.print(myClass[i].name);
  Serial.print("    Class: ");
  Serial.print(myClass[i].year);
  Serial.print("    gpa: ");
  Serial.println(myClass[i].gpa);
 }
}

void loop() {
}
```

You should be able to figure out the code for yourself now.

CHAPTER 11

The C Preprocessor and Bitwise Operations

In Chapter 4, Table 4-2 presented a list of the C preprocessor directives that are supported by Arduino C. In this chapter, we want to extend that discussion, plus cover a few additional details that should prove useful to you. In this chapter you will learn

- What the C preprocessor does

- What parameterized macros are

- What bitwise operators are

- What the standard C header files are

Preprocessor Directives

The ANSI C specification details the duties of the C preprocessor. It is the function of the C preprocessor to process the defined directives supported by the C compiler. Table 4-2 lists the preprocessor directives that Arduino C can translate. In the previous sentence, the word "translate" is not a typo, as that is exactly what the preprocessor does: it translates the directives you have written into your code with whatever you have designated to be the replacement. For example, consider the following preprocessor directive:

```
#define FIRESENSOR 145
```

which would likely appear near the top of your source code file. Now further suppose that you later write the line:

```
if (currentSensor == FIRESENSOR) {
   //...some code here to do something with the fire sensor state
}
```

The *if* statement here is what you see when you examine your source code. One of the first things the compiler does when you hit the compile button is run the C preprocessor. Conceptually, you can think of the C preprocessor pass as performing a global search-and-replace using all of the preprocessor directives you have written in your source code file. When the preprocessor finds the *if* statement, it substitutes the value 145 every time it finds FIRESENSOR in your source code. When the preprocessor has finished, the *if* statement is transformed and the compiler sees your source code as though you wrote the *if* statement as:

```
if (currentSensor == 145) {
   //...some code here to do something with the fire sensor state
}
```

The C preprocessor has translated all of your preprocessor directives into whatever substitution you wrote. Throughout this text you have used preprocessor directives to get rid of magic numbers in your source code. Rather than force you to flip back to Chapter 4, Table 4-2 is repeated here as Table 11-1.

Table 11-1. *Arduino C Preprocessor Directives*

Directive	Action
#define NAME value	Ascribes the identifier *NAME* to the constant *value*.
#undef NAME	Removes *NAME* from the list of defined constants.
#line lineNumberValue "filename.ino"	Allows the compiler to refer to any line numbers in the file named *filename.ino* to be referenced as line *lineNumberValue* from this point on by the compiler. Normally used in debugging. This is not in the Arduino C reference material, but the compiler recognizes it.

#if definedConstant expression operand	Conditional compilation. Example:
	
	`#if LED == 12`
	`        #define VOLTS 5`
	`#endif`
	
	This is not in the Arduino C reference material, but the compiler recognizes it.

#if defined NAME // statement(s) #endif	Allows for conditional compilation of statements if *NAME* is defined. The statement block ends with *#endif*. This is not in the Arduino C reference material, but the compiler recognizes it.
#if !defined NAME // statement(s) #endif	Same as *#if* defined, but processes the statement block only if *NAME* is not defined. This is not in the Arduino C reference material, but the compiler recognizes it.
#ifdef	Same as *#if* defined. This is not in the Arduino C reference material, but the compiler recognizes it.
#ifndef	Same as *#if !defined*. This is not in the Arduino C reference material, but the compiler recognizes it.

(continued)

Table 11-1. (*continued*)

Directive	Action
#else	Can be used with *#if* like as *if-else* statement, but to control compiled statements. Example:
| | ```
#if defined WINDOWS7
        #define BITS 64
#else
        #define BITS 32
#endif
``` |
	This is not in the Arduino C reference material, but the compiler recognizes it.
#elif	Used with *#if* for cascading *#if*'s
#include "filename.xxx"	Opens the file named *filename.xxx* and reads the contents of the file into the program source code. Usually, if double quotes surround the file name, the search for the file is in the currently active directory. If the file is not found there, the search resumes in the default include directory path. If angle brackets are used (*<filename.xxx>*), the search is confined to the default include directory path.

You already know the *#define* directive and have used it in several programs. What we need to do here is just expand the information in Table 11-1 to make it a little clearer.

#undef

The *#undef is used to turn off a previously defined #define preprocessor directive.* For example, suppose you have a source file with something like the following code in it:

```
#ifdef DEBUG
    Serial.print("The counter value is: ");
    Serial.println(myCounter);
#endif
```

This is a technique (called *scaffolding*, remember?) that you have used before to toggle debugging code into the program. If the source contains

```
#define DEBUG 1
```

at the top of the source file, then the two *Serial* object method calls are compiled into the program. You can also write the directive simply as

```
#define DEBUG
```

without the 1 digit, and it will still behave the same. Why? The reason is because we plan on using DEBUG in a *#ifdef* expression. A *#ifdef* doesn't care if there is a value or not, just whether it has been defined or not. Still, this old dog has always used the first form with the 1 digit present, so that's what we'll use in the examples that follow.
```

Now let's suppose the function that contains the debug code is named *ReadSensorCounter()* and that you finally have that function working perfectly. You could "shut off" the all of the debug code in the source file by simply removing or commenting out the *#define DEBUG 1* line in the program. Because the preprocessor would no longer see the *#define* for *DEBUG*, the *Serial()* debug code is not compiled into the program.

However, that's not an optimal solution because you may still have more debugging to do in other parts of the source file. If that's the case, cut-and-paste the *ReadSensorCounter()* function source code to the end of the source code file and add a *#undef* just above it in the source file, as seen in the following code fragment:

```
#define DEBUG 1
//
// A whole bunch of program lines
// that still need to be debugged
//
#undef DEBUG
ReadSensorCounter()  {
// code for the debugged function
}
```

When the preprocessor sees the *#undef* directive, it removes *DEBUG* from its list of *#define*'s. This has the effect of removing the *Serial()* calls from the (now debugged) *ReadSensorCounter()* function. However, because the *#undef* is at the bottom of the source file, all of the other *#define DEBUG* scaffolding code is compiled into the program because *DEBUG* is still defined everywhere above the point of the *#undef* directive. Therefore, the *#undef* directive gives you a way to undefine a previously defined preprocessor directive. By moving the source code for debugged functions after the *#undef* directive, you can leave in the scaffolding code you still need with undebugged code without cluttering up the debug statements with *Serial* output statements from code that already works.

If something happens down the road and the *ReadSensorCounter()* function starts acting up again, just remove the *#undef* and the *Serial* statements are automatically recompiled back into the program the next time you hit the compile button. By using the *#undef* directive, you don't have to retype in the *Serial* statements into the code again. While the *#undef* can be used for other purposes, toggling scaffold code into and out of a program is a fairly common use.

#line

The *#line* directive is used most often while debugging a program. The syntax is

```
#line lineNumberValue "filename.ino"
```

where *lineNumberValue* is the line number you want to the compiler to use from that point on in the source code file name filename.ino. Therefore,

```
#line 100 "C:\Temp\myCode.ino"
```

tells the compiler to reference the next line number as line 100 for the source file name *myCode.ino*. This directive is useful when your program reads in one or more header files. For example, suppose your source file begins with

```
#include <stdio.h>
```

and your program has an error on line 10. If file *stdio.h* has 22 lines in it and your program finds an error at source code line 10, the error message will say the error is at line 32. This can get confusing, especially if the compiler isn't really adept at counting source code lines when include files are used. Fortunately, the Arduino compiler does a good job of counting lines. In fact, it does not count the lines in header files. Not all IDEs behave this way.

As an experiment, however, try placing the *#line* directive in one of your programs and change the file name to the file that you are working on. You will see that the line number does change according to the line number you specify in the *#line* directive.

#if, Conditional Directives

There are a number of conditional directives, and they are very similar, so we can discuss them as a group. First, the expression

```
#if definedConstant expression operand
// Statement(s)
#endif
```

might be written as:

```
#if BOARD == ATMEGA168
    #define MAXEEPROM   1024
#endif
```

In this example, if *BOARD* is defined as *ATMEGA168*, then *MAXEEPROM* is set to 1024. The *#endif* directive is necessary to complete the directive for the compiler. You can have multiple statements controlled by the conditional directive.

The directive

```
#if defined BOARD
```

might be used as:

```
#if defined BOARD
        #define MAXEEPROM   1024
#endif
```

In this case, however, it doesn't matter how *BOARD* is defined, *MAXEEPROM* is set to 1024 as long as there is a *#define* for *BOARD*.

The directive

```
#if !defined expression
```

is the negative of the previous directive. That is:

```
#if !defined BOARD
        #define MAXEEPROM   1024
#endif
```

257

This says that if *BOARD* has *not* been #*define'*d in the program, *MAXEEPROM* gets set to 1024. This directive can also be written using the #*ifndef* in the same manner:

```
#ifndef BOARD
        #define MAXEEPROM    1024
#endif
```

The result is exactly as before: If *BOARD* has not been #*define'*d in the program, *MAXEEPROM* is set to 1024.

#else, #endif

All of the conditional preprocessor directives must end with a #*endif* directive. However, you can have an *if-else* type of directive by using #*else*:

```
#ifdef BOARD
        #define MAXEEPROM    1024
#else
        #define MAXEEPROM    512
#endif
```

In this case, if *BOARD* is defined, *MAXEEPROM* is set to 1024; otherwise it is set to 512. This gives you a little more flexibility for setting *MAXEEPROM*.

Finally, you can also use #*elif* to form a cascading *if* statement, as in:

```
#if BOARD == ATMEGA168
        #define MAXEEPROM    512
#elif BOARD == ATMEGA2560
        #define MAXEEPROM    4096
#else
        #define MAXEEPROM    1024
#endif
```

The #*elif* simplifies the code from what it would be if the directive was not used.

#include

The #*include* directive is used to read in header files into your program. As a general rule, header files do not contain executable code. That is, you should not use header files to define functions that you wish to use in your programs. Header files are properly used for data declarations, not definitions. (The exception is parameterized macros that can act like code definitions. More on that in the next section.) You have used the #*include* directive before, but I never fully discussed what it does. Simply stated, the #*include* directive

```
#include <stdio.h>
```

causes the compiler to read the *stdio.h* header file into your program as though its contents are part of your program's source code. Surrounding the file name with angle brackets (<>) causes the compiler to look in a compiler-specific default directory for the header file. With the Arduino IDE, the compiler looks in the \hardware\tools\avr\avr\include directory for the file. (For contributed libraries, like you find in the libraries subdirectory, those header files are included using either the double quotes or brackets. Not all

IDEs behave this way.) If you replace the brackets with double quotation marks (*#include "myheader.h"*), the compiler looks in the current working directory for the include file. Include files are a convenient place to store *#define*'s or other preprocessor information that is specific to the source file being compiled. It is also common to find function declarations (i.e., function prototypes) in header files, too.

You may wish to spend some time examining the standard header files supplied with the compiler, as there are a number of function declarations and parameterized macros that should prove very useful to you. Table 11-2 presents some of the "don't miss" header files.

Table 11-2. Standard C Header Files

Header file name	Description
stdio.h	Standard I/O header file with macro for file redirection and most file I/O
stdlib.h	Memory allocation functions, string conversions, value-to-ASCII conversions
string.h	A host of memory and string processing declarations
math.h	Math declarations, symbolic constants (e.g., pi), transcendental declarations
ctype.h	Character processing declarations (e.g., *isalpha()*)

It would be well worth your time to browse through all these files, as you are sure to find some nuggets that you can use in your programs. If nothing else, you will see function prototypes and macros that could prove very useful to you.

Parameterized Macros

If you look in the *stdio.h* header file, there's some pretty scary stuff, like this:

```
#define feof(s) ((s)->flags & __SEOF)
```

You already understand what the *#define* means, but what does all the rest of the line say? Recall what a *#define* does to the source code: it causes a textual replacement to occur in the source file. So, if you wrote a source line

```
int myEndOfFile = feof(fileStream);
```

that line would look like

```
int myEndOfFile = ((fileStream)->flags & 0x0020);
```

when the preprocessor pass finished because *__SEOF* was also *#defined* to be

```
#define __SEOF   0x0020          /* found EOF */
```

in the *stdio.h* header file. To understand what all of this means, you need to understand bitwise operators.

To help you understand bitwise operators, let's build a simple circuit that simply connects eight LEDs to the digital pins 4–11. We use a 220-ohm current-limiting resistor on each LED. (Any value between 150 and 680 ohms should work just fine.) The circuit is shown in Figure 11-1.

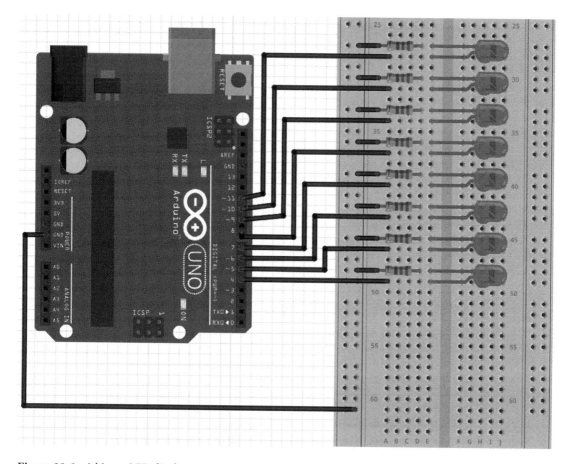

Figure 11-1. *A binary LED display*

Now, let's write a short program to demonstrate how binary data looks for a byte. The first attempt at the code is presented in Listing 11-1.

Listing 11-1. Simple LED Display

```
int ledPin[] = {4, 5, 6, 7, 8, 9, 10, 11};
#define ARRAYLENGTH(x)  (sizeof(x) / sizeof(x[0]))

void setup()
{
  for (int i = 0; i < ARRAYLENGTH(ledPin); i++)
  {
    pinMode(ledPin[i], OUTPUT);
  }
}
```

```
void loop()
{
  for (int i = 0; i < ARRAYLENGTH(ledPin); i++)
  {
    digitalWrite(ledPin[i], HIGH);
    delay(500);
    digitalWrite(ledPin[i], LOW);
  }
}
```

The purpose of this short program is really to see if the circuit works properly. If so, each LED lights in sequence for a half second, moves to the next LED, and then the process repeats itself. Note the parameterized macro *ARRAYLENGTH()*. We use this macro to control the number of elements that are read in the program's *for* loops. The breakdown of the macro is:

```
#define ARRAYLENGTH(x)        (sizeof(x) / sizeof(x[0]))
#define ARRAYLENGTH(ledPin)   (sizeof(ledPin) / sizeof(ledPin[0]))
#define ARRAYLENGTH(ledPin)   (16 / 2)
#define ARRAYLENGTH(ledPin)   (8)
```

The macro correctly returns eight elements for the *ledPin[]* array. It works by using the *sizeof()* operator to determine the total array size (i.e., 16 bytes) and then divides that number by the size of one element in the array (i.e., 2 bytes for an *int*). The really useful thing about this macro is that you can use it with any data type . . . it is a "typeless" macro. You could write the equivalent as a *const int* statement

```
const int arrayLength = (sizeof(ledPin) / sizeof(ledPin[0]));
```

but if you do, it can only be used with a specific array type. In this example, you could only use it with *int* arrays. The parameterized macro is more flexible.

The code should look pretty familiar to you by now. The *setup()* code simply sets all of the LED pins to be used for OUTPUT using a *for* loop. The *loop()* code simply walks through the LEDs and turns each one on and off for a half second. Pretty simple, but it is a good way to make sure that things are connected correctly, as we will expand this code in the next section to make it a little more useful.

Decimal to Binary Converter

Let's modify Listing 11-1 to accept a decimal number between 0 and 255 and display it on the LEDs as a binary representation. Listing 11-2 shows the modified program.

Listing 11-2. Decimal to Binary Converter

```
int ledPin[] = {4,5,6,7,8,9,10,11};
#define ARRAYLENGTH(x)  (sizeof(x) / sizeof(x[0]))

void setup()
{
  Serial.begin(9600);
  for (int i = 0; i < ARRAYLENGTH(ledPin); i++)
  {
    pinMode(ledPin[i], OUTPUT);
  }
}
```

261

```
void loop()
{
  char buff[4];
  int charsRead;
  int val;

  if (Serial.available() > 0) {
    charsRead = Serial.readBytesUntil('\n', buff, 3);
    buff[charsRead] = '\0';
    val = atoi(buff);
    if (val > -1 && val < 256) {
      DisplayBinaryDigit(val);
    }
  }
}

void DisplayBinaryDigit(byte num)
{
  for (int i = 0;i < ARRAYLENGTH(ledPin);i++)
  {
    if (bitRead(num, i) == 1) {
      digitalWrite(ledPin[i], HIGH);
    } else {
      digitalWrite(ledPin[i], LOW);
    }
  }
}
```

The code before and up to *loop()* is the same as Listing 11-1. In *loop()*, the code waits for the user to enter a number and press the Enter key of the *Serial* monitor using the *Serial.available()* method call. The *readBytesUntil()* method of the *Serial* object is very handy. The first argument (the newline character, '\n') says to keep fetching keystrokes until you read a newline character, but ignore anything after you have read three characters (the third argument in the method call). Each keystroke by the user is stuffed into the *buff[]* array, which is the second argument in the method call. The *readBytesUntil()* method returns the number of characters that were read into the character array, *buff[]*.

Because we want to convert what the user entered from *chars* to an *int*, we need to use the *atoi()* (ASCII to *int*) function from the standard C library. However, *atoi()* expects the argument to be a string, which means we must take whatever the user entered via the *Serial* monitor, and add a null to it to form a string. This is easy because *charsRead* holds the number of characters entered by the user. The statement

```
buff[charsRead] = '\0';
```

adds the *null* character in the proper element of the array. Because the return count does not include the '\n' character in its count, the previous statement overwrites the newline character with a null. For example, if you enter the digit characters 1 and 0, those two keystrokes are assigned to elements *buff[0]* and *buff[1]*. However, since two characters where entered (i.e., *charsRead* equals 2), the statement means *buff[2]* receives the *null* character, thus forming a string, and all's right with the world. The next line then uses the call to *atoi(buff)* to convert the characters entered by the user to an *int* with the value of 10. If the value is within 0 and 255, we call *DisplayBinaryDigit(val)* to display the value in binary (i.e., base 2).

The *bitRead()* function is used to read a specific bit in *num*. If the bit at location *i* is *HIGH* (i.e., a 1), the corresponding LED is turned on. If the bit is *LOW*, the associated LED is turned off. Control then returns to *loop()* and waits for another input by the user.

Turn back to Table 3-2 and you can easily understand the LED output you see when you alter the numeric values. You may want to run this program as you read the rest of this chapter. Figure 11-2 shows what the breadboard might look like after you build the circuit.

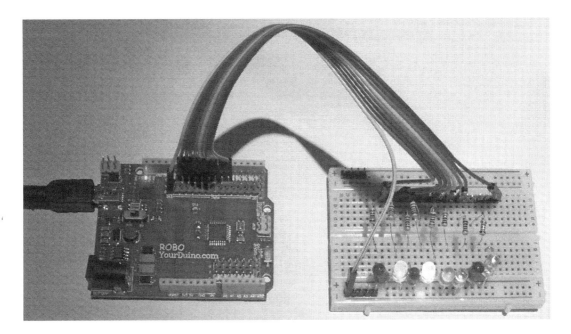

Figure 11-2. *Building the binary converter*

Bitwise Operators

Arduino C provides you with four bitwise operators: AND, OR, XOR, and NOT. The first three operators are binary operators and hence require two operands in the expression. The bitwise NOT operator is a unary operator and uses only a single operand. *Bitwise operations can only be performed on integer data* (i.e., no floating point data). Individual bits do not treat those bits as a (32-, 16-, or 8-bit) unit or number. It is not uncommon to find the bitwise operators being used in conjunction with various external hardware devices to extract information from the device. Some examples of each will help you to understand how bitwise operators work.

Bitwise AND

The bitwise AND operator is a single ampersand (&) and performs a binary AND between the corresponding bits of the two operands. Keep in mind that bitwise operators are single characters (e.g., &), whereas logical operators typically use two characters (&&). Confusing the bitwise and logical operators is a flat forehead mistake waiting to happen . . . and it will. Expect it to happen, and learn from it.

The result of the bitwise AND operation is such that the resultant bit is 1 if, and only if, both operand bits are 1. For example, suppose you have an external sensor that sends you information over a serial link to the µc board. To save time, the sensor packs two pieces of information into each byte. Assume the low *nibble*

(4 bits is called a *nibble* . . . for real, just like 8 bits are called a *byte*) contains the sensor's data and the high nibble contains the sensor number that generated the data.

The *truth table* for the bitwise AND is shown in Table 11-3. A *truth table shows you all possible results from a bitwise operation*. Reading the first row, if both bits are 0, the result is 0. If one bit is 1 but the other is 0, the result is 0. Only when both bits are 1 is the result 1.

Table 11-3. *Bitwise AND Truth Table*

Bit 1	Bit 2	Result
0	0	0
1	0	0
0	1	0
1	1	1

In code, the bitwise AND might look like this:

```
byte a = 10;        // 00001010
byte b = 6;         // 00000110
byte c = a & b;     // 00000010
```

Note that a result bit has a value of 1 only when both operand bits are 1. In this example, only bit 1 has a value of 1.

In Table 3-2, you saw how the bits contained in a byte are interpreted. Suppose the sensor device sent the byte

```
00110101
```

to your code. How would you determine what the data is and which sensor sent it? Simple! You would use the bitwise AND operator. The hardware specs tell you that the low 4 bits hold the data and the high 4 bits holds the sensor number that sent the data. We can separate the data using "bitwise masks" to extract the information. Because a bitwise AND sets a result bit if—and only if—the bit position of the data and of the mask are both 1, you find that:

```
00111010          // The sensor data--operand1
00001111          // The low nibble mask--operand2
---------
00001010          // Bitwise AND result using the two operands
```

The low 4 bits in the mask are all set to 1s because we need to know the data held in all 4 low bits (i.e., the low nibble). The rightmost bit in the sensor data is a logic 0, but the low bit of the mask is a 1. Because a bitwise AND only has a bit value of 1 when both operand bits are 1, the low bit of the result is 0. The second bit is 1 in the sensor data (*operand1*), and also a 1 in the mask. A bitwise 1 with 1 always results in 1, so the result is 1 for the second bit. The third bit in the sensor data byte (*operand1*) is 0 while the mask (*operand2*) is 1. Therefore, the result is 0. The fourth bit is 1 in the data and 1 in the mask, so the result is 1. Because we don't care about the high nibble when looking for the data, the rest of the mask is all 0's. If you look at Table 3-2, a byte with the binary value of 00001010 has a decimal value of 10. You now know that the data value sent from the sensor is 10.

So, which sensor sent the data? The device documentation says that the sensor number is held in the 4 high bits (i.e., the high nibble). To determine this, you redefine the mask to look at the high 4 bits:

```
00111010              // The data
11110000              // The high nibble mask
---------------
00110000              // Bitwise AND result-the device
```

If you only look at the high 4 bits (i.e., 0011), you can see that this would represent sensor number 3 of the device. (You will see in a moment exactly how to extract this information.)

As you can see, bitwise AND is often used to strip away unused bits from data so you can extract the information that you need.

Bitwise OR

A *bitwise OR operator* employs the single vertical bar (|, or *pipe*) operator and is used to set a bit when *either* operand bit has a value of 1. Only when both operand bits are 0 is the resultant bit 0. The bitwise OR truth table is presented in Table 11-4.

Table 11-4. *Bitwise OR Truth Table*

Bit 1	Bit 2	Result
0	0	0
1	0	1
0	1	1
1	1	1

In code, a bitwise OR fragment might be written as:

```
byte a = 10;      // 00001010
byte b = 6;       // 00000110
byte c = a | b;   // 00001110
```

Note that a *result bit has a value of 1 when either or both of the operand bits is a 1*. Contrast this with the bitwise AND.

Quite often a bitwise OR is used to set a bit when communicating with an external device. For example, perhaps the device has a communication register where a 1 in bit position 3 means it's okay for the device to send a byte to the controller board. Perhaps the device documentation says that the content of the communication register should be OR'ed with the communication's byte. In that case, you want to send a byte to the register with bit 3 set:

```
00000100      // Communication byte to device to set bit 3 (operand1)
00000000      // Look for a communication byte (operand2)
------------
00000100      // Bitwise OR result
```

As a result, the device knows that it's okay to send a byte of data back to the μc board. The bitwise OR is often used to read/set register bits. *bitwise OR is often used to combine data fields.*

Bitwise Exclusive OR (XOR)

The bitwise exclusive OR, also known as XOR, uses the carat operator (^). *An XOR operation results in 1 only when the two operands are different, and 0 when they are the same.* The truth table for bitwise XOR is shown in Table 11-5.

Table 11-5. *Bitwise XOR Truth Table*

Bit 1	Bit 2	Result
0	0	0
1	0	1
0	1	1
1	1	0

Using our code fragment

```
byte a = 10;        // 00001010
byte b = 6;         // 00000110
byte c = a ^ b;     // 00001100
```

note that a result bit has a value of 1 only when both operand bits are different.

What's interesting about an XOR operation is that if you call variable *b* the XOR mask, and XOR the result of the preceding code fragment (variable *c*) with the same mask,

```
byte a = 12;        // 00001100 - the result from the first XOR
byte b = 6;         // 00000110 - the XOR mask
byte c = a ^ b;     // 00001010 - the result; the original value
```

then the result is the original value for variable *a!* Because XOR operations have this effect on the data, you will often find XOR operations done on pixel data to invert an image. XOR'ing a second time restores the original image.

Bitwise NOT (~)

The bitwise NOT operator uses the tilde character (~) as its operator. The bitwise NOT is a unary operator; it only requires one operand. A bitwise NOT operation simply "flips the bits" of its argument. That is, all 0 bits become 1s and all 1 bits become 0s. The bitwise NOT operator truth table is shown in Table 11-6.

Table 11-6. *Bitwise NOT Truth Table*

Bit 1	Result
0	1
1	0

For example:

```
byte a = 1;      // 00000001
byte c = ~a;     // 11111110
```

Therefore, the bitwise NOT on the decimal value 1 results in a value of 254. The *byte* data type is an *unsigned* data type, so only positive value are possible (0–255).

This can cause some interesting problems if you use *signed* data with a NOT operator. For example,

```
int a = 1;       // 00000000  00000001
int  c = ~a ;    // 11111111  11111110
```

which sets the sign bit (i.e., bit 15), resulting in a value of –32,766 and not 65, 534. Because of the interpretation of the sign bit, most bitwise NOT operations are done on *unsigned* data.

Bitwise Shift Operators

C allows you to shift bits of an operand. There are two types of bit shifts: a right shift that uses the >> operator, and a left shift that uses the << operator. The shift operators are binary operators using the following syntax:

```
result = valueToShiftLeft << numberOfPositionToShift          // left shift
```

and

```
result = valueToShiftRight >> numberOfPositionToShift         // right shift
```

Let's take a look at each of these operators.

Bitwise Shift Left (<<)

The shift left bitwise operator simply shifts the bits to the left N bit positions, where N is the number of positions to shift the bits. For example:

```
byte a = 5;              // 000000101
byte result = a << 1;    // 000001010 = result
```

In this example, the bits are shifted left by one position. This changes the value of *a* from 5 to 10.

This behavior leads to an interesting fact: *rotating the bits one position to the left multiplies the original value by 2*. The statement

```
byte result = a << 2;    //  000010100 = result
```

shifted the bits two positions to the left. If you convert the binary value for *result*, you'll find that *result* now equals 20. Because each shift-left bitshift doubles the value, two positions causes a multiplier of 4 (i.e., $2 * 2 = 4$), which yields a final value of 20 (i.e., $5 * 4 = 20$). If you shifted the bits three positions, then *result* is 40 (i.e., $5 * 2 * 2 * 2$).

There is a *caveat* to this rotating-doubling fact: the topmost bit of each rotation "falls off the end." That is, any bit in the high bit position is lost when the shift-left takes place. Therefore, if you shifted any byte of data eight positions to the left, the value will be 0 because you "over shifted" all the data in the byte into oblivion.

Bitwise Shift Right (>>)

A bitwise shift right is the opposite of a bitwise left shift. With a right shift, *each bit moves one position to the right.* Any data in the lowest bit also "falls off the end." For example:

```
byte a = 10;                    // 000001010
byte result = a >> 1;           // 000000101 = result
```

As you would expect, a shift right by one bit position has the effect of dividing by two. However, if we take the result of 5 and shift it one more position to the right

```
byte a = 5;                     // 000000101
byte result = a >> 1;           // 000000010 = result
```

it produces a result of 2. This is also a divide-by-2 operation, but the lowest bit is lost in the shift so the result is 2, not 2.5. This is as it should be since integer division cannot have a fractional value.

Bit shifting is an extremely fast operation at the register level. That is, multiply-and-divide operations take many assembly-level instructions to arrive at a result. However, shifting the contents of a register is a single instruction. For that reason, some optimizing compilers look for "powers of 2" math operations on integer data, and do shifts instead.

One More Example

Recall from our discussion in the section on the bitwise AND operator a device with sensors that returned data to the μc board. Specifically:

```
00111010                // The data
```

The data returned from the device was 00111010. The high 4 bits was the sensor number of the device that sent the data, and the low 4 bits is the data value from the sensor. So, how can you extract the data and sensor number? Consider the following code fragment:

```
byte sensorByte = ReadDevice();     // sensorByte equals 00111010 after the call
byte sensorData = sensorByte & 15;  // 15 = 00001111
byte sensorNumber = sensorByte >> 4; // 00110101 >> 4 = 00000011
```

If you work through the statements, you will find that *sensorData* now equals 10, which is the value of the four lowest bits (1010). Bit shifting the data byte four positions to the right has the effect of "throwing away" the lowest data nibble, leaving a binary result of 00000011, or a value of 3. Therefore, you now know that sensor number 3 returned a data value of 10. This "bit packing" lets you transmit two pieces of information in a single byte rather than using two separate function calls to read the device.

It should be noticed that bitwise AND and OR have compound equivalents. That is, the statements

```
int a = 5;
// Some code
a =  a & 10;
// Some more code
a = a | 3;
```

may also be written as:

```
int a = 5;
// Some code
  a &= 10;          // Note abbreviated operator
// Some more code
  a |= 3;           // Same here...
```

Personally, I think the compound versions take a bit more thinking when you read them in code vs. the simple use of the operators. Still, you have the option if you wish to exercise it.

Using Different Bases for Integer Constants

Sometimes it is easier to understand what a statement means if a different numbering system is used. For example, you could rewrite the previous sensor data extraction statement as

```
byte sensorData = sensorByte & B00001111;
```

which expresses the constant as a binary value. (Note the B before the binary representation of 8-bit data.) Likewise, the same statement could be expression in hexadecimal as:

```
byte sensorData = sensorByte & 0x0F;
```

Many programmers who write code for μcs are comfortable with hex because it is so often used with assembly language programming. You can also express constants using the octal (base 8) numbering system if you wish. (You should use zero-Oh when using octal, as in 0O123, so the compiler is clear that you wish to use octal. The leading zero-Oh is unfortunate because zeroes and Ohs look very much the same.)

Whatever numbering system you decide to use with your integer constants, you should be consistent when using them.

Parameterized Macros . . . Continued

All the discussion about the bitwise operators was triggered because of a parameterized macro that appears in the *stdio.h* header file. (The macro name *feof()* comes from filestream end-of-file, which is used to sense the end of a file.) The macro was:

```
#define feof(s) ((s)->flags & __SEOF)
```

In that discussion, you also saw that *__SEOF* was *#define*'d as the hex constant 0x20.
Therefore, the expression expanded to

```
int myEndOfFile = ((fileStream)->flags & 0x0020);
```

which you now know can be rewritten as:

```
int myEndOfFile = ((fileStream)->flags & B00100000);
```

If you read the comment in the *stdio.h* header file, you will discover that the purpose of this statement is to mask off the end-of-file bit to see if the end of file (EOF) has been read. The statement uses a pointer to read the value of the flags variable and then masks off the sixth bit to see if EOF was read.

Why use a parameterized macro? The reason is because *macros generate inline code,* thus saving the overhead of a function call. If the macro is found in a tight loop, the time savings could be noticeable.

Summary

In this chapter we added a little more detail to the preprocessor directives that are available to you. You also learned about parameterized macros, as they are sometimes found in various header files. Also, you learned how to use the bitwise operators. Understanding how bitwise operators work is often needed when communicating with external devices over some form of data link. You will also find the bitwise operators useful if you do a lot of interrupt programming.

EXERCISES

1. Write a preprocessor directive that sets pin 14 to OUTPUT if the development system is using Windows to host the compiler or to INPUT under any other host system.

   Answer:

   ```
   #define WINDOWS 1
   // Some code...
   int pin14;

   #ifdef WINDOWS
        pin14 = OUPUT;
   #else
        pin14 = INPUT;
   #endif
   ```

2. Suppose you've written some macro that you want to include in your program. They are currently stored in a file named *myheader.h.* How would you write the statement to include the header file?

   Answer: The statement would be:
   ```
        #include "myheader.h"
   ```

   You would use the double quote marks instead of the angle brackets (<>) because the header is likely to be found in your development directory.

3. If you have an integer value *k* and wish to multiply it by 2 and assign the result into variable *j*, what statement would you use?

   Answer:
   ```
   j = k * 2;
   ```

   Just because you know how to shift bits doesn't mean that's the way you should do a simple multiply. If your code is doing something in a really tight loop and you want to see if bit shifting makes a difference, go ahead and experiment. However, if you do the multiplication with bit shifts, make sure you put a comment in the code to explain what you're doing. Keep in mind that it is estimated that 80% of software development time is spent on testing and debugging.

Anything you can do to make a section of code easier to read is usually a good thing. Using bit shifts in place of the multiply operator rarely makes things easier to read.

4. What types of data would you consider using for bitwise operations?

   Answer: You would use *byte*, *unsigned int*, and *unsigned long* data types. You would likely want to use *unsigned* data types so there's no interpretation problems involving the sign bit.

5. An external device returns data in the lowest six bits of a data byte. The top two bits can be ignored. How would you write the code to extract the data?

   Answer:
   ```
   byte myData = deviceByte & B00111111;
   ```

   You could also write the statement as:
   ```
   byte myData = deviceByte & 63;      // Decimal
   byte myData = deviceByte & 0x3F     // Hex
   byte myData = deviceByte & 0077;    // Octal—with a leading zero-oh"
   ```

   This would also work. Your actual choice depends upon what you think is easiest to read or perhaps some policy where your work dictates the format.

6. If you perform a bit shift operation that shifts bits "off the end," where do those bits go?

   Answer: I don't know either . . . rumor is they fall into a bit bucket.

7. Okay, at least you're reading the exercises . . . good for you! As a reward, let's modify Listing 11-2 to work with some of the bitwise operators. The lazy reader won't even know this program is here! First, however, *please* try to write the code yourself. The only way to learn is by doing when it comes to programming. The code uses the circuit in Figure 11-1.

   What we want is to test the bitwise operators for AND, OR, XOR, and NOT. These will be assigned the numeric values of 1 to 4, respectively. Because all but NOT are binary operators, the user will enter the bitwise test to use plus the two operands, separated by commas. For example, to perform a logical OR of the values 33 and 85, the user would type **2,33,85** into the *Serial* monitor. The program should then show the results on the LEDs from the bitwise operation. If you can code this on the first try, then you're ready for just about anything.

   Answer: The code is as follows.
   ```
   /*
     Bitwise operator test. The user can test the AND,
     OR, XOR, and NOT bitwise operators. The user enters
     test data using the Serial monitor in the form:
   ```

```
      TestToPerform,Operand1,Operand2

   As it stands, the comman operator separates fields
   in the input stream

   Dr. Purdum, December 24, 2014
*/

#define AND   1
#define OR    2
#define XOR   3
#define NOT   4

#define COMMA   ","    // Used to separate input arguments

int ledPin[] = {4, 5, 6, 7, 8, 9, 10, 11};
#define ARRAYLENGTH(x)  (sizeof(x) / sizeof(x[0]))
int GetBitwiseTestParameters(int *which, int *op1, int *op2);

void setup()
{
 Serial.begin(9600);
 for (int i = 0; i < ARRAYLENGTH(ledPin); i++)
 {
  pinMode(ledPin[i], OUTPUT);
 }
 Serial.println("Bitwise Operators: 1 = AND, 2 = OR, 3 = XOR, and
 4 = NOT");
 Serial.println("Enter Bitwise Operator COMMA Operand1 COMMA
 Operand2");
}

void loop()
{
 int whichTest = 0;
 int operand1;
 int operand2;

 GetBitwiseTestParameters(&whichTest, &operand1, &operand2);
 if (whichTest != 0) {
  ShowTest(whichTest, operand1, operand2);
  whichTest = operand1 = operand2 = 0;
 }
}

/*****
```

This function applies the operands and bitwise operator and displays
the results

```
parameter list:
  int which      which bitwise operation to use
  int op1        first operand
  int op2        second operand

Return value:
  void
*****/
void ShowTest(int which, int op1, int op2)
{
 byte result;

 switch (which)
 {
  case AND:
   result = op1 & op2;
   break;
  case OR:
   result = op1 | op2;
   break;
  case XOR:
   result = op1 ^ op2;
   break;
  case NOT:
   result = ~op1;
   break;
  default:
   break;
 }
 DisplayBinaryDigit((byte) op1);
 delay(1000);
 DisplayBinaryDigit((byte) op2);
 delay(1000);
 DisplayBinaryDigit(result);

}
/*****
```
This function takes the string entered by the user via the
Serial monitor and parses it into its relevant parts

```
parameter list:
  int *which     pointer to which bitwise operation to use
  int *op1       pointer to first operand
  int *op2       pointer to second operand
```

```
    Return value:
      void
*****/
int GetBitwiseTestParameters(int *which, int *op1, int *op2)
{
  char buff[10];
  char *ptr;
  int charsRead;
  int temp;

  if (Serial.available() > 0) {
    charsRead = Serial.readBytesUntil('\n', buff, 9);
  }
  if (charsRead > 9) {
    return 0;              // Too many characters
  }
  buff[charsRead] = NULL;   // Make into a string
  ptr = strtok(buff, COMMA);
  *which = atoi(buff);
  ptr = strtok(NULL, COMMA);
  *op1 = atoi(ptr);
  ptr = strtok(NULL, COMMA);
  *op2 = atoi(ptr);
}

/*****
 This function displays a byte value as a binary number
 on the LEDs.

 parameter list:
   int num        the value to display

 Return value:
   void
*****/
void DisplayBinaryDigit(byte num)
{
  for (int i = 0; i < ARRAYLENGTH(ledPin); i++)
  {
    if (bitRead(num, i) == 1) {
      digitalWrite(ledPin[i], HIGH);
    } else {
      digitalWrite(ledPin[i], LOW);
    }
  }
}
```

You can likely follow everything in the code, but in the *GetBitwiseTestParameters()* function, the use of the standard library function *strtok()* is a little weird. The function is a string "tokenizer" and is used to parse out substrings from a bigger string. For example, if the user wants to perform a bitwise AND test on the values 25 and 7, that test data should be entered in the *Serial* monitor as 1,25,7. Clearly, you need a way to extract, or parse, the numeric values 1, 25, and 7 from the input string. In this example, we are assuming that a comma separates each relevant numeric value.

In the *GetBitwiseTestParameters()* function consider the statement:

```
ptr = strtok(buff, COMMA);
```

This statement, when "filled in" with the input data, looks like this:

```
ptr = strtok("1,25,7", ",");
```

So, what we are saying is: "Ok, *strtok()*, start with the contents of the *buff[]* character array and see if you can find a comma in the string." Obviously, it finds a comma at *buff[1]*, but here's the tricky part: *strtok()* overwrites the comma with a NULL and returns a pointer to *buff[0]*. So, after the first call to *strtok()* completes, it's as though the code looks like this:

```
&buff[0] = strtok("1NULL25,7", ",");
```

This means we have created a substring with the content "1". The call to *atoi()* converts this substring using *ptr* to a numeric value and assigns 1 into the variable named *which*.

Recall that the first call to *strtok()* returns a pointer, which we assigned into *ptr*. However, look at the second call to *strtok()*:

```
ptr = strtok(NULL, COMMA);
```

The NULL for the first argument is actually a signal to the function to use its internal pointer on this call rather than an external pointer. (Do you think this internal pointer is defined with the *static* storage class? Why or why not?) That is, the internal pointer is actually a pointer to *buff[2]*. So, in fact, the second call works as though the call is

```
ptr = strtok(&buff[2], COMMA);
```

which, after the function completes its work, looks as though it was written as:

```
ptr = strtok(25NULL7", ",");
```

We can now use the same technique to change the string "25" to a numeric value via the call to *atoi(ptr)* and assign the numeric value 25 to *op1*. You should be able to figure out what the final call to *strtok()* does.

After the code in *GetBitwiseTestParameters()* does its job, control is sent to *ShowTest()* to display the results on the LEDs.

The *strtok()* function is very powerful and actually easy to use once you understand what it does. Also, the second argument can have multiple separators. For example,

```
ptr = strtok("This,is#a test of? the function.", ",#?.");
```

and *strtok()* would parse out substrings: "This", "is", "a test of", " the function". Why would you ever want to try and write the equivalent of *strtok()* yourself? Indeed, as you gain more experience, your knowledge of what library functions already exist will make you more and more productive over time. So, whenever you think you need to write a new function, google the task you need to accomplish just to make sure that someone hasn't already made it available to you in a library.

CHAPTER 12

Arduino Libraries

In Chapter 11, Table 11-1 presented a number of standard C header files that are available for use in your programs. Most of these header files are used in conjunction with their associated Standard C library and the functions they hold. A C *library* is nothing more than a group of (often related) functions that have been precompiled into what is called a *library file*. Conceptually, you can think of a library file as being organized like a book. At the front of the file is an index of each function name that appears in the library, followed by a byte offset that tells where the code for that function can be found in the file, along with the byte-length of the function. With this information, the compiler is able to extract the code for any given function from that library and insert it into your program.

What we want to do in this chapter is point out the library routines that are routinely shipped with the Arduino C compiler. We also want to provide some detail on how those library functions actually get placed into your program. In this chapter, you will learn

- The purpose of a linker

- What a library is

- The libraries that are standard with the Arduino C compiler

- How to create your own library

Let's dig right in and expand your knowledge about C libraries.

The Linker

The process of extracting the function you need from a library is performed by the *linker*, which is built into the Arduino IDE. Although I've simplified what actually happens a bit, the linker's responsibility is to "tie things together" after the compiler does its thing. (For additional details, see `http://openhardwareplatform.blogspot.com/2011/03/inside-arduino-build-process.html`.)

When the compiler sees a function that you have used, but whose source code is not in any of the source code files (e.g., *digitalRead()*), it adds the name of that function to a list of "unresolved externals". The compiler also marks the point in the program where that missing function's code should be added. Eventually, the compiler finishes its task, all intermediate files are generated, and finally the linker is invoked.

© Jack Purdum 2015
J. Purdum, *Beginning C for Arduino, Second Edition*: Learn C Programming
for the Arduino, DOI 10.1007/978-1-4842-0940-0_12

The linker finds the compiler's list of unresolved externals and starts looking through the library files for the missing functions. Visually, you might think of your program as a book. The list of unresolved externals are like book pages that are missing from the book, and each unresolved external in that list has the page number where those missing pages should be inserted into the book. It's the job of the linker to find those missing pages and insert them into your program at the proper place. So, how does the linker know which libraries to search?

Well, if there are no unresolved externals, the linker has nothing to do so the final code is generated for your program. In reality, however, there are almost always unresolved externals in a program. So, the linker first searches the default Arduino libraries (e.g., it finds *digitalRead()*). If there are still unresolved externals in the list, the linker then searches those libraries associated with the header files you've included in your code (e.g., *#include <Wire.h>*). When the linker is finished, all of the missing functions should be resolved and the linker has supplied all of the missing code to your program. If the linker tells you there are still "unresolved externals" or something "was not declared in this scope", it probably means you have forgotten to *#include* the header file for the library function you have used.

One of the beautiful things about C is that you are not bound to a set of built-in functions for doing things like math, I/O, or other commonly performed tasks. If you don't like the way something is done by a function in a library, you are free to write your own function to replace it. If you do write your own version of a library function, the compiler finds the code for the function in your source file and does not add it to the list of unresolved externals that is passed to the linker. That way, your version is used in the program and the linker never sees the function in the unresolved externals list. In other words, your code supersedes the library code.

Libraries

It is useful to divide the libraries that you have available to you into two groups:

- libraries that form the Arduino libraries and are distributed as part of the Arduino IDE

- all other libraries

Let's start with the Arduino libraries.

Arduino Libraries

To obtain information about the Arduino libraries, click the Help menu option in the Arduino IDE, and then select the Reference option. In a moment you will see a page similar to that shown in Figure 12-1. If you look closely at the figure, you will see the cursor sitting on the Libraries link near the top of the page. Right-click the Libraries link, and then select Open Hyperlink from the menu that pops up.

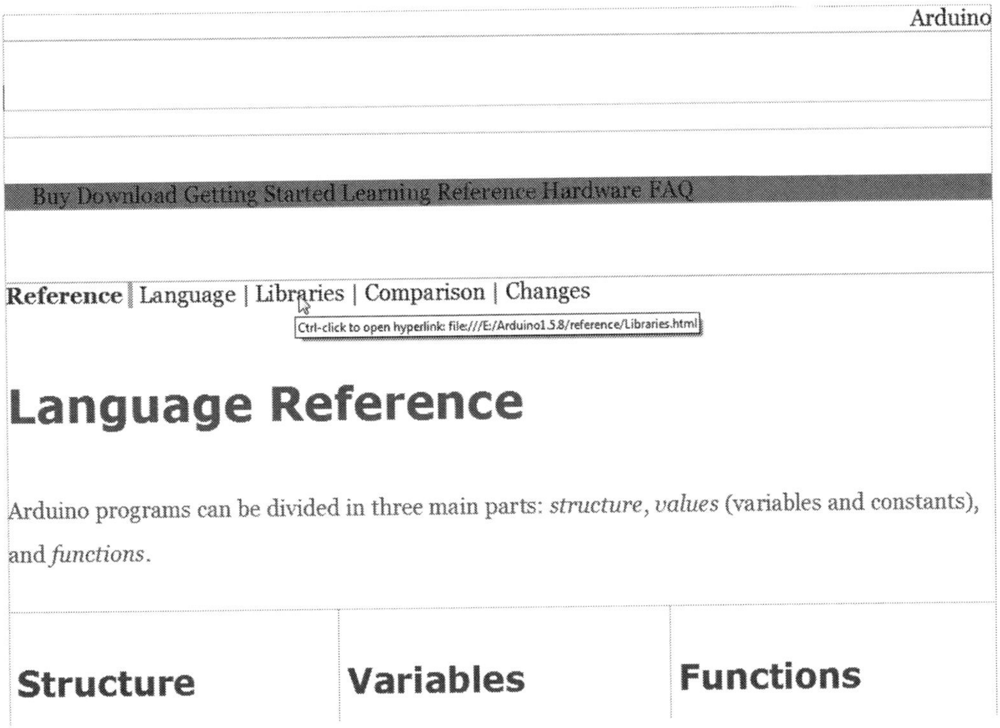

Arduino

Buy Download Getting Started Learning Reference Hardware FAQ

Reference | Language | Libraries | Comparison | Changes

Ctrl-click to open hyperlink: file:///E:/Arduino1.5.8/reference/Libraries.html

Language Reference

Arduino programs can be divided in three main parts: *structure*, *values* (variables and constants), and *functions*.

| **Structure** | **Variables** | **Functions** |

Figure 12-1. The Arduino reference page

After clicking the Libraries link, you will see a page similar to that shown in Figure 12-2. The libraries that are visible in Figure12-2 are some of the libraries that are provided and supported by the Arduino IDE. You will often hear these libraries referred to as the *Arduino core libraries*. In addition, there are a number of libraries that have been contributed to the Arduino support team and have been judged useful enough to be included in the libraries distributed with the Arduino IDE. These libraries are normally referred to as *Arduino contributed libraries*. What follows is a brief description of each of these two library groupings.

Reference | Language | Libraries | Comparison | Changes

Libraries

Libraries provide extra functionality for use in sketches, e.g. working with hardware or manipulating data. To use a library in a sketch, select it from **Sketch > Import Library**.

Standard Libraries

- EEPROM - reading and writing to "permanent" storage
- Ethernet - for connecting to the internet using the Arduino Ethernet Shield
- Firmata - for communicating with applications on the computer using a standard serial protocol.
- LiquidCrystal - for controlling liquid crystal displays (LCDs)
- SD - for reading and writing SD cards
- Servo - for controlling servo motors

Figure 12-2. Arduino libraries

The Arduino Core Libraries

Table 12-1 presents a list of the Arduino core libraries. These are libraries that are supported directly by the Arduino C support group. It serves no real purpose to rewrite the documentation for each of these libraries. You should, however, check the Arduino web site from time to time because the list of Core Libraries grows. Also, there are some libraries that are earmarked for specific Arduino boards (e.g., the Due) that are not normally distributed with the core, but are supported by Arduino.

Table 12-1. *Arduino Core Libraries*

Library name	Description
EEPROM	Functions to read and write to EEPROM memory
Ethernet	Functions for using Arduino-compatible Ethernet Shields
Firmata	Functions for communicating with external devices using a standard serial protocol
LiquidCrystal	Functions used in conjunction with LCD displays
SD	Functions for reading and writing data to Secure Digital cards
Servo	Functions to control servo motors
SPI	Functions for communicating with *Serial* Peripheral Interface bus devices
SoftwareSerial	Functions for serial communications using any digital pins
Stepper	Functions for controlling stepper motors
Wire	Two-wire interface (TWI/I2C) for sensor I/O communication

You can read up on these libraries yourself using the Arduino documentation as the need arises. However, that being said, there are some things that can pose some stumbling blocks along the way. For example, there are a number of Arduino-compatible shields (peripheral boards that plug into the Arduino μc boards) that use these core library routines. For example, I have used the SD shield and was lucky that it worked on the first try. Another programmer friend of mine used the same identical shield, but with a different SD card, and he couldn't even format the card. When I gave him my SD card, his code worked perfectly. The long and the short is that some SD cards simply don't work in some SD shields. The question then becomes: How do you find out which cards work and which don't? Indeed, how can you avoid common stumbling blocks that may arise when using these contributed libraries?

Using the Forums

The first stopping point you should visit at the outset of any project that is new to you is `http://arduino.cc/forum/`. This forum covers a multitude of Arduino topics, as can be seen by the partial listing in Figure 12-3. In these forums, you will find discussions on everything from using the Arduino to suggestions for improving the Arduino itself. These forums can be a real time-saver, and you should consult it anytime you begin a new project or if you are having trouble getting your code to work correctly. Many times I have found hints, tips, and suggestions that potentially saved me hours of research and trial-and-error time. Also, you will discover discussions on hardware interfacing issues (like the SD card problem I mentioned), which include ways to resolve them. The Forum should always be visited before you buy any interface device or shield. I'm positive the visit will save you time and money.

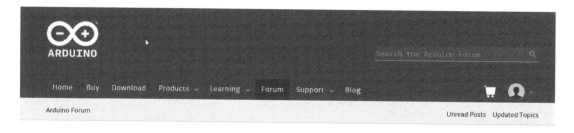

Figure 12-3. *Arduino Forum page*

Using a Core Library

Anytime you need to use one of the core libraries, simply use the Sketch ➤ Import Library menu option, as shown in Figure 12-4. (As you add more contributed libraries, the menu list grows to reflect those additions.) If you import a library, this menu selection alerts the compiler to look in the included library for any missing functions used in the program code. If there is a header file associated with the library, an *#include* preprocessor directive is automatically added to your source code file for the appropriate header file. You already saw an example of this when you wrote the code in Listing 10-4 from Chapter 10, which *#include*'d the *EEPROM.h* header file. (If you add a new library, you must restart the IDE to establish the necessary links to the new library.)

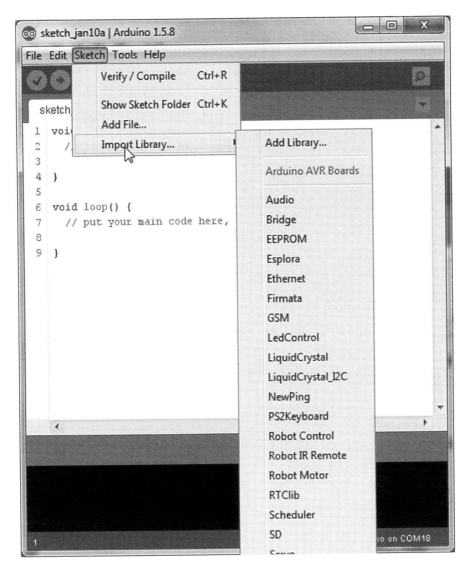

Figure 12-4. Importing a library routine

If you look closely at the list of libraries that are available in Figure 12-4, you will notice several libraries (e.g., Audio) that are not part of the Arduino Core library set. Where did these come from?

Contributed Libraries

If you reload the Libraries page depicted in Figure 12-2, you will see a large number of contributed libraries. For example, one of the libraries is called Tone. If you right-click the Tone link and select the Open Hyperlink option, you are directed to the page shown in Figure 12-5. If you look closely at Figure 12-5, you'll see a note stating: "The Arduino Tone Library is no longer maintained here. Please go here:", after which is another link to the Tone library.

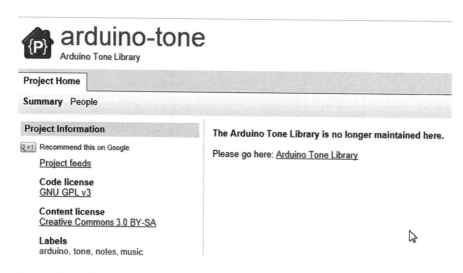

Figure 12-5. *The Tone page*

Click that link and you are taken to the linked page, as seen in Figure 12-6. If you click the Downloads tab, you can download the new Tone library.

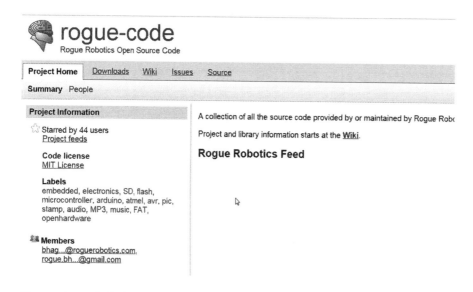

Figure 12-6. *The link page for the Tone library*

(Note that there are several other libraries listed on the Downloads page, including one for MP3 players. At the time of this writing, the third library in the list is the Tone library.) The Tone file is a ZIP file, which Windows can extract for you. Just double-click the ZIP file after you've downloaded it, and Windows Explorer will extract the files.

The extraction process produces a Tone folder that holds the set of files that are listed in Table 12-2.

Table 12-2. *Extracted Directories and Files from the Tone ZIP File*

Item	Description
examples	A directory that contains sample code on how to use the library
changelog.txt	A history of changes made to the library code
keywords.txt	A text file that tells the IDE how to handle keywords that are used with the library
Tone.cpp	The source code used to write the library
Tone.h	The header file for the library

The entire Tone directory should be copied into the *Libraries* directory of the Arduino IDE. Now close the Arduino IDE and then reopen it. Now when you select the Sketch ➤ Import Library menu option, you should see the new Tone library in the list of library options. If you click the Tone library, your source code file automatically has *Tone.h* added to it. (There is a new, built-in way to import libraries, too. See `http://arduino-info.wikispaces.com/Arduino-Libraries#NewLib`.)

Using a Contributed Library

Almost any contributed library contains a set of files similar to that shown in Table 12-2. The *examples* directory usually contains one or more sample sketches of how the library can be used; it is a great way to learn about any new libraries you wish to add to your IDE. Indeed, it is a good idea to try the sample sketches to make sure that your hardware functions properly with the contributed library. I purchased some shields/sensors that did not work with a related library. However, most of the vendors do know which libraries work with their sensors and shields. If you are buying over the Internet and are not sure of the compatibility of their sensor with a given library, e-mail them and ask. Reputable vendors will either say it is compatible, or they will direct you to a site that provides the proper library. If the vendor doesn't follow one of these options, find another vendor.

When you first install a library, take the time to read the header file(s) provided with the library. Often there are little nuggets of information buried in the header file. I remember an OLED library that must have had several dozen constructor calls buried within the header file, with a default that the programmer assumed would be the most popular. Of course, my OLED didn't use the default and my OLED did not have any identifying markings on it. After considerable trial-and-error, I found one constructor that worked. If I hadn't dug through the header file, I might have just assumed that the OLED was incompatible and moved on. The lesson is: It pays to read the header file(s).

Between the examples provided with the library and the forum mentioned earlier, you should have little trouble utilizing a library in your own code.

Other Libraries

Actually, there are "invisible" libraries that hold many useful routines that don't appear in the Arduino Library reference. (Many of these library functions are used in conjunction with the *Arduino.h* header file. This header file is automatically read into your program for any program you write, even though it doesn't appear in the source code file.) To ferret out these invisible libraries, you need to look into the header files that were presented in Table 10-1. Most of these header files are tied to the System V Standard C library files. Listing 12-1 is a partial listing of the code from the *string.h* header file. Almost everything you see in Listing 12-1 is a function declaration for library functions that you can use in your program.

Listing 12-1. The string.h Header File (Partial Listing)

```
extern void *memccpy(void *, const void *, int, size_t);
extern void *memchr(const void *, int, size_t) __ATTR_PURE__;
extern int memcmp(const void *, const void *, size_t) __ATTR_PURE__;
extern void *memcpy(void *, const void *, size_t);
extern void *memmem(const void *, size_t, const void *, size_t) __ATTR_PURE__;
extern void *memmove(void *, const void *, size_t);
extern void *memrchr(const void *, int, size_t) __ATTR_PURE__;
extern void *memset(void *, int, size_t);
extern char *strcat(char *, const char *);
extern char *strchr(const char *, int) __ATTR_PURE__;
extern char *strchrnul(const char *, int) __ATTR_PURE__;
extern int strcmp(const char *, const char *) __ATTR_PURE__;
extern char *strcpy(char *, const char *);
extern int strcasecmp(const char *, const char *) __ATTR_PURE__;
extern char *strcasestr(const char *, const char *) __ATTR_PURE__;
extern size_t strcspn(const char *_s, const char *_reject) __ATTR_PURE__;
extern char *strdup(const char *s1);
extern size_t strlcat(char *, const char *, size_t);
extern size_t strlcpy(char *, const char *, size_t);
extern size_t strlen(const char *) __ATTR_PURE__;
extern char *strlwr(char *);
extern char *strncat(char *, const char *, size_t);
extern int strncmp(const char *, const char *, size_t) __ATTR_PURE__;
extern char *strncpy(char *, const char *, size_t);
extern int strncasecmp(const char *, const char *, size_t) __ATTR_PURE__;
extern size_t strnlen(const char *, size_t) __ATTR_PURE__;
extern char *strpbrk(const char *_s, const char *_accept) __ATTR_PURE__;
extern char *strrchr(const char *, int) __ATTR_PURE__;
extern char *strrev(char *);
extern char *strsep(char **, const char *);
extern size_t strspn(const char *_s, const char *_accept) __ATTR_PURE__;
extern char *strstr(const char *, const char *) __ATTR_PURE__;
extern char *strtok(char *, const char *);
extern char *strtok_r(char *, const char *, char **);
extern char *strupr(char *);
```

For example, consider the following entry:

```
extern void *memcpy(void *, const void *, size_t);
```

I typed "memcpy" into Google and found a reference to the Linux manual for the library documentation (www.kernel.org/doc/man-pages/online/pages/man3/memcpy.3.html), which is always a good C Standard Library source. The description for the *memcpy()* function reads: *The memcpy() function copies n bytes from memory area src to memory area dest. The memory areas must not overlap. Use memmove(3) if the memory areas do overlap.*

Using the function declaration in conjunction with the Linux description, you should be able to figure out what *memcpy()* does. When describing functions, the System V Standard library wording uses *src* for the source object of a copy and *dest* as the destination object of the copy. The second parameter in the declaration uses the *const void* * attribute list, which says it must be the source of what is being copied. The reason it must be the source is because of the keyword *const*, which means the function cannot change whatever is being pointed to. It wouldn't make sense for the destination array parameter to be a *const* if the purpose was to copy something into it. The *const* keyword would prevent the copy from taking place. Therefore, the first parameter (*void* *) must be the destination of the copy.

The term *void* * is a common C idiom used to denote a "typeless" data type pointer in a function declaration. In other words, *memcpy()* does no type checking during the copy process . . . it assumes that you know what you are doing and that the pointers all point to valid data! Not paying attention to such details can produce a very bloody foot.

The *size_t* keyword is defined in the cplusplus.com reference as: *size_t corresponds to the integral data type returned by the language operator sizeof and is defined in the <cstring> header file (among others) as an unsigned integral type.*

This third parameter in the function declaration, therefore, is *n* in the *memcpy()* description, which tells how many bytes are to be copied. Voila! You now know about a very efficient standard library routine that does fast memory copies. As a general rule, most System V string functions that use a source and destination arguments place the destination argument first and the source argument second. Although there may be some deviations, under pressure this string convention is a good assumption to make.

You should spend a little time studying all the header files presented in Table 10-1, plus any others you may find interesting in the *include* directory. There are a lot of good information nuggets contained in those header files.

Writing Your Own Library

The day will come when you have developed a group of functions that you would like to group together as a library. As you know, placing functions in a library is a convenient way to capture the functionality of a routine without having the source code directly available in your program. In this section, you will learn how easy it is to create your own libraries.

Normally, a library contains more than one function, but there is nothing to prevent you from creating a library with just one function. For purposes of example, let's take the code from Listing 6-1 (repeated as part of Listing 12-3) that calculates whether a given year is a leap year or not; we'll convert this into a library so that we can use it in other programs. While most standard library routines return the Boolean value *true* or *false* as the return value for a leap year function, for reasons I mentioned in Chapter 6, my leap year returns either 1 or 0. If you don't like this, you are free to change it.

Listing 12-3 also contains code to calculate the day that Easter falls on for a given year. (The specific day and month for Easter depends upon the lunar calendar, so the date varies from year to year.) There are a number of "magic numbers" in the *GetEaster()* function that are dictated by the way lunar dates are manipulated. I've slept since I understood what these magic numbers are, so I've left them in "as is." The curious readers can research this themselves.

Before we discuss Listing 12-3, however, it makes more sense to discuss the header file used in the listing.

■ **Note** Because the Arduino IDE is set up to recognize *.ino* files, it is often easier to write the header and source code files using a simple text editor like Notepad. (You might want to try Notepad++, `http://notepad-plus-plus.org/`. Give it a try and you'll throw rocks at Notepad.) You can then move the necessary files to a folder in the Libraries directory after you have tested the files with a sample program.

The Library Header File

Perhaps the best place to start is with the header file associated with the library. Listing 12-2 presents the necessary format for creating the header file. The very first thing you need to do is decide on a name for your library. Obviously, you don't want to cause a conflict with existing libraries, so review those libraries that are in the *Libraries* directory and make up a different name for your library. We will use *Dates* for our library name.

The format that you must use for the header file is more or less etched in stone. Because of this format inflexibility, you should model any libraries you create closely to what is described here. First, most libraries start with a comment that tells the name and purpose of the library. That is followed by a *#ifndef* preprocessor directive. This is a bit of defensive coding that prevents someone from "double including" the header file information. Note that the matching *#endif* is at the very bottom of Listing 12-2. Whatever you use for the *#ifndef* name, you don't want it to collide with any other likely *#ifndef*'s. Usually, it's safe to use the library name followed by an "*_h*", as in:

```
#ifndef Dates_h
```

Now things get a little strange because the rest of the file uses C++ language syntax, not just C syntax. As you know, the Arduino compiler is capable of compiling C++ code, and this is the nature of this latest version of the Arduino IDE. There is no way to do justice to the C++ language here. Personally, I'm a huge fan of object-oriented programming (OOP), but that's another story. Although we can't delve into OOP here (we highlight some OOP principles in Chapter 14), you already know enough to get things to work in your new library.

The first thing you need to do is tell the compiler that you are going to compile some information into something called a class. A *class* is nothing more than a blueprint for something (i.e., an object) you are going to use in your program. Whatever properties or functions (aka, *methods* in OOP parlance) you place in the class are accessed by the programmer using the dot operator in much the same way you did with a structure. (Indeed, you've been doing this since Chapter 2 when you used the *println()* method of the *Serial* class.) In fact, a class is much like a structure, only a class is also allowed to have methods (i.e., functions) defined within it. The general syntax form is:

```
class YourLibraryName {
  public:
  // Things you want the outside world to know about
  private:
  // Things you want to use internally but not make available to others
};
```

In our library, we don't have any *private* elements of the class, so you can leave the *private* keyword out of the header file. (Or you can leave it in to document there are no *private* elements in our class.) The *public* elements of the class are those data items you do want the outside world (i.e., other programmers) to be able to use. The first thing I've placed in the *public* section of the class shown in Listing 12.2 is a *#define* for the ASCII character 0. As you know, when you touch the 0 (zero) key on your keyboard, an ASCII code is sent to the operating system. In this case, the code is the numeric value 48. We are using *ASCIIZERO* as a symbolic constant to get rid of the magic number 48.

Next, we define a structure with the tag *easter*, which holds the members that are used by the *Dates* library. Most of the members are *int* data types, but the last member, *easterStr[]*, is designed to hold a string presentation of a date in the MM/DD/YYYY format. One variable named *myEaster* is defined as a type *easter* structure. The structure variable is the only property (i.e., *public* data item) of this class. In the OOP world, a *property* is a variable that is defined within the class. To reinforce the idea of encapsulation, most class properties use the *private* storage class.

Near the bottom of the class are two function prototypes for the functions (usually called *methods* in C++) that you want to make available to users of your library. These prototypes allow the compiler to perform type checking on the functions when they are used in a program. Because this completes our library (and hence, the class definition), there is a closing brace and semicolon for the class declaration and the closing *#endif* for the *#ifndef* preprocessor directive you placed at the top of the header file.

That's all that's necessary for the *Dates.h* header file. Note that there is no "executable" code in a header file.

Listing 12-2. The Dates.h Header File

```
/*
  Dates.h - Library for finding is a year is a leap year
            and the date for Easter for a given year.
  Created and modified by: Dr. Jack Purdum, Dec. 25, 2014
  Released into the public domain.
*/
#ifndef Dates_h            // If we haven't read this file before...
  #define Dates_h          // ...read it now. This prevents double-including

  #include "Arduino.h"    // Not needed for our code, but often included

  class Dates
  {
    public:
      #define ASCIIZERO 48      // character for 0 in ASCII
      struct easter {
        int month;
        int day;
        int year;
        int leap;
        char easterStr[11];
      };
      struct easter myEaster;
                                // Function prototypes:
      int IsLeapYear(int year);
      void GetEaster(Dates *myEaster);
  };
#endif      // Don't forget this!
```

The *GetEaster()* function is passed a pointer to an *easter* structure. It is assumed that the *year* member of the structure has been filled in prior to the call to *GetEaster()*. A pointer to the structure is passed so the function can fill in the month and day for Easter. The function also fills in *easterStr[]*, which is a MM/DD/YYYY representation of the date for Easter. Because *easterStr[]* is *null* terminated, it may be used as a string upon return from the function.

The Library Code File (Dates.cpp)

The *Dates.cpp* is a C++ file (hence the *.cpp* secondary file name) that contains the necessary code to make your library functional (see Listing 12-3). The first line of the source file contains a preprocessor directive to *#include* the *Arduino.h* header file. (In earlier versions of the compiler, this was called *Wprogram.h*.) This header file grants access to the standard data types and constants used by the Arduino C compiler.

As mentioned before, this header file is automatically added to all of your programs, but is not added automatically for library source files; you must add it yourself. Immediately after is an *#include* for the header file you just defined, *Dates.h*. (This actually makes the include of *Arduino.h* in the header file unnecessary, but it is usually added by convention.) After the *include* files, the actual code for the library functions is written.

The source code for *IsLeapYear()* begins with a comment of the same form that you have used when you wrote previous functions. The line

```
int Dates::IsLeapYear(int year)
```

looks a little strange because of the *scope resolution operator* (::) used in C++. Simply stated, this operator makes sure that any name conflicts that might arise with other functions finds that the *IsLeapYear()* method is associated with the *Dates* library. Any C++ book or online tutorial can give you more details about the scope resolution operator if you are interested. The actual code for *IsLeapYear()* has already been discussed in Chapter 6.

Listing 12-3. The Dates.cpp Source Code

```
#include "Arduino.h"
#include "Dates.h"

/*****
   Purpose: Determine if a given year is a leap year. Algorithm
            taken from C Programmer's Toolkit, Jack Purdum, Que
            Corp., 1993, p.258.

   Parameters:
     int year            The year to test

   Return value:
      int                1 if the year is a leap year, 0 otherwise
*****/
int Dates::IsLeapYear(int year)
{
  if (year % 4 == 0 && year % 100 != 0 || year % 400 == 0) {
    return 1;   // It is a leap year
  } else {
    return 0;   // not a leap year
  }
}
/*****

   Purpose: Determine the date for Easter for a given year.
            Algorithm taken from Beginning Object Oriented
            Programming with C#, Jack Purdum, Wrox, 2012.

   Parameters:
     struct easter *myData     Pointer to an easter structure

   Return value:
     void
```

```
   CAUTION: This function assumes that the year member of the structure holds the
            year being tested upon entry.
*****/
void Dates::GetEaster(Dates *myData){ // This is line 44
  int offset;
  int leap;
  int day;
  int temp1, temp2, total;

  myData->myEaster.easterStr[0] = '0';     // Always a '0'
  myData->myEaster.easterStr[2] = '/';     // Always a '/'
  myData->myEaster.easterStr[3] = '0';     // Assume day is less than 10
  myData->myEaster.easterStr[10] = '\0';   // null char for End of string

  offset = myData->myEaster.year % 19;
  leap = myData->myEaster.year % 4;
  day = myData->myEaster.year % 7;
  temp1 = (19 * offset + 24) % 30;
  temp2 = (2 * leap + 4 * day + 6 * temp1 + 5) % 7;
  total = (22 + temp1 + temp2);
  if (total > 31) {
    myData->myEaster.easterStr[1] = '4';     // Must be in April
    myData->myEaster.month = 4;              // Save the month
    day = total - 31;
  } else {
    myData->myEaster.easterStr[1] = '3';     // Must be in March
    myData->myEaster.month = 3;              // Save the month
    day = total;
  }

  myData->myEaster.day = day;                   // Save the day
  if (day < 10) {                    // One day char or two?
    myData->myEaster.easterStr[4] = (char) (day + ASCIIZERO);
  } else {
    itoa(day, myData->myEaster.easterStr + 3, 10);  // Convert day to ASCII and...
  }
  myData->myEaster.easterStr[5] = '/';     // Always a '/' and overwrites null from
itoa()
  itoa(myData->myEaster.year, myData->myEaster.easterStr + 6, 10);    // Convert year to
ASCII...
}
```

The remainder of the source code deals with determining the day of Easter for a given year. Note that the user of this library function is expected to pass in a pointer to a *Dates* object. The code then fills in the members of the structure contained in the *Dates* class with the appropriate values. If a pointer was not used, there would be no way to return all of the required values to the caller. By using a pointer, you can fill in the *day*, *month*, and a string representation of the Easter date (*easterStr[]*) in the function.

Setting the Arduino IDE to Use Your Library

So far, you have two source code files for your library:

- the *Dates.h* header file

- the *Dates.cpp* library source code file

You can move these two files into a folder you created and named *Dates* in the *libraries* directory of the Arduino IDE. Figure 12-7 shows how this directory might look on your system. Notice how we have a *Dates* folder near the top of the directory. If you opened that directory, you would find the *Dates.h* and *Dates.cpp* files.

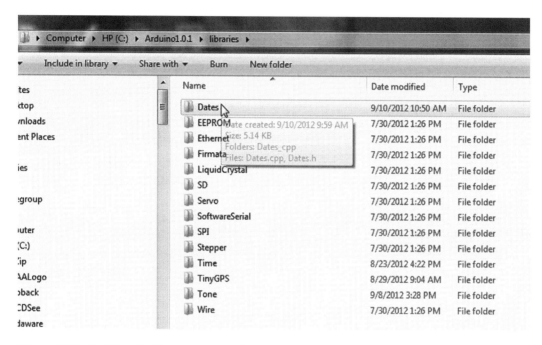

Figure 12-7. The Libraries directory of the Arduino IDE

With those files in place in the *Libraries* directory, close the Arduino IDE and then reopen it. This action will register the new *Dates* files with the IDE.

A Sample Program Using the Dates Library

Listing 12-4 presents the code to exercise your new library. The program begins with a *#include <Dates.h>* directive. You can type this line in yourself, or you can also use the Sketch ➤ Import Library ➤ Dates menu selection, which would automatically add the *#include <Dates.h>* to your source code file for you. The program then defines a *Dates* object named *myDates* for you to use in the program. The *setup()* call simply establishes a serial link so that you can see the output produced by the program.

Listing 12-4. A Program to Test the Dates Library Routine

```
#include <Dates.h>
Dates myDates;

void setup() {
  int i;
  Serial.begin(9600);

  for (i = 2000; i < 2016; i++) {
    Serial.print(i);
    Serial.print(" is ");
    if (myDates.IsLeapYear(i) == 0)
      Serial.print("not ");
    Serial.print("a leap year and Easter is on ");
    myDates.myEaster.year = i;
    myDates.GetEaster(&myDates);
    Serial.print(myDates.myEaster.easterStr);
    Serial.print("  ");
    Serial.print(myDates.myEaster.month);
    Serial.print("  ");
    Serial.print(myDates.myEaster.day);
    Serial.print(" ");
    Serial.println(myDates.myEaster.year);
  }
}
void loop() {}
```

The code inside the *setup()* function uses a *for* loop to print out the leap year and Easter data for the years 2000 through 2016. Note how the library routines are called using the dot operator. That is,

```
myDates.IsLeapYear(i)
```

says: Load your backpack with variable *i*. Go to the *myDates* object, insert your key (the dot operator), enter into the class black box, and call the *IsLeapYear()* method. Once inside the class method, the code unpacks your backpack, extracts the data, and shoves it into the *year* property. The call to *GetEaster()* works much the same, only we pass the lvalue of *myDates*. This allows us to use indirection via the pointer to permanently change the state of the members of the *myDates* object. You can tell that these values are permanently changed by the way they are referenced in the *Serial.print()* calls. A sample run of the program can be seen in Figure 12-8.

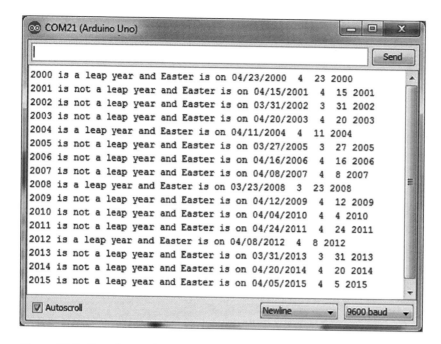

Figure 12-8. Sample run of the Easter dates program

Adding the Easter Program As Part of the Library

If you look in any of the other libraries in the *Libraries* directory shown in Figure 12-7, you will see a folder named *examples*. The purpose of this directory is to provide the programmer with one or more examples of how to use the library. You should create a subdirectory named *examples* below the *Dates* library folder and move the program found in Listing 12-4 into that directory. (As always, the **.ino* file must appear in the directory of the same name.) Your *Dates* directory should now look like Figure 12-9 and the program from Listing 12-4 should be located in the *examples* directory.

Whoa! Where did the *keywords.txt* file come from? That's the subject of the next section.

Name	Date modified	Type	Size
examples	9/10/2012 8:23 PM	File folder	
Dates.cpp	9/10/2012 7:34 PM	CPP File	3 KB
Dates.h	9/10/2012 7:30 PM	H File	1 KB
keywords.txt	9/10/2012 8:22 PM	Text Document	1 KB

Figure 12-9. The Dates directory

The keywords.txt File

The Arduino IDE lets you add keywords for syntax highlighting if you wish to do so. For the *Dates* library, the *keywords.txt* file contains the following lines:

```
Dates          KEYWORD1
IsLeapYear     KEYWORD2
GetEaster      KEYWORD2
```

Note that the format used in the *keywords.txt* file is pretty fussy. That is, in the first line, *Dates* is immediately followed by a Tab space, and then *KEYWORD1*. This change causes the class name *Dates* to appear in the color reserved for *KEYWORD1* keywords in your source code files. Using the entries shown here, the word *Dates*, for example, takes on the same color as *for*, *which*, *else*, and so forth, when it appears in the source code window of the Arduino IDE.

The next two lines cause the functions defined in the *Dates* library to have coloring as defined by *KEYWORD2*. As before, a Tab space must separate the function name from the *KEYWORD2* constant. When you view your source code, the words *IsLeapYear* and *GetEaster* take on the same color at any other class methods you may use. The two function names, for example, will now have the same color as *print* in *Serial.print().*

For the *keywords.txt* file to take effect, you need to close and reopen the Arduino IDE.

Keyword Coloring (theme.txt)

Some of the colors that the Arduino IDE uses in its editor are difficult for me to see. I don't know if the reason is some degree of color blindness or simply eyes that are getting worn out from too much use. Whatever the reason, I started digging around to see if I could change the default color scheme.

If you look in the *lib\theme* directory just below where the Arduino EXE file is located (the exact location depends upon where you installed your compiler), you will find a file named *theme.txt*. This file holds the definitions for the colors used in the text editor of the IDE. If you are going to play around with the colors, it's a good idea to save a backup copy of the original file. I used *Notepad++.exe* to make the changes. If you have the IDE open, you should close it before making the changes suggested next.

First, I loaded up *theme.txt* and then did a Save As menu option using the name *themeBackup.txt*. That way, if I screw something up, I can always go to this file and rename it back to *theme.txt*—and I'm back where I started.

Next, I used Notepad++'s Edit ➤ Find menu option (or Ctrl+F) and typed in **Keyword1**. The result of that search is shown in Figure 12-10. (If you use a different editor, like Wordpad, it may look different than Figure 12-10. This is because of the way the end of lines are treated in different editors. If you use Wordpad, make sure you save the file as a normal text file and not a .doc (or some other) file type.) If you look closely at Figure 12-10, after the equal sign, you will likely find the entry *#cc6600,plain*. I changed it to *#0000FF* because it's easier for me to see. Experiment with different color combinations until you're happy. Keep in mind, however, that this color change applies to all files you use in the IDE, not just your library.

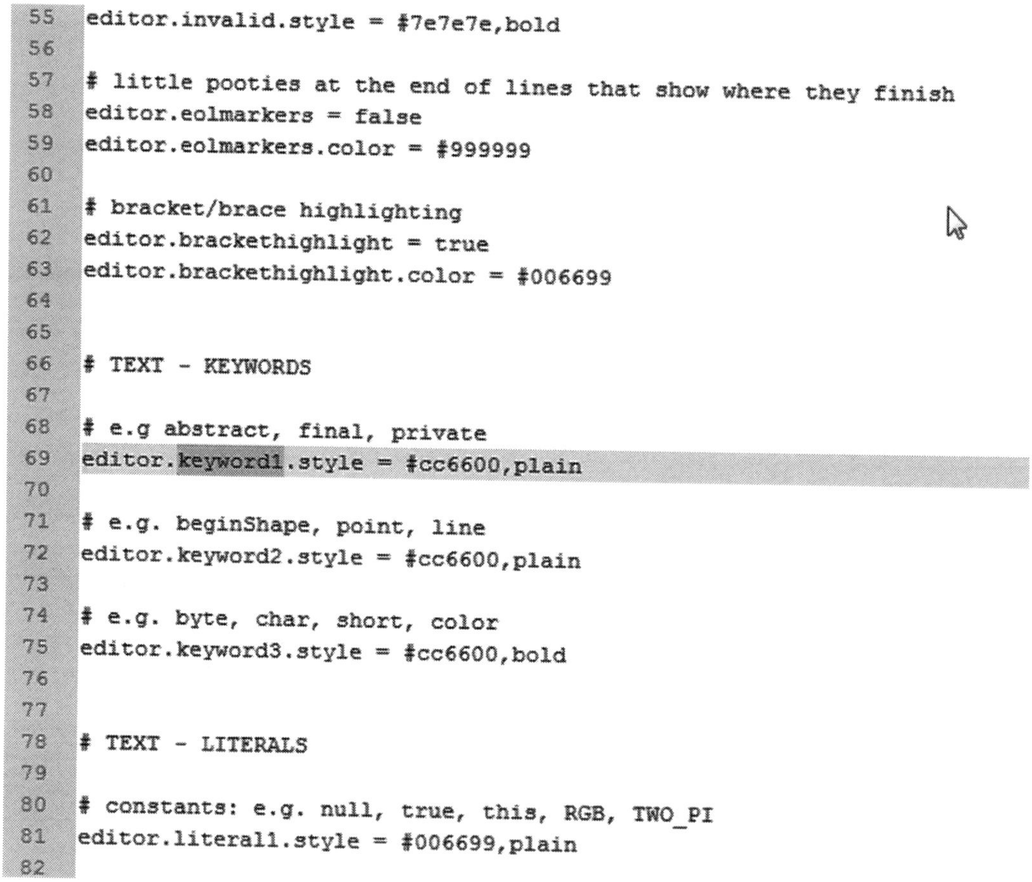

```
55  editor.invalid.style = #7e7e7e,bold
56
57  # little pooties at the end of lines that show where they finish
58  editor.eolmarkers = false
59  editor.eolmarkers.color = #999999
60
61  # bracket/brace highlighting
62  editor.brackethighlight = true
63  editor.brackethighlight.color = #006699
64
65
66  # TEXT - KEYWORDS
67
68  # e.g abstract, final, private
69  editor.keyword1.style = #cc6600,plain
70
71  # e.g. beginShape, point, line
72  editor.keyword2.style = #cc6600,plain
73
74  # e.g. byte, char, short, color
75  editor.keyword3.style = #cc6600,bold
76
77
78  # TEXT - LITERALS
79
80  # constants: e.g. null, true, this, RGB, TWO_PI
81  editor.literal1.style = #006699,plain
82
```

Figure 12-10. *Using Notepad's Find option to locate Keyword1*

The *cc6600* value is actually the hexadecimal number for the red-green-blue (RGB) value used by the editor for *keyword1* words in the source code file. Because my RGB value has no red or green component, *keyword1* words now show up in blue. (Prior to my change, the color value was #CC6600, which one of my students called "baby-poo orange"!) Notice that the actual entry for *keyword1* looks like:

```
editor.keyword1.style = #0000FF,plain
```

If you change the word "plain" to "bold", the keywords are displayed in bold font. (The answer to Exercise question 5 at the end of this chapter has a URL for a page that has a nice color chart and corresponding hex values.)

I also found the "e.g." examples in the themes file misleading. For example, *keyword1* uses "e.g. abstract, final, private" as the example of text coloring. A more common example would include the keyword *void*, which you will see as the function type specifier for the *setup()* and *loop()* functions. Keyword2 is used for coloring common data types (e.g., *char*, *int*, etc.) and method names for class objects (e.g., *begin* in *Serial.begin()*). Keyword2 is used to color function (e.g., *setup, loop)* and class (*Serial*) names. I find the code easier to read when I vary these keywords. You may not, so experiment and see what you think.

While I was playing around with the themes file, I also changed *keyword2* (which now equals FF0000) and *keyword3* (which now equals 009900) using the same Notepad++ search method. When I was finished, I did a Save As and used the file name *theme.txt*. I then reloaded the IDE and, voila! All of the color changes I made become the default colors for the editor. If you don't like the changes, you can always go back and try some new colors. If worst comes to worst, you can rename the *themebackup.txt* file to *theme.txt* and you're back to the default IDE colors.

Summary

The goal of this chapter was to make you feel more comfortable using the nondefault libraries that are shipped with the Arduino IDE. You should understand what the standard, core, and contributed libraries are from an operational standpoint. You should also understand the part that header files play in conjunction with library files. Indeed, you should spend some time looking through all of the header files available to you. The *string.h* file is just one example of the treasures you will find in the header files. Also, you should be comfortable creating your own libraries and adding them to the Arduino IDE. Finally, you learned how to use the *keywords.txt* and *theme.txt* files to alter the way the editor visually presents keywords in your source code.

EXERCISES

1. If you were trying to explain the concept of libraries to someone who was just learning about programming, how would you explain it in one sentence?

   Answer: A library is a collection of pre-written functions (methods), usually grouped under a common theme, that you can use in your own programs.

2. What is a core library?

   Answer: Core libraries are those libraries that the compiler routinely uses when compiling programs. For example, the *Arduino.h* header file is automatically included in your source code for all programs that you write. This header file enables the compiler to draw from various libraries. There are a number of contributed libraries that are also automatically installed.

3. What is a contributed library?

   Answer: These are libraries that have been supplied by users of the Arduino system. Because Arduino is an open source project, users are encouraged to share whatever code they develop. Contributed libraries are one result of this code sharing.

4. What does *strncpy()* do?

   Answer: I'm not going to tell you. It comes from the *string.h* header file, so it is a routine stored away in a library and hence you can use it in your programs. The easiest way to answer this question is to google the function. You should get used to doing this whenever you see a function that you don't know about.

5. Suppose you wish to change some of the colors stored in the *theme.txt* file, but you don't know what the RGB hex values are? How can you decipher the color codes?

Answer: Once again, go to the web and start looking. That's what I did and I found
www.2createawebsite.com/build/hex-color-chart-grid.html, which makes it easy
to pick a color you like. There are quite a few colors to choose from . . . 256³, or over 16.7
million! Google is your friend.

6. Where should you place a library that you've written and you want to make
    permanently available to the IDE?

    Answer: You should place your library in the *Libraries* directory and it should have a
    directory structure as follows:

```
Libraries
    YourLibraryName
        examples
        YourLibraryName.h
        YourLibraryName.cpp
        keywords.txt
```

examples contain the source code for at least one example of how to use your library.

CHAPTER 13

■ ■ ■

Interfacing to the Outside World

One of the first things most Arduino programmers want to do is "see" something that was produced by their program. Sure, the *Serial* monitor is okay for a while, but eventually you will want to display program output on something other than the *Serial* monitor. After all, dragging your PC around with you everywhere kind of limits what you can do with your Arduino.

One of the most popular displays is either a 2×16 or a 4×20 LCD display. These are widely available and fairly inexpensive, usually running around $5. The Arduino web site has a great discussion about using these displays (http://playground.arduino.cc/Code/LCD), and because they can display both alpha and numeric data, it's pretty easy to find a lot of source code available that use these displays. In fact, googling "Arduino LCD display source code" turns up more than 390,000 hits!

So, rather than kick a dead horse again, I thought I'd discuss an 8-digit 7-segment LED display instead. Figure 13-1 shows a typical example that uses the MAX7219 chip working through the *Serial Peripheral Interface* (SPI) protocol to your Arduino. The program for this LED display could also use the newer MAX7221 chip, but those are more expensive, so I concentrated on the MAX7219 chip to control the display. With a little Internet shopping, you should be able to buy this display for less than $3.

Figure 13-1. *An 8-digit, 7-segment LED display using the MAX7219*

© Jack Purdum 2015
J. Purdum, *Beginning C for Arduino, Second Edition*: Learn C Programming
for the Arduino, DOI 10.1007/978-1-4842-0940-0_13

The Serial Peripheral Interface (SPI)

The SPI protocol is used to communicate with one or more peripheral devices. In most applications, the Arduino serves as the master device that holds dominion over the peripheral devices. The communication is accomplished using four lines that are shared among the devices. These four lines are as follows:

- *MISO*: This is the Master In, Slave Out line for sending data from a slave to the master

- *MOSI*: This is the Master Out, Slave In line for sending data to the peripherals

- *SCK*: This is the *Serial* Clock line that synchronizes the data transmission by the master

- *SS*: A pin on a device that the master uses to select the device

Because of the SPI popularity, most Arduino boards bring these control lines out to a single header called the *In Circuit Serial Programming* (ICSP) header (see Figure 13-2). You'll notice that the SS line is missing from the ICSP header. (The SS pin is most often used when a slave device is controlled by an external master.) However, you can use just about any digital pin to control the select line. (If possible, still avoid pins 0 to 3 because of the USB communications and interrupts that often use these pins.)

If you want more information about the SPI protocol or the ICSP, two good sources are at http://arduino.cc/en/Reference/SPI and http://en.wikipedia.org/wiki/Serial_Peripheral_Interface_Bus#Mode_Numbers.

MISO 1   2 +Vcc

SCK 3   4 MOSI

Reset 5   6 Gnd

Figure 13-2. *The ICSP header pins*

An SPI Program

Let's write a program that simulates a counter timer. The display shows the approximate time that has elapsed from when the program was started to the present. The reason that we say "approximate" is because we are using *delay()* to track the time. I've already mentioned that *delay()* is a nice easy function to use, but it's not very accurate, plus it uses interrupts that could "block" certain applications where you need an ISR. The IDE sample program, Blink Without Delay, is a better example of how to code something where you need to work with interrupts. Rather, the program presented here is used to show how you can display up to eight numeric digits easily and at a fairly low cost.

The program starts with a zero count, which for this program means that all displays are initialized to zero. Starting on the left edge of the display, the code uses the first two digits to represent hours. Clearly, the max number of hours is 99. The remaining pairs of digits are for minutes, seconds, and hundredths of a second. The hundredths-of-a-second display digits are an illusion; they are there simply to make the output from the display a little more interesting. If you look at the function named *BumpFrame()* in Listing 13-1, you'll see a call to *delay()* of:

```
delay(10);
```

Because the last two digits represent hundredths of a second, and 1000 milliseconds is one second, we simply divide 1000 by 100 to get a delay of 10 milliseconds between display updates. Clearly, that's not going to be accurate because it takes time to execute the program instructions. You could improve the accuracy by counting the program instructions and the time it takes to execute each instruction, but that's an H-bomb-to-kill-an-ant for our purposes. All I want to do is show you how to interface to an inexpensive LED display.

Listing 13-1. Countdown LED Display

```
/*
   Program is a quick-count stopwatch. The code starts with zero and
   counts up from there. No protection rollover. Base code by Blair Thompson.

   Modified by Dr. Purdum, 12/26/2014
*/
#include <LedControl.h>      // From Arduino LedControl library

int DIN    = 10;
int LOADCS = 11;
int CLK    = 13;

int ledBrightness = 5;     // range is 0-15.  0=lowest, 15 = full power

// DIN, CLK, Load/CS, 8 digits
LedControl myLEDs = LedControl(DIN, CLK, LOADCS, 8);
int hundredths0, hundredths1;
int seconds0, seconds1;
int minutes0, minutes1;
int hours0, hours1;

void setup()
{
  pinMode(DIN, OUTPUT);
  pinMode(CLK, OUTPUT);
  pinMode(LOADCS, OUTPUT);

  myLEDs.shutdown(0, false);                 // Wake 'em up

  Reset();
  myLEDs.setIntensity(0, ledBrightness  ); //set the brightness
}

void loop()
{
  BumpFrame();  // Bump the necessary display digits
}

/*****
   This function increments the hundredths of a second counter and
   rolls to the next digit as needed.

   Parameter List:
     void
```

```
  Return value:
    void
*****/
void  BumpFrame()
{
  delay(10);     // Count to 99 from 0 every second

  myLEDs.setDigit(0, 0, hundredths0++, false);  // Update last digit
  if (hundredths0 == 10) {
    hundredths1++;
    hundredths0 = 0;
  }
  if (hundredths1 < 9) {                        // Time to roll over?
    myLEDs.setDigit(0, 1, hundredths1, false);  // Nope
  } else {
    hundredths1 = 0;
    myLEDs.setDigit(0, 1, hundredths1, false);  // Yep
    BumpSeconds();
  }
}


/*****
  This function increments the seconds counter and
  rolls to the next digit as needed.

  Parameter List:
    void

  Return value:
    void
*****/
void  BumpSeconds()
{
  seconds0++;         // Bump the seconds count
  if (seconds0 == 10) {
    seconds1++;
    seconds0 = 0;
  }
  myLEDs.setDigit(0, 2, seconds0, true);     // update units

  if (seconds1 < 6) {
    myLEDs.setDigit(0, 3, seconds1, false);  // Update tens
  } else {
    seconds1 = 0;
    seconds0 = 0;
    myLEDs.setDigit(0, 3, seconds1, false);  // Reset and update minutes
    BumpMinutes();
  }
}
```

```
/*****
  This function increments the minutes counter and
  rolls to the next digit as needed.

  Parameter List:
    void

  Return value:
    void
*****/
void  BumpMinutes()
{
  minutes0++;                // Works the same as seconds, only for minutes:
  if (minutes0 == 10) {
    minutes1++;
    minutes0 = 0;
  }
  myLEDs.setDigit(0, 4, minutes0, true);

  if (minutes1 < 6) {
    myLEDs.setDigit(0, 5, minutes1, false);
  } else {
    minutes1 = 0;
    minutes0 = 0;
    myLEDs.setDigit(0, 5, minutes1, false);  // Need to update hours
    BumpHours();
  }
}

/*****
  This function increments the hours counter and
  rolls to the next digit as needed.

  Parameter List:
    void

  Return value:
    void
*****/
void  BumpHours()
{
  hours0++;               // Works same as minutes…
  if (hours0 == 10) {
    hours1++;
    hours0 = 0;
  }
  myLEDs.setDigit(0, 6, hours0, true);

  if (hours1 < 6) {
    myLEDs.setDigit(0, 7, hours1, false); // Nothing left to bump, so reset
  } else {
```

```
      hours1 = 0;
      hours0 = 0;
      Reset();
    }
}

/*****
  This function resets the digits to zero

  Parameter List:
    void

  Return value:
    void
*****/
void Reset()
{
  myLEDs.setDigit(0, 0, 0, false);
  for (int i = 1; i < myLEDs.getDeviceCount(); i++) {
    myLEDs.setDigit(0, i, 0, (i % 2 == 0) ? true : false);
  }
}
```

You can read about the LedControl library and download it at https://github.com/wayoda/LedControl. One of the nice features of the library is that it allows you to configure the control pins the way you want to define them.

You probably don't need me to make too many comments on the code, as there's not a whole lot going on. A global LED control object named *myLEDs* is defined and initialized to work with our eight-digit display. Next, we define a bunch of *int* variables that essentially give names to each of the eight seven-segment displays. The *setup()* function does little more than set the control pins to *OUTPUT*, set the LEDs to active mode, set the display brightness, and clear the display. The *loop()* function only has one statement: *BumpFrame()*.

BumpFrame() is responsible for incrementing the hundredths-of-a-second digits of the display. If the units component (*hundredths0*) is equal to 10, the tens component (*hundredths1*) is incremented and *hundredths0* is set to 0. This process continues on until the count is 99, at which time the two digits are set to 0 and *BumpSeconds()* is called. In other words, the hundredths of a second "rollover" to the seconds segments of the display.

If you look at the code for *BumpSeconds()*, it works pretty much the same as the way the hundredths-of-a-second digits were incremented, only using a rollover value of 60 (seconds) instead of 100. Indeed, *BumpMinutes()* and *BumpHours()* are the same, only using different units of the display. The algorithm is essentially the same. Once the display shows 99:59:59:99, the code calls the *Reset()* function and the count starts over.

The real point of this program is to show how easy it is to use the SPI interface to control an inexpensive eight-digit display. Also, you can turn off the display for whatever time period you need and only display the number on a given criteria. Because LEDs are relatively power hungry, being able to turn the display off easily can be useful. These displays are a good choice if you only need to display fairly large numbers. In most cases, these displays cost less and are more easily viewed than a 16×2 LCD display.

Interrupts and Interrupt Service Routines (ISR)

Anyone who has been around a two-year-old child for more than a couple of hours knows what an interrupt is. If you've raised your own kids, you also know what an Interrupt Service Routine (ISR) is— ranging from diaper changes to chasing away those monsters that live under the bed. Simply stated, *interrupts are notifications that something wants immediate attention. The nature of that attention is contained in the code that comprises the ISR.*

Interrupts offer an alternative to the polling process mentioned in Chapter 5 when we talked about loop structures. Recall that I discussed how you might use a loop to monitor fire sensors in a building. The code visited each sensor, and if no fire was sensed, the loop moved to the next sensor. This process of moving from one area of interest (i.e., a sensor) to the next is called *polling*. The problem is that if you have thousands of sensors in the poll list, and it takes a few seconds for each sensor to get an accurate reading, it could take over a half an hour to make a complete pass through the sensor list. If you're unlucky enough to have a fire start immediately after a visit to that sensor, the fire is going to get a half-hour start before anyone knows something's amiss. Not good. Because of such limitations, critical applications like a fire system would not use a polling algorithm for the fire system. Instead, the system would be based on sensors that can generate an interrupt.

The Arduino family supports two types of interrupts: external (hardware) and pin change. External hardware interrupts are triggered by some type of signal on a pin. Hardware interrupts can be triggered in four different ways:

- on a low signal state
- on a change in signal state
- on the rising edge of a signal change
- on the falling edge of a signal change

Because these interrupts are hardware based, they are very fast. Although external interrupts are fairly easy to work with, the bad news is that the Arduino boards have a limited number of pins designed to respond to external hardware interrupts. The good news is that all of the Arduino pins can be used with pin change interrupts. You simply designate the pin(s) you wish to use and attach them to an ISR. Table 13-1 shows the external interrupt pins for several popular Arduino boards.

Table 13-1. Arduino External Interrupt Pins

Board	Int0	Int1	Int2	Int3	Int4	Int5
Uno, Mini, Nano	2	3				
Mega 2560	2	3	21	20	19	18
Leonardo, Micro	3	2	0	1		

If you look at the LCD examples that are distributed with the Arduino IDE, you'll find that they use pins 2 and 3 as part of the data communication between the display and the Arduino. The use of those pins is not etched in stone, so we prefer to move them so pins 2 and 3 are left for hardware interrupts should a sketch need them. If your design does not require all of the digital pins to be used, we'd suggest leaving pins 0–3 open. As you know, pins 0 and 1 are used by the *Serial* object to communicate with your PC via the USB cable. Now you know that pins 2 and 3 are available for external hardware interrupts. While these pins can be used in your program for digital use, as a rule we leave them empty just in case we want to use an external interrupt down the road. Figure 13-3 shows how the pins are mapped for the Atmel 328 chip.

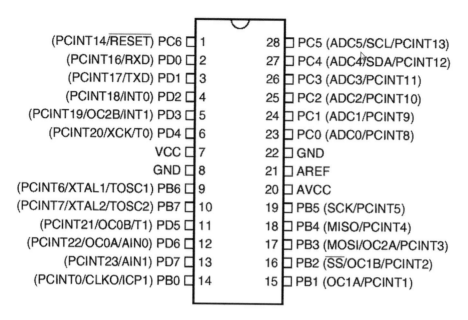

Figure 13-3. *The Atmel 328 chip*

Note how INT0 and INT1 are actually tied to pins 4 and 5 on the chip. However, most boards arrange the pinouts so they appear to be digital pins 2 and 3. Pin 1 on the chip is actually the Reset pin, whereas pins 2 and 3 are the RXD/TXD used by the *Serial* object for communication over the USB link.

There are three ports defined for the Atmel 328 (or 168) chip. These ports allow for faster, low-level manipulation of the I/O pins associated with each port. The three ports are defined in Table 13-2. Note that PORTB, PORTC, and PORTD are symbolic constants that you can use in your programs. Also note that only PORTB forms an 8-bit port.

Table 13-2. *Port Pin Assignments*

Port Name	Pins	Comment
PORTB	14-19 and 9,10	Labeled PB* in Figure 13-2.
PORTC	23-28, 1	Labeled PC* in Figure 13-2. Avoid pin 1, the Reset pin. (These are also the analog pins, ADC0 – ADC5.)
PORTD	2-6, 9-13	Labeled PD* in Figure 13-2. Avoid interrupt pins 2 and 3, and *Serial* pins 0 and 1.

PORTB is labeled PB0 through PB7 in Figure 13-2, and corresponds to pins 14–19, but then skips to pins 9 and 10 for the last to bits of the port. PORTC is labeled PC0 through PC6 in Figure 13-2, but PC6 is rarely used because it is the CPU Reset bit. PORTD is labeled PD0 through PD7, but you will usually avoid pins PD0 and PD1 since these are used by the *Serial* object. PD2 and PD3 correspond to the interrupt pins, INT0 and INT1, respectively.

Each port is controlled by three registers: the Data Direction Register, the PORT Data Register, and the port PIN registers. Therefore, DDRD would be the Data Direction Register for Port D, PORTD (as seen earlier) is the Data Register for port D, and PIND is the PIN register for port D. All of the PIN registers are read-only.

Interrupt Details

To appreciate how interrupts work, we need to learn some low-level details about the Arduino boards that are based on the Atmel 328 CPU. (We'll concentrate on the 328 chip, as that's the most popular.) First, we need to understand the External Interrupt Control Register A, EICRA. This can be seen in Table 13-3.

Table 13-3. *The External Interrupt Control Register A*

Bit	7	6	5	4	3	2	1	0
EICRA					ISC11	ISC10	ISC01	ISC00
Read/Write	R	R	R	R	R/W	R/W	R/W	R/W

The two interrupts available on the 328 chip are INT0 and INT1. The EICRA controls what triggers these two interrupts, as described in Table 13-4. In this table, ISC00-01 describes the parameters for INT0, whereas ISC10-11 is for INT1.

Table 13-4. *Interpretation of Bit Patterns*

Description	ISC11	ISC10	ISC01	ISC00
The low level	0	0	0	0
Any logical change	0	1	0	1
Falling edge	1	0	1	0
Rising edge	1	1	1	1

Therefore, if the EICRA register of a 328 processor holds binary 00000010; INT0 will be using the falling edge of the signal to trigger the interrupt. A bit pattern of 00001110 says INT0 is using a falling edge trigger, but INT1 is using a rising edge trigger. Make sure you understand why these bit patterns determine how INT0 and INT1 work before you move on.

The determination of which interrupt is being used is set using the External interrupt Mask Register (EIMSK). This is presented in Table 13-5. If the 0 bit is set (i.e., 1), INT0 is active. If the 1 bit is set, INT1 is active. Obviously, you can also have both interrupts active at one time by setting both bits.

Table 13-5. *The External Interrupt Mask Register*

Bit	7	6	5	4	3	2	1	0
EIMSK	-	-	-	-	-	-	INT1	INT0
Read/Write	R	R	R	R	R	R	R/W	R/W

Table 13-6. *The External Interrupt Flag Register*

Bit	7	6	5	4	3	2	1	0
EIFR	-	-	-	-	-	-	INTF1	INTF0
Read/Write	R	R	R	R	R	R	R/W	R/W

When an edge or logic change occurs on either the INT1 or INT0 pin and triggers an interrupt request, the appropriate bit in the External Interrupt Flag Register (EIFR) is set (see Table 13-6). If either of the corresponding interrupt pins is set in the EIMSK register, control branches to the ISR. The ISR code determines what the interrupt actual does. The EIFR is cleared when the ISR code is executed.

An External Interrupt Program

Now let's take a simple example where we wire a switch to pin 2. The ground leg of the switch has a 10K resistor between the switch and the ground pin on the Arduino. Anytime we press the switch, we want program control to immediately jump to our ISR. Listing 13-2 shows the source code for our interrupt program.

Listing 13-2. A Simple Interrupt Program

```
#include <avr/interrupt.h>

#define LEDPIN   13

volatile int state = LOW;

void setup() {

  DDRB = DDRB | B00100000;  // Set pin 6 of Port B to output, but…
                            // PORTB6 is digital pin 13
  PORTD |= (1 << PORTD2);   // turn On pin 2 of PORTD

  EICRA |= (1 << ISC00);    // set INT0 to trigger on ANY logic change
  EIMSK |= (1 << INT0);     // Turns on INT0

  sei();                    // turn on interrupts
}

void loop() {
  unsigned long i;
  unsigned long sum = 0;
  for (i = 0; i < 4000000; i++)  // Do this just to have
    sum++;                       // something to interrupt!
}
ISR(INT0_vect)
{
  state = !state;           // Flip its state
  digitalWrite(LEDPIN, state); // interrupt code here
}
```

The first thing we do is #*include* the header file that contains the symbolic constants for using interrupts. Next we define *state* as a *volatile int* variable. The *volatile* keyword is actually a message to the compiler to generate code that forces the *state* variable to be reloaded from memory every time it is accessed, even if it is currently sitting in a register. That way we can ensure that the code doesn't use an "out-of-date" (i.e., cached) value for *state*. It's a good idea to use the *volatile* keyword with any variable that is part of the ISR.

The next statement

```
DDRB = DDRB | B00100000;   // Set pin 6 of Port B to output, but...
                           // PORTB6 is digital pin 13
```

is used to set bit 6 of PORTB high by using the Data Direction Register for Port B (DDRB). If you count the digital pins in Figure 13-2, starting with PD0, and count to PB5, you'll find out that bit 6 of PORTB is the 13th digital I/O pin. Sound familiar? Yep... it's the LED pin. In other words, the preceding statement is the low-level equivalent of:

```
pinMode(13, OUTPUT);
```

Indeed, you could replace the low-level statement with the *pinMode()* call, and it will work exactly the same.

The next statement

```
PORTD |= (1 << PORTD2);   // turn On pin 2 of PORTD
```

is used to turn on pin 2 of Port D. Now refer back to Figure 13-2 and look for PD2 (i.e., pin 2 of Port D). Well, whaddaya know... PD2 is also the pin for INT0! So the statement is simply activating the INT0 interrupt.

The first of the next two statements

```
EICRA |= (1 << ISC00);   // set INT0 to trigger on ANY logic change
EIMSK |= (1 << INT0);    // Enables INT0
```

can be understood by looking at Table 13-4. Because we are setting bit ISC00 to 1, we are setting the External Interrupt Control Register A (EICRA) to use any logic state change on INT0 to trigger the interrupt. The |= operator performs a bitwise OR on the current state of EICRA, which has the effect of maintaining the bit pattern that prevailed before this statement is executed. That way, the statement only affects the ISC00 bit in the register. The call to *sei()* "sets external interrupts," which enables the interrupts.

If you look at the call to *ISR(INT0_vect)*, it is the ISR we wrote for INT0. Note how the parameter to the ISR (i.e., *INT0_vect*) determines which interrupt is being defined. As you can see, the ISR does little more than toggle the state of the onboard LED. It does this by doing a logical NOT on the current value of *state*. Recall that we defined *state* using the *volatile* storage specifier to force the compiler to reload *state* each time it is referenced. This ensures that *state* remains "in sync" with what we are trying to do.

Three more little bits of advice about ISR.... First, use the *volatile* storage specifier with any variables used in the routine, for the reason we just mentioned. Second, keep the ISR as short as possible. The reason is because while your ISR is running, everything else is on hold until your ISR finishes. Third, while your ISR is running, no other interrupts can take place. This often means that any libraries you might use that have their own ISRs (e.g., *Serial* methods) are comatose while your ISR is active. This is another reason to keep yours as short as possible. You'd hate to have your light sensor ISR turning on a couple-hundred hallway lights in the morning while the fire ISR is trying to tell you that the tenth floor is on fire.

The code in *loop()* is just there so something is going on when you press the button. If you just put in an empty *loop()*, most of the time the compiler optimizes it away. Oh, one more thing. If you run this program, it sometimes appears that the button press gets out of whack with what you think should be happening. This is probably caused by "switch bounce." If you look at a switch closure on a fast oscilloscope, you will see that the voltage bounces between HIGH and LOW before it settles down to its "real" state. There are ways in both hardware and software to get rid of switch bounce. A quick session with Google will show you a bazillion ways to cope with switch debouncing.

An Alternative Interrupt Program

Let's have the same goal as the previous program; namely, blinking the onboard LED when we press a switch connected to pin 2. This time, however, remove the 10K resistor and just directly wire one leg of the switch to GND on the Arduino and the other side to pin 2. Arduino pins to default inputs, which means they do not explicitly need to be defined using the INPUT symbolic constant and *pinMode()*. Internally, this means each pin behaves as though it has a high impedance (e.g., 100 megohm) resistor wired in front of each pin. As a result, it takes very little current to change the pin state, which is beneficial in some situations. However, it also means that unconnected pins can change state in a seemingly random fashion, as such pins "float" between the HIGH and LOW states.

However, internal to the Arduino are 20K pullup resistors that can be activated by software. (The exact value of the pullups varies by chip type. Check your chip's documentation if this is a critical factor to your circuit.) You can access these pullup resistors using a *pinMode()* call with the INPUT_PULLUP symbolic constant. Because of this configuration, with a switch connected to a pin with INPUT_PULLUP active, an open switch reads HIGH, and it reads LOW when the switch is pressed.

Listing 13-3 is the code that illustrates another way to implement an interrupt. The code is very similar to Listing 13-2, except we rely on the *attachInterrupt()* function to do most of the work for us.

Listing 13-3. Alternative Interrupt Program

```
#include <avr/interrupt.h>

#define LEDPIN   13

volatile int state = LOW;

void setup() {
  pinMode(LEDPIN, OUTPUT);
  pinMode(2, INPUT_PULLUP);

  attachInterrupt(0, myISR, CHANGE);
  sei();                    // turn on interrupts
}

void loop() {
  unsigned long i;
  unsigned long sum = 0;

  for (i = 0; i < 4000000; i++)  // Do this just to have
    sum++;                       // something to interrupt!
}

void myISR()
{
  state = !state;
  digitalWrite(LEDPIN, state);/* interrupt code here */
}
```

The statements

```
pinMode(13, OUTPUT);
pinMode(2, INPUT_PULLUP);

attachInterrupt(0, myISR, CHANGE);
```

set the LED pin to OUTPUT and turns on the pullup resistor for pin 2. (Can you get rid of these magic numbers? If so, then do it!) The *attachInterrupt()* function has the interrupt number as its first argument. In our example, we are using interrupt 0 (INT0). The second argument is the name of the ISR that tells the program what to do when an interrupt occurs. In our case, we simply toggle the LED using the ISR named *myISR()*. The third argument tells what signal condition should cause the interrupt. We have used the CHANGE symbolic constant to trigger the interrupt whenever the state of the switch changes.

When you run the program and press the switch, the LED blinks on and off. Note, however, that if you are using a push button switch, pushing it in turns the LED off and letting it go turns it back on. (If you have a real "bouncy" switch, it may strobe several times.) The reason is because we are using the CHANGE symbolic constant to trigger the interrupt whenever the state of the switch changes. What would happen if you changed this to trigger on a rising or falling edge signal?

The code in the *loop()* function is there to show that we can do something else while the interrupt is active. Again, if we just used a simple empty loop, the compiler optimizes the loop away, which is why we use *sum* in the loop. If you wish, you can put a *Serial.print()* statement in *loop()*, but don't forget that because the *Serial* object itself uses interrupts, your interrupt will have to wait until the *Serial* object finishes its interrupt code before you can hope for yours to activate.

Ultrasonic Sensor Program

Many of the Arduino Starter Kits detailed in Appendix A include an inexpensive ultrasonic sound sensor (see Figure 13-4.) These sensors are based on the idea that a transmitted sound takes a known amount of time to travel a given distance. For example, at 72 degrees Fahrenheit, sound travels 1131.7439486730823 feet/second, or 344.9555555555555 meters/second. Therefore, if the sensor emits a ping and a wall is 1131.74 feet away, it takes approximately 2 seconds for the sound wave to make the round-trip from the sound emitter to the wall, and back to the sound receiver. (These inexpensive sensors are pretty much deaf at 1100 feet. Ten feet is a more realistic range.)

Figure 13-4. *Ultrasonic sensor*

If you look closely at Figure 13-3, you can see that the sensor is controlled by just two pins: a trigger ping and an echo pin. The idea is that one device emits a sound and the other device detects that sound. By measuring the time interval in between sending and receiving the ping, you can measure the distance to an object. The distance range is approximately 1 inch to 12 feet, with an advertised accuracy of about 0.25 inches. The cost of these sensors is about $2.

The code to use the sensor is presented in Listing 13-4. You can probably figure out the code without my help. I chose to use pin 8 for the trigger pin and pin 10 for the echo pin, but you can choose whatever pins you wish.

Listing 13-4. Ultrasound Sensor Program

```
/*
  Code is taken from
      http://www.arduino.cc/en/Tutorial/Ping
  and was written by David Mellis and modified
  by Tom Igoe.

  Modified by Dr. Purdum for sound speed at
  72 degrees F.
  1/2/2105
*/

int triggerPin = 8;
int echoPin = 10;

void setup() {
  Serial.begin(115200);
  pinMode(triggerPin, OUTPUT);
  pinMode(echoPin, INPUT);
}

void loop(){
  long roundTrip;
  float cm;

  digitalWrite(triggerPin, LOW); // Trigger a short low pulse
  delayMicroseconds(2);          // before the HIGH pulse
  digitalWrite(triggerPin, HIGH);
  delayMicroseconds(10);
  digitalWrite(triggerPin, LOW);

  roundTrip = pulseIn(echoPin, HIGH);
  cm = microsecondsToCentimeters(roundTrip);
  float inch = cm / 2.54;        // Figure out inches
  Serial.print(cm);
  Serial.print(" cm or ");
  Serial.print(inch);
  Serial.print(" inches");
  Serial.println();
  delay(1000);
}
/*****
  This function calculates how far the pulse travels to
  strike and object and return. The air temp is assumed
  to be 72F.

  Parameter list:
    long microseconds    the time of the pulse
```

```
    Return value:
      float              centimeters to and from target
      *****/
float microsecondsToCentimeters(long microseconds){
  return (microseconds*0.034495)/2;
}
```

Because the trigger pin (*triggerPin* = 8) sends the pulse, we use *pinMode()* to set the pin for *OUTPUT*. Pin 10, *echoPin*, uses *pinMode()* to set the pin for *INPUT* since it receives the pulse.

The documentation for the sensor says to send a short, low pulse immediately before sending out the pulse of interest. You can see this near the top of *loop()*. There is a 10-microsecond pulse, after which the sensor is set to LOW. The statement

```
roundTrip = pulseIn(echoPin, HIGH);
```

waits for the pin to go HIGH to start its timing cycle, and stops timing when the pin goes LOW. It returns the length of the pulse in microseconds. The documentation says *pulseIn* works with pulses from 10 microseconds up to almost 3 minutes. The call to *microsecondsToCentimeters()* is passed the number of microseconds it took to make the trip from and back to the sensor. For that reason, the actual distance to the object is half that time, which is why the function adjusts the conversion from time to microseconds by dividing by 2. The floating point constant reflects the speed of sound when the temperature is 72 degrees Fahrenheit. Figure 13-5 shows a sample run of the program as I moved a book forward and backward in front of the sensor.

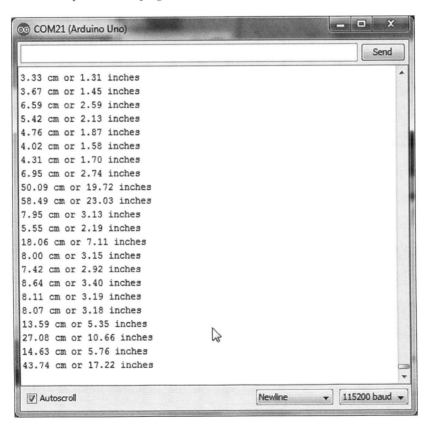

Figure 13-5. Sample run of ultrasonic sensor program

313

Although sensors like the one shown in Figure 13-3 are often used in robotics types of equipment, that's not the reason for showing you how to use it. Rather, I wanted to show you how simple it can be to use a sensor in a program. Many other types of sensors, from light sensors to audio detectors, are just as easily interfaced to an Arduino. Many of the starter kits include a variety of sensors, including the ultrasonic sensor. I saw an ad on eBay for a collection of 37 sensors for less than $50. Depending upon your interest, pick up a few sensors and experiment with them.

A Programming Problem

A time will come when you have a sketch working but you'd like to modify it to make it even better. When I first started working with the Arduino, I needed to display more information than would fit on a standard 2×16 LCD display. I needed the first line of the display to tell the origin of the data presented on the second line. Although not my actual program problem, let's say you need the first line of the LCD to say: "From: Jill" and the second line to show the message. No problem … as long as the message is 16 characters or less. But Jill tends to have long messages, so you need to be able to show the entire message while keeping the first line unchanged. How are you going to do this?

As you know, you can address the LCD cursor, position it where you want it on the display, and then print characters to it starting at that position. So, my first hack at the solution was to divide the message for the second line into 16-character chunks and simply scroll through the message. My first thought was to insert a *delay()* call after a 16-character chunk was displayed, and then display the next 16-character chunk. That worked fine, but looked kinda clunky; plus some people read faster or slower than other people. So, my next hack was to display a message chunk until the user pressed a key on the *Serial* monitor. For my specific application, this worked okay, but what if I faced a similar problem down the road and didn't use a PC as part of the solution, or I didn't want the user to have to press a key or switch? Then what? Okay, what's your solution? No, really—stop, think for a few minutes, and design a solution that you feel overcomes whatever shortcomings you perceive.

The first thing you have to realize is that my solution may be a lesser solution than your solution. After all, if I had all the "perfect" answers, I'd be rich and not writing books during my retirement. (Well, I'd probably still be writing, as I actually enjoy it.) Either way, you should try to implement your solution before you read about mine. So, go build your solution and come back after you have it working. Then you'll be able to compare the two.

My Solution

Before I get into my solution, I need to point out that there is one LCD display I absolutely love to use. It's a 16×2 white-on-blue LCD using the Inter-Integrated Circuit (I2C) interface from Yourduino (http://yourduino.com/sunshop2/index.php?l=product_detail&p=170). The display is reasonably priced ($5.75), is very fast, and uses only two pins. It took me less than 30 seconds from out-of-the-box to completely working. If you want an easy-to-use LCD display, it doesn't get any easier than this one. I'm sure there are other I2C LCD displays available on the Internet, too.

Anyway, my solution was to implement horizontal scrolling of the second line. The Yourduino display takes advantage of an LCD library written specifically for an I2C display. You can download the library from https://bitbucket.org/fmalpartida/new-liquidcrystal/downloads.

(You may have to rename any library that has the same matching folder name.) The library, however, does not implement horizontal scrolling, so we need to write that function ourselves. To do that, let's diagram how we want it to work. We'll assume that the message we want to display on the second line is 40 characters long. The second line of the LCD can be thought of as 16 boxes, each capable of holding one character:

1	2	3	4	5	6	7	8	9	10	11	12	13	14	15	16

We'll assume that the message is: "We will meet for lunch at noon at the Twin Lakes Restaurant." Therefore, our initial state of the display looks like this when we display the first part of the message that fits on the display:

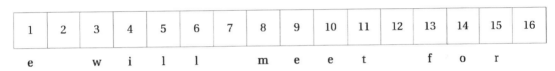

After a moment's pause, we need to push all of the letters on the display one position to the left and update position 16 with the next character in the message. Therefore, we want the display to look like this:

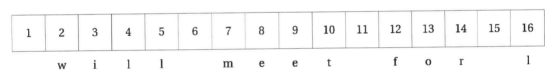

After another small pause, we want to push things left again so that the display shows this:

1	2	3	4	5	6	7	8	9	10	11	12	13	14	15	16
	w	i	l	l		m	e	e	t		f	o	r		l

We keep repeating this process until the entire second message is displayed. After the complete message is displayed, we can either stop or redisplay the entire message again.

So, how would you code this algorithm? You should fall back to the Five Program Steps. The Initialization Step should create the LCD object for the display, and we likely will need to define some global variables. It seems likely that we will need *char* arrays for the first and second message lines (*msg1, msg2*), and perhaps symbolic constants for rows and columns. Because we want the message to scroll at a readable speed, we will likely need a delay of some stated milliseconds while the message is scrolled. That delay value, too, will likely be a symbolic constant since we will want to experiment with the length of the delay.

The Input Step collects the message to be displayed. In our test case, we are just going to hard-code a message string during testing. In actual use, the message could come from any device that is capable of delivering a character stream. It could be the *Serial* object, a database connection, a Wi-Fi connection, an SD card reader... whatever. The point here, however, is to develop a function capable of horizontal scrolling.

The Process Step involves reading the input stream and formatting the characters into the strings that can be passed to the Display Step. It is the Display Step that is the focal point of this exercise. As usual, there is no Termination Step.

So, how do you want to scroll the display? We know we need to "slide" the message from right to left behind a fixed 16-character "window." This suggests a *for* loop to march through the message array in some fashion. So, let's use that as a starting point.

315

Listing 13-5 presents our scroll program. There's really nothing unusual about the global definitions or *setup()*. The *Serial* object is actually not used, but I added it in case you wanted to add some debug print statements while testing. Note how I use *#define DEBUG* to toggle the scaffold code.

Listing 13-5. Scroll LCD Display

```
//#define DEBUG      // Uncomment if you want to add debug prints

#include <Wire.h>  // Comes with Arduino IDE
// Get the LCD I2C Library here:
// https://bitbucket.org/fmalpartida/new-liquidcrystal/downloads

#include <LiquidCrystal_I2C.h>
#define COLS      16
#define ROWS       2
#define PAUSE     300

// For the Yourduino I2C LCD display:
// set the LCD address to 0x27 for a 20 chars 4 line display
// Set the pins on the I2C chip used for LCD connections:
//                  addr, en,rw,rs,d4,d5,d6,d7,bl,blpol

                    // Set the LCD I2C address
LiquidCrystal_I2C lcd(0x27, 2, 1, 0, 4, 5, 6, 7, 3, POSITIVE);
char msg1[] = "From: Jill";
char msg2[] = "We will meet for lunch at noon at the Twin Lakes Restaurant";

void setup()
{
#ifdef DEBUG
  Serial.begin(9600);      // For debugging, if needed…
#endif
  lcd.begin(COLS, ROWS);   // init lcd for 16 chars 2 lines

}


void loop()
{
  int len;
  len = strlen(msg1);
  if (len > COLS) {        // Truncate From details if too long
    msg1[COLS] = '\0';
  }
  lcd.setCursor(0,0);      //Start at character 4 on line 0
  lcd.print(msg1);
  len = strlen(msg2);
  if (len <= COLS) {       // Second part short enough to fit?
    lcd.setCursor(1, 0);
    lcd.print(msg2);
```

```
  } else {
    ScrollDisplay(msg2, 1); // Need to scroll the message
  }
  delay(4000);
}

/*****
  The purpose of this function is to scroll a message across
  a line of the display.

  Parameter list:
    char msg[]          the message to scroll
    int row             the row for scrolling

  Return value:
    void
*****/
void ScrollDisplay(char msg[], int row)
{
  int i;
  int j;
  char window[COLS + 1];  // Enough room for message + null

  strncpy(window, msg, COLS);
  window[COLS + 1] = '\0';
  lcd.setCursor(0, row);       // Show first part...
  lcd.print(window);
  delay(PAUSE);

  j = COLS;
  do {
    for (i = 0; i < COLS - 1; i++) {  // Copy old part
      window[i] = window[i + 1];
    }
    window[i] = msg[j];              // Add new character
    lcd.setCursor(0, row);
    lcd.print(window);
    delay(PAUSE);
  }while (msg[++j]);

}
```

In *loop()*, we determine the length of the message string; and if the second part is too long to fit a single LCD display width, the *ScrollDisplay()* function is called. Within the *ScrollDisplay()* function, we define a *COL + 1* window (e.g., *window[]*) in which to scroll the message. Because we know the message is too long to display, we copy the first *COL* characters from the message to the display window using this statement:

```
strncpy(window, msg, COLS);
```

strncpy() is a standard library function that copies up to *COLS* characters from *msg[]* to *window[]*. The code then displays the first part of the message string held in *window[]* on the LCD display.

■ **Tip** I encourage you to study the standard C library string functions. See `www.techonthenet.com/c_` `language/standard_library_functions/string_h/`. You should study all the *str*()* and *mem*()* functions, as they solve a lot of common programming tasks. I would also encourage you to avoid the *String* class. While that class does bring a lot to the table, I find it bloats the code size rather noticeably. Use a *char* array instead.

The program then uses a *do-while* loop to scroll the rest of the message. Note how the *for* loop has the effect of moving each character one screen column to the left, giving the illusion of horizontal scrolling. When the loop completes, we update the last character position with a new character from the message. The code then sets the cursor and displays the *window[]* line. The *delay()* call is necessary to keep the display on the screen long enough to read. You can play around with the *delay()* argument to suit your preference. We used a *do-while* because we want to test for the end of a message after the current character is scrolled.

Conclusion

In this chapter I tried to show you how easy it is to interface your Arduino with the outside world. We haven't even scratched the surface. A little work searching the Internet will turn up hundreds of projects that use all kinds of sensors. Because of the Arduino's popularity, there are dozens of inexpensive sensors, shields, displays, and other add-ons available with which you can experiment. You can even use an OLED display that's less than 1-inch square, but is capable of 128×64 graphics! Dig around a little and you'll be amazed what you will find.

EXERCISES

1. Why is it not a good idea to use the *Serial* object when you are using interrupts in your project?

   Answer: The reason is because the *Serial* object itself uses interrupts, which means that other interrupts may be missed when the *Serial* object is active.

2. If *pinMode()* can be used to set pins, why should you bother learning about port manipulation?

   Answer: Direct port manipulation is a little faster and allows you to set multiple pins at the same time.

3. Along the same lines, why use port manipulation for interrupts when you can use *attachInterrupt()*?

   Answer: Same answer—it is more efficient and it can set multiple pins at once.

4. Why would you choose to use the SPI or I2C interface for an LCD display instead of the standard interface used in the IDE examples?

   Answer: The SPI and I2C interfaces use fewer pins, plus the interfaces can control multiple devices if needed. Note that using these interfaces requires the use of an LCD display that has the SPI or I2C hardware as part of the display.

5. The Arduino IDE allows you to use the *String* class instead of *char* arrays for strings. Why did I avoid the *String* class in this chapter?

    Answer: The *String* class makes a lot of string manipulation very easy, but at a price I'm not willing to pay. Write a program using the *String* class and then write the same program using a *char* array. In most cases, the *String* class version will consume about 30% more memory.

6. I asked you to study the *str*()* and *mem*()* functions. Why did I do that?

    Answer: Because those functions are used over and over in programs—so you need to learn how to use them. It will save you time (and probably memory) as you develop your programs. Indeed, learning about what's available in different libraries is probably one of the most efficient uses of your time that you can pursue while learning C.

7. Rewrite the *ScrollDisplay()* function in Listing 13-5 without using a *for* loop.

    Answer: I added this exercise to see if you could apply what you learned in question 6. The fact that you're reading this suggests that you are interested in doing the exercises. The benefit of that drive is learning a little bit more than those who just skip over the exercises. Please try to do this on your own before you read my solution. At the very least, explain to yourself how I got rid of the *for* loop and how it works.

```
/*****
 The purpose of this function is to scroll a message across
 a line of the display.

 Parameter list:
  char msg[]       the message to scroll
  int row          the row for scrolling

 Return value:
  void
*****/
void ScrollDisplay(char msg[], int row)
{
  int i;
  int j;
  char window[COLS + 1];   // Enough room for message + null

  strncpy(window, msg, COLS);
  window[COLS + 1] = '\0';
  lcd.setCursor(0, row);          // Show first part…
  lcd.print(window);
  delay(PAUSE);
```

```
      j = COLS;
      do {
        memmove(window, &window[1], COLS);      // No more for loop!
        window[COLS - 1] = msg[j];              // Add new character
        lcd.setCursor(0, row);
        lcd.print(window);
        delay(PAUSE);
      }while (msg[++j]);

    }
```

CHAPTER 14

■ ■ ■

A Gentle Introduction to Object-Oriented Programming and C++

The purpose of this chapter is singular: I want to teach you enough about object-oriented programming (OOP) and C++ so that you can look at the source code of a library header (*.h) file and its associated C plus-plus (*.cpp) file and have some idea of what the code is doing. To say that I (or anyone else) can teach you C++ in one chapter is either a lie or a *REALLY* long chapter. Still, it's worthwhile having an idea of what OOP is and what it brings to the programming table. This chapter builds on information contained in Chapter 12, so make sure that you have already read that chapter.

C++ is not the only OOP language available in the world of programming. Many other languages could be used (e.g., Java, C#, Visual Basic, Python, Ruby, etc.), and each has its own strengths and weaknesses. However, given that the Arduino IDE is built upon the Open Source C++ compiler, it's obvious that any OOP coding is done in C++. For that reason, the discussion in this chapter is couched in terms of C++. While there are some minor variations, most of what's said in this chapter applies to many other OOP languages as well.

The OOP Trilogy

The core of OOP programming and its benefits can be explained in terms of the OOP Trilogy: encapsulation, inheritance, and polymorphism. Let's take a quick look at each of these elements of OOP.

Encapsulation

You already have some idea of what *encapsulation* means: data hiding. When we discussed scope in Chapter 7, I explained how limiting the visibility of a piece of data by encapsulating it in the most restrictive scope level possible makes it easier to test and debug a program. Encapsulation means that access to a piece of data is restricted. By having restricted access, any time that piece of data has a bogus value, you at least have a well-defined starting point from which you can ferret out what the problem is.

Back in the "bad ole days," all variables had what we now call *global scope* and many languages (e.g., Basic) had "typeless" data. That is, any variable could hold string, floating point, or integer data. Debugging was a nightmare. Creating data types and then encapsulating by using the concept of scope made life much easier for the programmer. OOP simply carries encapsulation one step further by hiding the data in something called a *class*. (I explain what a class is later in this chapter.)

© Jack Purdum 2015
J. Purdum, *Beginning C for Arduino, Second Edition*: Learn C Programming
for the Arduino, DOI 10.1007/978-1-4842-0940-0_14

Inheritance

Inheritance is the ability to have a "ground level" description of a piece of data, and then further refine it to create a new type of data. For example, some time ago I was asked by a real estate investor to write a package that would track their real estate holdings. The investor has three basic types of buildings: residential, commercial, and apartments. Each type of rental property had its own special considerations. While the number of bedrooms affects both residential and apartment properties, it has no impact on commercial properties. Likewise, commercial properties had to have so many parking places, of which some fraction had to be for handicap parking. Also, bathroom facilities were affected by the square footage of the building. There were even snow removal restrictions that varied by property type. So, how do you minimize the complexity of the software?

You can reduce the complexity by looking for common features for all property types, and then worry about the details. For example, each property had an address, property taxes, purchase price, insurance cost, mortgage lender, mortgage amount, and so forth. We could create variables for these aspects of a property in something called *building*. We could then create some other object and track the details that make each building type different. Figure 14-1 shows this relationship.

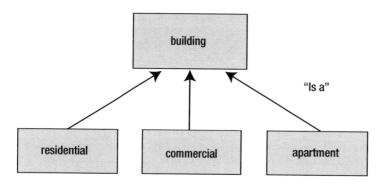

Figure 14-1. *Building types*

What we are showing in Figure 14-1 is that a residential, commercial, and apartment buildings are all a special type of a base type called *building*. In other words, these three special types of building "inherit" all of the basic elements shared in common for all buildings. The arrow pointing from each of the three specific building types is called an "is a" relationship, which says that each of those special building types inherits all of the traits of *building*.

OOP jargon often refers to *building* as the *base class*; the three building types are *subclasses* of the base class. You will also hear the base class called the *parent class* and the subclasses called *child classes*. The interpretation is the same for either set of terms. The important thing to note is that, instead of three sets of property taxes, mortgages, addresses, and types of variables, we can push that into a common denominator class (i.e., the base class) and simply let the subclass inherit those member's variables from the base class. By using inheritance of the base class, you've reduced the code for tracking those variables by two-thirds what they would be otherwise. Imagine the code savings if you are a university tracking 50,000 students!

Polymorphism

The concept of *polymorphism* literally means one thing has many shapes. In OOP programming, it means that a method can have a single name, but can behave differently based upon the arguments that are passed to it. You have used this yourself when you used something like the following:

```
int val = 10;
Serial.println(val);
Serial.println(val, HEX);
```

In this example, the *Serial* object's *println()* method is called twice, each using a different argument list. As a result, the first call prints *val* using the (default) base 10 numbering system, while the second version displays *val* in hexadecimal (base 16).

Sometimes you may read about method overloading. *Method overloading* is actually polymorphism in action because it allows you to "overload" a method name with multiple versions of its functionality based on its signature. As long as the argument list of the methods are different (e.g., different signatures), the compiler will be able to figure out what your intent is and generate the proper code even though the method names are the same.

The OOP Class

Perhaps the common denominator of all OOP languages is the concept of a class. A *class* is a formal description of something called an object. An *object* is simply a description of something that you are interested in. Let's create a simple example to illustrate what a class is.

Suppose you are looking for a new job. You make an application and the company wants to have a face-to-face interview. Because you live about a thousand miles away, the company calls you to set up the interview and arranges to meet you at the airport. During the discussion, you tell them that you're a female, about 5′4″ tall, blonde hair, slim, and that you will be wearing a black business suit and carrying a black attaché case. The company guys says he's male, about six-feet tall, graying hair, overweight, and will be wearing a gray business suit. You plan to meet near baggage claim.

During this phone call, you are both describing what we might call a *person object*. The person object has variables for height, sex, weight, clothing, and hair color. Does this sound familiar? Doesn't this data scheme sound a little bit like a C *struct*? You could declare a *Person struct* like:

```
struct Person {
    int height;
    int sex;
    int weight;
    char wearing[20];
    int hairColor;
};
```

Recall that each variable in the *struct* is called a member of the *struct*. A major difference between a *struct* and an OOP *class* is that a *class* allows you to add functions to the *struct*; something a *struct* does not allow. In OOP parlance, the functions that are contained within a *class* are called class *methods*. You've been using class methods from day one each time you called *Serial.print()*. *Serial* is the class object and *print()* is the class method. (I discuss the dot operator a little later.)

Why was I careful to say: "You could *declare* a *Person struct….*"? If you remember, the structure declaration is just a template for a structure variable. It's not until you do something like

```
struct Person candidate, interviewer;
```

that you actually *define* structure variables that we can use in our program. Now let's move our understanding of *struct* to a class.

Inside an OOP Class

Let's take a look at one of the more simple C++ libraries. Listing 14-1 presents the *EEPROM.h* header file. If you look at the first and last line of the file, you will see the *#ifndef-#endif* preprocessor directives, which we discussed in Chapter 11. Almost all library files have a similar starting format. In essence, what these preprocessor directives say is: "If *EEPROM_h* is not yet defined, read the contents of this file into the program. If it is defined, don't read this file."

Listing 14-1. The EEPROM.h Header File

```
#ifndef EEPROM_h
#define EEPROM_h

#include <inttypes.h>

class EEPROMClass
{
  public:
    uint8_t read(int);
    void write(int, uint8_t);
};

extern EEPROMClass EEPROM;

#endif
```

This is a bit of defensive coding to prevent us from "double including" the contents of a header file. If we didn't do this, we might get a bunch of duplicate definition error messages.

After including the *inttypes.h* header file, the code has the following statement:

```
class EEPROMClass
{
```

This statement says: What follows from the opening brace to the closing brace in this file is a *declaration* of what a *class* named *EEPROMClass* contains. The remaining lines say that there are two *public* methods named *read()* and *write()*:

```
  public:
    uint8_t read(int);
    void write(int, uint8_t);
};

extern EEPROMClass EEPROM;
```

The keyword *public* means that access to the following two methods is readily available through a *class* object.

Class object?

OOP and Class Objects

The *class* declaration code presented in Listing 14-1 is like a blueprint for a house. It tells you the features of the house and how it is to be constructed, but house blueprints are not a house. Just like you can't live in a set of blueprints, the declaration of a class is not something you can directly use in a program. To define a *class* variable that we can use, we need to use something like the statement:

```
EEPROM myEEPROM;
```

However, because each Arduino board only has one EEPROM memory bank, near the bottom of the header file you see the statement

```
extern EEPROMClass EEPROM;
```

which defines an object of the *EEPROMClass* and calls it *EEPROM*. The variable named *EEPROM* is an object of the *EEPROMClass*. (Recall that the keyword *extern* means the actual variable is defined in another file. In this case, it means that you will define the *EEPROM* object in your sketch. Look at one of the EEPROM library examples and you'll see how this works.) You now have defined a variable that you can use in your own program. Because of the *public* keyword in the class declaration, you can now use statements like

```
EEPROM.read();    // Access to the read() method using the EEPROM object
EEPROM.write();   //       "       write()        "
```

to read and write the EEPROM memory on your Arduino board.

One more analogy: A C++ class is like a cookie cutter. The members of the class describe the angles necessary to form the cookie cutter, ounces of dough, and so forth. By changing the angles, you can have diamond-shaped cookies, Christmas tree cookies, Halloween cookies, and so forth. The class members dictate the shape, whether it has sprinkles or frosting, whether it uses a *bake()* or *fry()* method, and so forth. Regardless of the class declaration, nothing happens until you press the cookie cutter (i.e., the class) into the dough (i.e., memory), and extract the actual cookie (i.e., the object of the class), and perhaps apply a method (i.e., *bake()*) so that you have something useful to dunk into a glass of milk. *The process of using a class declaration to define a class object is called object instantiation.*

Simply stated, a *class* is the set of blueprints for a house and an *object* of the class is the actual house itself. It is the class object that you use in your program.

public vs. private in a Class

The keyword *public* means that you can directly access that member or method through the class object. Suppose we modified Listing 14-1 as Listing 14-2.

Listing 14-2. The EEPROM.h Header File

```
#ifndef EEPROM_h
#define EEPROM_h

#include <inttypes.h>
```

```
class EEPROMClass
{
  private:
    uint8_t bankSize;

  public:
    uint8_t read(int);
    void write(int, uint8_t);
    void clear();
};

extern EEPROMClass EEPROM;

#endif
```

Notice that we added a new method named *clear()*. We placed this *prototype declaration* for the method in the *public* section of the header file so that it is accessible via the class object. That is, we could call it using *EEPROM.clear()*. We also added the lines

```
private:
  uint8_t bankSize;
```

to the class declaration. The keyword *private* means only methods defined within the class have access to the class member named *bankSize*. Perhaps the *clear()* method uses *bankSize* to clear the contents of EEPROM memory.

Wait a minute? If *banksize* is *private* to the class and hence not accessible outside of the class, how can it ever be changed? Ah ... great question, and this highlights one of the strengths of OOP design. If you want to be able to change the state of a *private* member of a class, like *bankSize*, you need to write a new method, perhaps called *SetBanksize()*, to be able to change the class member named *bankSize* while the program is running. (You could, of course, initialize the member to some value as part of its definition, such as:

```
private:
  uint8_t bankSize = 512;
```

However, by adding a new *public* method, you are allowing a *private* class member to be changed while the program is running.)

Big deal. . . what's the advantage of that? Why not just make the member *public*? Well, the advantage is that you can add some form of error checking in *SetBanksize()*, giving you better control over the data that gets "into" the class object. If you make *bankSize* a *public* member of the class, the programmer could stick in some stupid value (e.g., –513) they want and, perhaps, break something further down the line. By forcing *private* members to be changed through a *public* method that you control, you at least have a chance to catch bogus values before they get into your program. This approach makes testing and debugging easier, too.

Finally, it sometimes helps to think of class members as the attributes, or properties, of the class (e.g., weight, height, gender, etc.) Indeed, some programmers refer to class members as class attributes or class properties. As such, they are like nouns in a sentence: they describe what's in the class. Class methods, on the other hand, often describe some action that is performed on the class members: *read()*, *write()*, *clear()*, *setCursor()*, and so forth. Because they are action-based, they are like the verbs in a sentence. Because the class members describe the object and methods provide a means of changing those members (especially when they are defined using the *private* storage specifier), changing the value of a member implies changing the *state* of the object. Think about it.

Now let's look inside the *EEPROM cpp* source code file.

The EEPROM.cpp File

Listing 14-3 shows what's in the *EEPROM.cpp* source code file. Not much there, actually. The first few lines use the *#include* preprocessor directive to read in the necessary header files needed by the code. The *#ifndef* preprocessor directive in the header file prevents us from "double including" the three include files found in Listing 14-3. Note that we include the *EEPROM.h* header file we discussed earlier.

Listing 14-3. The EEPROM.cpp Source Code File

```
/*
  EEPROM.cpp - EEPROM library
  Copyright (c) 2006 David A. Mellis.  All right reserved.

  This library is free software; you can redistribute it and/or
  modify it under the terms of the GNU Lesser General Public
  License as published by the Free Software Foundation; either
  version 2.1 of the License, or (at your option) any later version.

  This library is distributed in the hope that it will be useful,
  but WITHOUT ANY WARRANTY; without even the implied warranty of
  MERCHANTABILITY or FITNESS FOR A PARTICULAR PURPOSE.  See the GNU
  Lesser General Public License for more details.

  You should have received a copy of the GNU Lesser General Public
  License along with this library; if not, write to the Free Software
  Foundation, Inc., 51 Franklin St, Fifth Floor, Boston, MA  02110-1301  USA
*/

/*************************************************************************
 * Includes
 *************************************************************************/

#include <avr/eeprom.h>
#include "Arduino.h"
#include "EEPROM.h"

/*************************************************************************
 * Definitions
 *************************************************************************/

/*************************************************************************
 * Constructors
 *************************************************************************/

/*************************************************************************
 * User API
 *************************************************************************/

uint8_t EEPROMClass::read(int address)
{
        return eeprom_read_byte((unsigned char *) address);
}
```

```
void EEPROMClass::write(int address, uint8_t value)
{
        eeprom_write_byte((unsigned char *) address, value);
}
```

```
EEPROMClass EEPROM;
```

The first line of code is

```
uint8_t EEPROMClass::read(int address)
```

which is the start of the definition of the *read()* method. The line is no different than the function signatures you read about in Chapter 6. It states that the *read()* method is designed to return a *uint8_t* data type. If you look inside the *Arduino.h* header file, you will find that *uint8_t* is another way of saying: "*unsigned* 8-bit integer data type". So what does the following mean?

```
EEPROMClass::
```

The double-colon (::) is called the *scope resolution operator* and its purpose is to tell you which class contains the current method being examined. In other words, to verbalize the statement

```
uint8_t EEPROMClass::read(int address)
```

you might say: "The *read()* method is a member of the *EEPROMClass* class, takes an integer argument named *address*, and returns an *unsigned* 8-bit integer." If you want another word pattern for the scope resolution operator, you could substitute: "contains the member method named". So a less complete reading of the line would be: "The *EEPROMClass* contains a member method named *read()*." In other words, the scope resolution operator tells you the class for which a given method is defined. After all, a *write()* method from the *EEPROMClass* is only one class that uses the name *write()* for one of its methods. Many other libraries use the same *write()* name (e.g., Serial, Wifi, Servo, SD, etc.) but the scope resolution operator allows the compiler to keep everything tied to the proper class.

Note the last statement in the *EEPROM.cpp* file:

```
EEPROMClass EEPROM;
```

This is the same as the last line in the header file, minus the keyword *extern*. This makes sense when you remember what *extern* means. The *extern* keyword is telling the compiler that the variable named *EEPROM* is defined in some other file, but let me use it in this file as an *EEPROMClass* object. In the header file, therefore, *EEPROM* is a data *declaration* statement. If that's the case, and it is, then some other file must *define EEPROM*. That's what this last statement in *EEPROM.cpp* does: it *defines EEPROM* so we can actually use it in our programs (i.e., it has an lvalue).

If you load the *eeprom_read.ino* sample program in the IDE, you will find that the first line in the *loop()* function is:

```
value = EEPROM.read(address);
```

Because variable *EEPROM* is an object of the *EEPROMClass*, you can use it to access the *read()* method of the class using the dot operator. The dot operator is used in much the same way as you used it with a *struct* variable. With a class object, however, you use the dot operator to bridge the gap between the class object and one of the object's members or methods. Simple!

These two files also illustrate another important fact about a properly constructed library: *a well-designed header file does not contain executable code*. That is, header files contain data declarations, not data definitions. Nor do header files contain definitions of class methods. Header files may contain data declaration for a class, but the instantiation of a class object is relegated to the associated *.cpp* or program (**.ino*) files.

Add julian() to Dates

Sometimes it's useful to know the number of days between two dates. For example, it's common to send an invoice that states "2-10 net 30". The interpretation is that the billed company can deduct 2% of the invoice cost if they pay the balance within 10 days. Otherwise, the full amount is to be paid within 30 days. Calculations like this need to know the number of days between two specified dates. At the heart of such calculations is determining a Julian date. A Julian date specifies the number of days from January 1 to a specific date.

If you think about it, the only wrinkle is that you have to correct for leap years. Otherwise, it's pretty simple. Listing 14-4 presents the code for the *julian()* method.

Listing 14-4. The julian() Method

```
/*****
   Purpose: Determine the numbers of days between the given date
            and Jan 1 of the same year. Algorithm taken from C
            Programmer's Toolkit, Jack Purdum, Que Corp., 1993,
            p.257.

   Parameters:
     int day          The day to test
     int month        The month to test
     int year         The year to test (e.g., 2015)

   Return value:
     int              The number of days, including the one given
*****/
int Dates::julian(int day, int month, int year)
{
   static int runsum[] = {0, 31, 59, 90, 120, 151, 181,
                          212, 243, 273, 304, 334, 365};
   int total;

   total = runsum[month - 1] + day;
   if (month > 2) {
     total += IsLeapYear(year);    // Adjust for leap year
   }
   return total;
}
```

The code is straightforward. The array *runsum[]* is a running total of the number of days from January 1 to the start of the next month. Question: Why did I define the array using the *static* storage modifier? If you leave the *static* modifier out of the definition of the array, then each *Dates* object you instantiate creates its own copy of the array. That is,

```
Dates myBirthday, yourBirthday;
```

instantiates two *Dates* objects. If we omit the *static* keyword, the *runsum[]* array is created for each object. However, since we never change the contents of the *runsum[]* array, why not share it with all instantiations of a *Dates* object? That's exactly what the *static* storage specifier does: It allocates memory for only *one* copy of the array and all *Dates* objects share that single array definition. The good news is that this saves us 24 bytes of memory for each *Dates* object our program instantiates. The bad news is that the compiler will *always* create that one copy of the array even if you never instantiate a single *Dates* object. Still, why would you include the *Dates* library if you didn't intend to use it? True, you might not use the *julian()* method, but the array is still going to be created anyway. If that's the case and you're really hurting for free memory, you can always cannibalize the *Dates* library and just extract only those methods you need.

Note how we use *IsLeapYear()* to adjust the day count when it is a leap year. It's calculations like this that make returning an *int* from the method easier to use than returning a *boolean*.

Before you can use the *julian()* method of the *Dates* class, you need to modify the *Dates* header file so the compiler knows a new method has been added to the class. How do you do that? Pretty simple, actually. Just add the method's signature to the header file, as the following snippet shows:

```
int IsLeapYear(int year);
void GetEaster(Dates *myEaster);
char *DayOfTheWeek(int day, int month, int year);
char *GetDayOfWeek();
int julian(int day, int month, int year);   // New method!
```

Obviously, the method prototype appears in the *public* section of the header file so we can access it using the class object's dot operator.

No doubt you noticed that there are two methods presented in the snippet that we haven't discussed yet. (You did notice, didn't you?) I added these two new methods simply to show how to use a private member of a class. The next section discusses these two methods.

Adding a private Class Member

The following code snippet is extracted from the *Dates.h* header file:

```
class Dates
{
  private:
    char today[4];            // Hold string for day of week

  public:
    #define ASCIIZERO 48      // character for '0' in ASCII
```

The snippet shows where we placed the definition of the *today[]* character array. It is used to hold a string representing the day of the week (e.g., "Fri") and we have made it *private* to the class. All of the day abbreviations use 3 bytes of memory, but we need the 4th byte for the *null* termination character. Again, defining *today[]* in the *private* definition section of the *Dates* class means that only members of the class can access it directly. So, how can we access *today[]*? Well, that's the purpose of the *GetDayOfTheWeek()* method. As you will see, this example is a bit contrived and a little on the RDC side, but it still makes a point. The code for both methods is presented in Listing 14-5.

Listing 14-5. The Day of the Week Method

```
/*****
  Purpose: Determine day of the week for given date. Algorithm
           taken from C Programmer's Toolkit, Jack Purdum, Que
           Corp., 1993, p.259.

  Parameters:
    int day         The day to test
    int month       The month to test
    int year        The year to test (e.g., 2015)

  Return value:
    char *
*****/
char *Dates::DayOfTheWeek(int day, int month, int year)
{

  const static char days[7][4] = {"Sun", "Mon", "Tue", "Wed",
                                   "Thu", "Fri", "Sat"};

  int index;

  if (month > 2) {
    month -= 2;
  } else {
    month += 10;
    year--;
  }
  index = ((13 * month - 1) / 5) + day + (year % 100) + ((year % 100) / 4)
          + ((year / 100) / 4) - 2 * (year / 100) + 77;
  index = index - 7 * (index / 7);
  strcpy(today, days[index]);
  return today;
}

/*****
  Purpose: Get the object's current day of the week

  Parameters:
    void

  Return value:
    char *         A 3 character string for the day

WARNING: This method is coupled tightly to DayOfTheWeek() and
         assumes it was called prior to calling this method.
*****/
```

```
char *Dates::GetDayOfWeek()
{
  return today;
}
```

Note the warning in the *GetDayOfWeek()* description. It points out that the method can only return something useful if *DayOfTheWeek()* was called first. This is necessary to do that so the *today[]* class member gets set. This is a bad design because it couples the two methods together so much that one can't work without the other. But, as I said, I'm doing it for teaching purposes, and teaching using a bad example can also be instructive. (Could you improve on this bad design? Sure. Move the method prototype for *DayOfTheWeek()* into the *private* section of the class, and place the actual method call as the first line of *GetDayOfWeek()*. Because *DayOfTheWeek()* is now *private*, it cannot be called outside the class, thus making it a *helper function* for *GetDayOfWeek()*. However, you would now have to pass in the month, day, and year as parameters to *GetDayOfWeek()*. It's still a little clunky, but it would work.)

The actual algorithm for determining the day of the week is based on the lunar calendar and is fairly complex. However, you should be able to explain why the *static* storage modifier was used for the *days[][]* array. If not, go back and reread the previous section so you do understand why. You do *not* want to appear unprepared when this discussion comes up at the next cocktail party.

The *today[]* class member has the day of the week for the date that was passed to the *DayOfTheWeek()* method. The *GetDayOfWeek()* method can then be called to extract the day from the *today[]* array, even though *today[]* is *private* to the class. You may hear other programmers refer to methods that access *private* members of a class as *accessor methods*.

Constructors and Destructors

When you use C++, things aren't always what they seem. As we mentioned before, a class declaration does not automatically instantiate an object of the class. You must do that yourself. With the *Dates* class, you can define a *Dates* object using the syntax:

```
Dates myDates;
```

The result is a *Dates* object that you have instantiated (or defined) with the name *myDates*. What is not so obvious is that, behind your back, the C++ compiler created a constructor method for you that is responsible for defining the members of the *Dates* class as part of an invisible background process. The constructor automatically sets all values types to 0 and all reference types to *null*. So when you defined the *myDates* object, there's a lot of quiet, sneaky, stuff going on that you didn't write. This is the way things are supposed to happen when you use C++. The problem is that in the Arduino world, you don't have any control over the way the default constructor behaves.

Consider the code in Listing 14-6.

Listing 14-6. Using the Dates Library

```
#include "Dates.h"

Dates myDates;          // This calls the default constructor

void setup() {
  int i;
  int total;
```

```
  Serial.begin(9600);
  //Dates myDates;        // Default constructor, no initializer
  //Dates myDates(2015);  // Constructor with initializer

  for (i = 2000; i < 2017; i++) {
    Serial.print(i);
    Serial.print(" is ");
    if (myDates.IsLeapYear(i) == 0) {
      Serial.print("not ");
    }
    Serial.print("a leap year, Easter is on: ");
    myDates.myEaster.year = i;
    myDates.GetEaster(&myDates);
    total = myDates.julian(3, 5, i);
    Serial.print(myDates.myEaster.easterStr);
    Serial.print("  jullian days to May 3: ");
    Serial.println(total);
  }
}
void loop() {}
```

We have added two constructors to the *Dates.cpp* file and added their prototypes to the associated header file. The two constructors are presented in Listing 14-7. We have left off their descriptions to keep the listings as short as possible. The first constructor has no argument list, whereas the second one is the syntax for initializing the *year* member we added to the *private* section of the header file.

Listing 14-7. Adding Two Constructors to Dates.cpp

```
Dates::Dates(void)
{
    Serial.println("We're in the constructor.");
}

Dates::Dates(int year):year(year)
{
    Serial.println("We're in the init constructor.");
}
```

When we run the version using the default constructor presented in Listing 14-7, the output looks like Figure 14-2. Even though the default constructor is called, no output is seen. The reason is because the *Serial* object hasn't been initialized yet.

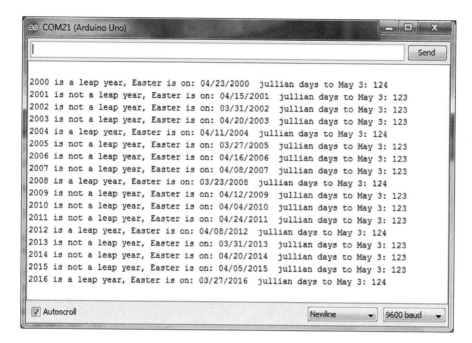

Figure 14-2. *Using the Default Constructor*

Now, comment out the global definition of *myDates* and uncomment the first definition inside of *loop()*, recompile, and run the program. The output appears in Figure 14-3. If you look at the first line in Figure 14-3, you can see that the no-initializer constructor has been called. If you uncomment the constructor that passes the year as an argument in *setup()*, the proper constructor is called. You should be able to convince yourself that the parameterized constructor could also be written as what's shown in Figure 14-3.

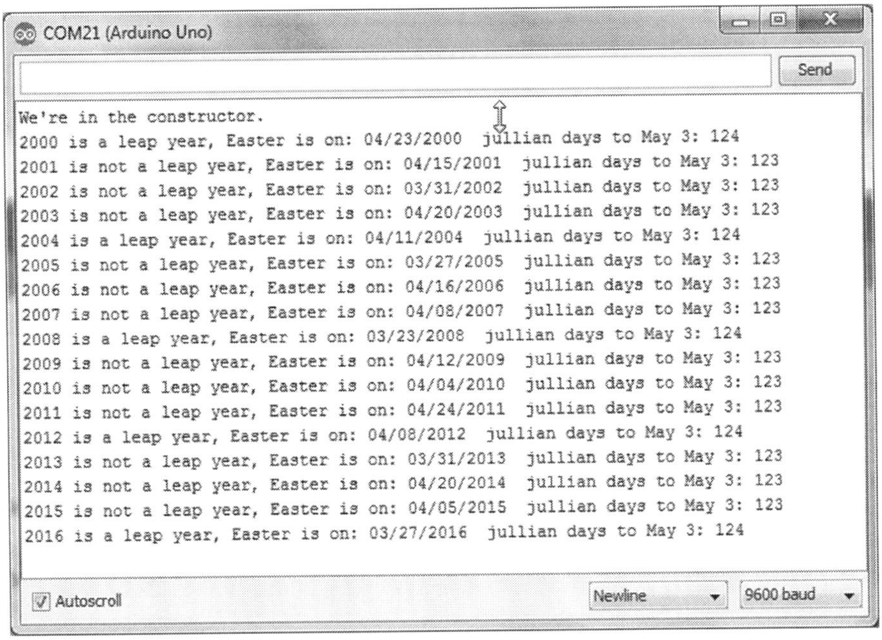

Figure 14-3. Constructor in setup()

```
Dates::Dates(int yr)
{
   Serial.println("We're in the init constructor.");
   year = yr;
}
```

So, when do you write your own constructor, and when do you just rely on the default constructor? If you have a reason to have a class start with specific values for its members, then you can write a constructor that meets your specific needs. If you can live with the initial state of the object having its members with the values 0 or *null*, there's no reason to write your own constructor. For example, I once wrote a membership program for a club in Indianapolis. Because virtually all of the members were from Indianapolis, I initialized the *City* and *State* members of the class to "Indianapolis" and "IN" as default values for any new object instantiated from the class. Because people do make mistakes, anything you can do to minimize their inputs is usually a good thing.

You can also call a *destructor* in C++, which should free the resources associated with the object. The syntax is

```
Dates::~Dates(void)
{
}
```

and the destructor is called when the object goes out of scope. Note the tilde operator, (~). You can also call it directly, as in *myDates.~Dates()*. The goal of a destructor is to allow the resources associated with the object to be released for reuse.

Truth be told, most Arduino programmers do not use constructors or destructors. We only present this small discussion about them so you know they exist. If you need to initialize a class member with a value, most Arduino programmers create a method that initializes the member. This is, for example, the exact purpose of the *Serial.begin()* method of the *Serial* object. You use the *begin()* method to set the default state for the baud rate to 9600 baud (in most cases). However, if you feel you need to override the default constructor for your class, you should research the topic thoroughly. We've only presented enough here for you to shoot yourself in the foot.

That said, you should be able to read the header and *.cpp* files you find in the *libraries* subdirectory and get a pretty good feel for what the code does. Don't be afraid to experiment with the library code; especially the code you find in a library's *examples* directory.

Conclusion

Well, our journey through the C language has come to an end. However, that doesn't mean you are done learning about C. I've been using C for almost 40 years now and I am still learning new techniques. Anytime I have a new programming task, my first stop is an Internet search on the topic of concern. There are a lot of incredibly bright people out there writing some very good code. Likewise, there is even more RDC out there, too. Hopefully, as you learn more and more, you'll appreciate elegance of finely crafted code and appreciate the efforts of those whose shoulders we all stand on.

EXERCISES

1. What is the OOP trilogy?

   Answer: The OOP trilogy is encapsulation, inheritance, and polymorphism.

2. If you wish to make a polymorphic method, what condition must be true?

   Answer: The method signatures must be different.

3. If you have a *private* class member and wish to be able to change it, how should you do it?

   Answer: Write a class method (i.e., an *accessor method*) that can be called to change the *private* member of the class. This affords you the chance to perform error checking on the new value, too.

4. If a *private* class member is *int gender* and another member is a *boolean pregnant*, how would you handle an input for *gender* as Male and pregnant as *True*?

    Answer: This type of error checking is called *consistency error checking* and it is not easy to be complete on consistency error checking because there are ill-defined cases. For example, if *gender* is Female, and *pregnant* is True, that seems reasonable until you notice that she's 87 years old. How far you carry such error checking depends upon the cost of being wrong vs. the cost of making sure it's right.

5. How is encapsulation enforced in the OOP world?

    Answer: If you truly want to encapsulate a variable, you should make it a *private* member of a class and then use a *public* accessor method to provide the means of changing its state. Any error checking should be part of the method. Once done, the only way to gain access to the *private* member is through a class object using the dot operator and the class method.

6. Do I have to use a class header file and a class *.cpp* file?

    Answer: Technically, no. You could write everything in a single cpp file. However, that's probably not a good idea and it would be best for you to stick with the **.h* and **.cpp* model for now.

APPENDIX A

Suppliers and Sources

This appendix presents information about where you can go for further information on some of the many Arduino-compatible boards, sensors, and other peripheral devices.

Starter Kits

These are great if you're just getting started, as most include an Arduino-compatible board.

- **16Hertz LLC** (www.16hertz.com). The Ultimate Starter Kit (see Figure A-1) has just about everything you'd want to begin working with an Arduino Uno, including the board at a very competitive price (about $60). The package includes a variety of sensors, displays, LEDs, and even a small stepper motor and assorted jumpers. The company also sells Starter Kits with fewer components at lower prices.

© Jack Purdum 2015
J. Purdum, *Beginning C for Arduino, Second Edition*: Learn C Programming for the Arduino, DOI 10.1007/978-1-4842-0940-0

Figure A-1.

- **HelloJack03** (http://stores.ebay.com/hellojack03). This UNO R3 starter kit is the top-selling kit on eBay, containing 40 types of the most widely used components, all fully compatible with Arduino. This kit also comes with 26 tutorials for beginners. It is very competitively priced.

Figure A-2.

- **OSEPP** (http://osepp.com). The company offers a number of Arduino-compatible boards and sensors. Their Starter Kit is complete and includes an Uno-compatible board. They also have a nicely packaged robotics kit that has everything you need to build a small robot, including their Uno-compatible board, motors, wheels, and so forth. It also comes with very good documentation for building and using the robot.

Figure A-3.

341

- **Yourduino** (http://Yourduino.com). This company sells their YourDuinoRobo1 Arduino-compatible board with a variety of starter kits. The company also sells an I2C 16 ×2 LCD display that I really like. Their Yourduino RoboRed is a very nice Uno clone and I really like how they have brought out the I/O pins so that they can be used with female jumpers as well as the standard headers. They have several different starter kits priced for just about anyone's pocketbook.

Figure A-4.

Shields, Boards, Sensors

Figure A-5.

- **4D Systems** (`www.4dsystems.com.au`). This company has a wide product line of high-end displays with pretty amazing graphics capabilities. While a lot of the graphics power comes from onboard electronics, it probably makes sense to use the ATMega2560 family with these displays. The company has online support for a variety of microcontrollers.

- **Seeed Studio** (`www.seeedstudio.com`). Suppliers of many reasonably priced μc boards, sensors, and shields. They submitted their Seeed Mega 2560 and SD shield for evaluation. Their 2560 Mega board has one of the smallest footprints I've seen for this board. I have also purchased several of their other shields, and everything has been of very high quality and performed as advertised. They also sent a robotic kit that has everything you need to build a robot. These are extremely high-quality, machined parts that should produce a rugged and durable system.

Figure A-6.

- **Diligent Inc.** (www.digilentinc.com). The Max32 board takes advantage of the powerful PIC32MX795F512 microcontroller. This microcontroller features a 32-bit MIPS processor core running at 80Mhz (quite a bit faster than the Atmel clock speed), 512K of flash program memory, and 128K of SRAM data memory. In addition, a USB 2 OTG controller, 10/100 Ethernet MAC, and dual CAN controllers that can be accessed via add-on I/O shields and 83 I/O lines. There is a modified IDE that is an Arduino look-alike and available for Windows, Mac, and Linux. (The board supports all three.) The modified IDE can be downloaded free at https://github.com/chipKIT32/chipKIT32-MAX/downloads. I tried several of my sketches and all ran without modification on the ChipKit Max32. However, the compiler has some differences ... most of them good! For example, an *int* data type for this board uses 4 bytes of storage and a *double* is 8 bytes, versus 2 and 4 for most Atmel boards. Depending upon your app, this could be a real plus in terms of range and precision. If you need a bunch of I/O lines and a very fast processor, this is a great choice and clearly worth investigating. I also found the placement of the reset button to be very convenient.

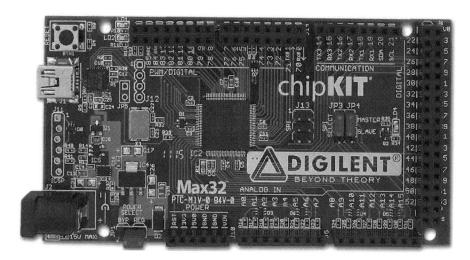

Figure A-7.

- **Nextion** (`http://imall.iteadstudio.com`). TFT displays allow inputs to be entered from the display screen. This display, however, avoids the rat's nest of wires that TFTs usually require, and replaces them with its own serial interface using a single port. The device includes an editor so that you can design your own interface objects. An onboard SD card stores custom data. There are two sizes: 2.4″ and 4.3″, which makes them small enough for many different applications. The cost ranges between $20 and $35.

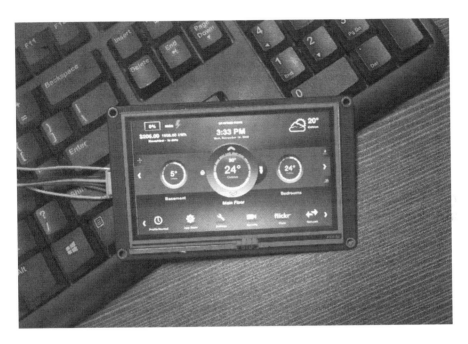

Figure A-8.

- **Tinyos Electronics** (http://tinyosshop.com). This company supplies an Atmega328- compatible board, which is shown in Figure A-9. As you can see, relative to the pen cap in the photo, this is one of the smallest boards I received, but it ran all of my sketches perfectly. The board is well constructed and reasonably priced. Also note that the chip is removable. This means you could load software onto the board, remove the chip, and place in a bare-bones board with only a chip and a few other components if you wanted to do so. I used this board a lot while writing this book, mainly because of its size. The company also sells a wide variety of shields, sensors, and other products for the Arduino boards.

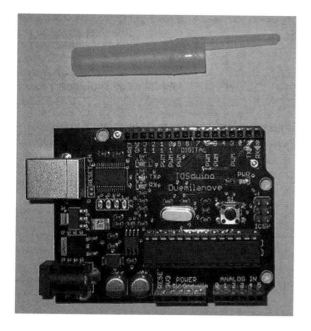

Figure A-9.

- **Cooking Hacks** (www.cooking-hacks.com). This company supplies a GPS module that is depicted in Figure A-10. I find this a very interesting piece of hardware and I hope to do more work with it once this book is put to bed. The web site also provides a tutorial on using the module, as well as downloadable software for testing purposes.

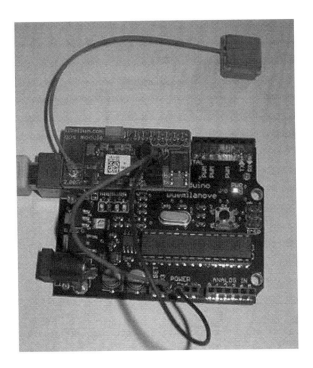

Figure A-10.

Specific Parts Sources

There are a number of places where you can go to purchase electronic components for your projects. Some of the ones I have used are listed next. You should also use eBay and Amazon as sources and references for parts. With more than 100 purchases on eBay, including from many foreign suppliers, I have never had a problem.

Bezels

RMF Products (`www.bezelsource.com`). This company is one of the few that offers bezels for LCD displays and other components. It's pretty tough to make an LCD project look professional without something to hide the fact that you didn't cut a perfect hole in the project box. The bezels come in different sizes and include a filter (if you want to use it) and mounting hardware. Depending on the size, you can buy them quantity one for $7.50 to $8.00. However, if you have a minimum order totaling $25, the cost drops to about $2 each. I would opt for about a dozen to get the minimum order size. You will likely use all of them anyway, or you can sell them to friends (e.g., ham radio club) for their projects.

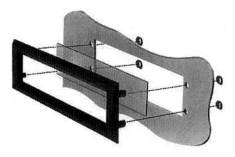

Figure A-11.

Jumper Wires

Leo Sales Ltd. Good quality jumpers with/without connectors. Carried by numerous domestic stores. Search the Internet for the closest supplier to you.

Project Cases

Parts Express (http://parts-express.com). Component supplier with good project cases. A variety of other useful parts, too.

Domestic Parts Suppliers

- **All Electronics** (www.allelectronics.com). Components supplier.

- **Debco Electronics** (www.debcoelectronics.com). Components supplier and a fun place to shop. A mom-and-pop place that's like the old hardware stores with bin after bin of parts.

- **Digi-Key Electronics** (www.digikey.com). Components supplier. No minimum order.

- **Jameco Electronics** (www.jameco.com). Components supplier.

- **Kbell Engineering** (http://plasmadyn.en.hisupplier.com). Source for the Leonardo Pro Mini board.

- **Martin P Jones & Associates** (www.mpja.com). Components supplier. Their monthly e-mail specials are interesting. They are a good source for all components, including power supplies.

- **Mouser Electronics** (www.mouser.com). Components supplier.

- **Radio Shack** (www.radioshack.com). Components supplier. Great for when you forgot to order that one part that makes it all work. Sadly, the company may not even make it to press time.

APPENDIX B

Electronic Components for Experiments

In this appendix, you are given a short list of the components that you need to implement the experiments mentioned in this book. Chapter 1 also discusses what you need. The major items are repeated here, plus a few other thoughts you may want to consider.

Microcontroller Board

No big surprise here. You probably already have a board. If not, Appendix A presents some board options that you should consider, as I have used all the boards mentioned there and any one of them would be a good choice. So, which one should you choose? It depends. For the most part, I rarely have run out of flash memory or EEPROM. There are times when I bumped into the SRAM limit, but not all that often. For some projects, I used a 2560 board because of the larger number of I/O pins and more memory. In certain situations, more pins is a better solution than multiplexing. Again, it depends upon your needs. You should be able to purchase a low-end Arduino-compatible board for less than $10. You can find an Atmega2560 board for around $15. Personally, I start all projects with the least expensive board and "move up" if the project demands it.

Solderless Breadboard

This is a necessity if you plan to do any experimentation. I like the board shown in Figure 1-2 because it's large enough to hold a lot of components but small enough to fit easily on my work desk. It also has points for connecting an external power supply. You should be able to buy a breadboard with over 2000 tie points for less than $20. In most cases, you'll find deals that even throw in a bunch of jumper wires, too.

Electronic Components

This is a catchall category that includes LEDs, jumper wires, resistors, and so forth. Keep in mind that the power supplied by the Arduino I/O pins is very limited. As a result, I created a small "power supply" (see Figure B-1) that uses an LM7805 to provide 5 volts at currents of about 1 ampere. There is a connector seen near the top-right edge of the board that accepts input from a 5V "wall wart" capable of supplying up to 1.5 amps of current. I bought a lot of 10-piece LM7805 voltage regulators on eBay for less than $2.50, including shipping. My guess is that with the perf board, the two electrolytic capacitors, the resistor, and the LED, I have less than $1 tied up in the board. There are two pins at the left edge of the board that supply 5 volts. The mini board is plugged into my breadboard when I feel that I need more power than what the USB cable can provide.

© Jack Purdum 2015
J. Purdum, *Beginning C for Arduino, Second Edition*: Learn C Programming
for the Arduino, DOI 10.1007/978-1-4842-0940-0

Figure B-1. *A small voltage regulator circuit*

For the simple circuits described in this book, all you'll need is a few LEDs and some resistors. Chapter 13 does discuss some specialty sensors and parts if you wish to construct those projects, but Appendix A can still be used as a source for the parts. All the components used in this book can be purchased locally at your favorite parts supplier. If you need to save every penny, check online to see if your area has a local amateur (i.e., "ham") radio club. They sometimes have flea markets that are a great source for inexpensive electronic components. If you have a local college or university nearby, check if they have an engineering or physics department. They may have ideas for finding local parts. If those avenues fail, there is always online purchasing.

Online Component Purchases

I am often asked if I feel confident in purchasing electronic items and components online. Definitely, yes. I have purchased items online from the suppliers mentioned in Appendix A, and I have never had a problem. Quite honestly, I always check eBay to get an idea of the market price for any item I don't use on a regular basis. If nothing else, eBay makes it easy to find out the price of things. When possible, I support my local shops. Also, Amazon carries many items you find on eBay, usually at fairly competitive prices. It's worth checking both sources.

Perhaps the second most often question I get asked is my experience using eBay to purchase items online. I know that I have made more than 100 purchases on eBay for various items. Of those purchases, I have never had one bad experience, especially with the electronics/component purchases I've made. Do I buy from China? Absolutely. Although I've made "bulk" purchases (e.g., 100 resistors or capacitors) from domestic suppliers, I've also made bulk purchases from China without a problem. While it's nice to be able to drive to my local Radio Shack, Micro Center, or Debco and buy that odd part I didn't have at home, when I needed 125 blue LEDs for a 5×5×5 LED cube project, I shopped around. Not too long ago, I purchased 150 LEDs with dropping resistors for less than $10. True, it took about eight days to get them, but they were postage paid and exactly what I ordered.

Where you buy your components is up to you. If I was a bazillionaire, I probably would just pay whatever the price is to have the item(s) tomorrow. Alas, unless you people start buying tens of thousands of copies of this book, I will still need to shop around for a good price. After a while, you'll find a few suppliers that you're happy with and you'll tend to use them over and over.

Experiment!

Lastly, I would hope you enjoy experimenting, even if you don't consider yourself an expert. True, electric circuits can be harmful, so you do need to be careful, especially with 120V circuits. Even a wall wart supplying 5 volts and low current deserves respect. Still, I would hope you're willing to try things on your own. I've smoked my share of resistors and sent more than one LED to supernova heaven, but I learned things during the process. My interest in electronics started before I got my amateur radio license in 1954, and it's never waned since. I hope that you find your microcontroller projects to be just as much fun as I have mine.

Experiment and enjoy!

Index

W

 X

 Y

■ **Z**